MODERNIST STAR MAPS

Bringing together Canadian, American, and British scholars, this volume explores
the relationship between modernism and modern celebrity culture. In support
of the collection's overriding thesis that modern celebrity and modernism are
mutually determining phenomena, the contributors take on a range of transatlantic
canonical and noncanonical figures, from the expected (Virginia Woolf and
F. Scott Fitzgerald) to the surprising (Elvis and Hitler). Illuminating case studies
are balanced by the volume's attentiveness to broader issues related to modernist
aesthetics, as the contributors consider celebrity in relationship to identity,
commodification, print culture, personality, visual cultures, and theatricality. As the
first book to read modernism and celebrity in the context of the crises of individual
agency occasioned by the emergence of mass-mediated culture, *Modernist
Star Maps* argues that the relationship between modernism and the popular is
unthinkable without celebrity. Moreover, celebrity's strange evolution during the
twentieth century is unimaginable without the intercession of modernism's system
of cultural value. This innovative collection opens new avenues for understanding
celebrity not only for modernist scholars but for critical theorists and cultural
studies scholars.

Aaron Jaffe is Associate Professor of English, University of Louisville, USA.

Jonathan Goldman is Assistant Professor of English, New York Institute of
Technology, USA.

T0383644

For our families

Modernist Star Maps
Celebrity, Modernity, Culture

Edited by

AARON JAFFE
University of Louisville, USA

JONATHAN GOLDMAN
New York Institute of Technology, USA

LONDON AND NEW YORK

First published 2010 by Ashgate Publishing

2 Park Square, Milton Park, Abingdon, Oxon OX14 4RN
711 Third Avenue, New York, NY 10017, USA

Routledge is an imprint of the Taylor & Francis Group, an informa business

First issued in paperback 2016

British Library Cataloguing in Publication Data
Celebrity star maps : celebrity, modernity, culture.
    1. Fame – Social aspects. 2. Fame in literature. – 3. Celebrities in mass media.
    4. Modernism (Aesthetics)
    I. Jaffe, Aaron. II. Goldman, Jonathan.
    306'.0904–dc22

Library of Congress Cataloging-in-Publication Data
    Modernist star maps: celebrity, modernity, culture / edited by Aaron Jaffe and Jonathan Goldman.
    p. cm.
    Includes index.
    ISBN 978-0-7546-6610-3 (hardback: alk. paper)
    1. American literature—20th century—History and criticism. 2. Modernism (Literature)—United States. 3. Popular culture—United States—20th century. 4. Celebrities—United States—20th century. 5. English literature—20th century—History and criticism. 6. Modernism (Literature)—Great Britain. 7. Popular culture—Great Britain—20th century. 8. Celebrities—Great Britain—20th century. I. Jaffe, Aaron, II. Goldman, Jonathan (Jonathan E.)

    PS228.M63M63 2010
    700'.4112—dc22

            2010003478

ISBN 13: 978-0-7546-6610-3 (hbk)
ISBN 13: 978-1-138-25736-8 (pbk)

Contents

List of Figures

List of Contributors

Nancy Armstrong is Gilbert, Louis, and Edward Lehrman Professor of English at Duke University. Her books include *Desire and Domestic Fiction: A Political History of the Novel* (1987); with Leonard Tennenhouse, *The Imaginary Puritan: Literature, Intellectual Labor, and the Origins of Personal Life* (1992); *Fiction in the Age of Photography: The Legacy of British Realism* (1999); and *How Novels Think: The Limits of Individualism, 1719–1900* (2006). She edits the journal *Novel: A Forum on Fiction.*

Judith Brown is Assistant Professor of English at Indiana University. She is the author of *Glamour in Six Dimensions: Modernism and the Radiance of Form* (2009).

Edward P. Comentale is Associate Professor of English at Indiana University. He is the author of *Modernism, Cultural Production, and the British Avant-Garde* (2004) and a coeditor of *T.E. Hulme and the Question of Modernism* (2004), *The Cultural Politics of Ian Fleming and 007* (2005), and *The Year's Work in Lebowski Studies* (2009).

Steven Connor is Professor of Modern Literature and Theory at Birbeck College, London, and Academic Director of the London Consortium. He is a writer and broadcaster for radio and the author of books on Dickens, Joyce, postwar British fiction and postmodernism, as well as, more recently, *Dumbstruck: A Cultural History of Ventriloquism* (2000), *The Book of Skin* (2003), and *Fly* (2006). *Next to Nothing*, an historical poetics of the air, and *Paraphernalia: On Magical Ordinary Objects* are forthcoming, and he is currently writing a philosophy of sport. His Website at www.stevenconnor.com includes many lectures, broadcasts, and unpublished works.

Lois Cucullu is Associate Professor of English at the University of Minnesota. She is the author of *Expert Modernists, Matricide, and Modern Culture: Woolf, Forster, Joyce* (2004) and articles in *Modernist Cultures, Signs, Novel: A Forum on Fiction, differences*, and *Texas Studies in Literature and Language.*

James C. Davis is an Associate Professor of English at Brooklyn College, City University of New York. He is the author of *Commerce in Color: Race, Consumer Culture, and American Literature, 1893–1933* (2007), and a 2008–2009 Fellow at the Leon Levy Center for Biography, where he began writing a biography of Eric Walrond.

Michael D. Garval is Associate Professor of French at North Carolina State University, Associate Editor of *Contemporary French Civilization*, and author of *"A Dream of Stone": Fame, Vision, and Monumentality in Nineteenth-Century French Literary Culture* (2004).

Loren Glass is an Associate Professor of English at the University of Iowa. He is the author of *Authors Inc.: Literary Celebrity in the Modern United States, 1880–1980* (2005). He is currently working on a history of Grove Press.

Jonathan Goldman is Assistant Professor of English at the New York Institute of Technology. He is the author of *Modernism is the Literature of Celebrity* (2010) and has published articles in *Novel: A Forum on Fiction* and *Narrative*.

Faye Hammill is Senior Lecturer in English at the University of Strathclyde, Glasgow. Her research areas are Canadian literature and interwar middlebrow culture. Publications include *Literary Culture and Female Authorship in Canada 1760–2000* (2003; winner of the Pierre Savard Prize), *Canadian Literature* (2007), and *Women, Celebrity and Literary Culture Between the Wars* (2007). She is a coeditor of *Encyclopedia of British Women's Writing 1900–1950* (2006), and was editor of the *British Journal of Canadian Studies* from 2004 to 2009. Currently she is leading the Middlebrow Network, funded by the Arts and Humanities Research Council.

Allan Hepburn is Associate Professor in the English Department at McGill University. His books include *Intrigue: Espionage and Culture* (2005), and *Enchanted Objects: Visual Art in Contemporary Fiction* (2010). He has edited a collection of essays entitled *Troubled Legacies: Narrative and Inheritance* (2007), as well as three volumes of archival and ungathered materials by Elizabeth Bowen: *The Bazaar and Other Stories* (2008), *People, Places, Things* (2008), and *Listening In: Broadcasts, Speeches, and Interviews* (2010). He has also published essays on Joseph Conrad, James Joyce, F. Scott Fitzgerald, Edith Wharton, Nancy Mitford, Louis Begley, and other novelists.

Aaron Jaffe is Associate Professor of English at the University of Louisville. He is the author of *Modernism and the Culture of Celebrity* (2005), coeditor of *The Year's Work in Lebowski Studies* (2009). He is working on a book on modernism and risk.

Deborah M. Mix is Associate Professor of English at Ball State University. She is the author of *"A Vocabulary of Thinking": Gertrude Stein and Contemporary North American Women's Innovative Writing* (2007). Her essays have appeared in journals including *American Literature*, *Contemporary Literature*, and *Sagetrieb*.

Stephen Watt is Professor of English and Associate Dean, College of Arts and Sciences, Indiana University. His major interests include Irish Studies, drama and performance studies, and higher education in twenty-first-century America. His most recent book is *Beckett and Contemporary Irish Writing* (2009), and he is working on a new book on memory and contemporary drama.

Annalisa Zox-Weaver is a Lecturer in English at USC, having recently defended her dissertation called *Seeing Through Evil: Women Modernists and Their Fascist Dictators*. She has published in *New German Critique* and is editing a collection of essays about the photographer Lee Miller.

Acknowledgements

This project germinated in 2003 when the two of us discovered our shared interest in the topic, which led eventually to a panel at the annual meeting of the Modern Languages Association in 2005. There, with Jennifer Wicke, whose mentoring and encouragement proved decisive, we discovered quickly that the topic appeals to a broader academic audience. A host of other scholars contributed to this project over the years, most notably at the 2006 Modernist Studies Association conference, in Tulsa, where we chaired a seminar devoted to modernism and celebrity. Its participants included Lois Cucullu, Faye Hammill, Andrea Fontenot, Loren Glass, Karen Leick, Jessica Lucero, Heather Lusty, Marina MacKay, and Claire Russell. This book is indebted to the work and ideas discussed during our session. There are others who made the volume possible: Taylor Hagood and David Anderson read portions of the manuscript and offered critical commentary, and Anne Diebel provided important editorial assistance. Most importantly, we are hugely grateful to Ann Donahue at Ashgate, who supported our vision and has been invaluable to us and others in modernist studies, and our other allies: our contributors. These scholars' insightful and energetic essays not only made this volume a joy to work on but also taught us more about interpretive community than we imagined there was to know.

Introduction

Aaron Jaffe and Jonathan Goldman

Name That Star

In 1940 a proposal was made to rename the stars: out with the dusty obscurities of antiquity—Polaris, Betelgeuse, Epsilon Ursae Majoris; in with something altogether more modern. This initiative to "make it new" came from one A.P. Herbert, a prolific if minor English modernist, a poet, satirist, author of suspense novels, member of Parliament, and general eccentric, one who shared a literary agent with W.B. Yeats. In his pamphlet *A Better Sky, or, Name this Star*, he discards all the exasperating Latin, Greek, and Arabic, advocating instead a scheme for renaming heavenly bodies after famous historical figures. Herbert's scheme concentrates heavily on the literary and philosophical personnages who had come to define modernity—or, at least, had come to define an account of the development of the modern world understood from a particular mid-twentieth-century point of view (i.e., firmly Eurocentric, male, Anglophone). Not restricting himself to individual stars, Herbert saw fit to rewrite the familiar constellations as more modern groupings: statesmen (Charlemagne, Cromwell, etc.), tyrants (Attila, Hitler), storytellers (Chaucer, Conrad), scientists (Euclid, Einstein), poets (Milton, Byron), and more, also forming geographical districts of modern nations, cities and islands, reflections of planet Earth's own divisions. His decisions were systematic: thus the constellation Orion, long a navigational beacon, becomes "The Sailor" (Columbus, Cook). Herbert published *A Better Sky* as a pamphlet that included a foldout, redrawn star map.

Herbert begins his slim volume with a complaint: "We know shockingly little about the stars—we the ordinary man, woman, and child" (1). His reinscription of the skies, he rationalizes, will encourage astronomical apprehension by providing more familiar mythologies by which we can identify the stars. He wanted to bring the heavens closer to earth. But his purpose was multifold: by bridging the distance between humanity and the stratosphere, he attempted to ensure that the night sky would reflect his own culture: "This is a good way to learn not only about the stars of heaven but the story of the earth" (5). That his constitutes a more meritorious star chart, he announces by brushing away the irrelevancies of the ancients: "Let us have done with all this unworthy stuff" (3). Thus Herbert was trying to designate astral immortality to the correct cultural figures by linking them to heavenly cartography.

This redistricting and renaming of the star map was by no means an isolated gesture. Rather, Herbert was participating in a widespread cultural impulse, what the authors of the current volume recognize as a modernist impulse, to revise the

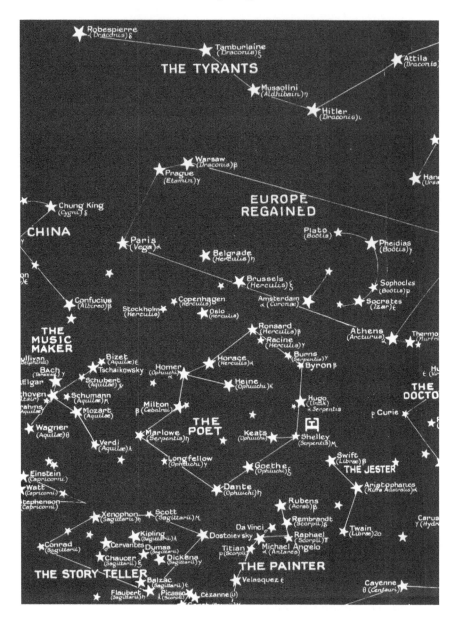

Fig. I.1   Detail from A.P. Herbert, *A Better Sky, or, Name this Star* (1940). Used with permission.

cultural function of those entities looming above "the ordinary man, woman and child." Herbert's rethinking of famous historical figures as stars, his appropriation of stardom to confirm the humanist traditions of the west, is an idea that could only happen in the waning years of the modernist period, at a moment when both the exploding Hollywood star system and Joyce's transformation of the myths of Odysseus into 1904 Dublin each exemplified a cultural desire to reconsider the relation between reputation and reality. Out with Ulysses and Sarah Bernhardt. In with Leopold Bloom and Clara Bow. In the first half of the twentieth century, those spheres of culture considered variously high (Joyce), low (cinema) or merely bizarre (Herbert) engaged in a radical re-envisaging of who would be elevated above the normal. Herbert found a distinct way to make the popular argument that through the lens of the early twentieth century, we celebrate a very different cast of characters.

Indeed, Herbert's *Better Map* compels a rereading of a no less famous statement of modernist thinking than that uttered by Virginia Woolf and repeated by scholars for the ensuing 80 years and counting: "On or about December 1910 human character changed." For all the service Woolf's celebrated line provides the prophecies of modernist aesthetic rupture, let us not forget that it identifies character, not aesthetic form, as the pertinent metamorphosis. For every epochal instance of form erupting in the works of Woolf, Joyce, Eliot, Stein, Pound, Faulkner, Barnes, and other modernist icons, for all the clarion calls to a return to form from modernism's critical flanks, is it possible that what was so startling were, in the end, only new kinds of characters? Responding to Arnold Bennett's accusation that her generation was inept at creating "real, true, and convincing" characters, Woolf answers with the demonstration of one Mrs. Brown, "one of those clean, threadbare old ladies [of] extreme tidiness": "There she sits in the corner of the carriage—that carriage which is traveling, not from Richmond to Waterloo, but from one age of English literature to the next" (423). Woolf's point is not to revive old debates about the immutability of character but undercut the terms of Bennett's indictment. As Woolf has it, any attempt to construe "character in fiction," heroically laid bare inside narrative, is outmoded by the state-of-the-art person glimpsed, however partially, extradiegetically, in the real world outside of books.

The accidental companion Brown is plucked from oblivion by none better than the "solitary, ill-informed, and misguided" author herself, that is, Woolf measuring an arm's length of distance between herself and the pedestrian across the railcar. The blandly named Brown offers not only an encounter with class difference but also a provocation with a form of excruciating obscurity. The anonymity is signaled, for instance, by the following remark, overheard by the omniscient author: "Can you tell me if an oak tree dies when the leaves have been eaten for two years in succession by caterpillars?" (421, 424). The non-sequitur, if nothing else provides a tremendous inducement for aesthetic production, Woolf suggests: "Few catch the phantom; most have to content with a scrap of her dress or a wisp of her hair" (421). Reality—if that's still the right word, rather than, say, ordinariness or banality—is outstripping the Bennetts of the world at their imaginary work; literary fortunes now depend on pursuing the "real" spectral bodies outside of fiction who augur different forms of identity, professionalism, personhood, and personality, different ways of claiming the status of the subject.

The shift at issue in this book, the transition which Woolf marks with so much assiduous imprecision, could be likened to the tipping point of celebrity culture itself. A nobody, from nowhere, from negligible origins, obscure for the sake of being obscure, Mrs. Brown enters public life "on or about" the moment of suffragist militancy and London's first encounter with post-impressionist art, yet she is not as yet traveling unaccompanied through public space. It would be surprising to find this "pinched," long-suffering female character firebombing mailboxes or frequenting the Grafton galleries. Over there "in her corner opposite," she presumably reads about such outrages over her daily bread, but she is not reading Woolf's books—nor Bennett's, truth be told—and yet what her appearance lacks in glamour and sophistication it makes up for in novelty. Here, it may be form, but it is the form of a character that allows Woolf to get in line with Pound's dictum to make it new—Woolf's "it girl" here a nonentity chosen for readers precisely for her unnerving normalcy.

The stroke of Mrs. Brown's sheer randomness comes through Woolf as an event of disorienting insignificance, as gauche as a naked light bulb: "very clean, very small, rather queer, and suffering intensely" (425). Then, with the same alacrity, the lady vanishes: "I watched her disappear, carrying her bag, into the vast blazing station. She looked … at once very frail and very heroic. And I have not seen her again, and I shall not know what became of her" (425). Ex nihilo, going nowhere, and—more to a point first observed in Daniel Boorstin's landmark book, *The Image*—known for knowness, she is, in the end, celebrated for nothing in particular save this uncanny familiarity without qualities. When we see candid photographs of celebrities—Steve McQueen posed with an unfamiliar person at a party, for example—one of the most disturbing things is the inevitably odd inclusion of ordinary, unknown faces. What is she doing next to him? Indeed the response has become so much a part of our sense of the celebrated that *Granta* dedicated much of its Autumn 2002 special issue on celebrity to exactly this: celebrities posing with fans. This disruption of the familiar in the stuff of celebrities is what Richard Schickel is getting at when he aptly describes them as "intimate strangers." This juxtaposition itself is a brush with the ubiquity of celebrification, yet it also suggests that knowness always seems to teeter on the brink of oblivion.

Woolf, like Baudelaire according to Walter Benjamin, is "more concerned with implanting the image in the memory than with adorning or elaborating it" ("Some Motifs in Baudelaire" 183).[1] Departing the train at London's Waterloo Station, lost in a massing urban crowd there is no need to mention, her character evokes what Benjamin describes as love "at last sight," a sense of her "being spared, rather than denied, fulfillment" (185–6). The famous "on or about 1910" line, with its odd prepositional muddiness, delivers its full meaning on a unstable spatial and temporal threshold, narratively speaking, conveying delay—missed

---

[1]   In *Tame Passions of Wilde*, Jeff Nunokawa connects this passage with Dorian Gray.

opportunity and belatedness—and restlessness. The latter sense cannot help but point to the transient mass audience's structures that the character embodies, mirrors, and heralds. Her background consequently resembles more typology than *bildung*: "The Victorian cook [who precedes her] lived like a leviathan in the lower depth, formidable, silent, inscrutable; the Georgian cook [who is her double] is a creature of sunshine and fresh air; in and out of the drawing room, now to borrow the *Daily Herald*, now to ask advice about a hat" (422). Matthew Arnold's Wragg—Brown's far more menacing Victorian relative—was never held up for celebration; she remained in the custody of newspapers and *Culture and Anarchy*. Woolf's character, a cipher of consumption in a post-literary age, is in the open and on the loose. Mass culture's personality takes form as a woman, who provides, *pace* Andreas Huyssen, a fantastic new sounding board "on or about" matters concerning newspapers and fashion. Well in advance of Andy Warhol, or even Gertrude Stein, Woolf places celebrity's extreme case on the jagged edge between oblivion and ubiquity: a celebrity for everybody, a celebrity who heralds the potential for celebrity for anybody.

Among the many potent forms of cultural experiment in play in the modernist period, the one that has been repeatedly underestimated—repeatedly left to non-academic, celebratory commentary—is celebrity culture. This books aims to correct this oversight. During early decades of the twentieth century, celebrity and our attitudes about it crystallized. As they did, older cultural formations (fame, aristocracy and rank, hero worship, the crowd) were smuggled along and transformed. The essays collected here demonstrate the folly of imagining the modernists immune to the explosion of mass-mediated celebrity around them. At the same time, this volume as a whole seeks to uncover the hidden role of modernism as a vanishing mediator in emergence of celebrity as cultural dominant. What the concept of celebrity offers modernist studies is an organon for the seemingly disparate concerns central to the "new modernisms": the settling of the canon wars, the turn to material modernisms, new critical bibliographic and text studies, the historical turn to examination of bodies, things, affect, performance, new media, cultures of consumption, and the economies of culture. What the concept of modernism offers celebrity studies—rooted in the disciplines of communications and cultural studies—is a theoretically rich explanation for a historical shift more often assumed than interrogated.

The General Theory

At the end of the last century and into this one, as celebrity has become visible as a ubiquitous, planetary form of cultural value, the scholar, the critic, and the cultural historian have sometimes struggled to keep pace. The topic presents astronomical possibilities for unreflective engagement on its own terms. At academic conference panels, for example, someone asserts, for argument's sake, that the first modern celebrity was, say, Charles Lindbergh, or the Biograph Girl, or Harry Houdini, or

Sarah Bernhardt. In response, an interlocutor jumps up and demands why Mark Twain, or Benjamin Disraeli, or Charles Dickens was not first proposed. Another jumps up (the two taking cues from the Oxford dons attending Stein's "Composition as Explanation" lecture) and suggests P.T. Barnum, or Lord Byron, or Jonathan Strange, or Alexander the Great. The search for origins for celebrity *per se* starts to sound suspiciously like the familiarly mythologized, *ex nihilo* origin story of the individual celebrity. Exit nobody, enter celebrity personality: the moment Jack Nicholson dons a football helmet on the back of Captain America's chopper, or Faye Dunaway bobs her hair, puts on a beret, and picks up a gun. Too often we speak through—but not about—the discourses of celebrity and the business at hand becomes celebration and celebrification rather than concept or critique. In the process these famous characters are treated without a conceptualized distinction between what it meant to be a renowned international tyrant in 1814 and the significance of an actress whose fame sells war bonds in 1918.

That is just to say that celebrification, even or perhaps especially within academic circles, tends to elide the historical differences between who, what, and how cultures once elevated its characters. But celebrity in the form we recognize it best is a phenomenon of a particular moment, one shared with the period of literary modernism, identified here as spanning the end of the nineteenth century and the mid-twentieth century. After all, a consultation with the *OED* suggests that, in P. David Marshall's explanation, "the use of the term *celebrity* in its contemporary (ambiguous) form developed in the nineteenth century" (4). Etymology aside, the path many scholars have taken to navigate away from infinite regression implied by the backwards glance from Lindbergh to Byron leads through Leo Braudy's *Frenzy of Renown*, a work responsible for the phrase "the democratizing of fame," which denotes the splintering off of fame from traditional hierarchies of state-sanctioned achievement. This schism between fame and celebrity emerges into legibility in the nineteenth century, and virtually explodes across the star ferment in the early twentieth. Those following Braudy's cues have produced a certain consensus about the golden age of celebrity. These range from the hyperbolic—Richard Schickel claiming that, "there was no such thing as celebrity prior to the beginning of the twentieth century" (31)—to the more materially historical—Jib Fowles' pointing out that, "[p]revious to … the nineteenth century, the famous were primarily people who wielded social power, such as religious figures, state leaders, or military commanders" (10). The tendency to mark a general shift, aligning fame with tradition and celebrity with novelty, can be traced to the seminal work on this topic by the Frankfurt School. Leo Löwenthal, in 1943, for example, surveying biographies published in the United States since the beginning of the twentieth century, noted a "considerable decrease of people from the serious and important professions and a corresponding increase of entertainers" (111). Löwenthal argues further that biography as a form—even the sort he categorizes with more than a whiff of cultural austerity as having "serious and important" subjects—undergoes a stylistic mutation consonant with new social prerogatives of entertainments and culture industries.

Given the centrality of visual culture—from image to spectacle—to these concerns, it is no accident that the general account treats photography and cinema as central, if not the decisive, technological factors behind celebrity. As Leo Braudy writes, "[t]he photograph, with its exaltation of a momentary state of physical being, and the motion picture, which further emphasized its subject's immersion in a passing time, helped create the more uneasy relation we now share with those in the spotlight," in contrast with earlier, pre-photographic conceptions of fame (554). Granting that celebrity is, to a high degree, a consequence of the cultural penetration of photography also supports the case for celebrity's genesis as early as the mid-nineteenth century, as everything from illustrated newspapers to studio portraits brought mechanically reproduced images across divisions of privilege and into ordinary experience. As Nancy Armstrong has shown, by the 1860s, photographic portraits "were no longer reserved for people of birth, wealth, or prominence" and thus could contribute to the elevation to celebrity status of figures of less traditional categories (129). Certainly, this volume follows the broad contours of this account, but taking notice (in the essays of Goldman and Brown) of visual culture's uneven development in the subsequent period, it reasons a case for a long gestation and a complex causality. Hammill's examination of *Vanity Fair*, for instance, explores the innovations in publication and distribution networks that made mass circulation middlebrow magazines of the 1920s and 1930s such a critical nexus for elite and popular form of cultural value. Moreover, in this volume, Zox-Weaver and Comentale argue for more explanatory weight to ascendant nonvisual communication technologies such radio and recording machinery, and, in similar ways, Mix, Hepburn, Jaffe, and Watt contend that new technique and scalability in monetary systems, theatricality, advertising, and publicity played key parts in establishing not only patterns for the popular consumption of celebrity but also, as Davis, Garval and Glass explore, its sub-routines and niches.

If Braudy's *Frenzy* is the magisterial study of fame, the paradigmatic transhistorical survey of a perennial theme from antiquity to the present, then Richard Dyer's *Stars* is the definitive treatment of cinematic celebrity—a narrow cultural studies analysis of the mechanisms of the Hollywood star system. Fame is august, venerable, and impressive by reason of old age; celebrity, in contrast, has attention deficit disorder. Neither has much to say about the historical seam between fame and celebrity. For Braudy, it's all about modulation of a uniform sacralizing impulse, the eternal return of ancestor worship; for Dyer, the specific apparatus is all, the system's collective production and its socio-political meaning. Following Dyer—but not so much his pioneer queering of these issues in *Heavenly Bodies*—the 'General Theory of Celebrity' adheres to a model abstracted from the Hollywood of the studio system era, supporting a visually defined, contemporary manifestation of the "star image." It is a version stemming from yet unreserved for the movies; Roland Barthes might see in the mass-reproduced mask of Greta Garbo a "Platonic Idea of the human creature" (56)—a moment redressed by Judith Brown's essay here—but also views the brain of Albert Einstein as "the image of knowledge reduced to a formula" (69). Braudy, Barthes, and Dyer behold celebrity for its unearthliness, taking the character out of the celebrity and releasing the star to the skies.

Accordingly, in the hands of P. David Marshall, S. Paige Baty, Chris Rojek, Ellis Cashmore, Graeme Turner, and others situated in faculties of sociology, communications, and media studies, celebrity functions as a symptom of, and a synonym for, post-modernity in various incarnations. Rejecting the notion that celebrities are anchored by "real" people or subjectivity, for instance, Marshall, channeling Foucault and Baudrillard, reads celebrities as capacious semiosis banks, powerful simulacra worked by remote control to "legitimate and illegitimate domains of the personal and individual within the social" (56). Rojek, too, despite a robust rogues' gallery that includes a celebrity alphabet from Ali G to Ziggy Stardust, closes with this perfunctory postmodern moral about celebrity's semiotic emporium and *res publica*:

> As long as democracy and capitalism prevail there will always be an Olympus, inhabited not by Zeus and his court, but by celebrities, elevated from the mass, who embody the restless, fecund and frequently disturbing form of the mass in the public face they assemble. (199)

Rojek's celebrity menagerie performs a unified function as a pantheon for a secular society. That there is an absent particularity in the general theory may be said to derive from its insubstantial incorporation of major celebrity work performed by the literary, which, at the moment of celebrity's manifestation, was undergoing its own shifts into more idealized realms. As Loren Glass has argued, the "focus on the modern culture industries of film, music, and television, in which the individual agency behind the celebrity persona is clearly vitiated," obscures celebrity's genealogical relationship with authorship, a connection implicit in Marshall's adaptation of Foucault's author-function (3). Literary celebrity has received explicit attention in historical studies such as Glass's *Author's Inc.: Literary Celebrity in the Modern United States, 1880–1980*, David Haven Blake's *Walt Whitman and the Culture of American Celebrity*, Joe Moran's *Star Authors: Literary Celebrity in America*, concerning the contemporary American scene; and, John Frow and James F. English's "Literary Authorship and Celebrity Culture," focusing on the contemporary British analogue. And, like this volume, Mike Garval's *'A Dream of Stone': Fame, Vision, and Monumentality in Nineteenth-Century French Literary Culture*, Jaffe's *Modernism and the Culture of Celebrity*, and Faye Hammill's *Women, Celebrity, and Literary Culture between the Wars* attend to some of literary celebrity's transatlantic constellations and cosmopolitan ambitions.

Highlighting some of the difficulties of a general theory derived from spectacular entertainers, these studies raise the problem of authorial agency "when writers themselves strive, not only through media appearances but in their very practice as writers, to manipulate the form and function of celebrity and short-circuit some of its usual effects" (Frow and English 44). Attention to celebrity authors helps bring into relief how the afterlife of authorial agency is implicated in the struggles of multiple constituencies—and, not least the celebrities themselves—to produce, circulate, and consume the bodies, personalities, and meanings of anybody and everybody: starlets, jocks, eggheads, pop stars, dictators, astronauts, nobodies, you name it.

One of the particular achievements of Glass's book could be described as its American Studies conjecture that authorship helped consolidate celebrity during the industrial transformation of the United States in the mid-nineteenth century. Building on the important work of scholars such as Mark Rose, Glass shows how magazine and book industries provide a means for personalities to go national. "Literary" celebrities such as Barnum (for whom forgoing the copyright on his autobiography speeds its promotional work) and celebrity authors such as Twain (who self-incorporates to shore up control of his authorial image and bequeath it to his daughter) exist as "signature literary" personalities providing a thin edge that wedge the ideologies of intellectual property and the right to privacy into national consciousness.[2] Twain's unease with these conditions—his attempts to control the author-function through capitalizing his name as so many shares—is a foretaste of the cultural contradictions of modernist authorship in a transnational framework. To this conjecture, we should perhaps add the Bela Lugosi Corollary, recalling the legal decision against Lugosi's heirs that, however vexingly, enshrines in legal precedent the crypto-modernist point that personality rights—the celebrity image, in so many words—are inferior property to that of copyright—based in the textual stuff of authors—and cannot be passed to heirs.[3]

The Special Theory

Concerning the shift from fame to celebrity, our general preposition, simply put, is that celebrity names the form that fame takes under conditions of modernity. Celebrity serves as an allegory of the triumph of mass commodity and mass consumption, readers, audiences, and fans, and, most saliently, the triumph of a mass idol as a fantasy of discretely defined individualism. The burden of bringing modernism and celebrity into a shared frame of reference means more than charting new economic frontiers, communications technologies, forms of publicity, and institutions. It entails scrutiny to specific changes in the literary. This brings us to the purview of modernist studies: altered mode and means of character, personality, theatricality, intellectuality, and publicity; extraordinary, uncanny, incredible, amazing kinds of stories encountered in esoteric, complex, unorthodox, sometimes pulpy, often cosmopolitan media contexts. For reasons identified by Moran, Glass, Hammill, and others, celebrity authors provide a special case, and for good reason. Celebrity is, as Jaffe has argued, authorial/literary self-fashioning *in extremis*. In that they share what we might call the cultural logic of celebrity, modernist literature, and popular cultural production, even if pitched to

---

[2]   See Adam Goldman's excellent documentary, *The Mark Twain Company* (1998).

[3]   See Lugosi v. Universal Pictures (1979) 25 C3d 813 <http://online.ceb.com/ CalCases/C3/25C3d813.htm>. For a consideration of Lugosi's case, see Gary Don Rhodes, *Lugosi: His Life in Films, on Stage, and in the Hearts of Horror Lovers.*

different audiences, address the same set of historical concerns. It turns out that the study of not only literary celebrity, but literature of celebrity's moment, exposes both celebrity's reach into the corners of society and modernism's suffusion into the mainstream. On this basis, this book both builds on and critically reassesses academic work that has attempted to chart the relation between modernism and popular culture. Once we view modernism's model of the author alongside the production of popular celebrity, we can conceptualize the relationship between these supposedly divergent spheres of culture as more of a collaboration than a parting of the ways of cultural production.

To see what modernism shares with popular celebrity, we need to understand how the modernist aesthetic pressures authorship; in terms not only of the production of the inscrutable art object but also the choreography of consumption, reception, and promotion. We need to understand modernist technique, that is, not merely as a difficult way of encoding popular material for a specialized domain of art, but as an expression of the same need for the subject to become an object that drives popular culture. Such an understanding of modernism, revealed in the Woolf's treatment of her stranger on a train, brings it in close proximity to celebrity, allowing us to historicize modernist style as a means of self-production within the text that accompanies, and in fact supersedes, the self-production of marketing and promotional activities. It is through style, and the attendant productions of originality and difficulty, that high modernism is thought to define itself and achieve at once its convergence with and separation from mass culture. The style of Mrs. Brown, the form of anonymity that allows her elevation above the norm, shows us modernist's participation in the great reaction to the changed historical conditions that create celebrity as well.

Some 20 years before Woolf's changed character, the literary and celebrity worlds already had the extraordinary case of Oscar Wilde's Dorian Gray. Unlikely as it may seem to compare Wilde's vision of splendidly preternatural male adolescence with Woolf's of common and ubiquitous female senescence, it is worth remembering that Gray and Brown are both set in motion as figurations of their times as a change to the individual. "There are only two eras of any importance in the world's history," Basil tells Lord Henry: "The first is the appearance of a new medium of art, and the second is the appearance of a new personality also. What the invention of oil painting was to the Venetians, ... the face of Dorian Gray will some day be to me" (11). In so many words, Gray supplies a similar chronotope to Brown, giving bodily form to temporal conditions when new forms of being human come into sight, already (1889) a modification of Barthes' Platonism. The moral of the story—one, at any rate—is that the rapid decrepitude that awaits Dorian bares the full metonymic weight of his youth cult/sentimental education in fashion. When Benjamin writes that "fashion defends the rights of the corpse," it is perhaps Dorian whom he means ("Central Park" 79).

Taking a page from Wilde, celebrity turns away from the form/content split of an archaic aesthetic system, replacing it with a new vocabulary in the terms of Gray's portraitist: medium and personality. Character, in effect, steps into the "real world," becoming too big to be contained by literary works and authors. The reconception seems at first to bypass a litany of modern bourgeois agonistics but, in the end, the effect heightens the moral vertigo: face/value, leisure/work, outside/inside, surface/depth, public/private, eminence/prominence, object/subject, exterior/interior; and, borrowing a final dualism from Steven Connor, extimacy/intimacy. If personality "simply" means the face of Dorian, metonymically, it has superhuman powers of extension that rapidly reorganize all human artifice into second nature: image, gesture, fashion, talismanic objects of selfhood, wisps of hair, scraps of clothes, handbags, signatures, trademarks, brands are all placed under the command of personality:

> To him Life itself was the first, the greatest of the arts…Fashion, by which what is really fantastic becomes for a moment universal, and Dandyism, which, in its own way, is an attempt to assert the absolute modernity of beauty, had, of course, their fascination for him. His mode of dressing, and the particular styles that from time to time he affected, had their marked influence on the young exquisites of the Mayfair balls and Pall Mall club windows, who copied him everything he did. (146)

The role of medium may be productively understood in terms of what Samuel Weber calls mass mediaura, authenticity of the real person arrives via mass mediated market place. If, as Basil has it, "newspapers [become] the nineteenth-century standard of immortality," mass mediauras, as the medium and measure of invention, replace immortality with ubiquity as the cultural desiratum (8).

We want to return to this shift, which is a critical limit between the concepts of fame and celebrity. Morality re-enters the picture, through the fan's affective relationship with (a) character. "What the invention of oil-painting was to the Venetians, … the face of Dorian Gray will some day be to me." "To me," Basil says possessively, as if he already registers that this ascendant character relegates the artist/author to a sub-species of the fan—in contrast to the earlier-modern moment of renaissance Venice. The epochal power of a medium for a multitude becomes individualized as a fan's individual encounter with an epochal personality. Basil's observation calls to mind fan cults, as does the warehouse of talismanic paraphernalia Dorian acquires (relics, ties) or the sentimental education set in motion by the loan of a certain yellow book from Lord Henry. In effect, Dorian supplies an extra-literary protagonist and plot for Lord Henry's "exquisite raiment," a kind of fan scrapbook conceived with a hole in the shape of Dorian Gray (141–2).

This quality resonates with a number of elements of Wilde's novel that expose a new porosity of intra- and extra-literary domains. The condition bears on the fate of Sybil Vane in particular, who provides the novel's answer to the Brown-Wragg axis of obscurity. Sordid news of her "lonely death in the tawdry dressing-room," buried in the pages of *The Standard*, establishes the kinship. The death of a "third-rate actress with a pretty face" is said to be caused by a "dreadful thing they use at theatres," meaning prussic acid or white lead, but the wording contributes to a sense of a murder in—or, even, by—the lower genres of the society of the spectacle, which is not quite the same, *pace* Bill Brown, as Sister Carrie's encounter with a camera. The interpretation that Lord Henry ("the lad was his own creation" as much as Basil's) proffers and Dorian all-too-readily adopts also confuses art and real life, albeit on a higher register of the generic continuum: Vane is, he argues, "less real" than the heroines of Shakespearean tragedy (naming Ophelia, Desdemona, and Cordelia), describing her instead as "a strange lurid fragment from some Jacobean tragedy" (65, 116–17). Dorian accepts the logic, but rejects the review. For him, Sybil realizes "a wonderful tragic figure sent on to the world's stage." Her suicide overcomes her hackneyed and sensationalist commonplaces, as formulated in a derivative way: "When she knew its unreality, she died, as Juliet might have died. She passed again into the sphere of art" (119, 98). Vane's failure is to misunderstand her quite ordinary self, behind the masque of the stage heroine, as real, and not just real, but bourgeois-real. It is akin, as Lois Cucullu points out in her essay here, to mistaking growing up for the objective, when it is clear in Wilde's world that it is an adolescent fascination with style and performance that makes the novel tick.

It has been evident from Basil's painting and Lord Henry's book that the "real" Dorian was always more affective in art than life, but to show Sybil in these terms reveals the extent that this perception is specific neither to the medium nor the personality. These issues now play across the frontiers of audience structures and generic expectations. And it is, after all, Sybil's interpretation of Dorian that holds sway in the end—the sinister fantasia that Prince Charming now "rules life for us," which owes more to unclassical folk mythology than attic grace. This interpretation traverses the various aesthetic domains, making a rake's progress through increasingly public, debased, and diffused spaces, moving from the salon and coterie to the theatre and the street, the last being governed by the most chatty, dispossessed, and transient of creative practices, namely, fashion and gossip:

> As [Dorian] strolled home, smoking his cigarette, two young men in evening dress passed him. He heard one of them whisper to the other, "That is Dorian Gray." He remembered how pleased he used to be when he was pointed out, or stared at, or talked about. He was tired of hearing his own name now. Half the charm of the little village where he had been so often lately was that no one knew who he was. (249)

Here, at the point of maximum semiotic diffusion—"liquid life," in Zygmunt Bauman's phase—it is not merely the differences between notoriety and fame that are irrelevant. So too are the differences between known-ness and un-known-ness. In short, the dilemma of Britney Spears: maximum semiotic diffusion equals semiotic red shift, the celebrity universe's cold death. The celebrity's struggle looks a lot like the struggle of the earlier hero, laboring *fama semper vivat* against oblivion. The celebrity also struggles against oblivion, but the instrument he or she uses is ubiquity. Indeed, Marshall's fundamental methodological premise is that celebrities are not people, but rather "an effective means for the commodification of the self" (26). Celebrities are not like you and me; they are both more ubiquitous and less human. They are more than this, of course; they are also more like fictional characters than you or I. The implication of this two-pronged conclusion for personality and medium is one of the morals of Wilde's celebrity fable.

The conjunction of modernism and celebrity is now, to quote Norma Desmond in *Sunset Boulevard*, ready for its close-up. The close-up reveals a special relationship, a homology conjoining two vanishing mediators in scenes of the presentation of value under conditions of modernity. For the last decade or so, scholars of the so-called "new modernisms" have turned their attentions to the facts of modernism: matters of production and consumption, material culture, historical context, institutions, sundry cultural goods, things. Taking their cues from particular developments in cultural studies and the archive fever initiated by new historicism, modernist scholars on or about 1999 initiated a kind of gentrification. As urban pioneers, they discovered old housing stock, added granite counters, hardwood floors, fresh paint, avant-garde showerheads, to make it new. Make it new, again, it seemed:

> According to the theoretical assumptions and critical practice endorsed by the "New Modernisms," no longer was the work of art to be considered in isolation from the biographical, cultural, and ideological circumstances that impacted its production and reception. And no longer was modernist studies the exclusive province of white male academics examining the work of their artistic, racial, gender inscribed, and ethnic counterparts in England and, sometimes, the United States. Though analysis of the lives and work of such 'canonical' artists such as Ezra Pound, T.S. Eliot, and James Joyce continues to be a part of modernist studies, attention has shifted to the cultural circumstance in which they wrote or to an interrogation of the premises by which they and other white male writers have been designated central in a landscape populated by artists and thinkers heretofore excluded from critical consideration by matters of race, ethnicity, gender, economic circumstances, geographic location, and ideology. (Charles 179–80)

This book comes out of the shared observation by its editors that all this rediscovery of *biographical, cultural, and ideological circumstances* entails something like the invention of personality for modernism. Modernist studies finally were ready for Mrs. Brown.

It is no coincidence that these developments and the concomitant turn to alternative modernisms come not only in the wake of queer theory, elaborated as it is around the queer recovery of certain modernists—James, Wilde, and Stein, above all—but also the reassessment of Hemingway, Eliot, Woolf, Cather, Barnes, Loy, Proust, and Joyce. As Jaime Hovey observes in *A Thousand Words: Portraiture, Style, and Queer Modernism*, "when queer theorists such as Judith Butler or Judith Halberstam began to use modernist texts such as Larsen's *Passing* and Radclyffe Hall's *The Well of Loneliness* to theorize more generally about gender as performance and performative, they abstracted twentieth-century gender from the art and literature that helped formulate it" (2–3). An essential concern for the essays in the volume entails, what Hammill describes elsewhere as, the problem of a "history of literary celebrity … rendered in strikingly male terms," and, to Hammill's point, we hasten to add that this history has often been rendered in strikingly queer erotics. The link between literary celebrity and the discourse of hyperbolic manliness—exemplified in Dale Peck's *Hatchet Jobs*, for instance—is an atavistic hangover of a fame game extending from Braudy at least, as far back in modern times as Thomas Carlyle's *On Heroes, Hero-Worship and the Heroic in History* (1841). Where Jaffe has argued that literary celebrity in the restricted high modernist context is caught in a punitive bind between the feminized work of publicity and masculinist work of authorship, Hammill, recovering an expanded field of women author–celebrities including Anita Loos and Mae West, reads "new paradigms for female literary success."

Consider, on the model of Loos and West, not only figures such as Loy and Stein, but also the likes of Cléo de Mérode, a nearly forgotten, shadowy version of Sarah Bernhardt, discussed by Garval, or Elvis Presley, discussed by Comentale, who exemplify possibilities for ludic, unliterary exceptions to the Bela Lugosi corollary by traversing the personality/authorship impasse. Or consider further Cucullu's assertion that celebrity, in the guise of Dorian Gray, actually marks a transition from a Victorian high serious *eminence grise* to the playful moment of adolescence. From gossip to publicity, from Hammill's sophistication to Brown's glamour, from Oscar Wilde to David Bowie,[4] celebrity organizes and legitimizes powerful affective energies—libidinal, anonymous, queer—in the cultural field, yet, again and again, as the essays in this volume repeatedly confirm, it proves an equivocal and unstable measure of a cultural good. For fame, this is unequivocally the case—bad fame is called notoriety, after all—but celebrity does its handiwork whether its experienced as gain or loss, fortune or hazard.

This kinship between the modernist, the celebrity, and the commodity, the idea that modernist celebrity can, "like gas engines or soda crackers or other consumer goods, be mass manufactured" (Leff xiii)—as opposed to an idealized, organic form of renown, drives the approaches in this volume. The purview does not merely include the degree and pursuit of fame and renown of the producers of modernist works—although these have been addressed productively, to be sure, and by some of the authors of the present volume—but comprises how the structures and discourses of celebrity underwrite the thematic, aesthetic and ideological modernist project.

Celebrity has until recently remained compulsively overlooked by modernist scholars—a cultural hazard no one wanted to touch. As Steven Connor observes, discussions of celebrity tend to neglect the very negativity, indeed the violence, structuring the celebrity/public relationship, and modernist scholars until very

---

   [4]   Or, from the modernists to the mods, as Todd Haynes's *Velvet Goldmine* elegantly encapsulates it. We're grateful to Andrea Fontenot for bringing this connection to our attention.

recently have fallen into a similar impasse because celebrity seems to erode cardinal modernist myth of discrete individual subjectivity. Celebrity was ignored, because, in part, it bears on aspects of authorship, authorial self-fashioning, and cultural authority that modernist studies have often been uneasy about having in the open. Even ground-breaking work about marketing modernism can be seen as complicit in lionizing not just the textual objects of scrutiny but also their creators. This book seeks to breaks free of this entrenched mode, working to explore the interstitial forms of celebrity and modernist affect, identity, commodification, value effects, personality, charisma, and theatricality. The present volume attends these concerns directly, arguing that the relation between modernism and the popular is unthinkable without celebrity. Moreover, celebrity's cunning passage into the twentieth century—whether manufactured in Hollywood studios, the Duke University English department, the famous "little magazines" that published modernists' writings or the infamous mass-market magazines that published their photographs—is unimaginable without the intercession of modernism's system of cultural value. Rather than merely spotting celebrity thematics in modernist texts or sighting modernist celebrities in popular culture, the essays collected here seek to chart the frequencies of these jointly emergent, mutually influential forms of cultural value.

The astrology of celebrity modernists and modernist celebrities collected in *Modernist Star Maps* charts characters, authors, impresarios, svengalis, divas, literary failures, sellouts, failed cases, con artists, playwrights, movie stars, directors, promoters, publicists, television stars, personalities. A quick scan through the index reveals names recurring through the essays: Oscar Wilde, Dorian Gray, Lord Harry, Virginia Woolf, Baroness Orczy, Tarzan, Orlando, Jay Gatsby, David Belasco, Eric Walrond, Erskine Caldwell, Frank Crowninshield, Marilyn Monroe, Gertrude Stein, the Tramp, Cléo de Mérode, Samuel Beckett, Douglas Fairbanks, Leni Riefenstahl, Rolf Harris, Rudolph Valentino, Marcel Duchamp, Adolf Hitler, and Elvis Presley. A book with scholarly essays on Elvis and Hitler necessarily calls to mind Don DeLillo's *White Noise* and its parody of bogus cultural studies. In effect, *White Noise* indicts Hitler Studies and Elvis Studies for being devoid of literary value—for lacking rigor, historical sense and critique. Hitler Studies, for instance, is so obviously fraudulent that its professorial originator in the novel, J.A.K. Gladney, has not yet mastered German, and what he passes off as "scholarship" merely accelerates the unreflective circulation of stale Hitler gossip. Whereas celebrity and celerity are related etymologically, celebrity, commentary and critique are not. Moreover, it is worth noting Benjamin's distinction:

> If, to use a simile, one views the growing work as a funeral pyre, its commentator can be likened to the chemist, its critic to an alchemist. While the former is left with wood and ashes as the sole objects of his analysis, the latter is concerned only with the enigma of the flame itself: the enigma of being alive. ("Goethe's Elective Affinities" 298)

Benjamin's simile might be understood as a figuration of cultural value in all its forms—fame, celebrity, notoriety, renown, reputation, and so on. Whereas celebrity studies in the J.A.K. Gladney vein merely stokes the embers of cultural value, the essays in this book attempt what Benjamin likens to chemical and alchemical analysis: commenting on the materiality of the tinder and residue and critiquing "the enigma of the flame itself" in terms of its curious life and afterlife. Part of the difficulty of conducting a reception history of cultural value *per se* is its very immateriality. Yet, the "perseity" of the object—to borrow a term Garval elaborates in his chapter—belies a material genealogy in a tissue of textual and paratextual citations, allusions, anecdotes, commodities, biographical debris, and cultural forms that once existed outside the legitimate purview of serious literary study, but have long persisted as a kind of celebrity white noise.

The essays here go to extraordinary lengths to rematerialize their objects. They engage, in effect, in what Stephen Watt calls in his chapter here, the study of "reverse influence":

> For much of the previous century, the discipline of literary criticism was obsessed with [...] the effect of past writers and texts on later ones—and post-graduate students just a generation or two ago were trained in the protocols of tracing influence and literary reputation. A revised cultural criticism needs to privilege the opposite process, defining the ways present aesthetic conventions and thematic preoccupations modify, even deform, the past. (PAGE#?)

Taking up the gauntlet, *Modernist Star Maps* seeks to explore both how our contemporary notion of cultural value turns our telescopic attention on certain figures of the past and ways to chronicle history alongside the preoccupations of our moment. The volume is therefore split into three sections: Part 1, celebrity modernisms, a selection of chapters exploring critical constellations of celebrity modernists and modernisms; Part 2, modernist celebrities, celebrity as a modernist vernacular and material form; Part 3, interstellar afterimages, the surprising durability, uncanny deaths, and deformations, and late theories of these forms.

Theories of celebrity in general and in the particular have tended to focus upon specific performers or audiences/fans worshiping at distinct celebrity sites. While the system of celebrity requires its discrete celebrities, a pressing need exists to understand the constellatory structure of celebrity, the extent to which it relies upon configurations of multiple celebrities and scenes of encounter and address. This collection departs from earlier academic treatments of celebrity by resisting the tendency to engage the phenomenon *in medias res*, to view celebrity as a symptom and a synchronic occasion for a larger diagnostic survey. Instead we trace the history of celebrity as a form of valuation diachronically, back to that early crisis of literary professionalism of the late nineteenth and early twentieth centuries known as modernism. With this in mind these essays argue for celebrity as a decisively relational, even diacritical, mode of valuation.

PART 1
Celebrity Modernisms

Chapter 1
Adolescent *Dorian Gray*: Oscar Wilde's Proto-Picture of Modernist Celebrity

Lois Cucullu

Fame is the thirst of youth.
—Lord Byron, *Childe Harold*'s *Pilgrimage*, 1812–1818

Be Happy and You Will Be Virtuous.
—Grant Allen, "The New Hedonism," 1894

That the name "Oscar Wilde" still raises eyebrows after more than a century testifies to the longevity of Wilde's notoriety. Throughout the 1880s and 1890s, and up to his conviction for gross indecency, Wilde was celebrated as an aesthete, artist, dandy, playwright, raconteur, savvy editor, and all around public personality. His success at meshing public persona and literary production is arguably unrivalled by any of his English literary peers. The net result of his self-promotion, so characteristic of celebrity culture, is that Wilde's public persona assumed a life of its own, surpassing even his bodacious fashioning of self-image. As his career progressed, it became increasingly difficult to separate the artist, his work, and his persona. We get an early glimpse of the workings of this fame machinery alongside the orbit of Wilde's rising status in the wry sketch that tracks the artist's early career, "Days with Celebrities, Mr. Oscar Wilde," published in 1882 in the weekly magazine *Moonshine*.[1] As it comically records, Wilde was acclaimed and mocked, as he would be later castigated following his trials, imprisonment, and penurious death, as a celebrity in English society when the very category and term, as scholars and critics have shown, were just gaining traction in the popular vernacular. Indeed the scholarly community writing on celebrity has rightly come to regard him, along with a handful of his contemporaries on either side of the Atlantic, as helping to inaugurate the phenomenon of celebrity culture that is one hallmark of twentieth- and twenty-first-century modernity.

---

[1]   For a discussion of the sketch and representations of Wilde's image, see Joseph Bristow's "Introduction," *Wilde Writings* 18–25. I wish to express my sincere appreciation to Joseph Bristow, to the National Endowment for the Humanities, and to UCLA's Clark Memorial Library for the 2007 Summer Seminar "The Oscar Wilde Archive." The writing of this essay has been greatly enlivened by the productive colloquy our group of scholars daily enjoyed.

Fig. 1.1   "Days with Celebrities, Mr. Oscar Wilde," *Moonshine* (January 28, 1882).

But the irreverent *Moonshine* caricature tells us more about Wilde and celebrity culture than first meets the eye. Taken as a perhaps playful forerunner of today's paparazzi relentless hounding of the rich and famous, it not only highlights the conflation of artist, work, and image in one deft sketch. It also significantly points to the looming collapse of the barrier separating private from public life that mass media would aggressively come to exploit—no activity being too mundane or too private to escape public scrutiny, especially if it smacks of scandal. And, for Wilde, nowhere does the breakdown of public/private appear more wounding and the public appetite for exposé more voracious than when his private homosexual liaisons become common knowledge during the course of his trials. Such is the machinery of fame that we witness the legal assault on his juridical person and, in the same moment, the public attack and stigmatization of his public persona with Wilde the man having to bear the brunt on all fronts. Ironically, what both fuels and hastens his physical downfall is *The Picture of Dorian Gray* (1890, revised 1891).[2] At his first trial and thereafter, this story serves as evidence of Wilde's profligacy and his sodomitical associations, associations that persist down to the present. So while the novella continues willy-nilly to be read as a melodramatic parable of deviance, moral corruption, and self-destruction, it persists more radically as Wilde's uncanny foretelling of his own cultural rise and physical ruin. Even in this more tolerant century, *Dorian Gray* popularly serves both as Wilde's decadent back-story and his epitaph, and, conversely, the castigation of Wilde as an abject homosexual still haunts the reception of *Dorian Gray*.[3] More than a hundred years after Wilde's death, his notoriety and fate remains intertwined with Dorian's and Dorian's with his. Indeed, one could well argue that more than the diverse body

---

[2]   Because Wilde has served as *cause célèbre* for Foucault's famous transformation of the act of sodomy into the homosexual actor, contemporary scholars have sought to parse the entanglement of Wilde as author, public persona, and homosexual, an entanglement, I submit, that is characteristic of the culture of celebrity. Daniel Novak has most recently pushed the discussion back on itself. He persuasively makes the case that Sir Edward Carson the prosecutor in the first trial turns Wilde into his sexual acts and turns his written act of the fiction *Dorian Gray* into the juridical body: "rather than turning the act into a subject, Carson attempts both to turn the subject into an act, and to transform the *fictional* subject into a juridical body" (4, original emphasis).

[3]   Bristow in his introduction to *The Picture of Dorian Gray* (hereafter *Dorian Gray* or *DG*) in *The Complete Works* provides the literary and publication history of the two texts, to include their reception, which, it is fair to say, was controversial from the outset. And even though Wilde attempted to tweak the popularity of the *Lippincott's* story by aestheticizing the novel version with an elegant book design, for example, the magazine version, as Bristow points out, had already painted Wilde as a popular storyteller, a legacy the novel never overturned (lviii). Let me note that given my purpose of connecting Wilde and *The Picture of Dorian Gray* to modernism and celebrity culture, I have chosen here to cite the revised 1891 text published as a novel, which continues to circulate as a cultural artifact and literary text, instead of the 1890 story published in *Lippincott's*, though the two texts are included in volume three of *The Complete Works*.

of work he created, more even than his great social comedies, Wilde's continuing celebrity owes to this singular gothic tale.

Given the role *Dorian Gray* has played as well as Wilde's pivotal position in the arts, at the end of the Victorian era in the midst of the great social, cultural, and technological upheaval that modernism would register, there remains more to Wilde's impact on celebrity formation that I wish to pursue here than merely observing the conflation of artist and *objet d'art*, collapse of private and public boundaries, and emergence of the scandal-mongering mass media and their gossip-happy audiences. In my earlier work, pressuring Andreas Huyssen's famous critique of "the great divide," which called attention to high cultural products versus their putative other, mass cultural ones, I shifted focus away from modernists' artifacts to concentrate on the agents themselves by linking elite literary modernists and their devotees and disciples in the arts and academia to the rise of expert culture and the concomitant secularization of knowledge. Maintaining that hierarchy and the monopolization of knowledge became de facto as critical in the literary arts as it was in the sciences, I showed how modernists, as competitors in a burgeoning knowledge market, sought to distinguish their work as *sui generis*, and themselves as a class apart consistent with experts in other fields. Modernists sought prestige for themselves as artists and cultural capital for their experiments as nonpareil representations of the travails of modernity. In this essay, pursuing Jonathan Goldman's cogent point that "signature styles of modernism and celebrity produce similar forms of cultural value" (*Modernism Is the Literature of Celebrity* 3) I consider the material and temporal conditions that conferred value on these two cultural phenomena in order to add to the collection's conversation about the stage that modernism and celebrity culture came to share.

To accomplish this, I want to consider modernism and the cult of the celebrity in relation to my current work on youth culture and adolescence. Over the course of this essay, in terms of modernism, I will suggest that it is not enough to see the shift from a Victorian to a modernist sensibility on strictly technical or aesthetic grounds as traditionally presented. Nor is it sufficient to understand it primarily as generational conflict, even though for many, such as the Bloomsberries, a belief in their superiority as a generation underpinned their brash pronouncements about their stylistic innovations: think here of Lytton Strachey's *Eminent Victorians*. By similar token, it is not enough to place the *frisson* within the sociological frame of dominant versus newcomer elaborated by Pierre Bourdieu in such works as *The Field of Cultural Production* and *Distinction*. Though these models retain considerable explanatory power, there remains more to the contention of a rupture with the past and embrace of the new advanced by modernist radicals from F.T. Marinetti to Ezra Pound, from Mina Loy to James Joyce. I contend that an underlying change equally profound and uniquely embodied was taking place, and it was happening around the dynamic of age itself. Most particularly, it occurred in the new and sweeping emphasis on youth and its categorical excrescence, that of adolescence, the impact of which shaped modernism no less than celebrity culture. So though celebrity may be a quintessential twentieth-century phenomenon as

P. David Marshall and Richard Schickel have persuasively contended, and while it may be inextricably linked to modernism as the editors of this book have asserted, it is no less true that the celebrity and modernism arise at roughly the same juncture in which the age of the adolescence begins. I will suggest that these phenomena are more than coincidental; they are mutually enabling—a point I shall make by reference to Wilde's *The Picture of Dorian Gray*. My claim is that the preoccupation of this *fin de siècle* text with age and, in particular, with the desire to indulge and prolong youthful potency rather than simply succumb to the decay of aging or surrender its beauty to the static province of art, gives us insight into a dynamic model that modernists and celebrities alike will increasingly trade on—one that will grant continuing cultural standing to their public personae and value to their aesthetic works.

To trace this paradigmatic shift occurring around age, first, I will explain how I approach the category of adolescence since it argues for a more nuanced treatment than the natural and social sciences provide and commonplace assumptions allow. For starters, whether one takes the developmental narrative pioneered in G. Stanley Hall's *Adolescence* (1904), which understands adolescence as the penultimate stage in universal human maturation, or whether one subscribes to such progressive narratives as the one advanced much later in noted historian John Gillis's *Youth and History* (1974), which sees adolescence as the necessary prolongation of youth brought on by the democratization of education, all adhere to some version of age segregation. I suggest, on the contrary, that the category is neither absolute nor, strictly speaking, age or time bound. Limited not just to the biological mandate of puberty or to the modernization of education, adolescence should more properly be seen as a dynamic model, the modern embodied counterpoint to senescence (aged subjects) on one hand, and the material counterpoint to obsolescence (outdated objects) on the other, that are together intrinsic to the rise of commodity culture and consumerism. In its preoccupation with the new and the ephemeral, and in its obsession with youthfulness, adolescence functions in the late modern period as the cultural apparatus *par excellence* for the perpetuity of the new that Walter Pater had imagined in *The Renaissance* and that Ezra Pound's dictum "*faire nouveau*" would make the anthem of aesthetic modernism. As such, adolescence first comes to define, out of proportion to its alleged duration, that which late modern individuals will most prize and, then, to provide the cultural space that all will wish to occupy, never leave, or re-enter. Celebrity culture will thus thrive on it, modernism will launch its manifestos based on it, advertising will interweave it into the very fabric of material life, while in the social sciences, sociologists and psychologists will make it constitutive of our modern psyches and lived relations, with anthropologists supplying correlatives of faraway idyllic primitivism and economists extending the credit necessary to fund it. Over time, adolescence will become too huge a motor of twentieth-century industry and youth capital too valuable an asset to restrict to one age group.

So to begin with, we need to push the definitional boundary of adolescence beyond the received wisdom found in the natural sciences, which sees adolescence as a biological phase of human maturation, and beyond that in the social sciences, which attaches socialization and psycho-sexualization to the biological process. Rather, I propose that we view adolescence as a modern cultural phenomenon and an engine of modernity that puts in motion new forms of capital under the sign of youthfulness—the desire for lasting beauty, sexual potency, heightened consciousness, and uninhibited and unlimited gratification. Adolescence, in staking out that which late modern individuals most admire of youth and desire for themselves, enables new expressions of subjectivity to arise in tandem with a consumerist culture increasingly prone to novelty and innovation, to the conspicuous acquisition of objects, as identified by Thorstein Veblen's *The Theory of the Leisure Class* (1899), and supported by an unfettered mobility to seek them out and the leisure time to indulge them. Properly understood, it is the apparatus *par excellence* for the cult of the new. It thus is perfectly in tune with the epoch Lord Henry Wotton extols in *Dorian Gray* as "a new Hedonism." This, he asserts to the novel's eponymous youth "is what our country wants" (*DG* 187).

One measure of the success of the new hedonism that I am associating with adolescence is to consider that, while at the beginning of the twentieth century adolescence is deemed to cover ages 12 to 25, by the end of the century scholars no longer agree on an age limit (some put the span at 12 to 34 years of age) or on what it actually comprises. Indeed, while scholars still agree that adolescence begins with puberty, there is little else they see eye to eye on. To put this ambivalence in context, let me offer this overview of G. Stanley Hall's seminal 1904 work *Adolescence: Its Psychology and Its Relations to Physiology, Anthropology, Sociology, Sex, Crime, Religion and Education.* The first extensive scientific survey in English, this two-volume study had a number of profound effects. For the public at large, as well as for the scientific community, Hall's work established adolescence as a decisive category of everyday human experience and *the* critical phase of maturation that was, importantly, a period of great instability. In turning adolescence into a distinct and worthy object of knowledge, moreover, Hall superimposed adolescence over the biological model of puberty, and, for all intents and purposes, supplanted its relevance, rendering puberty a mere marker of the onset of adolescence. The thrust of his work effectively gave adolescence its own privileged social and cultural space to develop and the scientific space to be investigated. All were conscripted into it and the future success, of the individual and the species, depended on it. Hall didn't single-handedly invent adolescence or engineer its magnitude, but he did give a name to and the privileged space for this twentieth-century cultural phenomenon to flourish and be studied as science.

A committed Darwinist, Hall filled this space with late nineteenth-century notions of human evolutionary progress. For him, every human retraced or recapitulated the evolution of the species as a whole, thus from simple to complex organism, from instinct-driven to reason-governed individual, from savage primitive to civilized adult. As his contemporary Freud on the other side of the Atlantic would see polymorphous perversity leading to normative heterosexuality in his 1905 essays on sexuality, Hall categorized adolescence as "the period of sexual maturity" leading to marriage (II.40). Given the implicit telos, Hall asserted that adolescence constituted a second birth, one of as great consequence as an infant's biological birth (I.xiii, 81). What is at stake we may gather from this passage in which he avers that adolescence "is preeminently the age of sense, and hence prone to sensuousness not only in *taste and sex*, where the danger is greatest, but in the domain of each of the sense species." And continues, "whatever our philosophy, it is never so nearly true as at this age, that there is nothing in the intellect that does not get there through the senses, for now the chief activity of the mind is working over the *sense capital* thus acquired" (I.38–9, italics added). The great dangers of "taste and sex" and the exercise and accumulation of "sense capital" are those that Hall's study aims at identifying and disciplining, for as he explains: "adolescence is the price modern man must pay for the prolonged prenubile apprenticeship to life" (II.108).

That this apparent economic apprenticeship of the senses—acquiring and spending sense capital to reach maturity—occurs over a protracted period, Hall significantly attributes to sexual evolution and to what he views as humankind's increasing advancement, both of which he ascribes, in a curious turn, not to nature per se, but to modern times. Put simply, the "progressive increase of this interval is," in Hall's judgment, "another index of the degree of civilization" (II.232). In other words, human evolution is fundamentally progressive and dependent on civilization's advance. The more civilized and the more modern humans become, the more prominent, prolonged, and charged "the period of sexual maturity."[4] The cost of modernity is protracted adolescence—with, however, two notable exceptions. Primitives and women, according to Hall, lacking the same evolutionary aptitude, are not advantaged by modernization in the same degree, but persist in a near perpetual state of adolescence.[5] Their virtually irremediable circumstance, while it necessitates greater disciplinary vigilance, does not, however, trouble his larger argument. Nor, significantly, does the logic that advanced civilization only

----

[4]   According to Hall, "for those prophetic souls interested in the future of our race and desirous of advancing it, the field of adolescence is the quarry in which they must seek to find both goal and means. If such a higher stage is ever added to our race, it will not be by increments at any later plateau of adult life, but it will come by increased development of the adolescent stage, which is the bud of promise for the race" (I.50).

[5]   Hall's bias toward women and primitives is illustrated in the very structure and of the study, with the topic of "adolescent girls" and of "adolescent races" occupying the final two chapters of the two-volume study, in all, 187 out of 1,337 pages. There is no corresponding chapter per se on "adolescent boys" or "advanced races." In the course of the chapter on adolescent girls Hall pleads for woman's "natural naïveté" and later states "that woman at her best never outgrows adolescence as man does, but lingers in, magnifies and glorifies this culminating stage of life with its all-sided interests, its convertibility of emotions, its enthusiasm, and zest for all that is good, beautiful, true, and heroic" (II.562, 624). And on the "adolescent races," of "the nearly one-third of the human race, occupying two-fifths of the land surface of the globe," he declares that: "Most savages in most respects are children, or, because of sexual maturity, more properly, adolescents of adult size" (II.648–9).

lengthens rather than reduces the period of adolescence for those most favored
with evolutionary potential. His argument tellingly ignores the rather conspicuous
fact that such positions muddle the distinction between culture and nature, thereby
undermining the alleged separation between human and non-human worlds. For
Hall the longer apprenticeship of adolescence for males in a modern society are
offset by the shorter duration for the evolutionary disadvantaged: women and
primitives … . Strikingly and from both directions, advantaged and disadvantaged,
adolescence moves from being an acute stage of human maturity to a chronic
condition of modernity.

From this recognition, it should come as no surprise that, for the social
sciences, the length of adolescence has continued to expand alongside twentieth-
century modernization. Nor should it be a surprise that scholars disagree about
what constitutes adolescence when human civilization (here read: technological
advancement and urbanization) becomes part of evolutionary biology.[6] In making
evolutionary theory essentially teleological, when it is at base dysteleogical, Hall's
study sets forth a cultural model that is at once andocentric, masculinist, racialized,
and recent. However culturally oriented the model, its driver, according to Hall,
remains nature and, more precisely, the natural instincts of immature human
subjects who must acquire and spend "sense capital" to become fully adult. Thus,
while the stated goal of his work is to supervise youth from puberty to marriage, a
gap that his own research acknowledges is widening, the net result of his study is
to sanction a stage of sensory and sexual experimentation, to license gratification
for an ever-expanding age group, and, in general, to make social misbehavior as
much a right as rite of passage. Is it any wonder that Lord Henry declares that
modern hedonism "is what our country wants" (*DG* 187)?

We don't have to look far afield in economic theory to find a corresponding
emphasis on modern hedonism, one that substantially departs from its connection
to utility as its main champion Jeremy Bentham had envisioned. As early as the
1860s, neoclassical economists like W. Stanley Jevons in England and Carl Menger
in Austria began developing models whose overall purpose, as Jevons states in his
The Theory of Political Economy, is to "*maximize pleasure*" (37, original emphasis).
Their marginal utility theories, as they became known, shifted emphasis away
from labor, production, and supply to stress instead demand, consumption, and
the personal over the public good. In granting individuals the privilege to choose
what to buy and how to make use of what they bought, these economists presumed
that utility resided with a rational purchaser who would make the most sensible
use of scarce resources so as to insure well-being and fend off misery. Intending to

---

[6]   Robert Emde's survey of selected scientific literature on adolescence in the *Journal
of the American Psychoanalytic Association* puts into question the very separation of
developmental stages and the endpoint of adolescence by acknowledging that "structural
change does not stop at adolescence" (60). He cites one study that even argues against "the
theory that turmoil is necessary for adolescent healthy functioning" and wonders whether
"Western culture had come to expect a state of disequilibrium in adolescence" (64).

provide a discrete mathematical basis to explain price, they rather made the science of economics dependent on the subjective choice of the individual. As a result these neoclassical economists, as Regenia Gagnier explains in *The Insatiability of Human Wants*, radically reoriented the Enlightenment's rational, mechanistic, and self-governing universe by focusing attention on the inconstant and idiosyncratic habits of distinct individuals who desire and consume things. And they did so at the very moment in which industrialization and urbanization were ascendant.

Once the consuming genie was out of the bottle, so to speak, it was left to succeeding generations of economists to reconcile consumer choice, which was impulsive and detached from the public good, with the abundance of goods made possible by the mounting productive capacity of industrial manufacture. Such economists as Hazel Kyrk, in *A Theory of Consumption* (1923), examining the theoretical model of her neo-classical predecessors, clearly identified their blind spot: "Choice is described as the result of deliberation and calculation," she remarks. "Impulse and habit, custom and instinct, are ignored. Rational thought is made the basis of human conduct and every one is supposed to be moved by conscious considerations" (139). Marginal utility, in its single-minded attempt to quantify the choices of individual purchasers, rested on the premise of rational agents, who, as Kyrk and others came to realize, often behaved quite differently. While producers might be counted to behave rationally in making financial decisions to increase profits, the same sobriety did not hold for consumers. They couldn't be relied on to act rationally, much less in their own self-interest, calculations that had been the bedrock of Benthamite utilitarianism (143). This admission, as Kyrk concedes, had economists struggling "to expurgate from their theory this concept of man as a pleasure-calculating machine," that is, to get rid of the concept of "hedonism," and to begin "*de novo*" (139). As she acknowledges, not only did hedonism strip choice of rationality, but it also leveled all choice to base instinct and, in the process, also leveled value. Every choice, even ones of moral consequence and common good, became subject to the whims of a discrete consumer who functions more like a desiring machine pursuing happiness wherever it leads than a thinking and compassionate human being, a point I shall take up below with *Dorian Gray*. As with Hall's treatment of adolescence, Kyrk's of hedonism points to a blurring of human and non-human worlds, in particular, a blurring of subjects and objects that carries over to value. Quoting B.M. Anderson's *Social Value*, Kyrk observes, "value was the 'shadow which consumption threw before.'" (150). If an object becomes desirable enough, value will rise. One problem with this equation is, of course, that desirable objects will come to exert greater and greater power over human subjects, resulting in the transformation that Leo Löwenthal describes as a shift from "idols of production" (a mania for humans producing things) to "idols of consumption" (a mania for things producing humans) laid out in his "The Triumph of Mass Idols" (115). As Gagnier remarks: "*Modern* man would henceforth be known by the insatiability of his desires, and Others on the road to modernity needed only to be inspired by envy to desire his desires, to imitate his wants to be on the road to his progress and his *civilization*" (94, original emphasis). In due course, however, what paves the "road to modernity" is not solely the envy of desiring others. National fiscal policies would also smooth this path in the democratization of desire and choice. In the growing swell of Keynesian economics that followed two devastating world wars and a worldwide depression, hedonism, instead of being expurgated from economic theory, became its underlying signature. Despite the constellation of problems surrounding them, Keynesian economics furnished neo-classical economics and hedonism the scale they previously lacked. Keynesian theories would transform the microeconomic model of marginal utility theorists into a "macro" model that encouraged businesses and governments alike to provide workers and citizens, respectively, the wages and credit to spend their way our of war and scarcity into peace and prosperity by consuming the desirable objects they helped manufacture.[7]

The convergence of these emergent economic forces and a progressive theory of modern civilization made adolescence—as hedonic license, protracted state, and knowledge object—an enviable form of vitality for all those Gagnier identifies on the "road to modernity," and, further, the ideal platform for consumption and an expanding commodity culture to function. It is here that the work of experts like Hall, his contemporaries and successors in the sciences as well as the arts, is critical. For they effectively confer on all undertaking this protracted march towards maturity a certain ontological autonomy and even existential angst, so that together with its promised profligacy, adolescence develops into the default condition of late modernity. In this respect, it represents one of the central contradictions Bruno Latour exposes in *We Have Never Been Modern*. With adolescence, we can trace the way that the boundary between nature and culture, between subject and object worlds had be written so that adolescence would appear as a separate and entirely natural event for human subjects. This forced separation occurs even though, as Hall's study makes clear, nature is suffused with cultural signification and economic forces, and even though culture, that exclusive field of human endeavor, is shown to be so saturated with nature and objects; not even its adult members can be counted as purely rational agents, much less their pubescent protégés.[8] In this privileging of impetuous vitality and unlimited materialism, its confusion

---

[7]   To realize recovery, as Keynes famously wrote to Roosevelt in his open letter of 1933: "Individuals must be induced to spend more out of their existing incomes; or the business world must be induced, either by increased confidence in the prospects or by a lower rate of interest, to create additional current incomes in the hands of their employees, which is what happens when either the working or the fixed capital of the country is being increased; or public authority must be called in aid to create additional current incomes through the expenditure of borrowed or printed money" (2).

[8]   For Latour, modernity manifests itself in twin separations, first of Nature from Culture, of objects from subjects, a process he calls "purification," which enables humans to rule as the sole agents of modernity. And, second, it manifests itself with the work of mediation or translation, a process in which the object and subject world intermix that both belies and makes possible the strict hierarchy of being by which humans continue to reign over the nonhuman. As Latour puts it: "[moderns] become the only actors in their own

over culture and nature, its preoccupation with sexual maturity, its blurring of subject and object worlds, we can begin to appreciate why, among the great crimes of the twentieth century, the least reconciled would be the interlocking pair made vivid in *Dorian Gray*—senescence and obsolescence. Against these modern exigencies, all struggle, as Lord Henry puts it, in "the silly hope of keeping our place" (*DG* 178). Modern youth and the new hedonism of *Dorian Gray* provide a singular act of translation of "keeping our place," which also points to the phenomena of modernism and celebrity. In Dorian's dilemma, the text discloses the contradictions that adolescence holds together as a handsome youthful subject exchanges places with a beautiful art object to circulate throughout metropolitan London in order to ask what constitutes value and where does value reside in a desire-driven, object-centered world?

To answer, let me begin with the obvious. What most stands out in the novel is the plotline in which for over two decades the eponymous Dorian *doesn't* gray. Not simply a glib observation, the fact remains that the text takes seriously the self-indulgent excursions of one remarkable exemplar of protracted adolescence across the purlieus of *fin de siècle* London. Despite its investment though, the text makes no brief for the democratization of desire tout court—this is not the story of everyone's desire but rather every desire of one, the handsome patrician ephebe Dorian Gray. Singularity that is the mark of the celebrity and of the modernist text is written into the very core of Wilde's tale. And singularity informs Dorian's characterization: his desires, caprices, and transgressions are at the center of the novel. And for this, the punning Wilde, who never missed an opportunity at clever turns of phrase to expose social problems, gives his youthful protagonist a name that will hold in tension the allure of the ancient Hellenic world and the gloom of a modern industrial city, the enticement of classical beauty and the dread of the hoariness of age, the aesthetics of beautiful objects and the drudgery of mere useful ones.[9] This tension the text will underscore by connecting Dorian to classical youthful beauty in its references to such mythic figures as Adonis and Narcissus, and historical ones such as Antinous, as the youth pursues his pleasures rather than undertake philanthropic missions to the East End. Above all, the tension registers the novel's homoerotic and tragic fascination with a good-looking male adolescent who enjoys exceptional vitality and mobility before he founders fatally.

Unlike his mythic Greek antecedents but consistent with his *fin de siècle* milieu, Dorian's awareness of his physical beauty, which leads to his self-adoration and self-centered manipulation of others, is manufactured and schooled. The composition of his beauty painted by his friend and mentor, the bourgeois artist Basil Hallward, is not complete until the cosmopolitan Lord Henry Wotton,

---

political destiny [the process of purification], while they go right on making their society hold together by mobilizing Nature [the process of translation or mediation]" (32).

   [9]   For derivations of the hero's name, see *DG* 370–72n. For "Dorian's" relation to martial manliness and fraternal comradeship, see Linda Dowling's *Hellenism and Homosexuality* 79, 124.

known familiarly as Harry, enlivens Dorian's momentous final sitting with his sexually suggestive banter. Harry's evocation of Hellenic beauty, his rebuke of his country's hypocritical abstemiousness, but especially his coy observations of Dorian's "rose-red youth and rose-white boyhood" elicit a visceral reaction from the youth in "the half-parted lips, and the bright look in the eyes" that allows Basil to finish his portrait (184). "I don't know what Harry has been saying to you," Basil confides, "but he has certainly made you have the most wonderful expression" (185). For the artist Basil, the picture captures Dorian's "simple and beautiful nature" together with the painter's own unabashed attraction, which makes him apprehensive about exhibiting the picture in public (180). For the aristocratic Harry, the painting affords opportunity to vilify narrow-minded rectitude and, above all, flirt—"Youth! Youth! There is absolutely nothing in the world but youth!" he exalts to Dorian (187). For the impressionable youth, however, the portrait has a more sudden and profound effect. While the text reports, "his own beauty came upon him like a revelation," the image that captivates Dorian, unlike Narcissus's reflection in a pool, is mediated by his pair of tutors (189). Basil's art and Henry's "panegyric on youth" pique Dorian's fascination and give value to the portrait. Stirred by their tutelage, Dorian perceives that "[t]he scarlet [will] pass away from his lips," "the gold steal from his hair," he will "be wrinkled and wizen," "broken and deformed," "will grow old, and horrible, and dreadful..." (189). His response, then, isn't to admire Basil's art for its own sake or even for the ideal of beauty it expresses. What he first reacts to is *his* likeness to the beautiful picture and not the other way around, a case of life, as Wilde was fond of saying, imitating art.[10] Embedded in Wilde's paradox and in the text generally is the acknowledgment that an image can be the source of intelligibility for subjects no less than for objects. And, in this instance, the intelligibility is eroticized, much as Walter Benjamin explained of the commodity fetish that surfaces in nineteenth-century Parisian commerce (7). Moreover, disarmed by this erotic intelligibility, Dorian cedes the portrait ontological precedence in this hierarchy of being. Such is commodity culture, as Rosalind Williams among others has noted, when "objects of consumption no longer related to a social hierarchy externally defined; instead, they [become] themselves the hierarchy" (184).

Dorian's deference to the painting assumes an added dimension, however, in his second and more curious response that "this picture will remain always young" (189). Again upon first seeing Basil's completed portrait, he might well remark on its beauty transcending time. To observe instead that "this picture will remain always young" whereas he "shall grow old" points to a different and unexpected temporal ordering (189). Not only does Dorian's comparison further blur the separation of subject and object worlds, but it does so by radically acceding organic

---

[10] His claim is most memorably stated in "The Decay of Lying," in which Evelyn declares: "it is none the less true that Life imitates Art far more than Art imitates Life" (*Complete Works* 1082), and, thereafter: "Life is Art's best, Art's only pupil" (*Complete Works* 1083).

development (youthfulness) to an inanimate object and, in the same moment, exempts it (always). Inanimate objects are infused with time, to be sure—they are new or old, wear out or break, are recycled or discarded, remain valuable or become obsolete—but they aren't mortal. Not so here, apparently. When Basil goes to destroy the picture, Dorian intervenes claiming the act would be murder and announces, "I am in love with it" (191). Once more, Benjamin's essay on nineteenth-century Paris is instructive in pointing out that a decisive element of the erotics of the commodity fetish consists of none other than "the sex-appeal of the inorganic," an attraction captured in Dorian's declaration of love (7). At the outset of the novel, in the moment Dorian voices his fatal compact, he sees himself objectified and subordinated by an art object that appears to him as an erotic subject that will forever remain young. In this topsy-turvy privileging of beautiful object over handsome subject, the picture, the mediated object, greatly admired by the two adult sophisticates, arouses their ephebe's desire so that what he comes to covet is the youthful beauty of an image that "will never be older than this particular day of June" (189). His declaration holds the germ of both the cult of celebrity and modernist art object, and their similar systems of cultural valuation based on exchange, in which, at one extreme, we can locate a Michael Jackson and, at that the other, a Bloomsday. That one is a famous human subject and the other a celebrated fictitious event matters not. Their value arises from, and circulates in, an overlapping economy of exchange and desire. And this economy, that a youth or a spring day in Dublin or a picture can stay young and have lasting value—that is, escape senescence *and* obsolescence—is the basis for the apparatus of adolescence that Dorian's journey launches with his sensory and sexual experimentation, licensed gratification, and uninhibited behavior. Within this psychologized and aestheticized exchange economy, Dorian will thrive so long as he remains desiring and desirable, so long as he is able to circulate in other words.

In Wilde's retelling of Pygmalion, in contrast to William Morris's version or Bernard Shaw's, there is a recurring melding of human subject and art object. Dorian moves through society as the adored beautiful object pursuing his whims wherever they lead while the immobile painting registers the abject decrepitude of an aging and defective mortal thing. What in another epoch might have given rise to a fable of an aristocratic youth's rakish exercise of his *droit de seigneur* or to an Elizabethan sonnet urging *carpe diem* to some youthful protégé, *fin de siècle* Dorian Gray performs a different cultural feat. Despite all its aristocratic affectations, the tale offers a gothicized romance of middle-class hegemony caught in the vise of its own contradictions.

From this moment forward, the novella both extols and worries about the prospect of Dorian's unchanging beauty. Over the course of some 20 years, there is a pervasive privileging of youth while the portrait registers the blemish of each adolescent indiscretion. Yet, given Dorian's freedom to indulge his senses without consequence to his physical appearance or vigor, more instructive than examining any transgression in itself is to question how it is, following Bill Brown's lead in his study of things, that "inanimate objects constitute human subjects, how they move them, how they threaten them, how they facilitate or threaten their relation to other subjects" (Brown 7).[11] Revealing in these terms is the cultural work of Dorian's first insult precipitated by his passion for the young actress Sibyl Vane or, more precisely, for her stage performances of Shakespeare's Beatrice, Portia, and Rosalind—adolescents all. As with his own self-infatuation in Basil's studio, so also in this "absurd little theater" in "a labyrinth of grimy streets," Dorian is entranced by the mediated portraits of Shakespeare's fêted ingénues (*DG* 211). The undue fascination they arouse in him is such that they, too, take precedence over the mortal human subject playing them, the adolescent Sibyl. Unlike her suitor however, Sibyl has no immunity from age and no compact to ensure her youthful longevity, not even the guarantee of class standing to rely on. For this young actress of limited horizons, her romantic feelings for "Prince Charming" become the be-all and end-all, such that she comes to view her portrayals as mere mimicry of passion, only a reflection of "what love really is," and is unable to carry on the artifice of acting (*DG* 242). The result is a stagy performance of arguably the most romantic of Shakespeare's heroines, Juliet. Her inability to perform strips her of the allure of her dramatis personae, and, in her young lover's eyes, she becomes undesirable. Where previously Dorian had planned to give her his name and make her "famous, splendid, magnificent" so that "the world would have worshipped" her, to make a celebrity of her in short, he now spurns "the romance of my life" and perceives instead "a third-rate actress with a pretty face" (*DG* 243). These star-crossed lovers come to their separate ends by the very incompatibility of their desires. Sibyl, for all her adolescent passion, holds dear a version of romance no less mediated than Dorian's, but hers points to domestic bliss, underwritten, we should duly observe, by an advantageous marriage to one of her social betters, the common staples of domestic fiction from Samuel Richardson's novels forward. The text tacitly suggests that these conventions, belonging to an earlier period, are outdated, are more congruent with the "idols of production" than those of consumption, which helps to explain, perhaps, why they go unrewarded. Along with Dorian, the text refuses the outcome of maturity and marriage, the exact one that motivates Hall's study of adolescence. Nor does their adolescent romance even lead to the exclusive heterosexuality that Freud would equate with adulthood. Quite the reverse, for Sibyl commits suicide and the adolescent Dorian continues to circulate, and, like the promiscuous and desirable commodity he is, in polymorphously perverse fashion. In this novel, there will be no "natural" death. For in an object-centered, desire-driven economy in which maturity leads to decay and obsolescence, the imperative is no longer merely to seize the day but to prolong it.

Yet the novel doesn't stop at a critique of romantic love, marriage, and sexual orthodoxy. Despite its blatant ephebophilia and its tacit espousal of paiderastia, the

---

[11]   Brown's ongoing analytical work on the culture of things, cited here from his introduction "Thing Theory" to the special issue of *Critical Inquiry*, challenges "our very capacity to imagine that thinking and things are distinct" (16).

text puts the aesthetic economy of classical Greece on notice as well. Hellenic culture may appear preferred to that of industrial England and its petty-minded philistines, but the classical values summoned appear to have more to do with casting legitimacy on the novella's adolescent hero and his milieu than with advocating a return to the Hellenic idealization of youth intimated in the opening scene at Basil's studio.[12] A similar process of legitimation operating in Dorian's collectibles helps make my point. Though the youth idolizes the sacred and precious objects he accumulates from earlier historical periods and imperial locales—the perfumes, music, jewels, "Delhi muslins," "ecclesiastical vestments"—enshrining these among his personal belongings gives pleasure and lends value to his mode of living but without any reciprocation. The religious or historical value of his collection doesn't alter his lifestyle, and, as the text informs, he doesn't submit to the systems they represent: "he never fell into the error of arresting his intellectual development by any formal acceptance of creed or system, or of mistaking a house in which to live, an inn that is but suitable for the sojourn of a night" (280). Beyond the gratification these objects temporarily furnish and beyond even the passkey their status provides to "the coterie of and for consumption," that Jennifer Wicke locates in her essay on Wildean and Bloomsburyairian economics, the objects more accurately enhance Dorian's aesthetic value and certify him as a desirable commodity (10).

In similar fashion, the text's many Hellenic references confirm the youth's desirability and his continuing value rather than promote a return to the rituals of a Hellenic past in which a beautiful youth's passage to maturity takes place under the guidance of noble tutelage. For one thing, despite all their erotic investment in Dorian or, rather, because of it, Lord Henry and Hallward are not up to the educative task. Of the pair of tutors, Harry proves dissolute. As the dilettante vendor of modern hedonism who dismisses fealty to any scruple and cloaks himself in class privilege at every turn, Harry indulges Dorian's sensual and sexual development and encourages his experimentation, most especially in his gift of the infamous book that so intrigues with its "exquisite raiment" and pageant of "the sins of the world," but with no greater purpose save Harry's own pleasure (*DG* 274). Such instruction hardly points to a revival of classical Greek ideals. But then, neither does Basil's guidance entirely satisfy. While Lord Henry instructs Dorian in prurient decadence, Basil pleads above all for decency. What this amounts to is Basil acting as spokesman for the bigotry of the English bourgeoisie, declared when he reproaches Dorian with rumors of his dissipation at their final encounter. Yet, tellingly, Basil's own allegiance to middle-class decency has meant, first, a

---

[12]   Cultural regeneration may have at first prompted the "[l]iberal partisans of Greek Studies," according to Dowling, but the effect of these studies on Wilde's generation at Oxford was to make homoerotic friendship and effusive expression of Hellenic ideals possible and defensible (35, 124–9). As a result, Dowling contends that "Dorian paiderastia" could thereby thrive among Wilde's set in the "indeterminate welter of late-Victorian psychosocial categories" before his trials (125–33). For the metropolitan milieu in which Wilde traveled, see Matt Cook's recent work *London and the Culture of Homosexuality*.

paralyzing anxiety over displaying his masterpiece of Dorian in public, lest his own homoerotic infatuation be revealed, and, second, an expedient removal to bohemian Paris, where, presumably, he will be safe to finish a second masterpiece: "a great picture I have in my head," he explains to Dorian (291). His artistic acuity notwithstanding, Basil acts on behalf of a society that Dorian derides as "the native land of the hypocrite" (294). Fearful enough that he withholds one great artwork and plans to flee England to complete another scarcely qualifies Basil as fit to educate.

I suggest that the shortcomings of Lord Wotton and Hallward's tutelary are only emblematic of a greater tension to reconcile one fading paradigm with another just coming into view, and neither represents a return to Hellenism. In point of fact *Dorian Gray*'s obsession with youth for youth's sake definitively upsets the Hellenic model of education in which the ephebe undergoes initiation to enter full manhood. In Wilde's novella, it is protracted adolescence, under the Hellenic brand, that is journey and destination in one—not the telos of maturity or of citizenship. The investments of the novel, flung at Basil in Dorian's biting rebuke of his mentor's late night counsel, point to an obsession with the youth and an excessive preoccupation with his good looks that lead him to his own vain reification: "you met me, flattered me, and taught me to be vain of my good looks," "introduced me to a friend of yours, who explained the wonder of youth, and you finished a portrait of me that revealed for me the wonder of beauty" (298). Such conduct does not promise a return to the Hellenic beau ideal but a distortion of it, and Basil's grisly murder gives proof, vividly dramatized in that symbolically resonant interior of the schoolroom where the sequestered painting has sedulously recorded every adolescent breach.

More than Hellenic traditions are at stake here, however. And just so we don't miss the point, Dorian's schoolroom is the scene of not one, but two histrionic stabbings. These dramatize the modern paradigmatic shift that worries the narrative: Dorian's gruesome homicide, first, of his mentor, and, second, his own ghoulish suicide, in which, by mysterious fiat, human subject and art object are miraculously restored to their proper and separate orbits. When his corpse is discovered, Dorian now utterly disfigured with age lies dead beside his picture, its pristine and beautiful object-self rejuvenated. With these violent deaths *Dorian Gray* chronicles the decadence and demise of a waning nineteenth-century paragon, that of the Victorian *eminence grise*, which takes the form of the visage that lords over the adolescent Dorian to register every youthful trespass by turning ever more gray and grotesque. That legacy, captured in the tension of the hero's two names, which is Dorian Gray's birthright, the adolescent brutally assaults and, in doing so, reveals its mortality and transience. But that is not all. For his brutal assault represents a final desperate attempt to reclaim the youth's humanity, and thereby to rescue human agency and reinstate the flawed Enlightenment separation of culture and nature, of subject and object worlds. Its victory, however, doesn't hold. The plot device, by which the desirable and desiring Dorian destroys himself by stabbing his picture, only reinforces the inescapable entwinement of subject and object. Suicide doesn't end desire; it only transfers it. The object, in fact, lives on, and no matter whether the picture comes into the possession of a private or public collection, it will certainly continue to be admired and imitated. With the publicity over its sensational lineage only enhancing its value, it will escape senescence and obsolescence. Setting aside all the gothic bluster of the novel, we can see that *Dorian Gray* straddles those two fateful moments that Jean Baudrillard identifies, so neatly crystallized in Brown's paraphrase: "just as modernity was the historical scene of the subject's emergence, so postmodernity is the scene of the object's preponderance" (14).

If this novel performs the cultural feat of divesting one paradigm—broadly "the historical scene of the subject" or parochially the Victorian *eminence grise*—and of previewing its fledgling replacement—that of the upstart adolescent—then there is considerable reason to resist the tidy moralistic ending that categorically punishes the transgressor Dorian, a punishment in which the character's literary creator has ever been implicated. To make the point, let me briefly revisit the dispute that precedes Basil's murder in which the artist confronts his young friend with the many sordid stories of his adolescent dissipation. The litany of misconduct Basil delivers is impressive in scope: "the boy in the Guards," "Sir Henry Ashton," "Adrian Singleton," "Lord Kent's only son," "the young Duke of Perth," "Lady Gwendolyn," and Lord Gloucester's wife (293–5). Repeating rumors whispered in drawing rooms and clubs, Basil assails Dorian for being the consummate seducer that which polite bourgeois society castigates on one hand, but on the other revels in reading about in the illustrated papers of the day. More damning still, he accuses Dorian of provoking "a madness for pleasure" (294). Boys, mothers, sons of noblemen, friends, even the sisters of friends, no one, regardless of station, sex, or age, is apparently immune; once smitten, pleasure appears irresistible and contagious and also fairly catholic in its effect. Scandal and notoriety ensue. But apart from murder, in his continuous desire for novelty—whether of pleasure, sensation, or emotion—which puerile transgressions of the Dorian's aren't anticipated by Hall's study of adolescence? And, what's more, given all his obvious cultivation, isn't his extended adolescence entirely justified using Hall's criteria? If we indict Dorian and his two more senior accomplices, the tutors Basil and Harry, for this infectious outbreak, mustn't we also implicate Hall and his compeers, tutors all, who, under the guise of science, implicitly endorse experimentation and sanction disequilibrium? But more to the issue of contagion, how exactly does taking the adolescent Dorian out of circulation, as transpires with his suicide, put an end to society's craving for stimulation and novelty once underway as Basil describes?

On a meta-critical level, this protean modern text, I suggest, patently gives us a picture of the apparatus of adolescence in full motion that will also fuel the phenomena of celebrity culture and of modernism. The iconic status of one "forever young" debaucher has certainly kept the machinery of Wilde's celebrity oiled and humming, and vice versa, as the novel has never been out of circulation. Though the next generation of artists suffered under censorship rather than from the harsh carceral punishment visited on Wilde, and as onerous as incarceration or even censorship notwithstanding is, which avant-garde or modernist art work has not benefited from the scandal of its contents or of its progenitor? The lists of twentieth-century great books are peppered with their names and titles. The banning weathered by such sexually explicit novels as Joyce's *Ulysses*, Lawrence's *Lady Chatterley's Lover*, and Miller's *Tropic of Cancer* only added to their prestige and, more importantly from a market standpoint, to their sales.

As to the question of how we come to terms with adolescence, its excesses, its enjambment of human and non-human worlds, that answer requires space greater than this initial foray to explain how adolescence functions. To offer some perspective, however, let me conclude with an instance of one of *Dorian Gray*'s celebrated literary offspring: Virginia Woolf's *Orlando*. In *Orlando* we have a novel that was a notable departure from Woolf's two previous innovative works that each centered on a senescent domestic heroine. Their successor, by contrast, based on Woolf's own high-spirited dalliance with an aristocratic woman, treats readers to a rollicking good tale of the protracted adolescence of another noble youth, whose peccadilloes over the course of some four centuries, which include no less than a sex change, make Dorian's portrait pale by comparison. Not only did the publication of *Orlando* give Woolf her first commercial success, and not without first raising fears of censorship. It also turned the maturing "Invalid of Bloomsbury" into something of a popular celebrity in her own right. Thus, if the sign of celebrity, as Marshall argues in *Celebrity and Power*, "is pure exchange value cleaved from use value," if "[i]t articulates the individual as commodity," then the apparatus of adolescence produces the temporal and material conditions for the sign of celebrity to flourish and the means by which a given celebrity whether as modernist author or avant-garde text may be valued and emulated (xi). This essay therefore suggests the need to gloss the quotation from Lord Byron that opens this essay. With the arrival of Wilde's *Dorian Gray* at close of the nineteenth century, it's no longer simply a matter of youth's thirst for fame but equally fame's thirst for youth.

Chapter 2
Orlando Pimpernel

Aaron Jaffe

According to Jane Austen's Sir Walter Eliott, the baronet in *Persuasion* (1818) whose favorite pastime is looking himself up in the book of minor blue bloods, the early nineteenth-century equivalent of Googling oneself, "a Mr. (save, perhaps, some half dozen in the nation) always needs a note of explanation" (26). The line speaks to the ways emergent plebian modes of high regard trade on the incredibility of and incredibility with older, aristocratic forms. Clearly, the irony is that it's the baronet who needs the note of explanation. He's already a relic in his own time. Not only is this is true because "common" names are already circulating with reputations preceding them but also because his sense of aristocrat renown is hollowed out, requiring literary support by recourse to reference books.[1] By the close of the nineteenth century, the phenomenon of being known for known-ness (to cite Boorstin's phrase yet again) is vast, and today, in the early twenty-first century, on this very day the signs are everywhere that celebrity is—not *a* but—*the* ubiquitous marker of cultural value.

Celebrity's cultural value already obtains in its particular ways in 1818 in connection to a scenario concerning aristocratic decay. As Tom Mole argues, in connection to Lord Byron,

> a recognizable modern culture of celebrity emerged in response to rapidly industrializing print culture in the late eighteenth century, which left readers feeling swamped with new reading material, yet estranged from its writers. The apparatus of celebrity was among the structures … developed to mitigate against this sense of information overload and alienation. It responded to the surfeit of print by branding an individual's identity to make it amenable to commercial promotion. (345)

This chapter's general thesis about celebrity is that it is aristocracy's "skeumorph," to adopt N. Katherine Hayles' word, a feature of an earlier social life now functionally dead yet somehow semiotically undead. It functions as a ghostly means of generic crossover—"for innovation to be tempered by replication," in Hayles' phrase (17). The goal here, then, is to provide a literary critical genealogy of celebrity in these terms, modern celebrity as an innovation tempered by replication. Genealogy, in this context, means something more than the usual metaphoric application, for in the genesis of celebrity it is precisely the concept of *gens* that is in play thematically.

---

[1]   See my *Modernism and the Culture of Celebrity*, 9–17.

The presentation of new kinds of celebrity characters in the proto-modernist period depends on hereditary value as an operative skeumorph. Specifically, I argue for a mutant genome that the pulp elitism of Virginia Woolf's *Orlando* (1928), intent on a superhuman overcoming of cultural patrimony, shares with the elitist pulp of Baroness Orczy's *Scarlet Pimpernel* (1905), set during the French Revolution and often considered the text that invents the modern superhero. These are two novels that go to extraordinary lengths to smuggle aristocratic values across the great divide. Like *The Scarlet Pimpernel*, *Orlando* aims for a settlement—a laying down of arms—to retain a form of aristocratic value for an altered audience structure, a settlement which raises questions concerning *character in fiction*, to crib the title of Woolf's famous essay.

What might it mean, for instance, to say that Orlando and the Scarlet Pimpernel the comic book progenitor, are relatives—even twins—separated at birth? More generally, how might the secret origins of this celebrity modernist be traced to the long decay of the aristocratic life-form in the context of nineteenth century constellations of literary professionalism and literary publicity? The aristocratic dimension of this transition involves a residual scene where cultural value is to be taken for granted, not argued over or debated about; the democratic dimension comprises a scene of negative freedom, the destruction of an old form of authority, namely, the literary authority of authors. It is well known that this force field implicates the dandy. Baudelaire writes of dandyism that it is "the last spark of heroism amid decadence," a spark that "appears above all in periods of transition, when democracy is not yet all powerful, and aristocracy is only just beginning to totter and fall" (500). When he calls the dandy a "declining daystar," "glorious, without heat and full of melancholy," he may be describing the emergence of the celebrity character type we could call Orlando Pimpernel (500).

Falling to Earth

On December 13, 1795, a meteorite fell near Wold Newton, Yorkshire. Orlando was nowhere in sight. He—or, was he already a she?—was far away, enjoying Ottoman hospitality, perhaps, while the Directorate was ruling in Paris, and 56 pounds of extraterrestrial heavy metal came crashing down on Topham's fields (Home 39). That Orlando was oblivious to these two events, the astronomical curiosity in Yorkshire and the revolutionary world-shattering in France, seems of little consequence except in light of a theory put forth by Philip José Farmer. In a curious appendix to his 1972 "biography," *Tarzan Alive*, "a veritable Ph.D. thesis on the real Tarzan," who is, of course, "alive and very busy to this day," as the cover blurb has it, Farmer proposes this event as the ground zero for genre and pulp heroes. Two coaches with fourteen occupants and four drivers passed close enough to the impact site on December 13, 1795, to be exposed to the meteorite's mysterious, mutagenic energies. The thud of the stone was so loud it bowled over a nearby field hand. It was heard miles away by the sons of the local vicar, who suspected it was terroristic ordinance from France. Yet, even if the carriage passengers were too enveloped in their luminously haloed talk to notice the big bang outside, their knowledge of shared exposure to this event is less relevant than its hidden effects on their respective genealogies. What anyway would the most well-bred and well-read carriage rider in the eighteenth century even know of meteorites, unseen radiation, or DNA?

Nonetheless, through a suitably labyrinthine simulation of archival research, improbable pseudonyms and impossible filiations (Lord Byron and Leopold Bloom, etc.), Farmer "recovers" an irradiated thread, a single tainted blood line, placing the Scarlet Pimpernel with the likes of Elizabeth Bennett, Fitzwilliam Darcy, and fifteen other literarily distinguished progenitors at the scene at the original event: "The bright light and heat and thunderous roar of the meteorite blinded and terrified the passengers, coachmen, and horses. But they recovered quickly … . They never guessed, being ignorant of ionization, that the fallen star had affected them and their unborn" (*Tarzan Alive* 248). Among the genetically altered offspring came an "outburst of great detectives, scientists, and explorers of exotic worlds, this last efflorescence of true heroes in an otherwise degenerate age." In this group are numbered Tarzan, Leopold Bloom, Doc Savage, James Bond, Sherlock Holmes, Phillip Marlow, and dozens of other minor and major celebrities of literary history (230–31). The sheer semic grandeur of this cohort of pulp protagonists can only be explained, according to Farmer, by "a single cause," "a nova of genetic splendor."

Wold Newton radiation, in effect, provides a common secret origin story. It not only predisposes its "offspring" to grey eyes and "intellect[s] like an anteater's tongue" ("long and sensitive, and poking into every dark hole and crevice, catching the termites of fact"), but it also seems to enable them to cross over into extra- and intra-literary territories. They are transported into "real life" like the sub-creations and hired characters in Flann O'Brien's *At-Swim Two Birds* or Tom Baxter in Woody Allen's *The Purple Rose of Cairo* (*Doc Savage* 238). Wold Newton signifies a kind of steampunk Area 51, an extraordinary domain, from whence a certain kind of modern pulp celebrity may be beamed into works by others authors. Such characters are celebrities of a sort; in many cases, they are, in fact, more well-known than their author-creators. Think here of the famous antipathy of the author Arthur Conan Doyle for the character Sherlock Holmes. One of the key premises of Farmer's "research" is that Doyle, Edgar Rice Burroughs, Bram Stoker, George du Maurier, Joseph Conrad, and so on, are not in fact authors but "literary agents." The irony is that, with real authors acting as literary agents, the characters—the ones with true literary agency—become real. And, in what may be the most sweeping act of ret-con ("retroactive continuity") in literary history, the seed Farmer plants at the base of this genealogical tree—the Wold Newton family, as it has come to be known—turns out to be none other than the unstable nucleus at the root of so many superheroic mutations.

At one point, Farmer calls this exercise "creative mythology": "I propose to show," he writes, "that Tarzan is, in many ways, the last expression of the mythical

Golden Age, that his life emulated, unconsciously [...] the lives of many of the heroes and demigods of classical and primitive mythologies and legends." (*Doc Savage* 199). There is also, I propose serious pulp dream-work for a speculative literary forensics of our own, a genealogical chrysalis deposited by the body-snatchers under a vast dormitory of sleeping modernist celebrity characters from Mina Harker to Mrs. Brown, from Trilby to Robin Vote, from Homer Simpson to Leopold Bloom, from Marlow to Philip Marlowe. In what sense can we say that all these new agents of hyperbole—"the fictional, the improbable, and the impossible," in Farmer's suitably hyperbolic phrase—possess a single genealogical commonality (*Tarzan Alive* xiii)? Must they all be related? The notion proceeds from a premise that all these characters are family relations, but what ground is there to positing on strictly typological evidence that it must be a family relation at work and then rooting out "distinguished ancestors" for all the "famous (and infamous) cousins" (*Doc Savage* 199)?

Let's take Farmer's fanciful conjecture seriously enough to say that these incredible protagonists have more than *a posteriori* affinity in common. There must be shared a *gens* somewhere—a secret common origin story encrypted in the genome of the imaginary clan, right? As Christopher John Smith has argued in *The Roman Clan*, "clan" may be a better approximation than "family, when kinship—the accumulation of genealogical information—is "largely fictive," as it certainly is here (2). Thus: the Wold Newton Clan can be understood as something like a social formation of fictive, high pulp protagonists—fantastic celebrity characters—*incroyables*, as Baudelaire called them—who are connected by an obscure logic of inheritance, condensed markers of character identity, and displaced audience knowledge about hyperbolic cultural value (2, 9). The symbolic significance of the meteor in all this is decisive. Its importance lies in the status of the Wold Newton meteor as the historical event that confirms for once and for all the existence of extraterrestrial matter. In effect, what is being displaced—repressed and transformed elsewhere—are the political events in France. In other words, the real radioactive "thing that fell from the sky" on or about 1795—the "real" fictional, improbable, impossible protagonist—is none other than the subject of the Declaration of the Rights of Man, approved by the National Assembly of France in 1789.

Orlando Alive

Did Orlando Miss the Wold Newton Meteor?

It's a different kind of question than *how many children had Lady Macbeth*, because it's not about the misapprehension of real psychological states in literary texts. Instead, the question concerns the porosity of fiction in itself—the penetration of fiction in fiction. Woolf's character obviously raises a problem for genealogy and not simply because Orlando, the one who does not reproduce, has no role in genealogical continuity. Orlando's problem is precisely the problem of genealogy, the problem of the family tree. Orlando just goes on.

In so many words, it's less cross-dressing than cross-over that matters in *Orlando*. The novel is a sustained apologia for crossing-over, a sanction for mixing fictional and non-fictional domains that pries character of a certain sort—celebrity character—loose from authors, on the one hand, and from hereditary value, on the other. It is not for nothing that Woolf's narrator is described as Orlando's biographer, echoing both Farmer's conceit and a common practice in fan cultures such as the Baker Street Irregulars who insist on referring to their hero's creator as Holmes's literary agent. *Orlando*, in fact, anticipates many of Farmer's ideas—not least in its mannered effacement of an author function.

Orlando herself—formerly Orlando himself—is shorthand for a thing fallen to earth, an amalgamation emitting generic radioactivity: that is, a message concerning an altered audience structure. Indeed, Orlando may well be hitchhiking on the dirty snowball that returned in or about 1910, the year that human character changed, or so Woolf observes in 1924. Four years later, Woolf is ruminating about the effects of this change on women and authorship. Paula Rabinowitz astutely notes an undercurrent of high pulpiness in the intervention about the female creativity in *A Room of One's Own*, for example:

> [W]hen Virginia Woolf invented the scenario for the modernist woman writer's entry into literary history in 1928, she resorted to cheap pulp narrative techniques—seduction, doubling, suicide, murder. Shakespeare's extraordinarily gifted sister, Judith, as imagined by Virginia Woolf, ends her short, overworked, frustrating life, having escaped London's theaters only to have men laugh in her face. Pregnant by Nick Greene, the actor-manager who takes pity on her, takes her in and takes her, she ends up killing herself one winter's night. (485)

Orlando, also published in this year, shares significantly in this argument which entails the invention of an artistically creative subject for a new cultural age. When we first encounter Orlando in "his" biography, he is not only seemingly settled as a he ("there could be no doubt of his sex, though the fashion of the time did something to disguise it") but firmly situated in the male metonyms of genealogy.

First, there's this "gigantic" ancestral house. One of the more obvious bona fides of male hereditary nobility, the house is the birthright that the named heir of the *gens* stands to possess—the certitude of the clan, the house, the name as mutually authorizing cultural inertia. More precisely, we first meet Orlando alone in the attic of this house, swinging a sword at a gruesome play-thing: a shrived head now strung from the rafters once hacked off a hapless African by one of Orlando's illustrious, unnamed ancestors. We never learn if this forbearer was Orlando's father or grandfather. Nor indeed do we ever learn the patronymic he shares with these knighted and benighted forefathers, but such uncertainties of house and name foreshadow the crisis of testate affected by Orlando's well-known transformation from "he" to "she."

The game in the attic at the novel's beginning carries a proleptic message about the complexities of Orlando's genealogy. As close as the novel gets to an origin story, this scene is more a scene of *qualitas occulta* than anything else. "It is dark, mysterious, and undocumented," writes the biographer about something or another. "Volumes might be written in interpretation of it; whole religious systems founded upon the signification of it" (*Orlando* 49).[2] Taken together, the skull and the attic point to the novel's combinatory generic agenda; the occultation of the respective male and female stands for the romance plot, namely, the adventure and the gothic. In effect, would-be gothic space—the repository of Bertha Masons, Fanny Prices, and other dispossessed female subjects—contains the evidence of the criminal madness of the imperial male adventurer—souvenirs of Kurtz's atrocities overseas. Orlando's house, Orlando's name—there is an uncanny lineage entwining the spoils of the manor with the spoils of imperial adventure.

Even more subtly, perhaps, possibilities of generic recombination play out almost immediately in iconographic terms. In the following passage, the subject of the biography is described as not so much pensive as posed before the attic's stained glass window:

> Orlando stood now in the midst of the yellow body of an heraldic leopard. When he put his hand on the window-sill to push the window open, it was instantly coloured red, blue, and yellow like a butterfly's wing. Thus, those who like symbols, and have a turn for the deciphering of them, might observe that though the shapely legs, the handsome body, and the well-set shoulders were all of them decorated with various tints of heraldic light, Orlando's face, as he threw the window open, was lit solely by the sun itself.... Happy the mother who bears, happier still the biographer who records the life of such a one! Never need she vex herself, nor he invoke the help of novelist or poet. From deed to deed, from glory to glory, from office to office he must go, his scribe following after, till they reach whatever seat it may be that is the height of their desire. Orlando, to look at, was cut out precisely for some such career. (12)

The information about genealogy is that—despite obvious ornamentation in male aristocratic signifiers—Orlando's has already been mutated. With signs of hereditary value (tinctures, shields, stains, weapons, coats-of-arms, emblems, totemic beasts) projected prismatically as if through a magic lantern, the rays cover Orlando's body phantasmagorically, yielding splendid, impossibly piebald and garish costumery. That is superhero fashion.

Heraldry, hyper-masculine discipline of research, applies neither an official symbolism for decoding nor guarantors of aristocratic privilege. The paraphernalia of nobility, knights, and aristocracy are muted and mutated; arcane rules about the impermissibility of color on color, metal on metal, and so forth are forgotten, forgettable, even boring. The martial leopard—already a fanciful hybrid of panther and lion—becomes totemic, forwardly projecting insignia, evocative of

---

2   Hereafter referenced as *O*.

a butterfly's wing. From this detail, it is apparent that engendering developmental dialectics have gone awry. Caterpillars do not become butterflies. Rather, a kind of persistent crystalis enfolds: the shape of Orlando's legs, for instance, will show off the Queen's garter so well, and the shape will also be retained through the metamorphosis of gender and time, when "the change of sex, though it altered their future, did nothing whatever to alter their identity" (*O* 102).

Baudelaire's timing of the decay of aristocratic value—butterflies becoming caterpillars in cultural, political, and aesthetic terms—is in play here. With the window thrown open—in the naked heliotropic glare as it were, seemingly unencumbered by the semiotics of aristocratic privilege—Orlando stands in intrinsic, autotelic splendor as Baudelaire's "declining daystar." The scene is not so much an invocation of natural aristocracy as it is a brilliance that defies the literary control associated with authorship: Fame minus Authorship equal Celebrity. The equation may be, in effect, the cardinal rule of Woolf's novel. That is, the organizing whimsy of Woolf's new character—her meditation on the invention of a creative subject for a new age—is not created or controlled by heritage but ready-made in a sub-literary crystalis that is simultaneously a functioning time capsule for an uncanny hereditary trace. Tellingly, in the opening scene, the biographer notes that Orlando's exceptionalism extends beyond both parental and authorial agencies. Nothing owed to a father's line, or a mother's nurturance, or indeed any formative labor whatever, parental, educational, professional, authorial, etc., Orlando is not progeny in any conventional sense. Even the Queen, whose early patronage sets Orlando's "career" in motion, is quickly exposed less as a mentor than as just another someone to be counted—with the biographer herself, of course—as one of Orlando's many enthralled fans.

Orlando's strange sub-literary "career" stretches across five centuries. It is a counterpoint of the curriculum vitae of a bourgeois biographical subject, multiple lifespans given to a reputation not made via achievements, positions, offices, publications, and awards. More importantly, maybe, Orlando's name is not produced as so much "intellectual property" of a creator. Instead, he or she is best imagined as a fictional concept that depends on ubiquitous repetition for power, a curious hybrid of agencies, which are not quite of a modernist author yet also no longer quite of a famous hero or aristocrat. This is, as I have argued with Jonathan Goldman in this volume's introduction, a relevant admixture for celebrity—or, at least, *Orlando*'s contribution to the discourse. What reveals the kinship with the Wold Newton clan is less Orlando's failure as a character in a bildungsroman as the character's insistent proximity to distinctive qualities of an author function and yet his or her simultaneous superfluity concerning it. If Orlando's first pastime entails hacking away at the moor's head, then the second, quite tellingly, involves stabbing away at a literary career, with "more perhaps than twenty tragedies and a dozen histories and a score of sonnets" already drafted when the novel begins.

"His" biography begins with Orlando scribbling away listlessly on *Aethelbert: A Tragedy in Five Acts*—a work destined for the fireplace, certainly. Not exactly hackwork—leave that for Nick Greene later—but it seems halfhearted at least:

Fig. 2.1   Panel of a Modernist Cenacle, from Jason's *The Left Bank Gang* (2005). Fantagraphics Books.

"once look out of a window at bees among flowers, at a yawning dog, at the sun setting, once think 'how many more suns shall I see set,' etc. etc. (the thought is too well known to be worth writing out) and one drops the pen, takes one's cloak, strides out of the room, and catches one's foot on a painted chest as one does so." The salient point is that Orlando is constitutively unable to realize authorial agency, or, more precisely, Orlando's author-function is constitutively under-realized. Even when success appears, it is compromised: the literary splash is made only when the 300-year manuscript of the "Oak Tree" reaches the able machinery of latter-day Nick Greene, the literary publicist.

In the opening scene, Orlando already proceeds straight from a desk in an attic garret to the place eventually associated with Orlando's most successful literary product, the oak tree in the garden of the ancestral house. What this transition is not, I submit, is a triumphal movement from literary workplace to the site of successful literary contemplation (finally!). Instead, I propose to read it as a post-romantic—indeed, post-human—substitution. This oak tree—returning with some regularity in the novel and, of course, another obvious signifier of genealogy—eventually replaces authorial subjectivity as Orlando's desiratum. The connection to genealogical wood is made explicitly when one of Orlando's inamorata is described as having "a family tree […], as old and deeply rooted as Orlando's" (*O* 25).

So, what does Orlando desire? One possibility offered is most certainly literary fame. The desire for fame ("glory," or, as Nicolas Greene pronounces it, "Glawr") is a persistent "fascination" for Orlando: "the very thought of a great writer stirred her to such a pitch of belief that she almost believed him to be invisible" (*O* x). The power of "invisibility" is an important detail I'll return to shortly. No other rationale is offered for Orlando's own literary efforts than the potential literary success offers as an improvement on aristocracy: "there was a glory about a man who had written a book and had it printed, which outshone all the glories of blood and state," "[t]o his imagination it seemed as if even the bodies of those instinct with such divine thoughts must be transfigured. They must have aureoles for hair, incense for breath, and roses must grow between their lips"; [there was] "an ineffable hope, that all the turbulence of his youth, his clumsiness, his blushes, his long walks, and his love of the country proved that he himself belonged to the sacred race rather than to the noble—was by birth a writer, rather than an aristocrat-possessed him" (*O* 64). Sean Latham has written on Woolf's interest in authorship as an aristocracy of writing. The superiority of authorship is that fame is produced and retained in one identity—in one person, one name—rather than reproduced in ever-branching genealogical plurality. Yet, in *Orlando*, the sentiment that Authorship is Aristocracy 2.0 is discredited by its being given full-throated support from Nick Greene, who, as many have observed, is hardly a paragon of Woolfian admiration. Furthermore, there is an obvious question: what value is there in immortal fame—that is to say posthumous fame—for someone as long-lived as Orlando?

At one point in *The Interpretation of Dreams* Freud compares dreams to famous people. More specifically, he compares the logic of dreams to paintings that pluck all famous thinkers or writers from the ages and deposit them in a single hall or on a mountain outcrop: Elvis, Bogie, and Marilyn in Hopper's diner. For Freud, these painted scenes exemplify—or, perhaps, just model—the way dreams synchronize and condense conceptual connections. Dreamwork gathers disparate things—thoughts, concepts—places them in a single time and space, and convenes a symposium or a republic of letters. Or, for that matter, an excursion to a meteor shower: or, a nap under an oak tree. Even though this particular connection is used as an example of the manner by which individual dreams are composed, it could easily be redirected into an observation about the dream-like condensation that constitutes the logic of the celebrity value itself—a "logical connection by simultaneity in time," as Freud puts it (423–4). Fan interest becomes an external radioactive power carrying all sorts of hidden side-effects "down to the details" for the cultural artifacts exposed to it. Farmer's pulp characters—whose "genes" all record exposure to the Wold Newton meteorite—provide a means of expressing a message about the ways certain fictional characters are suddenly charged with unaccountable, uncontrollable, and, significantly, authorially-invalidating value.

Further, Freud's notion that either/or cannot be expressed in dreams can be recast in terms of the most significant aspect of Orlando's character. It is notoriously difficult to write or talk about Orlando without first deciding on the gender of a pronoun. In effect, by choosing a "he" or a "she," the reader-critic takes sides in an argument that Woolf—or, the biographer persona, at least—ultimately leaves in uncertainty. If "he" is selected—selected as a "neutral" gender designation, not least—one denies the fact of the most significant event in the novel, the gender change. If "she" is selected—the more progressively feminist maneuver, without question—one denies the transformative event as an event. Its formative status is elided in the supposition that Orlando was always already a "she." The rule for the interpretation of Orlando seems to be, following Freud, to "treat the two apparent alternatives as of equal validity and link them together with an 'and,'" but with a corollary, following Woolf, that the "and" does not indicate that identity is pluralized—that despite a doubling of pronouns, singularity, in terms of identity and possession, rules. This dual insistence on pluralizing desire and experience through doubling and singularity is what adds the element of uncanny pronominal radioactivity to Orlando's case. As Nicholas Royle has argued, doubling is particularly uncanny because it raises issues of reproduction or cloning. The double seems to mean that the self can be self-reproduced forever; the double provides an immortal and indestructible agent. *Orlando and Orlando are the same; Orlando and Orlando is one; both he or she are a clone with a difference.* Bennett and Royle write that the double undermines the very logic of identity: it is "a promise of immortality (look there's my double, I can be reproduced, I can live forever) and a harbinger of death (look, there I am, no longer me here, but there: I am about to die, or else I must be dead already)" (39).

This effect is one reason that Orlando's longevity is defined again and again by missing things. Dilatoriness becomes a form of "invisibility." Missing Shakespeare on the way to being late for the encounter with the Queen is a case in point:

[T]here, sitting at the servant's dinner table with a tankard beside him and paper in front of him, sat a rather fat, shabby man, whose ruff was a thought dirty, and whose clothes were of hodden brown. He held a pen in his hand, but he was not writing. He seemed in the act of rolling some thought up and down, to and fro in his mind till it gathered shape or momentum to his liking. His eyes, globed and clouded like some green stone of curious texture, were fixed. He did not see Orlando. For all his hurry, Orlando stopped dead. Was this a poet? Was he writing poetry? 'Tell me', he wanted to say, 'everything in the whole world'–for he had the wildest, most absurd, extravagant ideas about poets and poetry–but how speak to a man who does not see you? who sees ogres, satyrs, perhaps the depths of the sea instead? So Orlando stood gazing while the man turned his pen in his fingers, this way and that way; and gazed and mused; and then, very quickly, wrote half-a-dozen lines and looked up. Whereupon Orlando, overcome with shyness, darted off and reached the banqueting-hall only just in time to sink upon his knees and, hanging his head in confusion, to offer a bowl of rose water to the great Queen herself. (17)

Orlando's lifespan makes Orlando a witness—or more properly a near witness—to the serial span of literary history. Instead of all the famous writers assembled in one place—i.e., in a canon—Woolf gives us a character whose very superhuman lifespan has the potential to do the same kaleidoscoping celebrity dreamwork. Yet, aside from a cursory, sidelong glance at Shakespeare here and an uncomfortable sideways encounter with Dryden there, Orlando most often misses the event. And, Orlando's ultimate non-event is, no doubt, the one most critical to the novel, the occasion of disinheritance: Orlando intestate. Literally, "she" is not there, when the *gens* passes over to the male heir, "him." The only way the self-positing of value can continue across this divide is through superhuman means: a celebrity court-case. If the garter fits, you must acquit.

In *A Room of One's One*, Woolf argues that female creating subject ("the woman composer") "stands where the actress stood in the time of Shakespeare," and gives us portrait of Judith Shakespeare as an actress undone by Nick Greene (59). In *Orlando*, she clarifies this to suggest that the performing subject may be a superior outcome than the creating subject in the time of Woolf, by positing a protagonist whose ultimate claim to cultural value is warranted neither as an aristocrat (through transcendent, elite family ties) nor as an author (through transcendent genius) but as a figure who is not quite one nor quite the other. Superhumanly fashionable, dilatory, and invisible—a singular plurality, to be sure—this illegitimate inheritor of an aristocratic *gens*, a mere sub-literary wannabe, provides an incipient definition of celebrity. In the end, in the time of Woolf, Orlando has done with literature; she sit under the oak tree, accessing earth and sky, as if patched in through a kind of giant radio-cosmopolitan antenna, and so realizing the triumphant synthesis Woolf describes in *A Room of One's Own*: "the androgynous mind is resonant and porous; that it transmits emotion without impediment; that it is naturally creative, incandescent and undivided" (108).

Crossing Over

Like Orlando, the Scarlet Pimpernel[3] crosses into literary history astride the Great Divide. Explicitly, in this case, this Great Divide is the French Revolution. This reason alone lets Phillip José Farmer put Sir Percy Blakeney at Wold Newton in 1795. And, considering the examples that accumulate in Orczy's novel, we should speak, perhaps, of a proliferation of Great Divides—all of which lie historically and symbolically somewhere between Dover and Calais in the depths of the English Channel: perfunctory breaches between "jovial, rubicund" England and blood-thirsty, revolutionary France; between elite aristocratic stability and mass democratic disorientation; between the glamorous performance of disguise and the guileless automaticism of Jacobinism; between high idealist adventure in the world of subjects and low materialist terror in the world of objects (27).

One sign of continuity between the SP and this genealogy is that, if nothing else, the Scarlet Pimpernel's name precedes him. Digging to the source is an arduous task, buried in layers beneath Raoul Wallenberg, Victor Laszlo, Pimpernel Smith, Zorro, the Lone Ranger, Superman, and Batman, Daffy Duck's Scarlet Pumpernickel, many theatrical and cinematic adaptations in the Errol Flynn swashbuckler vein, and a dozen or so sequels to the original 1905 novel. Despite the impressive print run and the reach of its cultural afterlife, there's virtually nothing about the novel in the way of academic criticism, so some background and summary may be appropriate. The *modus operandi* of the SP is often described as Robin Hood in reverse: the mysterious avenger who helps oppressed aristocrats stay one-step ahead of the guillotine. Whereas Orlando is remanded in an undisclosed location during this period of characterological upheaval, the Scarlet Pimpernel is in the thick of it. The three principal characters provide the novel's essential three principles: 1) the Scarlet Pimpernel, a.k.a. Sir Percy Blakeney, Baronet, mild-mannered, ineffectual and effete aristocrat; 2) Citoyen Chauvelin, the accredited agent of the French Republican Government, arch-enemy of the SP; and 3) Lady Marguerite Blakeney née St. Just, Blakeney's estranged and unaware wife, who focalizes the narrative. The SP's ultimate disguise is when he plays Marguerite's husband. In this, he is the rarity of the genus, who, like Superman, as others have observed, is really the "real" guy, whereas the "other" guy, the secret identity is actually the mask, the act, the performance.

The SP thus represents the principle of double identity. Its social logic is the League, his band of followers, who follow a code of absolute devotion, secrecy, and honor. Part of what makes SP uncanny, his "sheer supernatural agency," is that he is invisible. He hides in the open like Poe's purloined letter. In fact, it is decidedly the letter—the SP's Sobriquet—that has all the agency. "Heard of the Scarlet Pimpernel?" comments one character, "we talk of nothing else…We have hats 'a la Scarlet Pimpernel'; our horses are called 'Scarlet Pimpernel'; at the Prince of Wales' supper party the other night we had a 'souffle a la Scarlet Pimpernel.'

---

[3]   Hereafter Scarlet Pimpernel is referenced as SP.

[T]he other day I ordered at my milliner's a blue dress trimmed with green, and bless me, if she did not call that 'a la Scarlet Pimpernel'" (*SP* 68). What's next, one might ask, the Scarlet Pimpernel Happy Meal? The SP has literarily always arrived first. Here, we have a strategy of secrecy that depends on ubiquitous publicity and total commodity saturation.

If the SP hides in the open, it also means that his disguise functions both above and below the class schema depicted in the novel without fail within a kind of theatrically forced social enclosure, the country inn in England, the seedy bistro in France, even the clearing in the forests of France have this quality. In revolutionary France, this means the SP adopts a disguise beneath the putative discourse of human rights, under the radar of the citizens and their committee of public safety. In the first instance, the opening scene of the novel, the SP smuggles the fugitive aristocrats by disguising himself as an infected and decrepit body, "an old hag who said her son had the plague," transporting soon-to-be corpses (*SP* 6). In the last instance, the SP disguises himself as a Jew. Here's how he explains the logic: "I know these Frenchmen out and out. They so loathe a Jew, that they never come nearer than a couple of yards of him, and begad! I fancy that I contrived to make myself look about as loathesome an object as it is possible to conceive" (*SP* 266). Orczy is no doubt alluding to the Dreyfus affair—Dreyfus is not yet exonerated at the time the novel is written—another ironic historical counterpoint to "Liberté, Egalité, Fraternité," which is always invoked ironically here. In effect, the SP disguise in France, in the throes of radical redefinition of public life and its subjects, is to exist in a state such as that suggested by Agamben's "bare life," beneath the bios politicos.

More than Marguerite's redemption of her dishonorable past by acts of courage it is the fact that the sovereign of a social life, based on parties—distinction in the domains of fashion, wit, and beauty—is laid low. It is her being laid low that reconciles her with her husband: the "cleverest woman in Europe, the elegant and fashionable Lady Blakeney, who had dazzled London society with her beauty, her wit and her extravagances, present[ing] a very pathetic picture of tired-out, suffering womanhood" (255). In this state, pointedly stripped of her shoes (cf. shorn locks), she is left in the open by Chauvelin and his men: "It is no use mounting guard over a woman who is half dead," he says. She is stripped bare of her fashion: accursed in the open. The decisive moment when this happens is staged against an uncanny reorientation of the subject in space with nauseating vertigo:

> Oh! think! think! think!... [S]he heard nothing, she saw nothing: she did not feel the sweet-smelling autumn air, scented with the briny odour of the sea, she no longer heard the murmur of the waves, the occasional rattling of a pebble, as it rolled down some steep incline. More and more unreal did the whole situation seem. It was impossible that she, Marguerite Blakeney, the queen of London society, should actually be sitting here on this bit of lonely coast, in the middle of the night, side by side with a most bitter enemy; and oh! it was not possible that somewhere, not many hundred feet away perhaps, from where she stood, the being she had once despised, but who now, in every moment of this weird,

> dreamlike life, became more and more dear–it was not possible that he was
> unconsciously, even now walking to his doom, whilst she did nothing to save
> him. (246)

Marguerite, notice, does not process the natural landscape in romantic terms;
indeed, she experiences a negation of all its scenic potential rendered in—and at
the same time negated of—all its pathetic possibilities. The natural world does not
support her moment of high subjective crisis; it underscores her/its own unreality
and announces that the means of defining real has shifted into what is properly
understood as the domain of mass mediation and second nature. She experiences
the "weird, dreamlike" agency of fashionable society for all its unreality in its
most exquisite scene. In it she makes the long-shot wager about the presentation of
value in the context with no fixed social *a priori*—an encounter made possible, to
use the vocabulary of gambling that Marguerite herself employs, *not by birth but
by fortune*. It is precisely at this moment that Marguerite can see for herself what
she had been missing: not only that she is married to the Scarlet Pimpernel—much
more compelling than being married to his preferred costume, Percy—but also
that he has been with her all along—including right here disguised as the accursed,
up-to-this-point invisible Jew.

And so, with Chauvelin and the citizens chasing rumors elsewhere like
paparazzi sans-culotte, the SP and Marguerite proceed to the escape craft, docked
nearby, and the novel concludes chop-chop: "Half an hour later, they were on
board the Day Dream...Everything on board the Day Dream was fitted with that
exquisite luxury, so dear to Sir Percy Blakeney's heart, and by the time they all
landed at Dover he had found time to get into some of the sumptuous clothes which
he loved, and of which he always kept a supply on board his yacht." The marital
synthesis of the male and female principles of celebrity is confirmed—and the
Great Divide is forded, as it were—when Marguerite receives a pair of Pimpernel
shoes: "great was the little middy's joy when my lady found that she could put foot
on English shore in his best pair" (*SP* 271). From there to "a function at which
H.R.H. the Prince of Wales and all the elite of fashionable society were present,
the most beautiful woman there was unquestionably Lady Blakeney, whilst the
clothes of Sir Percy Blakeney wore were the talk of the *jeunesse dorée* [gilded
youth] of London for many days." As for the murderous Chauvelin, the ends he
comes to are about as profound or as trivial as not being invited to this or that "or
any other social function in London."

The proto-superhero plot proves to be a rather constrained, indeed foreshortened,
affair. It is not to be confused with the SP's secret history, *ab ovo*, the so-called
"Origin Story" of comic book lore, frequently a primal scene of paternal
abandonment, as Ang Lee's *Hulk* so usefully thematized. The Secret Identity is out
of the picture; the reader always arrives too late. Origin stories might be described
as analepses—on the model of prolepses. Gerald Prince notes that analepses have
a certain extent and a certain reach into history: an origin story like the SP's—like
Superman's or Batman's or, for that matter, Orlando's—has, both extent and reach

of several years of back-fabula and yet in terms of sjuzet it's always there. On the other end, the character, the modus operandi is always anterior of the text, that scene of value is always proleptically out of frame (5). The real truth is never completely unveiled so that the serial nature of the plot can continue on cycling the wager about its presentation of value in ubiquity.

The Left Bank Gang

The concept of the Great Divide comes from Andreas Huyssen's influential formula about a "categorical distinction" between high art and mass culture, a distinction which, Huyssen argues, has been internalized in the discourses of modernism and postmodernism themselves (vii). He proposes this concept in a reading of torn halves of Adorno, who "never saw modernism as anything other than a reaction formation to mass culture and commodification, a reaction formation which operated on the level of form and artistic material" (57). Huyssen restricts each to its characteristic synecdochal accommodation to a preferred narrative (57). In the case of modernism, in effect, the hero is the elite modernist art product staving off the forces of mass consumption, "with its tropes of crowds and floods and its association with the seemingly inscrutable logic of mass consumption [which Huyssen so sharply observes is] often gendered female," "a feminized mass audience with […] mob-like fluctuations in preference and its irrational assessments of value." Postmodernism moves the other way, registering the inclusive movement politics of civil rights, feminism, et al., in the forces of popular consumption pressing on the barricades of the aesthetic-legitimating the popular and democratizing the elite, accordingly (165ff.). In both cases, as a host of critics have noted, including Ástráður Eysteinsson, Bernard Gendron, and Lois Cucullu, Huyssen reserves interpretive primacy for the art object itself. Whether understood in terms of autonomous symbolic artifacts or the composite repackaging of economic goods—the emphasis comes at the expense of recognizing the agencies of other items of analysis, namely the cultural actors, characters, forms of subjectivity, and actual affect-bearing bodies—the Mrs. Browns, in other words—whose very agency seems displaced by the superhuman, character-like Great Divide itself.

For this reason, the vanishing mediator for Huyssen's position may be a much earlier essay on the same theme by Leslie Fiedler called "Cross the Border— Close the Gap" from 1970. In that piece, Fiedler makes it quite explicit he has the superhuman means for fording the chasms of the Elite and the Popular. It comes from the serial pages of genre forms. And, what's more, it's superhero comic books, in particular, that effect the change:

> [T]he Matter of Metropolis and the myths of the Present Future, in which the nonhuman world about us, hostile or benign, is rendered not in the guise of elves or dwarfs or witches or even Gods, but of Machines quite as uncanny as an Elemental or Olympian–and apparently as immortal. Machines and

mythological figures appropriate to the media mass-produced and mass-distributed by machines: the newsboy who, saying SHAZAM in an abandoned subways tunnel, becomes Capitan Marvel; the reporter (with glasses), who shucking his civilian garb in a telephone both is revealed as Superman, immune to all but Kryptonite–these are the appropriate images of power and grace for an urban, industrial world busy manufacturing the Future. (481)

In *Orlando*, Woolf reminds Fiedler and the rest of us that Wonder Woman— or, perhaps, Ms. Marvel—may be a more apt figuration for this audience structure. The circle may be closed when Woolf's Orlando appears in Alan Moore and Kevin O'Neill's steampunk graphic novel trilogy *The League of Extraordinary Gentlemen*, where his and hers is, according to Moore, the very same heroic name as Orlando inamorato and Orlando furioso.[4] Huyssen recognizes that Fiedler's project "reaffirm[s] precisely" one of the cardinal aims of the classical avant-garde, reconciling high culture and popular culture. The question is why it is that the pulp hero, in particular—the subject of genre fiction, par excellence—emerges from secret hiding places to do this work? One answer may be in the version of modernization that Fiedler underscores is driven not simply by the modern machine, Henry Adams' dynamo, but by the dynamic forces of mass communication technologies—cheap mass printing, telephony, photography, film networks, radio, television—that by sleight-of-hand promise seriality and ubiquity not as a path to mass media democracy but as a means of endless production of ersatz aristocratic aura and ersatz authorial immortality. Otherwise stated, this is one of the ways the modern's super-heroic character—in essence, Orlando Pimpernel—is expressed at the level of narrative. Her analeptic origin story paradigmatically, enters a scenario, an epochal instance of generational transience—and through proleptic seriality she appears uncanny and indestructible exceeding dangerous sjuzet at every turn.[5]

Moore and O'Neill's favorite protagonists—Mina Harker, Allan Quartermain, Orlando—all have on their side fictional indestructibility granted by anachrony and ersatz aura: they don't die. Even though *Dracula* appeared in 1897 and *King Solomon's Mines* was published in 1885, it is mistake to read these as merely adaptations nineteenth century characters or re-interpretations of nineteenth century texts. To take the steampunk aesthetic—an aesthetic to which Moore has

---

    [4]   Thanks to Jonathan Goldman for sharing his ideas about this link with me. Among the many signs of the genius of Moore's work—which figures Stevenson's Hyde, Stoker's Mina Harker, Haggard's Quartermain, etc., as a proto-superhero team—is that it enacts a convergence of two great literary innovations of modernity, the pulp form, and the modernist polysemic collage-text, and the significant linking of seriality and indestructibility. It is also important to note that the most durable "gentleman" is, in fact, decidedly female: Mina Harker. For background on *The League of Extraordinary Gentlemen*, see Jess Nevins's *Heroes and Monsters*—in particular his useful take on some of the issues discussed here in his chapter "On Crossovers," 175–84.
    [5]   Thanks to Benjamin L. Widiss for suggesting this connection.

Fig. 2.2   Panel of Orlando and the Moor's Head, from Alan Moore's
                The League of Extraordinary Gentlemen: Black Dossier (2007).
                Wildstorm. Illustrator: Kevin O'Neill.

significantly contributed—as a form of nostalgia for Victorianism is similarly
mistaken. More accurate is to observe that steampunk is invented out of a wholly
contemporary nostalgia for turn-of-the-century modernity, a nostalgia for the future,
to use Nina Boym's phrase, a nostalgia, in other words, for a literary modernity
without modernism. It is the same modernity without modernism that figured out
new ways of mobilizing literary properties on a vast, global scale (which I have
called elsewhere the Tarzan model—though Pimpernel model may be just as apt),
that Moore and O'Neill desperately want to recuperate for the present. 1898 is
the setting of the first two volumes of *The League of Extraordinary Gentlemen*;
when Harker and Quartermain return in 1958 in the third volume, having defeated
Dracula, Prof. Moriarty and Dr. Fu Manchu, a Martian invasion, and Big Brother,
and looking "younger," the enigma is what happened to both literature and the
League during the intervening 60 years. One answer, coming from an admittedly
unlikely source, the graphic novel by the Finnish artist Jason, *The Left Bank Gang*
(2005), is that James Joyce got plugged with lead by Zelda Fitzgerald in a botched
stick-up caper. Done in the funny animal idiom—Zelda, Pound, Fitzgerald,
Hemingway, and Sartre are all dogs; Joyce is a crow—the modernist "Gang" are
all starving comic artists living in Paris in 1920s.

Rather than represent the unrepresentable—the experimental, unclassifiable, and unsellable modernist comics the characters presumably create—the plot comes straight out of popular genre forms: elaborate noir, a triple cross (betrayals by Zelda and Jean-Paul, then by Zelda and Ezra), modernist bad guys, and numerous animal corpses. While it would be fitting for this allegory of the futility of a modernist league if the comic ended with Ernest and Ezra struggling on a rooftop with their satchel of cash dispersing to the wind, it actually ends a page later with an aptly Hemingwayesque aperçu, a plaintive line spoken to Hadley in a moonlit Parisian flat, in Jason's/Hemingway's signature deadpan style: "Please don't ever leave me" (46).

Chapter 3
Imposture in *The Great Gatsby*

Allan Hepburn

In F. Scott Fitzgerald's novels and essays, the desire for fame takes shape through theatrical emulation and imposture. In *The Great Gatsby*, emulation and imposture create renown, if not notoriety. Known for his shady business deals and his Long Island parties fueled with illegal alcohol, Jay Gatsby's notoriety is inseparable from his bid for greatness. That greatness, advertised in the title of Fitzgerald's novel, springs from Gatsby's impersonation of the manners, accents, and education of well-heeled Americans. Nick Carraway, engrossed in his own performance as a Midwesterner determined to make his fortune by selling bonds in New York, lords his good manners over Gatsby. In return, Gatsby draws on the resources of theatrical realism to make others believe in his authenticity. In imitation of the impresario and playwright David Belasco, Gatsby constructs an identity so faultless in detail that it appears true. Extending the principle of Broadway theatricality to personal relations, Gatsby stirs Nick's belief in imaginative possibilities as at a play. Theatricality moves out of the theater into the fabrication of identity. Nick and Gatsby adopt roles for themselves and for each other; they impersonate fantasies of the Midwesterner and the rags-to-riches businessman. Class status underlies the various postures and impostures that Gatsby and Nick strike. In this sense, American celebrity culture responds to upward and downward shifts in class. By the same token, imposture, as a trope of American identity, requires susceptibility to and mutual recognition of inauthenticity: illusions do not dissipate just because they are called illusions. By documenting the lies and illusions that contribute to Gatsby's grandeur—a huckster is most narratively compelling when his imposture is exposed—Nick sees through his neighbor's ruse but alleges that some necessary measure of phoniness constitutes American celebrity.

Some of the impetus for Gatsby's characterization derives from Fitzgerald's own anxieties about and meditations on celebrity. Throughout the 1920s, Fitzgerald was a cultural icon who summed up "the fizz and exuberance of [...] the Jazz Age" (Dickstein 302). As he knew from personal experience and as he describes in essays such as "Early Success" and "The Crack-Up," celebrity demands the sacrifice of integrity and vitality. "I had been thanking the gods too long," wrote Fitzgerald in 1936 in a valediction to his youthful success, "and thanking them for nothing" (*MLC* 145).[1] From the perspective of the mid-1920s, and especially in

---

[1]   For the sake of brevity, I use the following acronyms for titles: *The Beautiful and Damned* (*B&D*); *The Great Gatsby* (*GG*); *The Last Tycoon* (*LT*); *My Lost City* (*MLC*);

The Great Gatsby, Fitzgerald understood celebrity as a series of gorgeous impostures modeled on theatrical precedents. One earns fame for doing something well, but one becomes a celebrity through a broad apparatus of cultural articulations that may have little or nothing to do with the reason that one earned fame in the first place. In other words, a celebrity is someone who is famous for being famous. Although it is difficult to imagine a celebrity who does not possess a measure of fame, it is possible to be famous without being a celebrity. Of course the terms "fame" and "celebrity" blur together. Fitzgerald achieved fame as a writer in the 1920s before his appearances in newspapers as a *bon vivant* and prankster promoted him to celebrity status. Moreover, celebrity exists apart from authenticity; a writer, or for that matter a bootlegger, can achieve celebrity through stagecraft rather than genuineness. In *The Great Gatsby*, Fitzgerald posits celebrity as a mesh of illusions, purchased for the sake of putative greatness.

In his early years, Fitzgerald believed that his own destiny lay in theater. For the Elizabethan Dramatic Society in St. Paul, Minnesota, he wrote four comic plays that won him local renown. When he arrived in the East in 1911, Fitzgerald hurried to New York to see Broadway plays: "I saw a musical comedy called 'The Quaker Girl,' and from that day forth my desk bulged with Gilbert and Sullivan librettos and dozens of notebooks containing the germs of dozens of musical comedies" (*MLC* 3). In his freshman year at Princeton, work on the Triangle Club show *Fie! Fie! Fi-Fi!* preoccupied him so much that he flunked most of his courses. He collaborated on two more plays for Triangle: *The Evil Eye* in 1915–16 and *Safety First* in 1916–17. When he cobbled together *This Side of Paradise*, Fitzgerald incorporated material that he had written at Princeton, including a playlet called "The Débutante." Fitzgerald continued to think of himself as a dramatist at least until the failure of his play *The Vegetable* in 1923: "Although he would occasionally talk about writing another play, he never went beyond outlines" (Bruccoli 183).[2] Instead, Fitzgerald transmuted his talent for dialogue and scenic arrangement into novelistic narrative.[3]

Nevertheless, Fitzgerald's imagination remained structurally and metaphorically dramatic. His second novel, *The Beautiful and Damned*, exploits theatricality as

---

This Side of Paradise (*TSOP*); *The Vegetable* (*V*). Whenever context makes clear which text is under discussion, I omit these acronyms. The essays in *My Lost City* include selections that Fitzgerald proposed as a volume to Maxwell Perkins in the mid-1930s, as well as supplementary materials (West xiii). Wilson included many of the same essays in his edition of *The Crack-Up*.

[2]   In a letter to John Peale Bishop, conjecturally dated 1924 or 1925, Fitzgerald, deep in his cups, sketched out "a historical play based on the life of Woodrow Wilson" ("The Crack-Up" 265). Scenes of Wilson's career at Princeton, the governor's mansion, the battle front in 1918, and the peace congress are undermined by sophomoric high-jinks. Fitzgerald could not restrain his taste for farce when writing for the theater.

[3]   Alan Margolies argues that *The Great Gatsby* is a "dramatic novel" in terms of scenic distribution, the positioning of characters in light or darkness, and a relative unity of time (160–62).

a metaphor for class and notoriety. Three interludes in the novel are written in dramatic dialogue: "Three Men" (17–22); "The Ushers" (139–42); and "The Broken Lute" (239–51). Other passages adopt scripted dialogue instead of omniscient narration (25–7, 87). In these sections, objective representation breaks the archness and lyricism of the narrative voice (Stern 320). Throughout *The Beautiful and Damned*, malaise about the unreality of making money and ascending social ranks symptomatically appears in dramatic metaphors. As Gloria and Anthony Patch sell off bonds and grow poorer, their high living does not abate. They act out their wealthy pasts, as well as their expectations of inheriting Adam Patch's money in the future. In a spasm of ambition, Anthony promises to write a play for Gloria (126). Of course Anthony does not fulfill this promise; he rarely rouses himself to write anything at all, despite his claims to literariness. Theatricality governs his imagination. He keeps framed pictures of thespian beauties on his walls (10). He falls in love with women who use stagy gestures for self-aggrandizing effect. Anthony and Gloria's romance blossoms in an atmosphere of general theatricality. They hold hands at the theater, and study the theatrics of class-shifting Americans at a nightclub (127, 63–4). Anthony never achieves fame through writing a play, but he does achieve a certain celebrity by theatricalizing his ambitions and love life.

Anthony's propensity to theatricalize human interaction causes him to view city streets as theaters catering to his amusement: "'I like these streets,' observed Anthony aloud. 'I always feel as though it's a performance being staged for me; as though the second I've passed they'll all stop leaping and laughing and, instead, grow very sad, remembering how poor they are, and retreat with bowed heads into their houses'" (*B&D* 258). Anthony and Gloria cannot satisfy their need for self-promotion and theatricality. They stage fights in public places to attract spectators. At a train station, Anthony tussles with Gloria while commuters watch. The Patches validate their relationship, from which passion has ebbed, by drawing attention to their lapses of decorum. Although Anthony imagines the streets exists as a theater where he watches the drama of class unfold, he exploits public venues to stage his own fall from decorum and wealth.

Taking up Anthony's aphoristic tone, the narrator in *The Beautiful and Damned* remarks that "the public manner of all good Americans" combines "that of a Middle Western farmer appraising his wheat crop and that of an actor wondering whether he is observed" (85–6). The theatrical metaphor raises the specter of class mobility. Whether sliding up or down the social ladder, Americans act out the possibilities of the class to which they hope or fear they belong: farmer or actor; rich or poor; fan or celebrity. Class is theatrical insofar as Americans act up to grandeur or act down to trashiness. The Patches take on both roles. Initially, theatricality is a matter of artifice in *The Beautiful and Damned*. In fact, it defines class position: one acts because one lives in the future—the expectation of inheritance and better days— not because one lives in the present, and certainly not in the past. Because she has acted throughout her life, Gloria conjectures that she possesses all the resources of a skilled actress. Were she to act in movies, she could remain "a little girl" (360). Her desire to be a famous actress, for all its implied infantilism, ends with a disastrous screen test. Anthony's statement, "I hate theatrical things" (279), has to be taken with a grain of salt, for Americans aspire to celebrity status promised by acting in the theater or on film. For this reason, Fitzgerald resorts frequently to screen tests and screen time as tropes for fame. In *Tender is the Night*, Rosemary appalls Dick Diver by suggesting he have a screen test. When the movie producer Monroe Stahr calls Kathleen out of the blue in *The Last Tycoon*, she concludes that he wants to "put [her] in the movies" (*LT* 60). In a related scene in *The Great Gatsby*, Myrtle Wilson strikes a pose and beams "a brilliant smile" (35), as if she were being photographed. According to Fitzgerald then, all good Americans retain a touch of the actor, which is to say, a touch of the impostor.

As spokesman for flappers and slickers in the 1920s, Fitzgerald resorted to innocuous pranks to enhance his fame by theatricalizing his stature. A streak of vulgar grandstanding runs through his fiction and his life. In *This Side of Paradise*, a gang of Princeton undergraduates drives to the Jersey shore, where they eat meals in restaurants and leave without paying their bill. They con passers-by on the boardwalk by taking up "a collection for the French War Orphans which netted a dollar and twenty cents" (*TSOP* 78); instead of donating the money to orphans, they buy brandy. The undergraduates pull another prank at a movie theater by not paying (79). In *Tender is the Night*, the "slapstick comedy" (76) of one movable party in the streets of Paris culminates with a ride "on top of thousands of carrots in a market wagon" (79).

After Fitzgerald married Zelda in 1920, they indulged in tomfoolery as urban diversion. Kicked out of the Biltmore Hotel for disturbing other guests, the Fitzgeralds moved two blocks away to the Commodore Hotel, where "they celebrated their move by spinning in the revolving door" (Bruccoli 134). In a more sinister vein, Zelda, to protest Scott's flirtation with an actress, burned her clothes in a bathtub and flung a platinum watch—one of Scott's first gifts to her—out the window of a moving train (Bruccoli 256, 257). However juvenile these pranks may be, they express discomfort with and bewilderment about fame. Simultaneously, pranks consolidate celebrity in the sense that they draw attention, through a public or publicized commotion, to the people who commit outrageous acts. The Princeton undergraduates tear up their restaurant bills in *This Side of Paradise* as an expression of entitlement. The Fitzgeralds twirl in a revolving door as a youthful flouting of convention. Just short of being a nuisance, outrageousness stages fame as a law unto itself.

From childhood onwards, Fitzgerald was "adept at self-promotion" (Prigozy 4). He capitalized on youth culture by promoting himself as the spokesman of his generation. As Kirk Curnutt points out about the dissipated flappers in Fitzgerald's fiction, "This pursuit of youth inspired a reciprocal anxiety about the age at which one officially became 'out of date'" (44). As a record of their celebrity standing, Scott and Zelda kept scrapbooks of newspaper and magazine clippings about themselves. During the 1930s, they harvested almost no clippings; newspapers stopped devoting space to their self-promoting pranks. As Ruth Prigozy points out, obscurity was not permanent. Fitzgerald's star rose again with the posthumous publication of *The Last Tycoon* (1941) and *The Crack-Up* (1945), both edited by Edmund Wilson. In the 1970s and 1980s, Scott and Zelda were resurrected as the embodiment of "sensationalism and fleeting celebrity" (Prigozy 24). Prigozy concludes that, "the study of the Fitzgeralds and popular culture involves a dialectic between their public performance and public image on the one hand and their use of popular culture in their creative language on the other" (2). In the cultural logic of celebrity, the fascination with seeing oneself in the press vies with finding ways to make oneself talked about in the press.

In Fitzgerald's unfinished novel, *The Last Tycoon*, a group of Hollywood insiders measure their relative status against each other during an airplane trip. Monroe Stahr travels under an assumed name even though everyone on the plane recognizes him. The assumed name allows him a slight strangeness within the Hollywood crowd. Cecelia Brady, a producer's daughter who has grown up in Hollywood, comments, "We don't go for strangers in Hollywood [...] unless they're a celebrity. And they better look out even then" (*LT* 11). Strangers can enter the inside ranks of Hollywood only if they have become celebrities somewhere else first. Monroe Stahr, by contrast, adopts strangeness as a proof of his stardom. As Fitzgerald's appreciation of the subtleties of American celebrity culture increased during the 1930s, he identified celebrity as a closed system precariously balanced on the perception of stardom. Cecelia regrets that no movie stars fly on the Hollywood-bound plane: "High adventure might be among us, disguised as a movie star. But mostly it wasn't. And I always wished fervently that we looked more interesting than we did—just as I often have at premieres, when the fans look at you with scornful reproach because you're not a star" (*LT* 8). Celebrity culture depends on conspicuous visibility, extending even to the unmasking of a movie star on a plane trying to preserve his privacy. Conspicuousness in itself, however, as at a premiere, does not guarantee stardom.

In the wake of the success of *This Side of Paradise* in 1920 and his elevation to the pantheon of regular, highly paid contributors to the *Saturday Evening Post*, Scott Fitzgerald felt his relative celebrity acutely. In "Early Success," an essay published in October 1937, he writes regretfully about the "first wild wind of success and the delicious mist it brings with it. It is a short and precious time—for when the mist rises in a few weeks, or a few months, one finds that the very best is over" (*MLC* 186). Nick likewise remembers his thirtieth birthday and "the promise of a decade of loneliness" ahead in *The Great Gatsby* (143). Although he often eulogizes youth before it ends, Fitzgerald gives a sharper nuance to his own retrospective understanding of celebrity in "Early Success": "The man who arrives young believes that he exercises his will because his star is shining" (*MLC* 190). The sentence emphasizes causality, but a false one of astrological import. The young man's star shines, yet its shining has no relation to the young man's will, including his will to fame. The star, which metaphorically represents renown or destiny, shines of its own accord, no matter what the young man believes or does. Intuiting that his efforts have no bearing on the star of fame or destiny, the young man never knows for certain whether his actions and accomplishments are only so many impostures. The impostures might be the form that his will to fame takes, but they might also obstruct the path to fame. The young man, acting according to what he thinks is his destiny, emulates famous people or his notion of what fame ought to entail. The shining star provokes the young man to succeed, but emphasis in Fitzgerald's sentence falls on belief in destiny rather than destiny per se. In this regard, all personality contains histrionic or phony elements that fame, if and when it comes, exacerbates.

In his 1936 essay "The Crack-Up," a bitter reflection on the loss of vitality that accompanies middle age, Fitzgerald weighs the differences among literary, cinematic, and other kinds of success: "It seemed a romantic business to be a successful literary man—you were not ever going to be as famous as a movie star but what note you had was probably longer-lived—you were never going to have the power of a man of strong political or religious convictions but you were certainly more independent" (*MLC* 139). Fame can be measured by several factors: duration, degree, independence. No matter what consolations literary success brings, envy of movie stars nags Fitzgerald. In "How to Live on Practically Nothing a Year," he deliberately confuses his own celebrity with famous Hollywood actors. While changing money at a bank in Paris one day, he encounters a crowd of fans:

> I had evidently been recognized and an enormous crowd began to gather outside. The crowd grew and I considered going to the window and making them a speech but I thought that might only increase the disturbance so I looked around intending to ask someone's advice. I recognized no one, however, except one of the bank officials and a Mr. and Mrs. Douglas Fairbanks from America, who were buying francs at a counter in the rear. So I decided not to show myself and, sure enough, by the time I had cashed my check the crowd had given up and melted away. (*MLC* 43)

The dynamics of this celebrity sighting turn on recognizing and being recognized. While he bears in mind the ironic distance between his identity as a writer and his self-presentation in this celebrity drama, Fitzgerald claims to have "been recognized." He in turn recognizes no one, except a bank official and an American couple. The couple remain "a Mr. and Mrs. Fairbanks," not "the" Hollywood swashbuckling actor Douglas Fairbanks and his famous wife Mary Pickford. Fitzgerald clearly knows who they are, but the protagonist in this vignette pretends to be the center of the crowd's attention. Humor in this anecdote disguises Fitzgerald's understanding that fame has residual effects. Having been in physical proximity to Fairbanks and Pickford, he basks in their fame. He can perpetuate the moment of glory by telling the story and dropping names. Being close to a famous person is not inherently interesting except in a culture that valorizes celebrity as an indefinable yet essential quality.

Similar to how he imagines that the crowd around the Fairbanks has come to see him, Fitzgerald usually thinks that no one recognizes him when another famous person is nearby. Nevertheless, he emulates the star quality of Fairbanks and Pickford by momentarily displacing them, if only imaginatively, from fans' adoration. Fitzgerald imitates their hauteur from his anonymous, invisible corner. The charade of not noticing continues until the end of the anecdote. Fitzgerald pretends that the crowd disperses because he ignores them; in truth, the crowd dissolves because the famous movie stars leave. While manifestly ironic, Fitzgerald never concedes that the Fairbanks have a greater claim to fame than he does. The illusion of being the focus of adulation remains intact because Fitzgerald contravenes the rules of celebrity sightings. He does not act with the crowd because he assumes that he is the celebrity. He resists recognizing famous people at all. He shrinks from, and sloughs off, the veneration of the assembled fans in emulation of what truly famous people do.

Emulation propels the culture of celebrity. Being in proximity to famous actors and sharing the humdrum activity of changing money, Fitzgerald shares their aura. He typically kept his eyes peeled for celebrities during his travels. In his "Notebooks," he records "[m]eeting Cole Porter in Ritz" (*The Crack-Up* 223). Upon hearing that Edith Wharton was at Scribner's offices in New York one day, he burst into the room where she was and "knelt at her feet in homage" (Bruccoli 132). With alternating spikes of malice and jealousy, he sat near Isadora Duncan "giving one of her last parties at the next table" in a café on the Riviera (*MLC* 158); while Duncan wearily toasted oblivion, Fitzgerald stole salt and pepper shakers from his table. Impressed by Duncan's blasé attitude, he metaphorically tries to steal her limelight. Her fame blankets the theft, although Fitzgerald steals in order to draw attention to his status as a celebrity as well. The stolen salt and pepper shakers appear to commemorate the celebrity sighting as metonyms, although they stand in for the remote encounter with fame, not for Isadora Duncan herself. The ordinary shakers never belonged to Duncan; they mean nothing until Fitzgerald attaches a celebrity anecdote to them. Thus celebrity culture confuses metonyms and metaphors: salt and pepper shakers iconically stand for a brush with fame, regardless of the star's physical relation to the icon. Fitzgerald's celebrity stories follow a paradigm: he accidentally meets a star; he is invisible; seeking recognition, he pulls a prank; he tells the story of the encounter to prove that he shares star qualities.

Emulation of stars creates an identity. Speaking of his own personality, Fitzgerald claims in "The Crack-Up" that he is "more than average in a tendency to identify myself, my ideas, my destiny with those of all classes that I came in contact with" (*MLC* 141). According to his self-description in "The Crack-Up," Fitzgerald disappears into other people's personalities to the point that he loses his sense of self. He does not mean that, as a novelist, he empathizes with people to understand their point of view. Instead, he imitates others in order to escape his invisibility. Although capable of acting up in public, Fitzgerald never felt comfortable speaking *in propria persona* in front of groups (Bruccoli 150). He dealt with public gatherings by simulating the behavior of famous people. While disliking invisibility, Fitzgerald disliked conspicuousness even more. As *The Great Gatsby* intimates, the notorious—those who acquire fame for bad deeds or bad behavior—are too visible, whereas the famous seemingly exert no effort to attract attention. The dialectic of visibility and fame caused Fitzgerald to worry about his identity. In "Pasting It Together," a sequel to "The Crack-Up," he claims to have designated, to five different men, his intellectual conscience, his sense of the good life, his artistic uniqueness, his social relations and his political conscience: "So there was not an 'I' any more—not a basis on which I could organize my self-respect" (*MLC* 149).

The emptying out of personality, the urge to emulate, and the lack of self motivates the content of Fitzgerald's novels. In *This Side of Paradise*, Amory Blaine and his literary friends emulate Dorian Gray after reading Wilde's novel: "Kerry [...] simulated Lord Henry, following Amory about, addressing him as 'Dorian' and pretending to encourage in him wicked fancies and attenuated tendencies to ennui" (*TSOP* 52). They concoct identities from literary precursors. Kerry keeps up this performance in front of other undergraduates in the common room. As a result of this unwelcome publicity, "Amory became furiously embarrassed, and after that made epigrams only before D'Invilliers or a convenient mirror" (*TSOP* 52). Emulation itself does not embarrass Amory; attention does. Instead of curtailing his poses, he merely stops acting out his role as a Wildean wit in public.

In addition to Dorian Gray, Amory mimics Paul Verlaine, Algernon Swinburne, Samuel Johnson, and various swains from Broadway plays. In a disquisition on socialism addressed to rich Mr. Ferrenby in the back of his car, Amory recapitulates the ideas of Burne Holiday. Burne, devoted to social equality and Tolstoy's novels, opens Amory's mind in a way that Princeton professors never do. Amory concludes that "[b]eing Burne was suddenly so much realler than being clever" (*TSOP* 125). Amory does not want to adopt socialism or adulate Tolstoy. He aspires to merge his identity with Burne's by subordinating his personality to the stronger reality of Burne's convictions. Paradoxically, emulation, with its hint of inauthenticity, expands reality. By impersonating someone else, something "realler" materializes. Moreover, incarnating another person surpasses mere cleverness, for cleverness automatically follows from merging one's personality with someone else's. In his "Notebooks," Fitzgerald admits his tendencies to worship heroes: "When I like men I want to be like them—I want to lose the outer qualities that give me my individuality and be like them. I don't want the man; I want to absorb into myself all the qualities that make him attractive and leave him out" (*The Crack-Up* 169). Abject emulation allows accumulation of other men's admirable qualities. As with the emulation of stars, the person emulated does not even know that emulation happens.

Emulation happens inconspicuously. In *The Great Gatsby*, Nick, who spends an unpleasant afternoon in the company of Tom Buchanan, Myrtle Wilson, her sister Catherine, and the McKees, imagines a "casual watcher in the darkening streets" (49) looking up at the apartment where they sit. Nick projects himself into this watcher: "I was him too, looking up and wondering" (49). Not liking the company in the room, he merges in his imagination with someone hypothetically standing outside. Feeling himself invisible until Myrtle Wilson points at him as if he were her loathed husband, Nick adopts a position of watcher in the theater of Tom Buchanan's love life. In much the same way that Fitzgerald adopts invisibility in the presence of famous people, Nick observes people and speculates on their impostures from a position of agreeable taciturnity. Nick's taciturnity, however, camouflages envy and admiration.

Nick is a snob—a polite snob, but a snob nonetheless. His manners polished at Yale, he is "inclined to reserve all judgments" about people (*GG* 5). He means, in part, that judgment of his peers at college would have breached civility. He acknowledges the snobbery implicit in feigning sleep so that he does not have to hear the embarrassing confessions: "as my father snobbishly suggested and I snobbishly repeat, a sense of the fundamental decencies is parcelled out unequally at birth" (6). To claim that decencies are unequally parceled out presumes that one has received the lion's share of those decencies. These alleged decencies allow Nick to look down on people who have more money—Gatsby, Wolfsheim, Tom—but who have less social *savoir-faire* or tact than he possesses. Nick's good manners invite confessions; people apparently mistake his politeness for interest. In any event, he exercises good manners without calling attention to his decency. Like the "unknown men" who confess their "secret griefs" to Nick (5), Gatsby confides in Nick, although the truth of his confessions cannot be determined. After Daisy kills Myrtle Wilson in a hit-and-run accident, Gatsby, worn out by an all-night vigil outside the Buchanan's house, recounts the "strange story of his youth" (155). Unlike Nick, who remains "reserved" (5) in speech, Gatsby talks "without reserve" (155) on the subject of Daisy. Indeed, Nick and Gatsby perform their roles of impostor and polite listener with virtuosic insincerity.

Good manners reduce Nick to near invisibility, but his various gaffes also function to bring his character into heightened relief. His slightly embarrassing offences against politeness multiply in *The Great Gatsby*. At one of Gatsby's parties, Nick does not recognize his host and begs pardon for his rudeness (52). His comportment sometimes verges on the gauche. After accompanying Myrtle and Tom to their Manhattan apartment, Nick returns from buying cigarettes to find that his hosts have disappeared into the bedroom to have sex; he sits "discreetly in the living room" (34) reading a racy novel until they reappear. When Catherine confides that Tom and Daisy Buchanan cannot stand each other (37), Nick neither corrects this false information nor admits that he knows the Buchanans personally. By not interrupting or speaking up, Nick pretends to show decency, when, in fact, he tacitly judges the social acumen of others. When he sees Gatsby standing with arms outstretched on the darkened lawn of his East Egg estate, Nick does not speak to him because he understands that Gatsby is "content to be alone" (25). Not wanting to impose, Nick defies neighborliness and allows himself time to assess Gatsby's character.

Other characters compound Nick's gaffes. Jordan Baker infringes etiquette by shushing Nick so that she can eavesdrop on Tom and Daisy (20). Tom Buchanan rides away on his horse to prevent Gatsby from coming to dinner (110). Tom, distrustful of Gatsby's character, confronts him about his Oxford education and his murky career. He treats Gatsby with "well-concealed dislike" (122). Tom's dislike is not so well concealed, however, as to escape Nick's notice. In the end, Tom—who twists Daisy's finger, breaks Myrtle's nose, and instigates a car accident in which a chambermaid's arm is broken (16, 41, 82)—falsely insinuates to George Wilson that Gatsby killed Myrtle. Tom defies social courtesies, whereas Nick, out of politeness, facilitates the reunion between Gatsby and Daisy. By helping Gatsby realize his plan to see Daisy again, Nick betrays Tom, his Yale classmate and his cousin's husband.

Both Nick and Gatsby stage their politeness. When Nick meets Wolfsheim for the first time, he "politely" (74) inquires about a rhetorical question in a story. Politeness masks his distaste for Wolfsheim. Imitating Nick's punctiliousness, Gatsby inquires "politely" (103) after a reporter's request for information. At their first meeting, Gatsby asks Nick "politely" (50) about his war service. Even when Tom verbally attacks him, Gatsby responds "politely" (136). To prove he belongs in the privileged milieu of Long Island millionaires, Gatsby puts on a consistent performance of fine manners. Only rarely does Nick catch a flicker of his eye or an inconsistency in Gatsby's answers that betray a lie. Exasperated, Gatsby asks Nick directly, "What's your opinion of me anyhow?" (69) that causes Nick to squirm with embarrassment and to reply evasively. Were he to answer, Nick might reveal his likes, dislikes, and opinions; he would, in short, make himself conspicuous. Although critics traditionally read Nick as a "detached moralist" and a "reliable narrator-observer" (Carlisle 308), or a "weary narrator" who plays along with "Gatsby's game" (Weinstein 376, 377), the exchanges between Nick and Gatsby more exactly involve a contest between polite reserve and extravagant imposture.

Nick believes in Gatsby's hoaxes—the bootlegger's invented past and pretense of education—because of his susceptibility to the illusion of American-style success. Until he meets Gatsby, Nick does not find "romantic readiness" (*GG* 6) in anyone else. The incorruptibility of Gatsby's "single dream" (169), a heightened romantic ambition to recapture Daisy, captivates Nick. Just as Amory Blaine yields to the forceful personality of Burne Holiday, Nick merges his personality with Gatsby's. The gaudy gangster awes the reticent, hardworking Midwesterner. Gatsby's smile, with its "quality of eternal reassurance," causes the narrative to skitter uncharacteristically into the second person: "It faced—or seemed to face—the whole external world for an instant, and then concentrated on *you* with an irresistible prejudice in your favor. It understood you just so far as you wanted to be understood, believed you as you would like to believe in yourself and assured you that it had precisely the impression of you that, at your best, you hoped to convey" (52–3). Almost immediately, Gatsby transforms back into "an elegant young rough-neck" (53). While it lasts, Gatsby's smile mirrors Nick's commitment to social elegance and etiquette. Smiles reinforce charm. In *The Last Tycoon*, Monroe Stahr flashes "a kind fatherly smile" (30) as a sign of approval. The smile accepts the other person as he is. It mirrors the desire to be liked and included; the smile therefore signals complicity. A gesture of reciprocal enchantment, Gatsby's smile emulates and returns Nick's self-presentation.

Yet the smile is a con. Edgar Allan Poe, in "Diddling Considered as One of the Exact Sciences," claims that "diddlers"—Poe's word for swindlers—grin with self-satisfaction after cheating people: "Your true *diddler* winds up all with a grin. But this nobody sees but himself. He grins when his daily work is done—when his allotted labors are accomplished—at night in his own closet, and altogether for his own private entertainment" (Poe 237). Poe reckons that the swindler smiles to himself because his labor is its own reward. By contrast, Gatsby smiles at Nick in order to win his confidence. Even as a soldier, Gatsby practices imposture; he allows Daisy to believe that he has more money and social status than in fact he does (*GG* 156).

The impostor has a strong purchase on the American cultural imagination. Poe's "Diddling Considered as One of the Exact Sciences" and Herman Melville's *The Confidence-Man* set parameters for ways that con artists separate suckers from their money. The con artist is an impostor insofar as he presents himself in one guise, usually a trustworthy one, but has the low goal of defrauding people. Karen Halttunen divides mid-nineteenth-century confidence men into three categories: urban friends of country youths, demagogues, and gamblers. Furthermore, she asserts that American impostors before the Civil War expressed emerging anxieties about the shift from a vertically stratified to a horizontally leveled society (Halttunen 25). Attacking the middle-class values of hard work and thrift with his swindles, the confidence man embodies "inarticulate powers of contamination" (Halttunen 24), specifically the power to infect young Americans with hypocrisy. The impostor emulates the values of a class with money, education, or social distinction, in order to belong to that class.

The Shakespeare-quoting Duke and Dauphin in *Huckleberry Finn* share a range of confidence tricks that depend on class distinctions and a smattering of education. The Dauphin can peddle "patent medicines; theatre-actor—tragedy, you know; take a turn at mesmerism and phrenology when there's a chance; teach singing-geography school for a change; sling a lecture, sometimes" (Twain 99). The Duke, by comparison, prides himself on curing cancer, telling fortunes, preaching, and "missionaryin' around" (Twain 99). Twain captivated Fitzgerald's attention shortly before he wrote *The Great Gatsby*. He read Van Wyck Brooks's *The Ordeal of Mark Twain* and Albert Begelow Paine's biography of Twain; Fitzgerald admired the Duke and the Dauphin in *Huckleberry Finn* above all other characters (Bruccoli 135). The bald seventy-year-old Dauphin and the American-born Duke of Bilgewater tell preposterous lies. Similarly, Gatsby mystifies his origins and accomplishments. Nick occasionally doubts Gatsby's awkward equivocations. When he asks which part of the Midwest Gatsby hails from, Gatsby replies "San Francisco" (*GG* 70). Instead of guffawing, Nick answers, "I see" (70). He does not correct the factual absurdity or Gatsby's faulty grasp of geography. Like the Duke and Dauphin cobbling together lines from Shakespeare's plays, Gatsby gussies up his vocabulary with phrases—"old sport"—to evoke Ivy League chumminess and erudition.[4]

While a con man uses his imposture to deceive people and defraud them of money, the impostor does not inevitably have financial gain in mind. Gatsby hardly needs money from Nick. On the contrary, he offers to set Nick up with a lucrative business proposition. He replaces a dress that one of his guests tore (*GG* 47). A form of wizardry, Gatsby's extravagance brings people fleeting doses of pleasure and belonging. The "spectroscopic gayety" of his summer parties in West Egg breaks down the "staid nobility" of visitors from East Egg (49). For his part, Nick gives in to the magic of a Saturday night party after two glasses of champagne: "the scene had changed before my eyes into something significant, elemental and profound" (51). Nick usually detects hypocrisy in others. For example, he notices Englishmen on the make at Gatsby's party (46), and he diagnoses Jordan Baker as "incurably dishonest" (63). Yet he succumbs to Gatsby's charm.

Through his excesses and heightened vividness, Gatsby casts a spell over Nick. As Haltunnen remarks, the nineteenth-century confidence man usually corrupted Americans through demagoguery and mesmeric talents. In *The Age of Innocence*, Wharton, remembering New York in the 1870s, satirizes the mesmeric talents of the mountebank, Dr. Agathon Carver, who is gifted with "baleful eloquence" (184) and performs psychical research into "Inner Thought" (209). The impostor answers deep-seated psychological needs for community, belonging, and happiness. In this regard, Gatsby shares characteristics with P.T. Barnum and the Wizard of Oz: he creates enchantment through the grandiosity of his gestures. Emphasizing illusions and magic as aspects of his novel, Fitzgerald wrote to Ludlow Fowler in August 1924, while revising *The Great Gatsby*, "the burden of the novel" is "the loss of those illusions that give such color to the world so that you don't care whether things are true or false as long as they partake of the magical glory" (*Correspondence* 145). Fitzgerald means that Americans are indifferent to

---

[4]   Impostors often fake their educational credentials. For example, James Hogue, born in Kansas City, Missouri, in 1959, changed his name to Alexi Indris Santana and entered Princeton University as a freshman in 1988; he was just shy of his twenty-ninth birthday. Exposed in 1991, Hogue, who had received financial aid, was convicted of defrauding the university. He subsequently took another name and enrolled as an extension student at Harvard University. Hired to work at the Harvard Mineralogical Museum, Hogue stole $50,000 worth of gems. Violating the conditions of his parole for his earlier fraud, he trespassed on the Princeton campus in 1996 under the assumed name Jim MacAuthor (Samuels 72–85; "Bogus Princeton Student" 25). I cite this example because it happened for the most part at Fitzgerald's alma mater. But the phenomenon of imposture is widespread, especially at prestigious universities. An impostor named Philip Shaw joined a college and extracurricular clubs at Yale in 2003—without ever having been admitted as a student (Sullivan and Youngstrom). In April 2007, Marilee Jones, the Dean of Admissions at MIT, resigned because she had lied on her résumé; she claimed to have earned degrees at Albany Medical College, Union College, and Rensselaer Polytechnic Institute, but she had, in fact, no degrees from any of those institutions (Lewin n.p.).

truth as long as an illusion is credible. The suspension of disbelief opens up to the possibility of being pleasingly duped. Nick allows himself to be taken in by Gatsby's impostures. Whatever suspicions he entertains about his conspicuously consuming neighbor, he allays them. *The Great Gatsby* is, therefore, a novel about an impostor told from the point of view of the man who willingly subscribes to the "magical glory" of American self-invention.

Nineteenth-century impostors invent titles for themselves to legitimate their cons: Duke, Dauphin, Doctor. In *The Great Gatsby*, Nick shyly mentions that his family "descended from the Dukes of Buccleuch" (7). As if trumping Nick's claim, Gatsby extracts a photograph from his pocket to prove his background story; the picture shows Gatsby in Trinity Quad, Oxford, with the future "Earl of Doncaster" on his left (71). As when Fitzgerald finds himself in the same bank as Douglas Fairbanks and Mary Pickford, Gatsby's proximity to a titled aristocrat confers legitimacy. In this regard, Gatsby manipulates Nick's inherent snobbery and belief in the uneven parceling out of decency and class. The man in the photo could be any Oxford student. Nevertheless, Nick decides, with no evidence more substantial than a photograph, that everything about Gatsby "was all true" (71). Impressed by distinctions of pedigree, Nick accepts Gatsby's claim to authenticity because of an appeal to the English aristocracy. Through the small touch of providing visual testimony about his proximity to an earl, Gatsby perpetrates a hoax on Nick, and thereby wins his confidence.

Rather than falling into categories of impostor or plain dealer, Americans arrange themselves along a spectrum of impostures. Nick wants to pass with his richer friends while asserting that he is an honest Midwesterner. In this regard, he dupes himself as much as he dupes others. So, too, if Gatsby can take in Nick, he may be able to dupe Tom, Daisy, and various socially prominent people. If Nick believes his story, others might believe it as well. Impostors con people by affecting the manners or accents of the class they want to swindle. In general, the American impostor narrative in *The Great Gatsby* follows the rags-to-riches paradigm of Horatio Alger novels. The impostor emulates pedigree or success without possessing the required credentials for such entitlements. To disguise his past, the impostor assumes an alias, sometimes a flagrantly outrageous one. Plain Jimmy Gatz reinvents himself as Jay Gatsby: according to Nick, Gatsby "sprang from his Platonic conception of himself" (104). Nick qualifies this formulation: "he invented just the sort of Jay Gatsby that a seventeen year old boy would be likely to invent, and to this conception he was faithful to the end" (104). Gatsby may be faithful to his self-confected identity, but Nick exposes the doubleness behind the wizardry. In Nick's eyes, imposture has grandeur, even if the fabrication cannot be sustained indefinitely.

Fitzgerald understands imposture as a form of theatricality. As doubles for each other, or as a theatrical team, Gatsby acts as the conspicuous front man to Nick's fall guy. They perform their roles of preposterousness and susceptibility for each other. Just prior to writing *The Great Gatsby*, Fitzgerald dramatized swindlers and impostors in *The Vegetable*. In the second act of this talky and undramatic play,

Jerry Frost, after drinking bootleg gin, fantasizes that he has been elected President of the United States. Other characters double Jerry's imposture. His incompetent, dotty father serves as Secretary of the Treasury. The bootlegger Snooks transforms into the honorable "Ambassador to the United States from Irish Poland" (*V* 80). A far cry from being honorable, Snooks proposes a "straight swap of the Buzzard Islands for the State of Idaho" (*V* 99) as a solution to Jerry's difficulties with recalcitrant moralists from Idaho. A failure as an office clerk and as president, Jerry reconciles his character with his ambition by becoming a postman in the third act of *The Vegetable*.

Like *The Vegetable*, *The Great Gatsby* dwells on the overlap between theatricality and imposture.[5] Fitzgerald absorbs theatrical conventions and tropes into novelistic discourse. Nick initially thinks that Wolfsheim, "a denizen of Broadway" (*GG* 77), might be an actor. In Tom's apartment, Nick skims through "Broadway scandal magazines" (33). The scenic construction of the novel and Gatsby's repertory of expressive gestures—reassuring smile, outstretched arms, manly handshakes, goodbye waves—draw upon theatrical conventions. Gangster Gatsby sanitizes his dubious character by emulating stage romance and glamour. Indeed, having produced his parties like Broadway spectacles, he finally appears in front of his guests like an impresario. Actresses, chorus girls, directors, producers, composers, and socialites mix at Gatsby's parties. Vaudeville performers perform stunts. A woman who might be a Ziegfield's Follies understudy shimmies on the dance floor. Gatsby hopes to lure Daisy to his lavish parties in order to demonstrate that celebrities figure among his acquaintances. The plan backfires because Gatsby miscalculates Daisy's reaction to fame. When they glimpse an actress sitting beneath a tree in Gatsby's garden, Tom and Daisy experience "that peculiarly unreal feeling that accompanies the recognition of a hitherto ghostly celebrity of the movies" (111). The "ghostly" actress stirs an uncanny sensation, for Tom and Daisy recognize her without knowing who she is. Daisy exclaims over the number of celebrities at the party, but Tom, echoing Fitzgerald's sense of invisibility in the presence of stars, prefers to "look at all these famous people in—in oblivion" (112). According to Nick, Daisy is ultimately "appalled by West Egg, this unprecedented 'place' that Broadway had begotten upon a Long Island fishing village" (113–14).

In the fineness of detail brought to his parties and his image, Gatsby resembles David Belasco, the Broadway producer and playwright. The owl-eyed man in the library makes the comparison explicit as he holds up a real book: "It's a bona fide piece of printed matter. It fooled me. This fella's a regular Belasco. It's a triumph. What thoroughness! What realism!" (*GG* 50). Belasco is now remembered for

---

[5]   Even after *The Vegetable* failed, Fitzgerald thought that he would write again for the theater: "I'm going to write another play and I hope it'll be less disastrous than the last" (*Correspondence* 145). In the same letter, he links the failure of *The Vegetable* with the theme of disillusionment in *The Great Gatsby*. The rewards of writing short stories and, to a lesser degree, novels outweighed the possibility that fame lay for Fitzgerald in the theater.

writing *The Girl of the Golden West* and *Madame Butterfly*, but, as the builder of several theaters in New York and the producer of innumerable successful plays, his reputation in the 1910s and 1920s rested on the elaborate realism of his sets and the subtlety of his lighting effects. As Belasco states in *The Theatre Through its Stage Door*, published in 1919, "'the Belasco method' […] originates from the importance and emphasis I place upon every minute detail which makes for truth in my theatre" (241). As when Amory asserts that emulation of Burne creates a "realler" identity (*TSOP* 125), Belasco deploys the artifice of lights and details in the theater to approximate reality as nearly as possible. For a scene in a tenement in one play, Belasco could not achieve the authenticity he wanted with props, so he bought the furnishings of a shabby lodging house in New York and exactingly reconstructed the room on stage (Belasco 77). For another play set in a restaurant, he directed actors to flip real pancakes (Marker 61).

Belasco eliminated footlights and exploited the technical resources of electricity to achieve nuance in his lighting effects. He claims to have spent three months in the Sierra Nevadas to contrive the right blend of colors for the sky in *The Girl of the Golden West* (Belasco 56–7). The persuasiveness of a scene on stage, he argues throughout *The Theatre through its Stage Door*, depends on the balance and intensity of light: "when you use false lights and colors you do not stimulate imaginations, you only distort reality. And when you distort reality you have destroyed truth" (237). Fitzgerald knew about Belasco's realism, for he had a passing acquaintance with the impresario. In separate letters, Zelda mentions buying a coat for Belasco and Scott refers to one of Belasco's habitual sayings (*Correspondence* 246, 475). On the subject of lighting, Belasco declares that "romantic love suggests twilight or moonlight scenes" (227). He elaborates an atmospherics of lighting: "sunlit scenes imply happiness, moonlit scenes give a suggestion of romance, while tragedy or sorrow should be played in gloom" (Belasco 53–4).

Fitzgerald takes Belasco's hints on lighting to heart. The green light on the Buchanan's dock answers Belasco's schematic sense of color (Belasco 160). Sometimes Gatsby's house is ablaze with light and sometimes utter darkness swallows it up. Gatsby often appears beneath moonlight. At one party, the "premature moon" looks like it has been conjured by Gatsby "out of a caterer's basket" (*GG* 47); the moon rises as the party progresses (51). Lighting effects derived from Belasco filter Gatsby's romantic inclinations. When Gatsby remembers courting Daisy in Louisville, he conjures up a Belasco set of falling leaves, a sidewalk "white with moonlight," and a street mounting like a ladder to "a secret place above the trees" (117). When they kiss by moonlight, Daisy and Gatsby act out their theatrical roles as southern belle and transient soldier. Whatever romantic illusions Gatsby clings to five years after this brief romance, they commingle in a *mise-en-scène* of regret and yearning. Daisy may have loved him once; she may love him somewhat still. But no amount of stage moonlight can reconstitute their faded romance.

Nick professes scorn for Gatsby's phoniness, then praises him for making life grander: "If personality is an unbroken series of successful gestures, then there was something gorgeous about him, some heightened sensitivity to the promises of life" (6). The qualifying "if" that begins the sentence casts doubt on the proposition that an unbroken sequence of gestures does constitute a personality. Although Gatsby hopes that his array of studied, grandiloquent gestures authenticate his concocted personality, his impostures merely disguise his ascent through society. He is involved in bootlegging and trading stolen bonds. Knowing how to put himself in the best possible light—literally—he mimics the attitudes and accomplishments of wealthy classes. When he adapts theatrical effects to fake his credentials, he enhances the grandeur of American impostures in general.

Fame, as Fitzgerald understands it, has no inevitable connection to authenticity or talent. As he indicates in *The Great Gatsby* and his later essays that reflect on fame, imposture involves a dialectic of conspicuousness and invisibility. Whereas Gatsby makes himself highly visible through ingenious effects, Nick practices reticence in order to confirm his own credentials and integrity. In the first instance, the impostor can only fabricate an identity when no one is looking; in other words, inconspicuousness is necessary for self-invention. Nick's self-invention has touches of theatrical imposture as well. Nick understands Gatsby's imposture because he masks his own personality and motives with good manners. Responsible for stripping away the illusions that decorate Gatsby's life by narrating them, Nick promotes the possibility that inconspicuousness contributes to self-invention just as publicity does.

Thinking of the theatricality of identity, Fitzgerald claimed, "[t]here are no second acts in American lives" (*LT* 163). Success happens in the first act or not at all. Yet success carries the possibility that all Americans, like characters in plays, are capable of posture and imposture. To some degree, Gatsby duplicates the financial success of Dan Cody, with whom he yachted around the world for three years. According to his father, Gatsby could have rivaled James J. Hill, the railroad tycoon from St. Paul (*GG* 176). Never himself, Gatsby copies the achievements of financial titans. His reputation as a larger-than-life millionaire, a reputation that his romantic pursuit of Daisy enlarges, intimates that fame is always secondhand, insofar as it derives from prior examples of success. One has first to live outside the spotlight in order to steal it. Knowing that all Americans have a touch of the actor about them—he has invented his own gentlemanly identity—Nick aggrandizes Gatsby's life into a legend about imposture. As *The Great Gatsby* indicates, celebrity requires its impostors as well as those who endorse imposture as a credible American dream.

Chapter 4

There Has Been an Inward Change: In Search of Eric Walrond

James C. Davis

The pressure must have been enormous. Eric Walrond's plan to become a writer—a real writer of quality and critical acclaim—had succeeded. It had succeeded perhaps beyond his expectations, quite possibly beyond what he felt he deserved, and now he had to live with it. He had to live up to it. And he had to begin doing so in Wisconsin, of all places, in the dead of winter in February 1928. What in God's name had he gotten himself into?

In a few short years Walrond had managed an impressive ascent to literary celebrity. Born in British Guiana in 1898, raised in Barbados and Panama, he left his job as a reporter for the *Panama Star and Herald* and moved to New York in 1918, just as the Harlem Renaissance was gathering force. Winning a story contest in Marcus Garvey's *Negro World* catapulted him out of Brooklyn's West Indian community, where he had struggled to find anything but menial labor, and into Harlem's cultural ferment. But in time the limitations of writing for the house organ of the Universal Negro Improvement Association became more than he could bear. Garveyism demanded that artists and writers subordinate their aesthetic concerns to the cause of advancing its "race first" ideology, and Walrond began to chafe under this restriction and to question Garvey's leadership. In 1922 he dispatched his wife and three young daughters to Jamaica and signed on as a cook's helper aboard the S.S. Turrialba, a ship bound for the West Indies under the auspices of the United Fruit Company. The voyage would, as he predicted in letters to Alain Locke, prove decisive in inspiring his writing; it propelled him to complete the stories that make up *Tropic Death*, the 1926 short story collection for which he is best known. Upon his return, he established contact with Edna Worthley Underwood, a white poet and translator who agreed to represent him to the publishers she knew. As Walrond's agent, Underwood gave him renewed confidence in his writing ability and helped him place work in such places as *Vanity Fair*, *Forbes Magazine*, *The New Republic*, and *The Smart Set*. In early 1923, he published an article highly critical of Garvey in *Current History* and shortly thereafter resigned from *Negro World*. One of its chief competitors, *Opportunity* magazine, began to publish Walrond's work regularly that summer, and its editor, Charles S. Johnson of the National Urban League, soon brought him on board as the magazine's business manager.

These were heady days for Walrond and for Black writers in New York generally. While writing and working for *Opportunity*, Walrond grew close to a number of talented, enterprising young writers and artists based in Harlem. They included Langston Hughes and Countee Cullen, poised to become two of the most decorated African American poets, as well as Regina Anderson, Gwendolyn Bennett, and Harold Jackman. It was their collective effort, along with the support of Charles S. Johnson and Alain Locke, that brought about the momentous Civic Club dinner of March 1924,[1] the result of which was the publication of a special Harlem issue of *Survey* magazine and the *New Negro* anthology in 1925. Walrond's star was rising. He was extremely well regarded uptown, he served as a chaperone for white downtowners seeking to know Harlem, and he published widely.[2] A prolific book reviewer, he wrote about black writers for black publications (e.g., Rene Maran's *Batouala* for *Negro World*), about black writers for white publications (e.g., Walter White's *Fire in the Flint* and Countee Cullen's *Color* for *The New Republic*), and perhaps most interesting of all given the racial divisions of the time, about white writers for white publications (Carl Van Vechten and Haldane MacFall for the *Saturday Review of Literature*).

It is difficult to imagine the enthusiasm with which *Tropic Death* was received given the obscurity into which it has since fallen. Writing in the Jamaican journal *Savacou* in 1970, critic Kenneth Ramchand noted that while Claude McKay's *Home to Harlem* "is for many good reasons the novel with which discussion of the Harlem Renaissance begins ... the two stylists of the movement were Jean Toomer, strange author of the single work, a neglected master-piece, *Cane*, and Eric Walrond" (68). How striking, then, that so much ink has been devoted to reviving interest in *Cane* and Jean Toomer (among others) and so little to Walrond and *Tropic Death*, which has long been out of print. The 10 stories that make up

---

[1]   Johnson wrote to Locke in March, 1924, "I may have spoken to you about a little group which meets here, with some degree of regularity, to talk informally about 'books and things.' Most of the persons interested you know: Walrond, Cullen, Langston Hughes, Gwendolyn Bennett, Jessie Fauset, Eloise Bibb Thompson, Regina Anderson, Harold Jackman, and myself. There have been some very interesting sessions and at the last one it was proposed that something be done to mark the growing self-consciousness of this newer school of writers and as a desirable time the date of the appearance of Jessie Fauset's book was selected, that is, around the twentieth of March. The idea has grown somewhat and it is the present purpose to include as many of the newer school of writers as possible,—Walter White (who in a sense is connected with this group), Jean Toomer, and yourself." Alain Locke Papers, Box 164-40, folder 25, Moorland-Springarn Research Center, Howard University.

[2]   David Levering Lewis writes of the apartment at 580 St. Nicholas Avenue shared by Ethel Ray Nance, Regina Anderson, and Louella Tucker: "It served as a sort of [Harlem] Renaissance USO, offering a couch, a meal, sympathy, and proper introduction to wicked Harlem for newcomers on the Urban League approved list ... For Toomer and Hughes, it was an evening furlough from the literary battlefront. For Eric Walrond, making his rounds with fascinated whites, it was a genteel waystop, a relaxed forum for contact between Uptown and Downtown New York" (127–8).

Tropic Death, set in locations throughout the Caribbean, dramatize the struggles of ordinary people inhabiting and traversing the islands—struggles against social injustice in some cases, but more often struggles with difficult economic conditions and, as the title suggests, with the elements. They employ an impressionistic style and prominently feature local dialects and indigenous folk practices, reflecting Walrond's effort to forge a kind of Anglophone Caribbean modernism.[3]

What most impressed contemporary readers, however, was his refusal to idealize the peasants about whom he wrote or to allow his fiction to devolve into sentimentality or propaganda. "There is nothing soft about this book," wrote Langston Hughes, reviewing *Tropic Death* for the *New York Herald Tribune*. "I wish some of the stories were longer," he continued in a characteristically unadorned idiom, "What else happens to these people I never met before? The throbbing life and sun-bright hardness of these pages fascinate me." Robert Herrick also reviewed it favorably in *The New Republic*. Some found *Tropic Death* flawed but of great interest nonetheless, such as J.A. Rogers, whose review in the *Pittsburgh Courier* was the most critical, and Waldo Frank, who in *Opportunity* praised Walrond's "swift, angular approach to his subject" and the way in which "the reader finds himself seeing (and being moved by) Mr. Walrond's words" even as the language sometimes interfered with "the pictures and the dramas they are supposed to flesh" (352). Even W.E.B. Du Bois and Benjamin Brawley, two of the era's most genteel critics, were impressed by Walrond's book despite its many disreputable black characters and irredeemably fatalistic tone. Du Bois called *Tropic Death* "a distinct contribution to Negro American literature" and "a human document of deep significance and great promise" (152).

Not only was Walrond "considered by everyone to be a top-notch writer," in the words of Ethel Ray Nance, he was also by many accounts the straw that stirred the drink uptown: charismatic, gregarious, and above all a hustler. "He was certainly a person that held our little group together," Nance continued. "He had the faculty of bringing in interesting people and meeting interesting people. If Eric walked down the street, someone interesting was bound to show up" (13, 15). Walrond was so connected that Countee Cullen once kidded his white friend Van Vechten, "[W]ith your excellent entrée to all social functions of color, [you] must know more Lenox and Seventh Avenue gossip than even Eric Walrond."[4]

Despite it all, he was vulnerable to severe bouts of self-doubt and self-reproach. From the same pen that authored strident essays in *Negro World* and cosmopolitan sketches in *Vanity Fair* issued forth a series of self-deprecations in letters to

---

[3]   The scholar Carl A. Wade writes, "*Tropic Death* still delights, seventy years later, with its verbal artistry, shrewd subversion of colonial hegemony, uncompromising social realism, and its compassionate and universal vision. Literary merit apart, Walrond's text is perhaps the most comprehensive social document of West Indian life—especially migrant life—in the early years of the twentieth century" (70).

[4]   Carl Van Vechten papers, correspondence, June 29, 1925. James Weldon Johnson Collection, Beinecke Rare Books and Manuscripts Library, Yale University.

Underwood, Van Vechten, and Locke, for example, all of whom Walrond saw as having gone out on a professional limb for him. He worried to Locke about his contribution to the special Harlem issue of *Survey*, "I'm afraid I haven't been able to execute the assignment to the satisfaction of either you or Mr. Kellogg." Indeed, Walrond tells Locke elsewhere that his inadequacy as a writer has induced "a state of anxiety, melancholy, and depression." "All the winter I have spent in a rather profitless manner," he confesses, and "all I have to show for it is a loosely constructed, badly unadorned novel." It would be unfair, he goes on, to come visit Locke in Washington "in this high-strung, unnatural, morbid, discontented state of mind."[5] In addition to this tendency toward self-reproach, Walrond was deeply sensitive to perceived social insults and racial slights. Countee Cullen dedicated "Incident," one of his most famous poems on this theme, "for E.W." In short, the fragility of Walrond's ego is as evident as his prodigious talent.

In recognition of his fiction, Walrond received within a few short years a prize in the *Opportunity* short story contest, a book contract for *Tropic Death* with the highly regarded Boni & Liveright publishers, a spot in the inaugural volume of American Caravan, and three prestigious fellowships: a Harmon Foundation award (1927), a Zona Gale scholarship to study creative writing at the University of Wisconsin (1927), and in support of his proposed research on the history of the Panama Canal, a Guggenheim Fellowship (1928).[6] "Overnight he became famous," wrote Underwood, his former agent, "Praise and social honours were his, together with a secure and considerable income which he could count on for some time in the future" (36). For a writer as self-effacing and self-critical as Walrond, this rapid turn of events must have been at least as disorienting as it was satisfying.

This is what I see, anyway, when I look into Eric Walrond's eyes in a photograph (Fig. 4.1) from February 1928.[7] Granted, I am looking with an awareness of subsequent events, events that had not yet befallen the man in the photograph. But what I see is anxiety, wariness. He is not at ease. Perhaps his discomfort was merely a consequence of the stresses of travel. Having arrived in Madison but a few days

---

[5]   Correspondence with Edna Worthley Underwood, Leonard H. Axe Library, Pittsburg State (Kansas) University; with Alain Locke, Moorland-Springarn Research Center, Howard University; and with Carl Van Vechten, Beinecke Rare Book and Manuscript Library, Yale University.

[6]   The William E. Harmon Foundation gave awards "for distinguished achievement among Negroes" in various fields in the arts and industry from 1926 to 1930. Although the Guggenheim Foundation does not keep records of the races of its Fellows, I believe that Walrond was only the third African American recipient. Of the first 150 Fellowship recipients, the only other African Americans were Walter White (1927) and Countee Cullen (1928).

[7]   Walrond is at the far right. The other Harmon Award recipients in the photo are Anthony Overton (far left) and William Edouard Scott (next to Walrond), honored for achievement in the fields of Business and Fine Arts, respectively. Second from left is Shailer Matthews, Dean at the University of Chicago, who presented the awards. *Chicago Defender* (National Edition), 18 Feb. 1928: A12.

Fig. 4.1   Eric Walrond, far right, receives the Harmon Award. *Chicago Defender* (1928). Photograph: K.D. Ganaway.

earlier, Walrond traveled to Chicago on a hasty trip to collect his award. "I went up on a six thirty train, took my award at eight, and flew back to Madison on the two o'clock sleeper," he wrote to the Harmon Foundation director. Still, I have to think that the enormity and rapidity of his recent changes in stature were also weighing on his mind. The Harmon Foundation had given him very little money ($100) but a great deal of prestige, an imprimatur.[8] Over 2,000 people attended the Chicago award ceremony at which the photo was taken.[9] The Zona Gale Foundation had freed him from the daily pressures of work, giving him time and space in which to practice his craft, luxuries he had never enjoyed while taking courses at City

---

[8]   Over the course of its five years in existence, the other winners of the Harmon Award for distinguished achievement in literature were Countee Cullen, Nella Larsen, James Weldon Johnson, Claude McKay, Walter White, and Langston Hughes—distinguished company. The year that Walrond received the award, he was second to James Weldon Johnson while such notable writers as Georgia Douglass Johnson, Alain Locke, Benjamin Brawley, and Arthur Huff Fauset each received honorable mention.

[9]   This is the figure given in a letter from George Arthur, Executive Secretary of the Chicago YMCA to George Haynes, Executive Secretary of the Harmon Foundation, February 14, 1928. William E. Harmon Foundation, Inc., papers, Box 51, Manuscripts Division, Library of Congress.

College and Columbia University. And the Guggenheim Foundation had given him money, lots of it, more in all likelihood than he had seen before.[10]

For that matter, Boni and Liveright had advanced him $1,000 on a book about Panama, and they had begun advertising it. Their fall 1928 catalog included the following promotional copy for *The Big Ditch*:

> The building of the Panama Canal, that gigantic triumph of engineering over the most stupendous physical difficulties, lends itself to vivid telling as a human interest story. Strangely enough, though other accounts of the feat have been written, Mr. Walrond is the first author to bring out the drama of this as yet unsung epic of human heroism. He tells of revolutionaries, riots and the stirrings of racial consciousness among the varied nationalities engaged in the work. He tells of the titanic achievements of science, of human labor, of engineering. He describes the life and death battle against disease and insect pests which in that tropical climate present a more formidable front than armies of mere men. In this book, as in *Tropic Death*, the atmospheric quality is enriched by the author's memories of his impressionable boyhood years spent on the Isthmus. *The Big Ditch* is a colorful and dramatic, yet careful and authentic work. Mr. Walrond's high ability has been recognized not only by critics and the public, but also by the Trustees of the Guggenheim Fund, who have just granted him one of their fellowships for further research and writing in the West Indies and the countries bordering on the Caribbean.[11]

What is interesting about this blurb is that the book was nowhere near publication in the fall of 1928. In fact, it never was published at all. It's likely that the publisher, Horace Liveright, was in large part taking it on faith that this manuscript was in an advanced stage. That this was not the case only became apparent to Liveright, it seems, in the summer of 1928. He received a memo from Julian Messner, his chief financial officer, who alerted him that Donald Friede, formerly an editor at Boni & Liveright who had established a new firm, Covici & Friede, was interested in buying the rights to *The Big Ditch*. "I rather think you will be for this," Messner surmised, "even though we have not yet seen the manuscript nor been able to judge its value." Then he reminded Liveright, "We gave Walrond an advance of $1000." Liveright agreed immediately to the sale.[12]

Messner and Liveright must have known something was up. Perhaps Walrond had Friede snowed, or perhaps Friede just believed in him more than his former colleagues did. Friede had long been one of Walrond's strongest champions. When

---

[10]   The Guggenheim award was $2,500 for the first year and was renewed for a six-month extension at $1,250.

[11]   *Fall Catalogue 1928*. Boni & Liveright Publishers. Van Pelt Library, Columbia University, Rare Books & Manuscripts Division, 22.

[12]   "Dear Julian," Liveright wrote, "Yes, I am highly in favor of letting Friede take over Walrond's book if he gives us cash down for what we have advanced, together with our expenses in cataloguing, announcing, etc." Boni & Liveright Correspondence, File 309, Annenberg Rare Book & Manuscript Library, University of Pennsylvania.

asked by the Harmon Foundation to provide his reason for supporting Walrond's application for an award, Friede's endorsement was direct and unqualified: "Because I believe him to be the outstanding negro prose writer of this country, and because I believe that his work will in time place him among the important writers in America—both Negro and white."[13] It's extraordinary that Liveright— a notorious gambler on the books he published—was so quick to unload an author with a proven record at his firm at Messner's urging. Whatever he knew he didn't let on; publicity for *The Big Ditch* continued apace. *The Nation*, for example, listed it among its "Notable Fall Books" in 1928, and then again six months later among its "Notable Spring Books" of 1929. Boni & Liveright was asking $3.50 a copy for a book that didn't exist.[14]

At least, it didn't exist in saleable form.[15] Its author left Madison after one semester and sailed for the Caribbean on his Guggenheim money. In September 1928, he arrived in Panama. From here he would go on to Haiti, the Dominican Republic, the British West Indies, and Martinique. He returned to New York just long enough to gather his things and then shipped off again, this time for France, where he would spend the next two years. He never moved back to the U.S. His only visit occurred in the fall of 1931, a brief trip about which little is known except that he stayed with his parents in Brooklyn. *The New York Amsterdam News* saw fit to carry an article about his visit that celebrated him as "the young story writer whose volume of sketches on Caribbean life, 'Tropic Death,' was hailed by many critics as the flower of the new literary movement when published a few years ago." But the article's title, "Eric Walrond, Back in City, Feels No Homecoming Thrill," speaks volumes. "Of course I'm glad to see old faces again and to have the opportunity to talk with friends," Walrond told the reporter "with a shrug of the shoulders." "But there's no particular thrill in being here again," he continued, "Somehow, I feel different. There has been an inward change. Only urgent business brought me back to this country."

In one sense, his abandonment of the U.S., his contacts, and the career he had established parallels the very failure he was researching. The French diplomat Ferdinand de Lesseps made his name with a tremendous feat of engineering known as the Suez Canal, but when the his government called him into Panama in the 1880s he was overmatched by the diseases that ravaged his labor force and the sheer topographic scale of the project. The retreat of the de Lesseps crew left in its wake

---

[13]   Letter dated August 31, 1927. Harmon Foundation, Inc., Records, Box 51, Library of Congress.

[14]   *The Nation* 125: 3249 (12 Oct. 1928): 374; *The Nation* 126: 3276 (18 Apr. 1929): 471.

[15]   Several references to the manuscript of *The Big Ditch* occur in the correspondence between Walrond and Guggenheim Foundation secretary Henry Allen Moe in the late 1920s and early 1930s. Walrond seems to have provided Moe with something resembling a completed draft, which Moe then shopped unsuccessfully to *The Century* magazine in the hopes of serialization. In a letter to Moe several years later, he apologized for having submitted it to him prematurely.

several hundred tons of rusting machinery, a shabby railway, and some scratches in the earth, the deepening of which would soon become the task of Teddy Roosevelt and the United States Canal Authority. Eric Walrond, fresh off the success of *Tropic Death* and flush with accolades and awards, undertook a literary Panama Canal project that seems to have overwhelmed him. Intellectually, he was as well prepared as any writer of his time to execute the study, but temperamentally he seems to have been unfit. Because of his training he knew what it meant to write history well, and characteristically he set the bar for himself quite high. In addition, he recognized, more clearly I'm sure than any of his contemporaries, the centrality of the Panama Canal to the intertwined stories of the Black diaspora and Western modernity—that often suppressed but vitally important history evoked in Paul Gilroy's notion of the Black Atlantic. Given this historical awareness, given these inherited standards of intellectual rigor and excellence, and given, moreover, a personal investment as keenly felt as Walrond's was for Panama, few writers could have remained undaunted. Transfixed by the minutiae of his subject matter, he struggled to see the forest for the trees, or at least to render the forest so others could see it.

The Big Ditch ultimately became a series of excruciatingly detailed notebook entries whose refusal to submit to synthesis at Walrond's hand was a lifelong source of shame. They were, in fact, published eventually but the venue in which they appeared indicates the extent of the psychological troubles this once decorated writer now faced. *The Roundway Review*, which ran serial installments of Walrond's Panama history project in 1955–56, was a journal published by the Roundway Psychiatric Hospital (formerly the Wilts County Asylum) in rural Wiltshire, near Bath. Having left London during World War II and moved to the village of Bradford-on-Avon, Walrond continued to write, but succumbed finally to the chronic depression that had pursued him at least since 1940, when he referred to himself in a letter to Guggenheim Foundation secretary Henry Allen Moe as a "depression casualty."[16] Walrond was admitted to Roundway as a voluntary patient in 1952 and—in a melancholy echo of the entrepreneurial spirit he had shown in Harlem—helped start *The Roundway Review*, in which he published regularly until his discharge in 1957.[17] As recently as 1960, Walrond could be heard wrestling on the page with the shame of having disappointed his sponsors. He found occasion to write that year to Moe about having met Richard Wright and W.E.B. Du Bois in London at the funeral of George Padmore, the Trinidadian expatriate organizer and intellectual:

> The solicitude of both Richard Wright and Dr. Du Bois appeared early, and they both wanted to know in particular what had happened to "The Big Ditch." This was a reference to a project I have been under a crushing moral obligation to carry through to success...I did not tell either Richard Wright or Dr. Du Bois

---

[16]   Letter to Moe, June 20, 1940. John Simon Guggenheim Memorial Foundation papers.

[17]   On *The Roundway Review* and Walrond's role as assistant editor, see Steele, *Down Pans Lane*, Chapter 16. Walrond's Panama history was serialized under the title "The Second Battle."

that the initial effort, which I once inflicted upon you and for which I hope you have forgiven me, was poorly conceived based upon inadequate research and hurriedly produced. I do not even know how good a story I told them, by way of mitigation. I do remember intimating, however, that I have only one thing to live for (there was a moment in Wiltshire when I must have forgotten this), and in spite of my age and years of silence I have not lost sight of my objectives, or the high aims with which I set out as a Guggenheim Fellow such a long time ago.[18]

However, in a very important sense Eric Walrond was not a failure at all. Consider the intervening years, the time he spent in France, London, and Bradford-on-Avon that are beyond the scope of this essay. While he was not as prolific then as in the 1920s, neither was he entirely dormant, as historians have suggested.[19] His essays about the Harlem movement from which he had taken his leave appeared in periodicals in Madrid, Paris, London, and Kingston. His time in London involved active engagement in an anti-colonial movement of unprecedented reach and force, a movement galvanized by the work of expatriate West Indians such as Harold Moody, a Jamaican physician who founded the League of Coloured Peoples, and his secretary and countrywoman Una Marson, as well as a more radical Pan-Africanist group that included C.L.R. James, Amy Ashwood Garvey, George Padmore, Paul Robeson, and Kwame Nkrumah. Among other achievements, their activity laid the groundwork for a generation of Black British writers whose work would flourish in the post-World War II era. By overlooking Walrond's involvement in this Black expatriate scene in London and the anti-colonial movement that it sustained, scholars have not only perpetuated the obscurity of this particular writer, we've also missed a real opportunity to better understand the cultural contours of the Caribbean diaspora.[20] To be sure, the tumultuous, peripatetic nature of Walrond's career poses a challenge to inquiry, but the stories onto which his life and his writing open—the British colonies and the Panama Canal Zone, the Harlem Renaissance, the challenge to Empire and the construction of a vibrant Black British community—these are major stories of our

---

[18] Letter to Moe, June 11, 1960. John Simon Guggenheim Memorial Foundation papers. The letter itself does not specify at whose funeral this conversation took place, but all circumstantial evidence points to Padmore, who died in September, 1959.

[19] In his magisterial study *When Harlem Was in Vogue*, David Levering Lewis credits Walrond for helping shepherd the New Negro movement into being and having written some of its most exceptional fiction, but when it comes to following up on Walrond's post-Harlem career is content to leave us with this cliffhanger: "On his way to a weekend in the country with E.M. Forster, Richard Bruce Nugent encountered Walrond in a London railway station in late 1929. That was about the last heard of him" (234). Similarly, *The Essential Black Literature Guide* follows its discussion of Walrond's Harlem Renaissance accomplishments by stating, ingenuously, that he "travelled in Europe until his death in 1966."

[20] For a full account of Walrond's career in its entirety, see Louis Parascandola's excellent biographical introduction and bibliographic appendix in *"Winds Can Wake Up the Dead."*

time and it is extraordinary to find them so vividly chronicled and connected in one writer's lifetime.

To return, then, to the moment in 1928 with which we began—to Wisconsin and the *Chicago Defender* photograph—the pressure must indeed have been enormous. Walrond had led people to expect great things from him, and now they expected great things. "Eric Walrond was tremendous," recalled the poet and critic Sterling Brown in 1974, "[H]is *Tropic Death* was really quite a book. *Tropic Death* and *Cane* were the brilliant high marks in fiction" (Rowell 811). When Walrond was making his crossover move into white publications, *Success* magazine introduced him glowingly: "*Success* takes pleasure in presenting this new, young master of vivid narrative, believing that in him eventually is the making of one of the greatest novelists and short story writers of our day" ("New Generation" 68). He never lived up to that lofty billing, as we have seen, and as a result his work has been met with resounding scholarly indifference. Leaving New York, the New Negro movement, his friends, family, and business connections behind, he effectively sabotaged his career at its apex. His departure left even his closest friends mystified. Ethel Ray Nance, who probably knew Walrond as well as anyone in Harlem, wondered years later what could have prevented him from rising to the occasion. "I can't imagine Eric ever falling down on an assignment," she said, "I would have to hear it from him as to just what happened" (15). We can only speculate, finally, about his reasons, about why he underwent so decisive an "inward change." But as I have suggested here, it seems likely that a key factor was the high level of expectation with which a rapid ascent had saddled this enormously talented but highly temperamental writer—a West Indian émigré, arriving mid-winter in Wisconsin, alone, by way of Panama and New York.

Chapter 5
Erskine Caldwell:
Modernist Manqué

Loren Glass

The scholarly work on Erskine Caldwell is surprisingly scattershot. Author of *God's Little Acre*, one of the best-selling novels of all time, husband of and collaborator with photographer Margaret Bourke-White, Caldwell was an immensely popular author of the thirties and forties. When he published his first book of short stories with Scribners, he looked likely to become a canonical modernist on a par with William Faulkner or Ernest Hemingway, in whose company he was frequently mentioned at the outset of his career. Instead, Caldwell chose to focus on the mass market, teaming up with New American Library to become one of the most successful authors of the paperback revolution. His academic neglect is at least partly a product of this peculiar publishing trajectory. My intention in this piece is not so much to "correct" this neglect as to understand it, particularly in relation to Caldwell's earlier promise and popularity. I see Caldwell's career as a symptomatic case study in the politics and practices of literary reputation and authorial celebrity during the modernist era in the United States. In *Authors Inc.* I analyze these politics and practices as emerging from the tension between what Pierre Bourdieu calls the fields of restricted and large-scale cultural production. The former represents the relatively autonomous world of artists and writers who produce for an audience of each other; the latter represents the heterogeneous general public in which culture is circulated for profit. Using these broad designations as a methodological rubric, I formulate that

> the volatile passage from the restricted elite audience of urban bohemia and "little magazines" to the mass audience of the U.S. middlebrow became a signature career arc for American modernist writers. Along this arc, the model of the author as a solitary creative genius whose work goes unrecognized by the mainstream collides with the model of the author as part of a corporate publisher's marketing strategy. (Glass 6)

In essence, Caldwell traveled too far along this arc, moving beyond the middlebrow to the resolutely pulp, abandoning in the process any critical caché that might have allowed him to straddle fields, as Hemingway so effectively did. But, as I hope to show, Caldwell's very failure to maintain the tension that would keep other modernists safely consecrated even as their books also appeared in mass market form reveals the class politics that subtended the divisions of the cultural field in the modern United States.

One mode of maintaining this tension, as I argue further, is a masculine pose that allowed such authors as Hemingway and Faulkner to enter the literary marketplace while simultaneously disdaining it. Here, I rely on Andreas Huyssen's highly influential argument that many male modernists associated mass culture with femininity. Proceeding psychoanalytically, Huyssen then argues that fear of mass culture becomes a "fear of woman, a fear of nature out of control, a fear of the unconscious, of sexuality, of the loss of identity and stable ego boundaries in the mass" (52). I use Huyssen's useful theorization to argue

> that celebrity itself, in threatening the "stable ego boundaries" of the male author, figures as a psychosexual trauma in many careers of the modern era, and that the hypermasculine public posturing of authors such as London, Hemingway, and Norman Mailer can be understood as a symptomatic response to the feminized, and feminizing, literary marketplace. (18)

Caldwell's fiction is replete with paroxysms of misogyny and crises of masculinity, his early prose style is terse and seemingly without sentiment, and he publicly maintained a posture of resolute professionalism. However, he failed to synthesize these qualities into the kind of patriarchal authority that ballasted the canonization of his peers.

Indeed, it is the absence of crucial factors, both in Caldwell's writing and in his self-fashioning that illuminates the significance of those very factors in the more successful careers of his now canonized contemporaries. In the discussion following, I hope to demonstrate that Caldwell's failure to achieve lasting renown resulted not only from his unabashed embrace of the paperback revolution, which indelibly associated him with the mass market against which modernist authors— even those eventually published in paperback—worked to distinguish themselves, but also from an absence, in his writing, of the sort of stylistic mastery off of which could be read a magisterial author along the lines of Joyce or Faulkner. Finally, these failures of cultural distinction made it virtually impossible for critics to read Caldwell's relation to his principal subject matter—poor Southern Whites—in a way that could sustain their own class identity. Caldwell's failure to be canonized as a modernist, then, reveals more starkly the socioeconomic fissures that tend to be obscured by the consecration of his contemporaries. I will begin by reviewing Caldwell's biography, emphasizing its early parallels with and eventual divergence from the lives and careers of his contemporaries, and then I will conclude with an analysis of his two most well known texts—*Tobacco Road* and *God's Little Acre*— in order to show how their failure to sustain an indexical relation to an authorial consciousness enabled their shift from critical celebration to mass popularity to contemporary obscurity.

Caldwell's early biography traces an arc not unlike many members of his literary cohort. He grew up in genteel poverty in the rural south, the only child of a progressive Presbyterian preacher and a tenth-generation Virginia belle. Caldwell's father, Ira, was a tireless worker for the rights of the poor and a courageous advocate for racial equality in the Jim Crow South. Caldwell frequently accompanied him on his many professional travels, and the suffering and poverty he witnessed would later form the subject of much of his writing. The family moved frequently, so Caldwell was home-schooled by his mother, Carrie, against whose strictures he frequently chafed. Thus Caldwell grew up an only child, idealizing his father who would be the source of his political sympathies while struggling against his mother who would be the source of his literary proclivities. According to one biography, Caldwell "grew up largely in the company of women" and would become "a man almost consumed by efforts to prove his virility" (Miller 17). The similarities to Hemingway are unmistakable.

Although he did attend college, he was an extremely poor student, preferring to hang out in pool halls and hop freight trains. It would be in an obscure corner of the University of Virginia (UVA) library that Caldwell would discover a collection of modernist little magazines that would in turn launch his literary career. It was also at UVA that Caldwell met his first wife, Helen Lannigan, a first-year graduate student in French and daughter of the school's popular track coach, with whom he would have two children. Initially, he attempted to support his family as a cub reporter for the *Atlanta Journal*, an experience which he would later extol, again like Hemingway, as an ideal literary apprenticeship. One year later, the family moved to Maine and opened a small bookstore that became a gathering place for Portland's fledgling bohemian community. But Caldwell was doggedly determined to succeed in writing, abandoning his family frequently for weeks at a time to rent single rooms in which he could write without interruption. His first published story appeared in *transition*. Other early work would be published in *New American Caravan*, *Hound and Horn*, *This Quarter*, and *Pagany*. Thus, like Hemingway, Faulkner, and many others, Caldwell got his start in the little magazines.

These early stories brought Caldwell to the attention of Hemingway's editor Maxwell Perkins, and Scribners issued Caldwell's first anthology of short stories, *American Earth*, in 1931. *The New Republic* promptly published "two judgments" of the collection which conveniently adumbrate the contradictions that would determine, and eventually undermine, Caldwell's reputation. T.K. Whipple celebrates Caldwell's storytelling as "the true popular or vulgar oral literature of America, the germ, the unformed beginning of narrative" (3). And he warns that "these occult magazines ... are insidious poison for Mr. Caldwell," concluding "let us pray ... that he may be delivered from the highbrows" (4). Malcolm Cowley shares Whipple's populist appraisal of Caldwell's talent, but demurs about his publication venues, proclaiming that "the primary function of the little magazines is discovering talent," while their "secondary function" is "encouraging experimental writing" (5). Cowley concludes "Mr. Caldwell is a literary child of the 'occult' magazines" (5). Thus we can see that, before Caldwell even became well known, the arbiters of literary taste were debating the significance of his populist image and style. He not only wrote about the impoverished and uneducated, he seemed to write in a language derived from their own storytelling idiom. Whether this idiom in turn constituted "vulgar oral literature" or "experimental writing" would become one of the central indeterminacies of Caldwell's career.

This problem would become even more acute and complicated with the publication, in rapid succession, of Caldwell's first two novels, *Tobacco Road* (Scribners, 1932) and *God's Little Acre* (Viking, 1933), which remain his best known works. Both novels document the experiences of poor whites in the depression-era South in a tone precariously balanced between sociological description and grotesque satire; both generated highly publicized censorship battles. *Tobacco Road*, the story of Jeeter Lester, the befuddled patriarch of a family so degraded they don't even notice when they accidentally run over and kill their grandmother, was dramatized and became the longest-running play on Broadway up to that time; it was banned in multiple cities across America. *God's Little Acre*, the story of another addled patriarch, Ty Ty Lester, who obsessively digs for gold on his property as his family disintegrates into fratricidal violence, was also the subject of numerous obscenity charges.

The trial of *God's Little Acre* bolstered Caldwell's highbrow caché. His agent, Maxim Lieber, formed a "God's Little Acre Protest Committee" which included Malcolm Cowley, Lewis Mumford, Sherwood Anderson, H.L. Mencken and many other prominent writers, artists and journalists. If such endorsement affirmed Caldwell's literary credentials, New York City magistrate Benjamin Greenspan confirmed his sociological integrity, concluding that the book "contains internal evidence that it was written with a sincere attempt to present with truth and honesty a segment of life in the Southern United States" (People v. Viking Press 30). Thus these many censorship battles, occurring in the same decade as the landmark case of The U.S. vs One Book Called "Ulysses," enabled Caldwell to fashion himself as a highbrow champion of literary freedom, while also bringing extensive publicity not only to him, but to the plight of the Southern poor whose standard he seemed to bear.

Caldwell was now famous. In the North, literary critics and the general public embraced him, while in his native South he was frequently the object of vehement protest by politicians and journalists who denied the authenticity of his depictions. Indeed, it was difficult for supporters and detractors alike to parse the credibility of his main characters as well as his implied attitude toward them. Bennett Cerf wrote "I do not doubt for an instant that there actually exist people like the characters in Erskine Caldwell's *Tobacco Road* and *God's Little Acre*" (1). Kenneth Burke disagreed, calling Caldwell a "Maker of Grotesques" and claiming "what the decerebrated frog is to the whole frog, Caldwell's characters are to real people" (169). Malcolm Cowley would eventually conclude that there were "Two Erskine Caldwells," the "sociologist" who writes seriously about the plight of the poor, and the "imaginative" writer, who produces "impossible fancies and wild humor" (198). In his introduction to *The Pocket Book of Erskine Caldwell Stories* (1947), Henry Seidel Canby accurately predicted: "He is not a naturalist ... he is not a realist ... he is certainly not a romanticist ... . He will not be pigeon-holed easily by literary historians" (219).

In the wider public sphere there was a similar split. On the one hand, the dramatization of *Tobacco Road* was widely received as broad comedy, and the play's many critics insisted that, far from bringing attention to the sufferings of the poor, it simply allowed audiences to feel superior to them. On the other hand, Caldwell's obvious commitment to social justice, extensively and repeatedly proven by his unrelenting determination to challenge his critics and further illustrated by his move to social documentary in the later thirties, seemed ample evidence that he was motivated not by condescending pity but by righteous outrage, and that he intended his characters to be received as realistic portrayals, not comic grotesques. Indeed, it is difficult to improve on John T. Matthews' recent summation: "where the subject of poverty turned much other fiction about the South fervently political, Caldwell startled readers with grotesque comedy; while others grew sentimental, Caldwell preferred the salacious; when others committed to the social realism of reportage, Caldwell fashioned an indigenous magical realism" (206).

Nevertheless, Caldwell consistently denied that his depictions were intended to be humorous or exaggerated in any way. He insisted in the introduction to the Duell, Sloan and Pearce reprint of *Tobacco Road* that his book was about how "the everyday lives of people I knew were falsified and perverted by novelists who arbitrarily force human beings to conform, and perform, to artificial plot and contrived circumstances" (223); in the introduction to their reprint of *God's Little Acre* he confirmed that he was giving these people "the opportunity to tell the story of their lives in their own way" (225). And he embraced the popular front aspect of his image, as he spent the second half of the thirties engaged in sociological projects in collaboration with the photographer Margaret Bourke-White, who would become his second wife. The most well known of these—*You Have Seen Their Faces*—remains a landmark of the thirties documentary aesthetic, and was widely praised at the time as a unique innovation in form. His marriage to Bourke-White also catapulted him into the celebrity stratosphere, as he was now a rich man with powerful connections in both the culture industry and the political sphere. Caldwell was at the top of his game, having achieved the delicate balancing act of receiving both popular and critical acclaim.

But Caldwell's next novels, *Journeyman, Trouble in July*, and *Tragic Ground* (the first published by Viking; the second two by Duell, Sloan and Pierce), though they sold well and dealt with the timely topics of religious charlatanry, lynching and urban poverty, did not seem to realize his early promise, and were unanimously panned by the critics as lazy hackwork. Furthermore, in the forties Caldwell's novels began appearing in mass-market paperback form through New American Library on drugstore racks across the country. By the fifties, he was being widely celebrated as the world's bestselling author, with *God's Little Acre* the world's best-selling book; the critics abandoned him in disgust. Edward Wagenknecht, in *Cavalcade of the American Novel* (1952), dispenses with Caldwell in a handful of pages, affirming that he "seems destined for survival only in the mansions of subliterature.

His sales continue enormous—largely in twenty-five-cent, paper-covered editions, decorated with crude pictures of half-naked women—but his critical stock is so low that it is difficult to believe he ever enjoyed the acclaim which was given to him only a few years ago" (415). Thus while Hemingway and Faulkner were winning Nobel Prizes and becoming academic industries, Caldwell was becoming a legend in the publishing world as a purveyor of hillbilly porn for the paperback revolution.

Caldwell responded to his critical neglect with a series of autobiographical reflections expressing disdain for the "highbrow" critics and all they represented to him. Caldwell's first autobiography, *Call It Experience: The Years of Learning How To Write* (1951) is, by its own admission "less a personal history than it is an informal recollection of authorship" (v). The version of authorship Caldwell elaborates in this text combines an investment in the autonomy of the artist with a resolute dismissal of any form of literary distinction. Thus he claims, on the one hand, "I tried to write with only myself in mind as the reader, just as if no one else would ever read it" (45), while also affirming, "I wanted to succeed in my field, and to earn my living, just as if it had been any other profession or trade that men live by" (104). Furthermore, Caldwell chooses to eschew the political significance of his work, affirming that he "had no philosophical truths to dispense, no evangelistic urge to change the course of human destiny" (104).

Significantly, Caldwell's last chapter chronicles his encounter with Kurt Enoch and Victor Weybright of the American wing of Penguin books, "a brash newcomer in the publishing field" (176); Enoch and Weybright would soon break away from Penguin and form New American Library with Caldwell as their cash cow. He concludes this chapter with an anecdote recounting a visit to a writers' conference at the University of Kansas, which he attends after signing paperbacks at a drugstore in Kansas City. He is apparently snubbed by many authors at the conference: "because they felt that I had brought disrepute to the profession of authorship—and to the cause of higher education as well—by participating in such an undignified publicity scheme in Kansas City, and by autographing twenty-five cent books in a drugstore" (179). The locations are, of course, significant. He is snubbing the university—the institutions responsible for nurturing lasting literary reputations—for the drugstore—an institution which, until the advent of the paperback revolution, didn't even sell books.

Sylvia Jenkins Cook has affirmed that "Caldwell was consistent and masterful in selecting, omitting, emphasizing, and indeed inventing the elements of his own literary image," and it is worth affirming that Caldwell's careful selection of events in his professional life in this autobiography is matched by an almost complete omission of any events or people in his private life (255). His first wife, who proofread and edited all his early work and on whom he cheated openly, receives no mention; nor do his children, whom he used to beat ruthlessly. Bourke-White receives only passing mention, entirely in the context of their professional collaborations.

He has little trouble, on the other hand, representing his professional struggles in notably psychosexual terms. Thus in his next autobiography, really a collection of essays, *Writing in America* (1967), he affirms that he has "knowingly and purposefully ignored the existence of the critic, or, as he is sometimes called, the literary eunuch or procurer of the business" (11). Extending the metaphor, he calls the critic "the person who kicks the author's shins and flails the reader's spirits whenever consummation between them takes place without his active procurement" (11). By the time these essays were written, Caldwell had essentially been abandoned by the arbiters of cultural value in the United States, and he spent most of the sixties traveling the world keeping track of his lucrative international sales, sometimes under the auspices of the United States Information Agency, which hoped to capitalize on his worldwide popularity to enhance the image of the U.S. abroad during the Cold War.

Indeed, Caldwell became a shrewd businessman in his years of critical obscurity, scouring the planet for piracy and networking with agents everywhere from Poland to Japan. As he affirms in his final autobiography, *With All My Might* (1987), written shortly before his death, "I was never indifferent to any situation having to do with the publication of one of my books anywhere on earth" (325). *With All My Might* reveals even more emphatically his disregard for the operations of the restricted field of cultural production. As he elaborates early on,

> having previously concluded that the world should be divided with writers on the one hand and readers on the other.... I came to realize that a compromise would have to be made to accommodate a limited amount of reading... I decided to select one book by a contemporary author as being representative of his work...[T]he time would come when I would have to admit I had never read a page of such writers of the past as Nathaniel Hawthorne, Jack London, or Mark Twain. (61)

This is clearly unforgivable sacrilege for any author who aspires to be included in the canon of American literature. It is not surprising that Caldwell rarely appears on college syllabi.

Unlike *Call it Experience* or *Writing in America*, *With All My Might* touches on Caldwell's private life, opening with the cryptic, pseudo-psychoanalytic claim that "during most of my adult life I have often sought signs and manifestations from the past that might enable me to make wise decisions.... This has brought me to wonder if our entire life is spent in a subconscious search for that mysterious lost phase of existence" (1). He goes on to complain that his mother (like Hemingway's) dressed him in "unmanly clothing" (13), comments extensively on a photo he saw as a child of a teenage "masturbation club" (16), and provides considerably sanitized, though sexually frank, versions of his four marriages. He concludes with a notably defensive reflection on his career, again couched in clumsily erotic imagery:

> What I have resisted doing as a writer was glorifying the sensational and knowingly falsifying the anguish or the jubilation of men and women who have been brought to life and were captives of a story of mine. Like the physical body of a person real or imaginary, the human spirit should not be ravished and outraged in print by ghouls at large. (330)

Thus *With All My Might* attempts to portray a "true" version of the author in a bid for critical reconsideration. But, unlike the revelations of Kenneth Lynn's bestselling biography of Hemingway, which came out in the same year, *With All My Might* failed to generate any significant reappraisal of Caldwell's long-forgotten career.

Caldwell's concluding lines indicate the degree to which he still felt haunted by accusations of obscenity and sensationalism, while his opening lines indicate at least a suspicion that his work is psychoanalytically intelligible. I would now like to develop explicitly what is only implied in the relationship between these claims. At the peak of his popularity in the thirties, Caldwell's work had generated some psychoanalytic scrutiny, most of which can be traced to Lawrence S. Kubie's "God's Little Acre: an Analysis," which is partly a defense of Caldwell, and modernist literature generally, against the censors. Kubie sees Caldwell's text as an example of "morbid modern literature, a literature which attempts not merely a safe and literary escapade in sex, but rather a mirror of the moving realities of sexual problems in all their intricacy" (160). He focuses on the fact that there is "no living mother in the book" (162), and therefore he sees it as a regressive fantasy, "a story in symbolic language of the struggle of men to win some fantastic kind of sustenance out of the body of the earth" (163).

I am less interested in the accuracy of Kubie's analysis than in how he chooses to frame it. First, he insists that "it is necessary to stress the elimination of the author from our study" (165). In other words, the "sexual problems" depicted in the narrative are not Caldwell's. This bracketing of the author then leads Kubie to posit a correlative category of "healthy" readers, to whom such a book must be addressed:

> As long as there is a group of people who cannot be fooled or consoled by romance, whether it be cheap and tawdry or delicate and sophisticated…there will be a literature which seeks to write its way out of confusion and restraint into some pathway of passionate relief and happiness. (166)

In essence, Kubie strives to stabilize Caldwell's presumed authorial control by arrogating it to himself as a "healthy" reader. In order to do this, he must also categorize the text as "modern." Bracketing the author's biography and designating the text as modernist, then, are coordinated maneuvers.

As Aaron Jaffe confirms in a related context, "modernist texts repeatedly index literary work to authorial consciousness," a process whereby the "modernist work offers itself as a functional replacement for the biographical self" (30–31). Jonathan Goldman has similarly argued that modernist style "constitutes a new kind of author—as not only the art object par excellence but also the master choreographer of the culture that creates him" (86). I would now like to illustrate how Caldwell's most significant texts fail to achieve this indexicality.

I will start against the grain, by revealing the degree to which *God's Little Acre* is susceptible to biographical interpretation. According to one biographer, "Ira emerged in Erskine's mind an unblemished hero, while Carrie was held rigorously accountable for the strictures she placed on his behavior. Caldwell's resentment of his mother colored his entire life" (Miller 17). It wouldn't be difficult to crudely correlate Caldwell's misogyny in this text with his lifelong anger toward his mother, but I am more interested in the degree to which there is no figure to correlate with the father whom he idealized and therefore no position of paternal authority that can be imputed to the writer. Ty Ty Walden, like so many of Caldwell's characters, is an example of the type of figure with whom his own father had to struggle all his life. He owns land, but instead of cultivating it he obsessively digs for gold, saving one section, which he constantly shifts about in his mind, as the "God's little acre" of the title. As this title further indicates, Ty Ty is a religious man, and his peculiar wisdom dominates the dialogue of *God's Little Acre*. Much of this wisdom is coupled with the erotic imagery and innuendo for which the book became notorious. Thus one of the few things Ty Ty is thankful for is his daughter-in-law, Griselda, who "has the finest pair of rising beauties a man can ever hope to see. It's a wonder that God ever put such prettiness in the house" (30). He continues with what would become one of the more memorable lines from the text: "The first time I saw you…I felt like getting right down there and then and licking something" (30).

Lines such as these would eventually come to exemplify the genre of paperback pulp that *God's Little Acre* would help inaugurate, but it is important to affirm that they also form something like the religious substrate of the narrative. Later on Ty Ty's son-in-law, Will, who is killed attempting to turn the power on at the local cotton mill which has been shut down by a strike, and who is often considered the Christ figure in the text, will quote them during a truly bizarre scene when he strips Griselda naked in front of his wife and sister-in-law (Ty Ty's daughters). Combining piety and blasphemy, Will shouts: "He said you were the most beautiful woman God ever made, didn't he? And he said you were so God damn pretty, a man would have to get down on his hands and knees and lick something when he saw you like you are now" (157). After this astonishing scene and the off-stage (ostensibly oral) sex that follows, Griselda makes Will coffee:

> She put two spoonfuls into the coffee cup. She knew. It wasn't every woman who would know how much sugar to put in his cup. She's got the finest pair of rising beauties a man ever laid his eyes on, and when you once see them, you're going to get right down on your hands and knees and lick something. Ty Ty has got more sense than all of us put together, even if he does stay out there among those God damn pot holes digging for what he'll never find. (163)

I cite this paragraph in full because it effectively illustrates the aggravating indeterminacy of Caldwell's prose. He represents Will's thoughts through free indirect style, which would seem to provide the reader with some ironic distance from them, in turn indicating a stable authorial position apart from the antics of the characters. But Caldwell wants to anchor the wisdom of Will's thoughts in reference to Ty Ty, whom he refuses to ironize or mock throughout the text, despite the fundamental irrationality of his behavior. Here are Ty Ty's concluding thoughts:

> There was a mean trick played on us somewhere. God put us in the bodies of
> animals and tried to make us act like people. That was the beginning of trouble.
> If He had made us like we are, and not called us people, the last one of us
> would know how to live. A man can't live, feeling himself from the inside, and
> listening to what the preachers say." (208)

It is impossible to know how seriously to take these lines, since the text in which
they appear provides no stable perspective by which they might be evaluated.
Indeed, it is arguably the very absence of this perspective that enabled *God's Little
Acre* to slide from the literary to the pornographic to the forgotten.

Tobacco Road presents similar problems. Jeeter Lester, like Ty Ty Walden,
perpetually proclaims his religiosity, and likewise forms the flimsy moral center
of the book. He is particularly pleased when Sister Bessie, a "woman preacher,"
arrives at his house. Here is Caldwell's description of Bessie:

> There was no church building to house Bessie's congregation, nor was there an
> organized band of communicants to support her. She went from house to house
> in the sand hills, mostly along the crest of the ridge where the old tobacco road
> was, and prayed for people who need prayer and wanted it. She was past thirty-
> five, almost forty, and she was much better-looking that most women in the sand
> hills, except for her nose. (45)

At this point, there is a paragraph break and the tone shifts precipitously in a
manner characteristic of Caldwell's prose:

> Bessie's nose had failed to develop properly. There was no bone in it, and there
> was no top to it. The nostrils were exposed, and Dude once said when he looked
> at it it was like looking down the end of a double-barrel shotgun. (45)

The first paragraph appears sympathetic not only to Bessie, but more crucially to
the function she serves in the community, but at the end it shifts and by the time
we get to Dude (Jeeter's son, who will marry Bessie) we appear to be in the realm
of broad satire. Indeed, Bessie's shotgun nose is frequently returned to over the
course of the narrative.

Thus it is difficult to know how to take the wisdom Bessie imparts to Jeeter
later in the text, when he asks her to explain why his daughter has a harelip. Bessie
proclaims: "He knowed if He told you to stop fooling with Ellie May, you wouldn't
have cut off the root of evil like He said do. He sent Ellie May into the world with
a slit in her lip. He figured she would be safe from a sinner like you" (55). Jeeter
takes this advice seriously enough to consider castrating himself: "He was more
convinced than ever that God expected him to fix himself so he would not have any
more sinful thoughts" (109). But in the end he is too lazy: "He decided, however,
not to carry out his intentions just then. There was plenty of time left yet" (109).

At this point, we can posit a direct connection between Caldwell's novel and
his father's work with the poor. The Jeeter family was in fact based on a family
which his father had attempted to lift up out of poverty. He put the children in

school, got the father a job and encouraged the entire family to attend his church. The experiment was an abject failure, and Ira eventually wrote a series of articles about it called "The Bunglers" for the magazine *Eugenics*, in which he endorsed sterilization. He was particularly aggravated by the family's immunity to his religious exhortations, and their stubborn susceptibility to religious charlatanry. Bessie's folk religion and Jeeter's contemplation of castration thus both derive from Ira's struggles, but Caldwell refuses to come to any definite religious or sociological conclusions.

Indeed, it is clear that Caldwell could find no place for his father, or his father's God, in the world of the family he based on the Bunglers. Thus both *God's Little Acre* and *Tobacco Road* feature bewildered impotent patriarchs who perpetually proclaim allegiance to a God who has abandoned them. In this, they are of course of a piece with the generalized disenchantment of modernist literature. However, Caldwell refuses to make the necessary next move: to step into the breach and provide an authorial persona to take the place of God. As Bourdieu affirms, speaking of Flaubert: "God is dead, but the uncreated creator has taken his place" (189). This process must occur both within and outside the text. Thus when Flaubert famously wrote that "the author should be like God in the universe; everywhere present but nowhere visible" or when Joyce claimed that "the artist, like the God of creation, remains within or behind or beyond or above his handiwork, invisible, refined out of existence, indifferent, paring his fingernails," both men were simultaneously mandating a literary style and a mode of authorial self-fashioning. The modernist text, in its formal integrity and disciplined style, provides evidence of the author's godlike powers. The author himself, along with the critics who canonize him, is responsible for ensuring this indexical relation in the cultural field. Thus, in the thirties, Hemingway was consolidating his image as "Papa" while Faulkner was becoming the brooding patriarchal creator of Yoknapatawpha County. Neither Caldwell nor his critics could stabilize such an image which, I would argue, accounts for his disappearance from the canon of American modernism. By incompetence or intent, Caldwell didn't provide the stable position of literary authority that is necessary to make contemporaneous celebrity into posthumous fame.

Mark McGurl has recently argued that the American modernist novel can be understood in terms of William Empson's classic theory of the pastoral, "as a technology simultaneously of identification with the low—with the authenticity of the folk, the vigor of the primitive, the collective power of the social mass—and of distinction from the low" (8). In its sociological extensions, as McGurl convincingly elaborates, the formal complexity required to achieve this balancing act was essentially a technology of distinction whose function was to sort out those with the capacity to negotiate literary difficulty from those who could not; whatever its original aesthetic intentions, in other words, the modernist novel, in its social effects, is an intelligence test.

Modernist celebrity can be seen as playing an ancillary, or even compensatory, role in this sorting strategy, enabling authors to straddle high cultural distinction and mass cultural renown. Caldwell's brief celebrity, then, was constituted through an embarrassing exposure of modernism's ambiguous class politics. High modernists frequently wrote about the lower classes, but their self fashioning as authors placed them in a distanced dialectic of sympathy and irony toward their subject matter, and they were rarely read by those about whom they wrote. Caldwell's tone, on the other hand, was highly unstable, lurching between satirical grotesquery and sentimental pathos, and he was popular amongst the populations about whom he wrote. Thus I am, on the whole, in agreement with John T. Matthews' recent claim that "Caldwell reverses the sublimation of social difference and bodily sensation that allows the illusion of aesthetic purity. By deliberately confusing high and low, spiritual and physical, serious and comic, aesthetic and carnal categories, Caldwell strategically obliterates cultural distinctions that indirectly support social differences" (219).

I am less convinced, however, by Matthews's Deleuzian proclamation that Caldwell's "two best-known books zero in on the revolutionary potential of anti-Oedipal desire under modern capitalism" (217). Although Matthews begins his analysis by asserting that "Caldwell's grotesquely lascivious yet socially committed fiction has failed to find an interpretation adequate to its profoundly schizophrenic nature" (206), his conclusion forces him to agree with the standard interpretation of Will as the redemptive figure in *God's Little Acre*, who "flouts the codes that territorialize desire in the Oedipal family" (217). Such a conclusion, in my opinion, reads like a postmodern inversion of Kubie's analysis; it stabilizes authorial intent through bracketing authorial biography in the ultimate service of a liberatory psychoanalytic argument.

Rather, one can only conclude that Caldwell's work foregrounds an irresolvable contradiction: on the one hand, many modernist authors represented themselves as essentially sympathetic to a "common" man who would never read their writing; Caldwell, on the other hand, frequently seemed more condescending to the population, which nevertheless read him avidly. Caldwell's literary style and cultural celebrity, in other words, gives the lie to the bad faith of modernist reputations, without providing any stable alternative to them.

Chapter 6
Gertrude Stein's Currency

Deborah M. Mix

"Currency," in all its valences, occupied Gertrude Stein throughout her career, but perhaps most clearly so in the mid 1930s. Currency is synonymous with money, of course, but it also suggests being current or in vogue and having a kind of electric charge; to be current is to circulate, to signal a kind of value in a larger system. Between the publication and runaway success of *The Autobiography of Alice B. Toklas* in 1933 and 1936, Stein found both her finances and literary reputation in flux, in ways that both elated and alarmed her. She began to make money for her writing with *The Autobiography*, and she found herself drawing large crowds during her 1934 lecture tour of the United States. At the same time, however, her work from this era reveals that she was beset with anxieties about what these changes in economic and cultural status meant. Could a work that people paid money for also be a master-piece? Can one be both a genius and a celebrity? What are the forces that dictate one's position in these fields? What happens to the writer who finds herself judged to be "of the moment" when what she most values is work that she perceives as transcending it? For Stein, these questions prompted an uneasy negotiation with fame, money, and cultural authority that plays out across her mid-1930s writing.

In 1934, Gertrude Stein finally yielded to the entreaties of various friends and literary figures and agreed to undertake a lecture tour of the United States in response to the enormous popularity of *The Autobiography of Alice B. Toklas*. Although she had previously refused such suggestions—telling a reporter from the *Herald Tribune*, for instance, "There is not enough money in the world to persuade me to stand up before a horde of curious people who are interested in my personality rather than my work"—once she finally acquiesced, she found herself enjoying the prospect quite a bit (Mellow 452). "I am slowly but steadily getting pleased about getting over there and so is Alice," she wrote to Carl Van Vechten in July of 1934, and by October of the same year, she and Alice arrived in New York (qtd in Souhami 201).

Stein's American tour was widely publicized. Large crowds attended her lectures, she appeared in at least one newsreel, and she and Alice B. Toklas had the experience of seeing Stein's name up in lights on the Times Building: "Gertrude Stein has arrived in New York, Gertrude Stein has arrived in New York"

(Mellow 457).[1] Her work was mentioned, parodied, and even discussed in newspaper columns from New York City to South Carolina.[2] Stein's popularity had reached fad status earlier that year, with a *Vanity Fair* columnist suggesting that reading Stein's work, specifically the *Autobiography*, had become the newest craze, making light of Stein's work even as it acknowledges its significance, which seems to be the most common response to Stein's work at the time, even among its most dutiful readers. Her work—or at least a popular conception of it—was even judged useful for advertising purposes, with Steinian language appearing in print ads ("A rose is a pose is a rose is …") and shop windows throughout 1934, coinciding with the Broadway smash *Four Saints in Three Acts*, an opera Stein co-wrote with Virgil Thomson. Steven Watson explains that department stores recognized that "money was to be made in merchandising *Four Saints* chic," and thus Bergdorf Goodman, Gimbel's, and Wanamakers offered various women's fashions ("Four Wraps in Cellophane") and built store window displays ("Four Suits in Three Acts") to capitalize on Stein's popularity.[3] Alyson Tischler argues that these marketing strategies benefited the advertisers by associating their products with the newly fashionable Stein, but that they also benefited Stein, "not only because they provided her publicity, but also because they helped to explain her most difficult prose to the public" by "highlighting the similarity between the circularity of her writing and that of advertising language" (24, 22). Tischler may be right about the explanatory value of these advertisements, but in the end, Stein found herself to be reduced to the status of personality—albeit one people were eager to see—and allied with the temporary fashion of clothing and other trends, rather than recognized as a timeless genius, something she firmly believed herself to be.[4]

---

[1]   Stein recounts this moment in *Everybody's Autobiography*: "we saw an electric sign moving around a building and it said Gertrude Stein has come and that was upsetting … to so suddenly see your name is always upsetting … always it does give me a little shock of recognition and nonrecognition" (180).

[2]   Newspaper headlines sought to imitate Stein's distinctive style: "Gerty Gerty Stein Stein is Back Home Home Back" (Souhami 206). Tischler discusses in detail the ways Stein was represented in various newspapers.

[3]   See Tischler for reproductions of the "Rose is a Pose" and "Four Wraps in Cellophane" advertisements along with a photograph of the "Four Suits" window. Perelman cites a 1990s book club ad that trades in what he describes as Stein's notoriety in similar ways (141–2).

[4]   Tischler explains that *Four Saints* had "received little notice when published in *transition* in 1929 and then in Stein's collection *Operas and Plays* (1932)"; two years later, "*Variety* magazine reported that this opera was discussed in more newspaper columns than any production of the last decade" (24). Watson's history of the opera, *Prepare for Saints*, discusses the opera's reception in detail. According to Stimpson, until "the appearance of *The Autobiography of Alice B. Toklas*, only a few supporters knew that she was more than a bohemian character, an art collector, a language freak, or a joke. After 1933, though she delighted in her fame, she legitimately queried the reasons for her new success" (132).

Stein seems to have been thrilled and disconcerted in equal measure by her reception. She wrote to her friend W.G. Rogers, "Have we had a hectic time it is unbelievable … everybody knows us on the street, and they are all so sweet and kind it is unimaginable … I thought I might be news but not like that" (qtd in Souhami 209). Bryce Conrad has argued that Stein wrote the *Autobiography* as a way to "stage the recognition" of her work, using the narrative voice of Toklas as a way to assert the significance of Stein's writing, the ways it evinced the genius she believed she possessed. Kirk Curnutt makes a similar claim about the purpose behind her lecture tour, suggesting that Stein meant to take advantage of her celebrity status as a means to direct the public back to her work itself (223, 303). But rather than providing the proof of her value as genius, the *Autobiography* and her lecture tour offered confirmation only that she had become a celebrity. Stein chafed under the notion that people wanted to see her, rather than to read her work. She was repeatedly asked to talk about the famous people she knew—and whom she had written about in the *Autobiography*, gossip which in no small part accounted for the book's success—rather than to discuss her other writing. Despite evidence to the contrary, Stein insisted to her publisher, Alfred Harcourt, "Remember this extraordinary welcome that I am having does not come from the books of mine that they do understand like the *Autobiography* but the books of mine that they did not understand" (*Everybody's Autobiography* 6). She did manage to arrange U.S. publication for an abridged edition of *The Making of Americans*, a work she believed to be her magnum opus and which had previously been published only as excerpts in the *Transatlantic Review* and in small editions (an edition of 300 had been published in 1925, but it hadn't sold well); however, her more difficult work, which is to say the work besides the *Autobiography* and the later *Everybody's Autobiography* and also the very work co-opted by advertisers and newspaper columnists, still failed to find a wider audience.[5]

In short, Stein found herself to be a celebrity, a personality rather than a person. Stein had always believed that her writing was what made her worthy of attention and, more importantly, respect. However, in the wake of the success of *The Autobiography*, she was increasingly troubled by the sense that, as she wrote in *Everybody's Autobiography* (1936), "the American public were more interested in me than in my work. And after all there is no sense in it because if it were not for my work they would not be interested in me so why should they not be more interested in my work than in me" (50). Liz Stanley notes that the lecture tour put Stein face-to-face with "people who had already conceived and personified a 'Gertrude Stein' that she then had to learn to (appear to) be," something that Stein was ultimately unwilling to do (52).

She writes in an essay published in September 1934, "What happened to me was this. When the success began and it was a success I got completely lost …

---

5   *Everybody's Autobiography* did not enjoy the success of the *Autobiography*. Mellow notes that Random House printed a run of only 3,000 copies, and the reviews were "more circumspect" than the rave reviews for the first memoir (508).

Well you see I did not know myself … I was not I because so many people did know me" ("And Now" 63). Equally distressingly, Stein's relationship to her writing was also undermined: "[F]or the first time since I had begun to write I could not write and what was worse I could not worry about not writing and what was also worse I began to think about how my writing would sound to others, how I could make them understand, I who had always lived within myself and my writing" ("And Now" 63). In his examination of twentieth-century celebrity culture, P. David Marshall argues that in one iteration, "The success expressed in the celebrity posture is seen as success without the requisite association with work … Thus there is no substance to the sign of the celebrity … the celebrity sign is pure exchange value cleaved from use value" (xi). For Stein, use value equates with her identity as a genius, so the shift to celebrity status threatens the stability of genius as an intrinsic quality, for exchange value is determined by an arbitrary consensus that is likely to have little to do with the object of the exchange. She appears to have regained her equanimity by the time she arrived in the U.S. in October; when asked by reporters, "Why don't you write the way you talk?" she replied, "Why don't you read the way I write?" (Souhami 205; Mellow cites a slightly different version of this exchange [455]). Nevertheless, just two years later she writes in *Everybody's Autobiography*,

> Before one is successful that is before any one is ready to pay money for anything you do then you are certain that every word you have written is an important word to have written and that any word you have written is as important as any other word and you keep everything you have written with great care. And then it happens sometimes sooner and sometimes later that it has a money value I had mine very much later and it is upsetting because when nothing had any commercial value everything was important and when something began having a commercial value it was upsetting. I imagine this is true of anyone. (40)

Further, "If my writing was worth money then it was not what it had been, if it has always been worth money then it would have been used to being that thing but if anything changes then there is no identity and if it completely changed then there is no sense in its being what it has been" (84). In reading the latter passage, Loren Glass notes, "What money introduces into the reflexive calculus of identity is, quite simply, change, which would seem to violate the very principle of sameness on which identity is based. And this volatility vexes author *and* text, both of which seem unable to maintain any continuity between before and after the public's willingness to pay" (123). Glass is correct, but I want to suggest that Stein's anxiety about the stability of identity in the context of celebrity also points toward an anxiety about the nature of literary reputation, about the nature of genius and the idea—Stein's idea—of the "master-piece."

Stein firmly believed that she was the author of what she called "master-pieces," which she defined this way in a 1936 lecture: "the master-piece has nothing to do with human nature or identity, it has to do with the human mind and the entity that is with a thing in itself and not in relation … [T]hey exist because they came to be as something that is an end in itself and in that respect it is opposed to the business of living which is relation and necessity" ("What Are" 358). Stein's "entity," which is "a thing in itself and not in relation," is directly opposed not only to the non-master-piece but also to much of the rest of everyday life, all of which exists in "relation and necessity." Still, Stein explains, "every one in a curious way sooner or later does feel the reality of a master-piece" ("What Are" 358). Michael Szalay connects Stein's concerns expressed here to those expressed in another essay, "What Is English Literature," which appeared in *Lectures in America* the previous year. He notes that Stein's valorizing of the "autotelic artifact" allows her to place the master-piece outside of time, away from "relation and necessity," in a familiar, if conservative, formulation of literary value and canonicity (91). The master-piece for Stein, which is to say the kind of work she believed she was producing, was not subject to fashion or changing standards of literary value. That is, the master-piece exists outside of systems of exchange. To conceive of the master-piece otherwise would require Stein to recognize literary value as another system of exchange, an admission that would ally the master-piece too closely with the voguish trend, the genius author too closely with the celebrity.[6]

More specifically, the master-piece is not subject to the vicissitudes of the marketplace and money. Throughout the latter half of the 1930s, Stein returns again and again to the subject of money. In essays she wrote for the *Saturday Evening Post* and *The Geographical History of America*, published in 1936, and in *Everybody's Autobiography*, published the following year, Stein reveals herself to be deeply concerned with money and the nature of value in all its iterations. Certainly it is easy enough to imagine why money might have been of interest to anyone in the mid-1930s. In the depths of the Depression, most people's relationship to money changed. Stein herself found her monthly income, which came from her share of her family's investments, decreasing by 40 percent when Franklin Roosevelt moved the U.S. dollar from the gold standard to the silver standard in 1933 (H. Stein par. 13). She refers to the effects of this drop in a 1934 essay: "And then the dollar fell and somehow I got frightened, really frightened awfully frightened" ("And Now" 64). She goes on to assert that she began to write to help herself deal with her fears—and, more pragmatically, to try to earn some money. But I don't think the real crisis for Stein is about finance per se. Rather, the real crisis is the nature of value, and her ideas about money serve as a way for her to work through a much more vexed relationship to value, specifically to two concepts she believed to be mutually exclusive: genius and celebrity.

Money off the gold standard is, in a basic sense, detached from value, just as fame off the "genius standard" might be meaningless. It seems clear that Stein's approach to the concepts of both money and fame was in fact quite simplistic—to her mind, neither gold nor genius concerned itself with "relation and necessity."

---

[6]   This point of recognition is indebted to Aaron Jaffe's work on modernism and celebrity. Jaffe's formulation of the modernist "imprimatur" suggests that literary value was allied with controlled scarcity and thus stood in opposition to celebrity's ubiquity.

Bob Perelman asserts that Stein "addressed a culture that seemingly would have no way of receiving what she wrote" (142), but as Karen Leick and Tischler have both painstakingly demonstrated, Stein and her work were not only known but also discussed in substantive ways throughout the United States in the 1920s and 1930s. Via Toklas's narrative voice, Stein remarks with evident satisfaction in *The Autobiography*, "some day they, anybody, will find out that she is of interest to them, she and her writing. And she always consoles herself that the newspapers are always interested. They always say … that my writing is appalling but they always quote it and what is more, they quote it correctly" (70). This kind of attention seemed to satisfy Stein—in citing her work accurately, she believed, the newspapers affirmed her value as an important writer, as a genius whose work had currency. She doggedly sought publication for her work, not only via the small presses and little magazines commonly associated with literary modernism, but also via major presses and mainstream magazines, and remained "quite certain that readers could respond to her work in the manner that she desired" (Conrad 217). Given Stein's publications in a variety of middlebrow venues in the 1930s— venues that included the *Saturday Evening Post* but also *Vanity Fair*, the *Atlantic Monthly*, and the *New York Times Magazine*—along with the publication of her longer works by Random House, it seems clear that editors believed readers were prepared to "receive" Stein's work and were perhaps even eager to do so.

Other critics have argued that genius functioned as a kind of commodity for Stein, her "trademark," as Perelman puts it, "unfathomable and glamorous as art but as immediately available as the sign of goods in the store window," and Stein herself "never touches or is touched by history" (168, 167). Perelman goes on to read Stein as isolated, asserting, "her freedom from the trammels of society also meant her exclusion from society" (168). Yet even as Stein wanted affirmation that she was indeed a genius, part of a firmament populated by "Shakespeare … Walt Whitman, Henry James, and Poe," she sought that affirmation through engagement with the very forces of "relation and necessity" from which she believed the "master-piece" itself must be free (qtd in Conrad 219).

Stein's ideas about money are strikingly similar to her ideas about master-pieces—to her mind both master-pieces and money possessed inherent value not subject to the vicissitudes of the economy or popularity. She opens the first of five essays she published in the *Saturday Evening Post* between June and October of 1936 with this question: "Is money money or isn't money money" ("Money" 106). Throughout the essays, she seeks to assert money's intrinsic meaning: "Everybody who earns it and spends it every day in order to live knows that money is money" ("Money" 106). She plumbs the same set of issues in *The Geographical History of America*, writing, "I cannot begin too often begin to wonder what money is" (125). She concludes, "Money is what words are. / Words are what money is" (165). As tempting as it may be to read this passage as a kind of Saussurean declaration that, like money, words only "mean" as part of a larger system, what Stein seems to be suggesting is that there *is*, in fact, an intrinsic value to both money and words. She writes, "[P]erhaps money has to do with the human mind and not with human nature. Perhaps like master-pieces it concerns itself with human nature but is not related to it, oh yes yes" (189). As far as Stein was concerned, money was—or at least *should be*—a dehistoricized thing, isolated from the vagaries of human nature; to her mind money "remains constitutively outside the relations it determines" (Glass 129). Glass cites a passage from the *Geographical History* in which Stein avers, "money can be alone and at its best it is alone money is alone and the human mind and the universe" (Glass 129); in short, Glass explains, "[m]oney has no value because it is value" (129).

Just as the American celebrity system threatens to undermine the value of her words and her status as genius by misunderstanding which of her words or works matters most, so the New Deal, to Stein's mind, threatens to undermine the value of money. Stein wonders, darkly, "Is Franklin Roosevelt trying to get rid of money. That would be interesting, but I am afraid it is only human nature, that is electioneering and that is not interesting" (189).[7] Michael Szalay detects a "paranoia that Roosevelt was trying to evacuate money of meaning," a threat that, to Stein's mind, extends to the graver concern of literary value (89). If money's value can change—as it seemingly had when Roosevelt moved the dollar off the gold standard—what is to say that a true master-piece's value might not be subject to the same vicissitudes? What is to say that the gold standard of genius might not be replaced by the silver standard of celebrity, or even by no standard at all?

Stein was, by all accounts, extremely critical of Franklin Roosevelt and his New Deal, and was "attacked as a reactionary" by readers and friends (Hobhouse 211). Furthermore, as Conrad points out, her long absence from the United States meant that she had almost no knowledge of an economy built on "speculative capital of the sort wielded by the corporate interests that had defined market economics during the period of her thirty-year absence" (229). Perhaps because of both her inherent suspicion of Roosevelt and her lack of up-to-date knowledge about the American economy, Stein frames her *Post* essays through the logic of the domestic, opening her *Saturday Evening Post* essays with a comparison between the "father of a family" and the government: "[I]f there was any way to make a government handle money the way a father of a family handles money if there only was. The natural feeling of a father of a family is that when anybody asks him for money he says no. Any father of a family, any member of a family knows all about that" ("Money" 107). Her argument is that, within the context of an individual family, value is understood. A father, responsible for the family's pursestrings, understands the value of a dollar as internally consistent. Stein explains, "When you spend money that you earn every day you naturally think several times before you spend more than you have, and mostly you do not" ("Money" 107). At the level of the government, however, money loses its concrete value: "[W]hen you vote money away there is not really any difference between a million and three" ("Money" 106). It's not the patriarchal value of a family that interests Stein here,

---

7   Szalay develops Stein's "extraordinary if dizzying analogies between literary and governmental acts" (90; see esp. 89–93).

and in fact, as I will discuss, she's very suspicious of the relationship between patriarchal ideologies and political ones.[8] Rather, it's the small scale of the family that interests her—in her terms, a family is not an organization, and as such it can maintain a stable system of value, even in the face of forces, like the hyperbolic claims of children, which would seek to disrupt the stability of value.[9] She ends her first essay with an anxious entreaty to her readers: "So, now please, everybody, everybody everybody, please, is money money, and if it is, it ought to be the same whether it is what a father of a family earns and spends or a government, if it isn't sooner or later there is disaster" (107). Though the punctuation of the passage is typically muted, involving only commas and a single period, the diction betrays agitation in its repetition of "please" and "everybody" and in its ominous conclusion that "disaster" is imminent.

In talking about money, Stein is also talking about genius. In worrying about money not being money, Stein betrays her fear that what she understood as her genius might not be recognized as such. Where her genius should be the gold standard for her work, she discovered that her celebrity was offering a silver standard at best. She had believed that selling her work would affirm her genius, when instead selling her work only affirmed her status as someone with something to sell. In "What Are Master-pieces," Stein confesses, "One of the things I discovered in lecturing was that gradually one ceased to hear what one said one heard what the audience hears one say," underscoring her fear that the transformative power of celebrity is bound up with anxieties about identity and genius and about the stability of words themselves (356). Here, Stein reveals that the actual meaning of the text is undermined, made dangerously indeterminate, by the familiar dangers of "relation and necessity"; celebrity, guaranteed only by itself, is part of an unguaranteed circuit of value, its stability tenuous.

In the same way, Stein suggests that economic organizations, like the federal government, substitute arbitrary value for intrinsic value, but they seal over this operation through the institution of what she calls "organization." In the *Post* essays, Stein refers to (and seems to conflate) a variety of economic systems, from monarchy to communism to fascism, and in each case she attributes a creeping displacement of value to these systems, displacements that undermine the individuals who are pulled into the organizations. For instance, in her third essay, "Still More About Money," Stein discusses unemployment:

---

[8]   Szalay concludes just the opposite, arguing that Stein "favored a patriarchal model" (89). Hobhouse asserts that Stein's politics "were simply based on a dislike of being disturbed and general dislike of father figures" (210).

[9]   Stein includes just such a scenario, presented as a story about her nephew: "I remember when my nephew was a little boy he was out walking somewhere and he saw a lot of horses; he came home and said, oh papa, I have just seen a million horses. A million, said his father, well anyway, said my nephew, I saw three" ("Money" 106). Here we see the proper response of the father of a family, recalling the exaggerating child to the truth of the matter. The member of Congress, to Stein's mind, will too easily accept the shift from three to a million.

> One of the funny things is that when there is a great deal of unemployment you
> can never get any one to do any work ... Once unemployment is recognized as
> unemployment and organized as unemployment nobody starts to work. If you
> are out of work and you find some work then you go to work. But if you are
> part of the unemployed then you are part of that, and if work comes you have to
> change your position from the unemployed to the employed, and then perhaps
> you will have to change back again, so perhaps you had better just stay where
> you are. (109)

Here we see Stein attempting to explain why the ranks of the unemployed seem
to her to be consistently populated by the same people. People are organized
into a group—in this case the unemployed—and are reluctant to leave that
identity behind, even if it means finding steady work. This, Stein suggests, is the
end of organization: people are no longer willing or able to define themselves
independently of the system that defines them. To be "out of work" is to be lonely,
trudging through the streets in search of a job; to be "unemployed" is to be part
of a much larger group, one that shares the burden of unemployment and one in
which membership confers advantages—according to Stein, "ten francs a day"
plus free health care and a free burial (109). Where value had been located in
work itself, in doing the labor that leads to the paycheck, now value is extrinsic—
"ten francs a day" are conferred for doing nothing. Society, Stein suggests, has
shifted from a kind of gold standard—labor is inherently valuable—to one in
which value can reside anywhere, even in doing nothing.

Stein herself didn't experience unemployment per se, and the sheer arrogance
of a woman living off a family fortune commenting on the distinctions between
being "out of work" and "unemployed" cannot be sidestepped (particularly
when she frames the entire issue through the lens of Toklas's and her inability
to hire servants). However, she did have experience with what happens when
the organization itself becomes more powerful than its membership via her
disorienting experiences with celebrity and the organization that seemed to her to
detach her fame from the very work that merited attention. "It always did bother
me that the American public were more interested in me than in my work," she
writes in *Everybody's Autobiography* (55). "But now well now how can you
dream about a personality when it is always being created for you by a publicity.
How can you believe what you make up when publicity makes them up to be
so much realer than you can dream" (*Everybody's* 71). Stein's phrasing, even its
choice of an indefinite article, positions "a publicity" as a thing and as something
that is utterly separate from her (as opposed to "my publicist," for instance).
It is distressingly abstract (not "the publicity for my lecture tour") and irresistibly
powerful. "A publicity," in Stein's formulation, is a juggernaut organization, one
that sublimates the individual's personality to the one the organization creates for
her—their version is "so much realer than you can dream." Like the transition from
"out of work" to "unemployed," the personality before and after the intervention
of "a publicity" moves from a distinct individual to a cog in a larger machine.
The new personality has value only within the organization system; without

the organization, the "realness" of the personality collapses, but that very threat can strengthen the individual's fealty to the organization, slowly allowing the organization to supplant the individuals within it.

The analogy between celebrity and employment appears elsewhere in Stein's Depression-era writing too. For instance, in "The Capital and the Capitals of the United States of America" (published by the *New York Herald Tribune* in 1935), Stein distinguishes between the "hired man" and the "employee": the former is, first and foremost, a man who happens to be hired to do a job, whereas the latter has had his identity subsumed by the employer, becoming "some one whom some one employs ... and not on their own" (75). In this state, the individual's personality is likewise created by the organization, perhaps so subtly that the individual doesn't even recognize the shift. Szalay points out that Stein's vision links "transitory employment, which romantically recalls the self-indentured laborer of preindustrial America, to a vision of 'small' or 'invisible' government" (93). To Stein's mind, this was a time in which individuals forged their own identities rather than leaving the work up to organizations, like the government or "a publicity." "Stein herself had been packaged and sold by that very mode of organization," explains Conrad, "Stein had been given a market value that could not ultimately be tied to the value which she herself had located in her writing" (230).

Stein envisions the threat posed by organization as one that only increases, and not just for the author caught up in a publicity or the Frenchman caught up in unemployment. She traces a history of Western culture in which the rise of organization inevitably leads to trouble:

> The beginning of the eighteenth century, after everything had been completely under feudal and religious domination, was full of a desire for individual liberty and they went at it until they thought they had it, which ended up with first the English and then the American and then the French revolution, so there they were and everybody was free and that went on to Lincoln. Then they began inventing machinery and at the same time they found virgin lands that could be worked with machinery and so they began organization, they began factory organization and laborers organization, and the more they began organization the more everybody wanted to be organized and the more they were organized the more everybody liked the slavery of being an organization. ("My Last" 111)

The narrative here is nearly Marxist in its assertion that the rise of assembly-line production led to the demise of the individual and individual liberty.[10] Of course, Marxist revolution is precisely the opposite of the conservative reform Stein seems to be seeking via her critique of the New Deal. In her formulation, the organization that has gotten out of control is the federal government, which has undermined the reassuring stability of master-pieces and money.

----

[10]   Her apparently thoughtless analogy between industrialization and slavery along with the elision of slavery from her brief history of the United States merits scrutiny as well, however such attention is beyond the scope of this essay.

In Stein's formulation, any organization is inevitably doomed to collapse, though the damage it will do in getting to the point of collapse may be immense. Because the organization's power is backed by nothing—not gold, not genius—it is rapacious, ingesting space and resources at breakneck speed: "The virgin lands are getting kind of used up, the whole surface of the world is known now and also the air, and everywhere you see organization killing itself by just ending in organization" ("My Last" 112).

Organization that begets only more organization is, finally, the heart of the matter for Stein. And, she fears, the organization has come to replace the individual. To return to the father of a family, who understands the real value of money and knows how to spend it appropriately, we see Stein setting up its inverse, a kind of organization family, one operating on a national scale, heedless of the value of a dollar or of the individuals in the system. Since money isn't really money on the scale of the organization, the substitute father—the head of state—can offer his flawed judgment in place of that of the good father who knows the real value of a real dollar. Thus, rather than celebrating a patriarchal social model, Stein turns to a critique of patriarchal organization.

> There is too much fathering going on just now and there is no doubt about it fathers are depressing. Everybody nowadays is a father, there is father Mussolini and father Hitler and father Roosevelt and father Stalin and father Lewis and father Blum and father Franco is just commencing now and there are ever so many more ready to be one. Fathers are depressing ... The periods of world history that have always been the most dismal are the ones where fathers are looming and filling up everything. (*Everybody's* 137)

Once the patriarchal family reaches the scale of the organization, its nature is changed. Where a good father knows the difference between "a million and three" ("Money" 106), these fathers don't. While it's jarring to see Hitler and Roosevelt, communists and fascists, labor leaders and prime ministers set alongside as equals of a sort, Stein's interest isn't in any particular political or economic system at all. What's important for Stein, I think, is the way in which each of these men represents an organization, all of which she sees as dangerous to the stability of identity and value—the value of individual judgment, the value of a dollar, the value of literary reputation. It's difficult to say whether Stein is showing a particular prescience here, an awareness not only of how organizations have affected her—her pocketbook and her status as celebrity or genius—but also of how organizations might wind up exercising terrifying power in the coming years.

Despite this sense of anxiety, Stein seems unable to relinquish a sense of optimism for the future. As complex as her reactions to her celebrity were, they didn't stop her from seeking out publication, not just for her "genius" work but also for her more accessible writing. Despite her assertion that "I do want to get rich but I never want to do what there is to do to get rich" (*Everybody's* 132), she returned from her American lecture tour "several thousand dollars the richer," according to Carl Van Vechten (qtd in Curnutt 304). She also returned with an agreement from Bennett Cerf, who promised, "[W]hatever you decide each year you want printed you tell me and I will publish that thing ... just like that, he said, you do the deciding" (*Everybody's* 304). She seems, too, to have regained her balance, or at least her insistence on her genius, writing in *The Geographical History of America*, "Think of the Bible and Homer think of Shakespeare and think of me" (81). At the end of the *Post* essays, she gestures toward a future in which individuals will no longer seek to subsume themselves in the identity of an organization. Her vision is a bit naïve, but it is also quite appealing. "What are they going to try next, what does the twenty-first century want to do about it? They certainly will not want to be organized ... perhaps they will begin looking for liberty again and individually amusing themselves again and old-fashioned or dirt farming" ("My Last" 112).

PART 2
Modernist Celebrities/
Modernist Vernaculars

Chapter 7
Garbo's Glamour

Judith Brown

They [film stars] are so glamorized and vaporized and made to appear in print as somebody they aren't at all.

—*Silver Screen*, December 5, 1936[1]

[Garbo] seems not so much the artist as the medium through which forgotten things of a far past find expression.

—*Pictorial Review*, July 1933

The Birth of Personality

During the first decades of the twentieth century, theories devoted to the shaping of human subjectivity flourished: Virginia Woolf marked 1910 as a turning point in human character, T.S. Eliot declared his radical vision of "impersonality," and the entertainment industry—and popular culture more widely—was newly concerning itself with "personality," particularly in the spectacular and carefully contrived birth of the movie star. Warren Susman has argued that human character was undergoing revision during the first decade of the century: character, the old ideal of a former age, was transforming into something flashier and more engaging. "Personality," with its emphasis on charm, poise and likeability, became the watch-word of the modern age, bolstered by the publication of self-improvement manuals, the emergence of fan magazines such as *Photoplay* (first published in 1911), and the new industry of motion pictures. Charm, magnetism, and fascination quickly emerged as the desirable traits of the twentieth century, replacing such fogeyish terms as "virtue" and "strength of character." "Character," in the old morally-freighted sense, was practically declared outmoded. In this climate of refurbished human character was created a potent mix of public fascination and an almost magical potential to transform human form into something better, light-infused, and enduring.

Celebrity was produced in the alchemical mix of fame, wealth, public recognition, adulation, and the remove from the prosaic routine of everyday life. Together these elements produced an intoxicating distance across which the ordinary mortal could not reach. The celebrity was endowed with "personality," yet personality emerged as a screen effect, strangely devoid of human substance.

---

[1]   Quoted in *The Oxford English Dictionary*.

The new standards for beauty, a requirement for at least most celebrities, depended upon a mechanical principle: "Photogenic beauty rests its definition of perfection on a smooth, standardized, and lifeless modernism, a machine aesthetic in the guise of a human. Caught in time, it is a perfection that never ages, and experiences no mood swings. The idiosyncrasies of character are forged into the market-tested gleam of personality" (Ewen 89). Celebrity glamour—the effect of the merging of human object, market, and machine aesthetic—depended upon an evacuation of the recognizable limits of human life that enmeshed the "ordinary" citizen: glamour did not emerge from human warmth, morals, and the messy emotions that define the everyday; rather, in their place was the coolly aloof and beautifully coiffed personality, hovering over the multiple indignities of life on the ground.

What connects Woolf's call for reformulated character in fiction, Eliot's argument for the extinction of personality in poetry, and the newly marketed formation, the Hollywood star? Certainly all point to a shift in the presentation of the individual; a shift that is linked to the changing climate and changing needs of the twentieth-century subject. While the sharply divergent objectives of great art and box office profit should not be overlooked, Woolf's view of character, Eliot's call for impersonality, and the birth of the media-age personality share (rather surprisingly) some fundamental features, including the evacuation of detail in order to convey luminous (or radiant) form. The celebrity would not provide access to the lumpen details that might mar the effect of her gorgeous surface; rather, she would fascinate through the very absence of those details. In this essay, I look at the figure who comes closest to bridging the gap between modernist character and media-age personality: Greta Garbo. Garbo was all-personality and, at the same time, none, she who fascinated millions, remained a resolute mystery to her public, allowing no interviews, no publicity shots, offering no details about her life, instead choosing silence and, most famously, solitude (her most quoted line: "I want to be alone"). Nevertheless, she achieved a stature unsurpassed even in the contemporary world of the blockbuster and red carpet awards ceremonies watched around the world: "Those of us who were not present at the creation of her screen image have to reimagine the singular hold, both unprecedented and unduplicated, she exercised on audiences of the 1920s and 1930s," comments film historian Richard Schickel ("Afterword" 438). Garbo's celebrity tells us something about the desiring structure through which we produce the category of star: her ambition for celebrity was countered always by her resistance to it, her on-screen persona resolutely negated the qualities that suggest "personality." Garbo, Schickel agrees, "was always a creature of withdrawal, of silence—thus, ideally, of the silents— an actress who from the first moments she appeared on the screen defined herself by her refusals." ("Afterword" 441). She was pure magnetism, but a magnetism forged in negativity, as if the pull of the negative was what most profoundly encouraged the public worship she inspired. Rather than appeal to biography (the details of which Garbo mercifully denied us), or the system of capitalist relations that produced her celebrity, I wish to theorize the allure of Garbo's refusals— those withdrawals, silences, and exhausted performances that, according to critics then and now, defined her celebrity and made the image of Garbo so strangely compelling, so resolutely modern (even Woolfian), and so glamorous.

Just as Woolf "dredged up light buckets" to create the special luminosity of Mrs. Dalloway or Mrs. Brown, the photographer's art was one primarily constituted by light. Garbo's power rested, at least partially, in the lunar quality of her skin, the glow that erased the human detail and staged the tremendous and ethereal vitality of her eyes. No one better understood this than the generation of glamour photographers who worked in the studio system of Hollywood. Glamour photography, emerging in the 1920s and reaching its apex in the 1930s, was explicitly designed to produce the celebrity as beyond human, as intangible as light. The style of Hollywood portraiture would develop from the pictorialism of the early century which featured painterly lines in soft focus that were self-consciously artistic (called "fuzzygraphs" by detractors) to highly stylized photographs influenced by modernism.[2] These latter photos featured high contrast lighting (referred to as Rembrandt lighting) that sculpted its object, redefining facial features for maximum effect. The photographer was enlisted to take the ordinary mortal and transform her into something extraordinary and barely human. Glamour photography emerged as a powerful way to disseminate the star's image and was often acknowledged to be of more importance in creating a public image than the films themselves. (Dietrich, among other stars, would make this claim.) Celebrities were fashioned with brilliant illumination, floating out from black backgrounds, shining, hard, and hardly human. As the 1920s moved into the 1930s, the stars became ever-more-ethereal, more starkly lit, and more self-consciously glamorous, as retouchers went to work on their images after the studio session was over. Garbo worked at MGM with a number of Hollywood's best photographers, including Harriet Louise, George Hurrell, and Clarence Sinclair Brown. One notes, in these photos and in many of her films, that Garbo's face is best when sharply defined, when the frame is most severe, her hair pulled tightly back, the background dark, emphasizing the lines and contours that made her of this world and beyond it.

Garbo's celebrity thus depended upon competing visions of character and personality, as well as the developing technologies that lie at the definitional center of literary modernism; her extraordinary 16-year career in Hollywood fed an increasing appetite for the perfect, mediated image without the messy implications of human subjectivity. The celebrity didn't offer life; rather her superhuman image conveyed something more closely associated with static perfection and therefore death. Yet the power of her image lifted her away from the dulling aspects of everyday life and produced an intoxicating image that would enthrall those who encountered it. Garbo held a remarkable place in the modern psyche as she came

---

2   My information on glamour photography comes largely from the following scholars: John Jones; Robert Dance and Bruce Roberson; David Fahey and Linda Rich; and John Kobal.

to signify a kind of glamour in the early century that has not been surpassed—indeed *cannot* be surpassed—in our contemporary digital age.

In recent years, celebrity studies has emerged as a disciplinary field encompassing both biographical and discursive modes of criticism. One of the field's earliest formulations came in Daniel Boorstin's 1962 polemic, *The Image: A Guide to Pseudo-Events in America*, in which the writer decries our contemporary age of self-deception, in which we eagerly enter the "thicket of unreality." Boorstin chalks this up to "national self-hypnosis" and an ever-increasing addiction for illusion (3). The critic has no small task ahead of him, as he acknowledges when he winds up his introduction: "To dispel the ghosts which populate the world of our making will not give us the power to conquer the real enemies of the real world or to remake the real world. But it may help us discover that we cannot make the world in our image. It will liberate us and sharpen our vision. It will clear away the fog so we can face the world we share with mankind" (6). The terms Boorstin uses suggest a fog-free and unmediated world, which mark it, historically at least, as belonging to a world *avant* postmodernism where the authentic as a category still held meaning. We might agree with some of Boorstin's conclusions—the emptiness of the image, for example, and our demand for a daily flood of illusions—but today celebrity studies proceeds without the moral outrage that defines his tract, and instead offers a reading of contemporary culture as necessarily mediated by the lens of consumerist ideology and media conglomerates. Richard Dyer argues that celebrity constitutes more than empty mirage, and sees instead an "elaborate machinery of image-building" with economic, cultural, and historical importance (17). Others, including P. David Marshall, look to celebrity structures as telling us something about the ideologies under and through which we live and which provide us some sense of a shared culture.

I am interested, though, in preserving the idea of the celebrity as a ghostly and empty space, a tautology in Boorstin's terms, that frames an impossible desire for us, makes it almost close enough to touch, but resistant to the "real world" demands of its fans. If the celebrity may be understood as a negative space, a space that absorbs but does not produce meaning, how do we account for its singular power to provoke mass adoration? Celebrity studies as a field takes us a long way toward understanding the institutional foundations, "mass deception," and ideological underpinnings of celebrity, and recent work has included the inter-implications of celebrity and literary modernism, as Aaron Jaffe's work ably demonstrates; yet these studies do not address the strange impersonality of personality, the modernist inflections of the media-produced star. The aesthetic power of the celebrity over the modern subject who invests everything—and nothing, as I will show—in the image becomes crucial in interpreting glamour, particularly (though not exclusively) in the form of Garbo.

From Aura to Glamour

Of course 1910 also loosely corresponds to the era of the declining aura, in Walter Benjamin's terms, with the rise of technologies that substituted the reproduced copy for the original work of art. The aura described that mystifying or magical effect of art that connected viewer and artist, thus creating a relationship that was unique and authentic. The aura, like glamour, refers to a subjective experience, an effect of perception that draws from a historical and technological context. First appearing in his essay, "A Small History of Photography," Benjamin's aura was initially conceived of as an atmospheric trait, arising from the technical challenges of early photography. Already, however, the definition included the binary poles of distance and proximity: "What is aura, actually? A strange weave of space and time: the unique appearance of semblance or distance, no matter how close the object may be." The aura is produced in this fantasy of having, while its object remains unavailable. Benjamin makes clear the movement of contemporary society and its desire to possess the image: "Every day the urge goes stronger to get hold of an object at very close range by way of its likeness, it reproduction" (223). To behold an image in close-up is to possess it, to boast the sort of access that suggests intimacy with the object, even if the close-up represents only a fragment of the original. Details emerge that would otherwise go unnoticed, creating new and spectacular forms of previously familiar objects. A fresh understanding is, presumably, the result, yet the detachment of one moment from any other, its freezing in time, bears critical—even mortal—consequences. Paradoxically, then, the "form" that permits intimacy with the image also dislocates the image from time making it unattainable.

Benjamin imagined the aura to be a vestige of ancient experience still enmeshed in the enchantments of magic and cultic religion, yet also tied to the hierarchies of power. Mass experience was thus antithetical to the aura, indeed stripped the veil from the object itself: the experience of modern life, according to Benjamin, was defined by the shocks of the city, the experience of the crowd, and public demand for immediate gratification—all operating against the interests of the unique experience of aura. The nature of film worked to destroy aura due to the violence of editing, the relentless changing of the image, and the visual spectacle unrolling before the spectators' eyes, yet never reciprocating the gaze. Yet if, as Benjamin suggests, there can be no copy of the aura, how, one wonders, to explain the effect of Garbo, the screen icon adored by millions, and who rivaled religion in the fervor of her fan-base? I want to make the case here that Garbo's glamour (and glamour more generally) comes to stand in the place of the aura, signaling its death yet bearing its enchanted trace; glamour indeed becomes a twentieth-century response to the loss of both authenticity and spiritual belief. Glamour, emerging from the new possibilities of mass reproduction, maintains the qualities of ecstatic illumination while at the same time forgoes any possibility of depth or meaning. The movement from the sacred to the profane, from aura to glamour, thus comes amid the multiple pressures of the early century, its shifting subjectivities, technologies, and social relationships that both destabilized *and* energized modern cultural production.

Perhaps the best known of Garbo encomia, at least among academics, reinforces this point. Roland Barthes's exhilarated two-page essay is likely the most quoted piece on Garbo since its 1972 translation into English. The essay famously begins:

> Garbo still belongs to that moment in cinema when capturing the human face still plunged audiences into the deepest ecstasy, when one literally lost oneself in a human image as one would in a philtre, when the face represented a kind of absolute state of the flesh, which could be neither reached nor renounced. A few years earlier the face of Valentino was causing suicides; that of Garbo still partakes of the same rule of Courtly Love, where the flesh gives rise to mystical feelings of perdition. (56–7)

One is first struck by the hyperbole of Barthes's language, its effusiveness in the face of Garbo, the face that hovers silently, supremely, and indifferently over the text. The divine face "is not in the least expressive," lacking the emotion that characterizes Barthes's response to it. If Garbo is pure concept, as Barthes asserts—logical, cold, abstract—her remove is absolute, in the absolute language of mathematics or analytic philosophy. Barthes's rapture is in direct opposition to the coolness of the image he describes. This, perhaps, is where the pleasure resides, in the stark contrast between the absolute on the one hand and the entirely contingent or subjective on the other, or at least in the *imagined* absolute against the reality of one's feelings. One loses oneself in Garbo's image, Barthes writes, as one would in a philtre, a love potion. The homonym philtre/filter—or sex and lens—brings together two crucial explanations for Garbo's glamour: her sexuality emerges from the lens that captures her face in close-up, allowing a reading of her magnetism as it emanates from the photographic frame. A filter might also refer to the screen over the lens that produces its effects, reduces flaws, and makes the image even more alluring.[3] Whatever the definition of filter here, the ecstasy that Garbo inspires is sexual as if drunk from a potion, yet available only to the adoring eye.

The "face-object" of Garbo transcends the flesh, yet cannot escape its reality (as Garbo the woman most famously knew when she retired at 36 into the shadow of veils, large sunglasses, and cloistered celebrity). Yet Barthes deifies Garbo only as celebrity image, rather than as actress or as woman. He refers only to one aspect of her image, the face, and in so doing, invokes something mystical: "And yet, in this deified face, something sharper than a mask is looming: a kind of volunteer and therefore human relation between the curve of the nostrils and the arch of the eyebrows." Just as Garbo *almost* transcends flesh, she *almost* transcends gender. Hardly confined to the representation of one gender, her face eludes definition: "Garbo offered to one's gaze a sort of Platonic Idea of the human creature, which

---

[3]   An added dimension emerges when one considers that philtre is a term for the receptacle into which saints' relics were put during the Middle Ages.

explains why her face is almost sexually undefined, without however leaving one in doubt." The face, its smooth lines and clear expression, expresses nothing, will not be subject to the over-determination of later screen stars. Even ideologies of gender fail to limit its scope. Garbo eludes the "lyricism of Woman" that would confine many later faces, yet exudes a sexuality that is undifferentiated, Platonic, secret, and intellectual. There is arguably no lyricism of Woman in Barthes's description, one notes, but a lyricism that rejects heterosexual models and the ideology they answer to, and that explains more than her occasional cross-dressing her status as gay icon.[4] Garbo's lyricism may not attain to gender categories, but she will produce a lyric suspension that is, at the same time, subtlety *and* excess, sexual *and* sexless, mortal *and* sublime.

Barthes refers to Garbo's performance as Queen Christina, the sovereign in slacks who challenged gender norms (she falls in love with a man, for example, while cross-dressed as a man). The face-object of his account is that famous "choker" close-up that tightly framed Garbo's face from forehead to chin and concludes the film. Queen Christina has abdicated the throne, choosing love for a man over that of country (the individual over the collective, pleasure over duty). Antonio, her lover, however, will die on board the ship that was to sail them into a romantic future. Instead, alone in the closing shots of the film, Christina walks to the bow of the ship, taking her place as its figurehead, and looks out to sea. The final and famous close-up would run for 85 feet, filling the screen for almost a minute, as Christina stares into seemingly infinite space. Garbo had received the direction from Rouben Mamoulian to "think of nothing," to empty her face of any emotion, to reduce it to its most fundamental features. Garbo asked, "What do I express in this last shot?" and was answered, "Nothing. Absolutely nothing. You must make your mind and your heart a complete blank. Make your face into a mask" (qtd in Vierira 188–9).[5] In the face of this "nothing," audiences might recognize the queen's vast powers, her impulse to rule, her refusal to be ruled, reaching into the ineffable; here the face is not reducible to trivial emotion but instead remains mysterious, unreadable, yet entrancing to its viewer. The shot echoes an earlier close-up, before Christina has met Antonio, when she, resisting the pressure to marry and produce heirs is told: Your father would want it. The camera moves in, framing her face in the cold light of a window, and Christina responds: "Must we live for the dead?" Yes, comes the answer. Christina replies poetically, her face framed in profile, though she seems to speak to no one: "Snow is like a wide sea. One could go out and be lost in it, and forget the world and oneself." In this

---

[4]   Robert Dance and Bruce Robertson note that Garbo had, already by 1927, a female impersonator whose photographs are archived at MGM: "These images are amazing on two counts: first, because they were adopted by MGM publicity at all, but also because their adoption came so quickly: *The Temptress* was only Garbo's second American movie. But by then, she was already a star" (104).

[5]   For an account of the technical difficulty of shooting the enormous close-up and Mamoulian's conversations with Garbo about the final frame, see Vieira, 188–9.

earlier close-up with its expanse of snowy white cheek, and in the final "choker" frame, there is knowledge of death and the desire for blankness, or for obliteration. In the last shot, she faces that wide open sea and, perhaps momentarily, is lost in it, forgetting all. Deathliness is thus inscribed in this face, emptied of all emotion, as it seeks a forgetting that is absolute and nullifying.

There is something about Garbo's effect that is, as Barthes's essay demonstrates, hyperbolic in its intensity, in its extension beyond the boundaries of human capacity (the handbook of hyperbole, *The Guinness Book of World Records*, in fact bestowed the "most beautiful woman who ever lived" honor on Garbo in 1954). Perhaps this is the rhetorical, even literary, power of her face to which Barthes responds. What does this mean, a face with rhetorical power? Audiences seemed to insist on Garbo's authority over them, to exaggerate her power, to bow down, at least metaphorically, before her image. And Barthes does not hold himself apart from the mass here, but seems rather to perform his rapture in an effort to understand it (although he spares us his self-critique). Thomas Weiskel claims that hyperbole itself is a trope, an "overthrowing, overtaking, overreaching that is closer to simplification through intensity than it is to exaggeration"; this may well be, then, the appropriate trope through which to read Garbo's face, a radical simplification of an extreme power. Weiskel places hyperbole in relation to the sublime, but here it works to describe the kind of ecstasy evoked by Garbo's close-up in early-century film audiences. Most of the critical writing on Garbo today remains within the realm of the hyperbolic, now as part of a literary tradition that sees Garbo as a magnificent effect of the early century. More specifically, Garbo's face provides a link to an earlier era of enchantment, when the face itself was known without mechanical contrivance.

The qualities Barthes describes—the all-absorbing power of the image, its ability to transcend gender, its erotic charge—also characterize the rule of courtly love to which Barthes refers, as he knowingly pays tribute to and places himself within a tradition of adoration. Does celebrity simply enact this earlier version of iconic worship? The rule of courtly love, as Jacques Lacan has influentially argued, leaves open a vacuole, an empty space where Woman is situated. This is not just any woman, but a powerful, even cruel, force who punishes and exhilarates via her indifference. She is a manufactured "mythology," like the screen star, and exists within a mediated relation into which her supplicant eagerly enters. Celebrity, like the position of the courtly lady, presents a space of desire which one hopes, hopelessly, to fill. Garbo, like the courtly lady, occupies the vacant central space in the web of representation, yet she takes it a step farther as she undoes even the category of "lady" itself: she is Art, the Thing, and within the web of Hollywood-produced consumer relations, she holds a similar (if degraded) power as the Celebrity. Here then we come to the nexus of abstract terms: character is here degraded, made to conform to the requirements of the mass market in the form of personality. In this relation—the shared sign of best and worst, art and commodity culture—emerges the glamour of celebrity, and particularly the hyperbolic celebrity of Garbo.

The Divine

Gilbert Seldes, a pioneer in the genre of "cultural criticism" that emerged in the 1920s, recognized what equaled religious adoration by film fans: "For a long time after 1920, or at any rate since the beginning of the reign of Greta Garbo, women on the screen were idealized in form and feature like the Madonnas of the Renaissance painters. If you look at a Madonna and Child by Leonardo da Vinci, you will see the strong resemblance she bears to the Garbo types that dominated the screen for over a decade" (296). In a world recently vacated by spiritual meaning, the screen star offered a new figure radiating light, an illuminated image before which the public could bow. This is the sub-text in Garbo's 1932 vehicle, *Mata Hari*, the tale of the notorious World War I German spy ("Temptress of the Secret Service" ran the advertising copy) who seduced men in order to obtain their state secrets. Garbo was at the height of her career, and the role seemed perfectly suited to her on screen powers of seduction. Mata Hari's love for a young Russian officer will lead her, eventually, to death by firing squad, yet the film, as it plots her final act of espionage, seems most interested in investigating the work of glamour itself. In fact, the film is framed by death—beginning with the execution of three spies, and ending as Mata Hari herself is led off to her death. Yet the grey opening frames are quickly forgotten as the film's lavish sets and stunning costumes take up the viewer's attention.

Mata Hari is introduced as a celebrity, a "sacred dancer" to whom the lieutenant is powerfully drawn and before whom he will soon genuflect. She goes to his flat and, in the critical seduction scene, the young man darkens his future considerably when he pledges to put her before god, country, and honor, proclaiming: "I love you as one adores sacred things." Mata Hari, having achieved her desired effect on the man and not yet caring for anything but his state secrets, will demand that her lover put out the flame burning in front of an image of the Madonna. We know, as Mata Hari does, that the flame burns to guard the man from evil, and stays burning in honor of the promise he made to his mother on her deathbed. We also know that the extinguished light will signal to a man who waits below for a sign from Mata Hari. The seduction has begun and he may now enter the apartment to steal the military secrets in Lieutenant Rosanoff's possession. The documents will be spirited away, photographed, and returned to the darkened apartment. The secret agent, meanwhile, will be doing her work, plunged in figurative and literal darkness (the theme of darkness will be literalized later in the film when Rasanoff is blinded).

Garbo, it is true, is hard to resist in the seduction scene, gowned extravagantly as she is by Adrian, MGM's master costume designer, in draping velvet that falls from her shoulder, generously trimmed in flashing sequins. In earlier scenes, she is literally encased in lamé and jewels, armored against human warmth by the profusion of exquisite gems that adorn her long, lean body (Adrian's costume was extravagant in every way, costing about $2,000 and weighing 50 pounds). In this scene, she wears a glittering cap that frames her face, much like the shining halo that surrounds the face of the Virgin. Here we are not meant to overlook

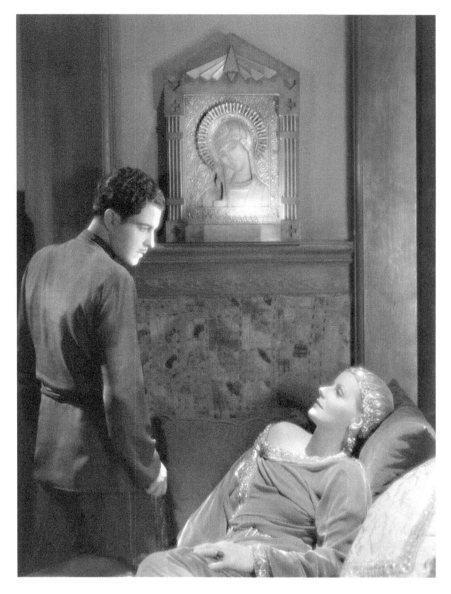

Fig. 7.1   Greta Garbo and Ramon Novarro, in *Mata Hari*, dir. George
Fitzmaurice (1932). © Bettmann/CORBIS.

the significance: this is the old world of faith, religion, and filial loyalty facing off against the new world of flashy surface, desire, and glamour. The Madonna doesn't stand a chance and the scene marks a critical shift as the naive soldier is drawn into the darkness whispering "forgive me."

Garbo, cast as a rival to the sacred, was playing a familiar role as Seldes's comments indicate. Her celebrity transcended that of most stars, propelled her to a sphere not only outside of ordinary human experience, but beyond that of most of Hollywood as well, just as her nickname, "The Divine," suggests. Critics in the years since Seldes's remarks have ecstatically, and routinely, claimed that Garbo's beauty resides in the ineffable, outside the lowly constraints of common life and the common word. Cloaked in carefully managed mystery, Garbo encouraged adoration that equaled or surpassed religious faith. *Mata Hari*, though a film of little consequence in film history, offered an interrogation of the role of celebrity, and particularly the celebrity of Garbo. The scene that pits one Madonna against another, then, operates as a paradigm for the shifting allegiances of the period, as well as a site of the complicated desires that motivate celebrity worship. Lieutenant Rasonoff's Madonna stands for one version of truth, enduring as the flame that burns before her, and that is snuffed out at the behest of the glamorous woman who rests languidly on a divan stacked with pillows below the sacred image. The pose is of course significant. Garbo's seduction rests on a horizontal plane, without any vertical display of energy that might detract from its air of exhaustion and ennui. Reclining on the divan, Garbo/Mata Hari imposes her will and demands the faith of those who gaze at her—her lover, the audience—in the darkness.

The horizontal pose, apparently, was routine for Garbo, or so argues Charles Affron in *Star-Acting*: "Garbo has been photographed supine in erotic scenes with all her leading men ... it is something of a trademark" (105). The 1926 image from *Flesh and the Devil* presents us with this supine Garbo, her face brightly illuminated against the swarthy John Gilbert who bends over her to deliver "the kiss" (the photograph accompanied a 1927 article in *Photoplay* called "The Evolution of a Kiss").[6] Garbo's face registers cool indifference, perhaps bored pleasure, to its viewer and to Gilbert. Her features—brows, lashes, lips—are starkly outlined against the white mask of her face. Gilbert, bowed down, wearing a high-collared officer's jacket, his eyes closed, his lips pressed against her cheekbone, is the picture of formal worship, while Garbo is more casual, less caring, there and not-there, her luminous face ghostly.

With their insistence on her static perfection, Garbo's films—posing the actress against statues, on beds, etc.,—underscore repeatedly her air of passive, even monumental, calm: "Her greatest moments are those nonverbal and nonverbalizable ones, when she somehow seizes the most transitory states and is able to pass them on to us in their purity, avoiding the words, gestures,

---

[6]   Bert Longworth was the stills photographer; the photographs were shot in September 1926, and reproduced in *Photoplay* in January 1927. See Robert Dance and Bruce Robertson for further information on the film's still photography, 228.

Fig. 7.2   Greta Garbo and John Gilbert, in *Flesh and the Devil*, dir. Clarence
              Brown (1926). © Bettmann/CORBIS.

and expressions of explicit translation" (Affron 168). Garbo, in fact, seems to
specialize in doing, expressing, emoting *nothing*, as the celebrated final shot of
Queen Christina attests. One critic, writing in 1950, recounts an anecdote:

> A folk tale of the days when Greta Garbo was becoming a star illustrates some of
> the difficulties of this early period. Her director was accustomed to working with
> untalented actors and depending on tricks and contrivances of the camera for his
> effects. Garbo, however, showed him how she could create a certain feeling by
> merely lifting an eyebrow. The director was not pleased. (Powdermaker 187)

Garbo was untouchable in her disdain for gesture, expression, movement, even
direction; she somehow managed to position herself outside even the requirements
of language as Clarence Sinclair Bull's photomontage of Garbo as the ancient
Sphinx (knowing and refusing knowledge) ironically illustrates.

Strangely, then, the unlikely combination of inertia (what one reviewer called
Garbo's "somnambulistic power") and indifferent sexual appetite produced her
remarkable appeal: "On the screen, Miss Garbo typifies the languor of passion.
She is the only woman in the world who has capitalized anaemia. When she glides,
or 'slouches' through a scene, with mouth partly open, and eyelids drooping,
it registers as exotic passion" (Tully 67). Garbo, then, is both "the epitome of

pulchritude, the personification of passion," *and* the phlegmatic sign of exhaustion: "Those who spend days at the studio often say that 'I'm tired' is almost her only expression" (67). A film viewer published a letter to Garbo in 1937 that stepped out of the mainstream and suggested some frustration with the pose of lassitude:

> Your fascination and your finesse in short your glamour, although it exercised an almost hypnotic influence on your public, could not quite hide the fact that, for some years, your acting was curiously uneven. And that in such films as Anna Christie, Mata Hari, and Grand Hotel, your playing was, more often than not, a highly finished piece of somnambulism. You were clever and sophisticated; but emotionally, Miss Garbo, you were walking in your sleep. (Qtd in Erkilla 602)[7]

Perhaps, Miss Canfield, the letter's writer, underestimates the power of ennui to fan the flames of public ardor. What could be so compelling about the display of exhaustion, what was repeatedly referred to as Garbo's "somnambulism"? Garbo worked on the premise of denial, leaving the audience alone with its fantasies and providing no extraneous clue to her interior state. As a blank, though beautiful, screen, Garbo enlisted the erotic energies of her audience to fill in the emotional absence of her performance while she maintained the aloof distance that defined her.

But is there more to indifference, to the sleepy performance of a star known for the subtlety of her technique, her closed sets and perfectionism? Indifference is defined by absence, the absence of interest or attention or feeling: is there something more in Garbo's multiple-layered absences that drive her celebrity appeal? Glamour, as I have been arguing, is backed by absence, suffused with longing and defined by the fantasy of distance. Garbo's stylized image, her indifferent gaze, perhaps reminded audiences—the consumers of and supplicants to her glamour— of their own precarious subjectivity that seemed tied to the relentless momentum of modernization. Indifference, or the "blasé attitude," according to Georg Simmel, necessarily characterizes the inhabitants of the modern city and is the sign of renunciation where "the nerves reveal their final possibility of adjusting themselves to the content and the form of metropolitan life by renouncing the response to them" (329). The "entire objective world" is devalued in this stance, and is met with "a slight aversion, a mutual strangeness and repulsion." Garbo's repeated desire to be alone, to sequester herself away from a public that numbered many metropolises crowding in upon her, shares some elements, we might imagine, with the aversion of Simmel's theory. Citing the reified urban subject, Simmel writes that

> ... this type of culture ... has outgrown every personal element. Here in buildings and in educational institutions, in the wonders and comforts of space-conquering technique, in the formations of social life and in the concrete institutions of the

---

[7]   Canfield letter originally published as "Letter to Garbo" in *Theatre Arts Monthly*, 1937.

State is to be found such a tremendous richness of crystalizing, de-personalized cultural accomplishments that the personality can, so to speak, scarcely maintain itself in the fact of it.

Personality, in the face of the crystallized impersonality of modern*ism*, suffers an eclipse: impersonality is both the cause and response, then, in Simmel's reading of the sociological effects of the urban. Audiences seemed to recognize in Garbo's indifference a shared experience of modern urban life, an aversion to its press of bodies, and a recognition of the lost-ness of personality, and so they responded with rapture to the "personality" of the screen star, which would, in the end, signify the death of personality itself. Garbo's magnificent face projected onto the big screen (no one could begin to surmise the mental life going on behind her impassive expression) thus a corollary to the mental states of her audience, each member in isolation—despite the collective or mimetic activity of the theatre experience—feeding on the expression of alienation they felt in modern urban life.

From Garbo's Face to Monroe's Figure

I want to conclude by considering a more recent advertisement that features the celebrity image and the word "glamour." The ad, appearing on billboards and in magazines in the mid-1990s, tries to revive the image of glamour, but chooses anachronistically, reflecting more the needs of the product for sale than the aesthetics of glamour. Marilyn Monroe looms in this ad with one word of copy, "Glamour," suspended in a bar of black below.[8] The word, paired with Monroe's colorful image (altered, with a tiny Mercedes Benz symbol on her cheek in place of her legendary beauty mark), works—at least in the advertising strategy—to sell the product with no further information. Monroe and the Benz are known quantities in the logic of this advertisement and their combination signals everything most desirable to the Benz customer—wealth, prestige, and an abundant sexual appetite.

"Glamour," that one word of text, provides the bond that connects product and image and suggests a kind of sexual satiation in their fusion. The word, emptied of the enchantment associated with the aura, signals only the erotics of consumption, allusively signifying desire and the fantasy of its fulfillment. Presence and absence work together in the ad, with the tight close-up of Monroe's face as seemingly present—bearing sexual promise with parted teeth, a little tongue, and beckoning, half-shut eyes—as the car is absent. One can see that Garbo's image would fail to sell the sedan, her long, hard lines wouldn't signal sensual comfort, her gaze is far too penetrating, even ironic. Monroe's image, rather, is all Woman as she suggests the genuine, the authentic, the vulnerable, the vital. Her face, digitally altered with the insignia of a high-end car, cannot be read without a knowledge of tragedy, a truncated lifetime, the embrace of gendered ideology, and without a vulnerability and openness that makes her the object of rapturous desire.

---

[8]   Mercedes-Benz of North America, *New Yorker*, 1997.

Unlike Garbo, there is nothing subtle, transcendent, or ambiguous about Monroe: she is the flesh made familiar, available, and present. Monroe suggests an immediacy of sensation, the smooth ride enveloped in the warmth, if not flesh, of newly tanned leather. Her parted lips remind one of the breath in her voice, her brand of appeal to a generation now able to purchase its fantasy. Monroe invites one to feast without stepping outside the clear lines of cultural expectation, without ambiguity, and without interpretation. Instead she reflects the satisfied retreat into a domestic ideology where Woman is flesh and productive mother (signified by Monroe's full breasts) without ambiguity or the complicated re-drawing of norms governing gender.

Monroe may whet the sexual appetites of a generation, but her image offers less to the literary appetite. Garbo's face—ambiguous, intellectual, undefined— offers more: Garbo's face, as Barthes would have it, gives us passage from an era of ritualized rapture to that of a less noble fascination. From aura to charm: in that transition is glamour, entangled in melancholic loss and desire whose magnitude is unspeakable, and continually spoken through our engagement with the image and all it seems to promise. The images of Garbo and Monroe, one emerging from the studio era of the 1920s and 1930s,[9] the other from the post-war atmosphere of buoyancy and domestic possibility, hinge then upon a competing aesthetic: Monroe's image offers sexual promise with the immediacy of purchase, while the figure of Garbo is less emphatically embodied, more abstract, impersonal, modern, and unambiguously glamorous.

---

[9] In fact, the era of Hollywood glamour would come to a close during the 1940s and we see this most obviously in the demise of glamour photography. Beginning in 1936, with the first publication of *Life* magazine and its new casual aesthetic, a demand emerged for more natural images of celebrity (in the home, with family, etc.,) that worked against the stark artificiality of George Hurrell's or Clarence Bull's carefully staged glamour. With the closing of the studio system soon after the war, stars were no longer viewed as immortal beings, but rather were now as human as anyone else (though with more wealth at their disposal). Candid photography, outdoor photography, and color photography reflected the evolving tastes of film fans and a new vibrant aesthetic (of *Life*, one might argue, over death), and eliminated even the trace of Benjaminian aura.

Chapter 8

In Good Company:
Modernism, Celebrity, and
Sophistication in *Vanity Fair*

Faye Hammill

Vanity Fair binds between the covers of a single magazine, the table-talk of a dinner party—at which cosmopolitan, well-bred, cultivated people discuss the news of their varied world—its arts, sports, letters, operas, theatres, dances, music, fashions, humor and gaieties. […] If you are a forward-minded American—and want to keep up with all the new movements of our day—and enjoy the work of our younger and more amusing writers and artists, you should read *Vanity Fair*.

—Advertisement, Vanity Fair, September 1918

In between the "little" and "big" magazines of the early twentieth century there was another group for which it is harder to find a label. In America, they included *The Smart Set*, *Vanity Fair*, *The New Yorker*, *The American Mercury* and *Esquire*. Described collectively by Sharon Hamilton as "American humor magazines with serious literary pretensions" ("Mencken" 101), by George O. Douglas as "smart" (1), and in other contexts as "quality" or "slick," these periodicals were influential taste-makers, and are intimately connected with the historical development of both modernism and celebrity culture. They traded extensively on the value of modernist signatures, and they also photographed and sketched modernists, speculated about their lives, analyzed their work, parodied them, mocked them and celebrated them. Their contributions to the fashioning of modernist careers are inflected by their complex attitudes towards both elite cultural capital and the operations of celebrity culture.

This essay explores the role of the "smart" magazines in mediating the discourses of modern(ist) fame. I chose *Vanity Fair* as a case study because it forms an ideal focus for an analysis of the interdependence, cooperation and also mutual distrust of modernist and celebrity cultures. A significant outlet for modernists, it published dozens of the writers and artists whose work now forms the modernist canon. The magazine was also an important conduit of the expanding culture of celebrity in interwar America, printing many portraits and star profiles, together with a regular "Hall of Fame" gallery celebrating achievement in the arts, entertainment and public life. My discussion examines the dynamic between *Vanity Fair*'s attention to the stars of popular culture and its commitment to disseminating experimental art, arguing that the interactions between modernist and celebrity systems of value in its pages can be read in terms of an organizing framework of sophistication. The sophisticated reading position which the magazine constructs for its audience disrupts conventional cultural hierarchies because it is defined, on the one hand, by knowledge about modernists and confidence in speaking of them, and, on the other, by a refusal to set modernists apart from other kinds of celebrities or to separate their work from other forms of cultural production.

Vanity Fair, Little Magazines and Mass Culture

In recent years, critics have focused intently on the role of little magazines in building writers' reputations, but important though this project is, it does not tell the whole story, and needs to be supplemented by analysis of the circulation of modernist cultural capital in larger magazines and newspapers.[1] Extensive research has, of course, been undertaken into modernism's commerce with popular culture and its operation in the marketplace, but apart from two excellent articles by Jane Garrity (on British *Vogue*) and Karen Leick (on the American daily press), there has been very little analysis of the influence of mainstream periodicals on the production of modernist artists as celebrities.[2] Leick points out: "It would have been difficult for any literate American to remain unaware of modernists like James Joyce and Gertrude Stein in the 1920s, since their publications in the 'little magazines' were discussed with such frequency in the daily newspapers and in popular magazines" (126). Her study demonstrates that the lives as well as the latest works of modernists were presented as news, and that their celebrity status was consolidated as much through the popular press as through the institutions of modernist literary culture. Turning to a British context, Garrity explores the Bloomsbury Group's status as a widely known "mass market phenomenon." She analyzes the showcasing of Bloomsbury in British *Vogue*, which was at the time "a fascinating cultural hybrid," juxtaposing distinctly highbrow material with fashion advertising and articles on homemaking (30). *Vogue* did not actually publish poetry and rarely included fiction, but it discussed modernists, photographed them,

---

[1]   I would like to thank Jonathan Goldman and Aaron Jaffe for invaluable comments on an earlier draft. Many thanks are also due to Karen Leick for sharing her unpublished research with me and for several useful discussions. The analysis of the role of little magazines in constructing and disseminating modernism is a rapidly expanding project, as, for example, the collaborative research programs based at Brown and De Montfort Universities demonstrate. See *http://dl.lib.brown.edu:8080/exist/mjp/index.xml* and *www. cts.dmu.ac.uk/modmags*. On little magazines in relation to modernist reputations, see Ardis (Chapter 5), Benstock, Edward Bishop, Churchill, Jaffe (especially Chapter 4), Materer, Morrisson, Nelson, Rainey.

[2]   Some further concise but helpful discussion can be found in Collier, while Boscagli and Duffy analyze photographs of Joyce published in *Time* and *Life*.

and ran features about their houses, in effect marketing high culture to an audience extending far beyond the intellectual elite.[3]

These two articles provide a model for my analysis, but my arguments are different because *Vanity Fair*'s attitude towards modernism does not correspond with those of the newspapers or the fashion magazines. Like these larger publications, the smart New York magazines gossiped about modernists and their careers, but unlike the popular press, they also published a great deal of avant-garde art and literature. The sheer amount of experimental poetry, fiction, painting and photography that appeared in the smart New York magazines is remarkable, and the way this material was presented deserves attention. There is not space here for a detailed account of the scope of modernist publishing in these outlets, but it is worth taking a sample from *The Smart Set*, *Vanity Fair* and *The New Yorker*, which were established in 1900, 1914 and 1925, respectively, and therefore intervened at different stages in the trajectory of modernism.[4] Their audiences were much larger than those of the little magazines, which ranged from approximately 200 to 9,000, but far smaller than those of the mass-circulation weeklies, which reached millions.[5] During the 1920s, *The Smart Set*'s circulation averaged at 30,000 and *Vanity Fair*'s at over 90,000.[6] *The New Yorker* initially had low sales (below 10,000 in some of the early months), but by the 1930s, it had become much bigger and more commercially viable than its rivals (see Douglas 130, 148). W.H. Wright, who briefly edited *The Smart Set* and transformed its literary standards, published early work by James Joyce, Ezra Pound, Ford Madox Ford and Frank Wedekind in 1913, while the editors who took over the following year, H.L. Mencken and George Jean Nathan, introduced writers including F. Scott Fitzgerald, Eugene O'Neill, Amy Lowell and Sinclair Lewis to

---

[3]   In the early 1920s, *Vogue*'s circulation was about 137,000. This is not far above *Vanity Fair*'s, but the *Vogue* readership increased rapidly over succeeding decades. More importantly, *Vogue*'s annual advertising revenue of three million dollars (six times higher than that of *Vanity Fair*) arguably moves it into the realm of the mass market. *Vanity Fair* relied on circulation revenue for 70 percent of its income; in comparison the little magazines tended to rely on circulation for around 90 percent of theirs (see Douglas 117; Rainey 98).

[4]   Condé Nast's *Vanity Fair* was a monthly, but two humorous weeklies had borne the same title, one in New York (1860–63) and one in London, from 1868. This last merged with *Dress* magazine to form the monthly *Dress and Vanity Fair*, soon renamed *Vanity Fair*. It became a casualty of the Depression in 1936, and was subsumed into American *Vogue*.

[5]   The two biggest American weeklies, *Collier's* and the *Saturday Evening Post*, reached 1 million and 2.1 million, respectively (Rainey 201n54). Compare *The Dial*, with a circulation of 9,000; the *Little Review* with 3,000 or *The Egoist* averaging 200 (Rainey 98).

[6]   See: Hamilton, "Mencken" 26; Peterson 271. Audience sizes varied, of course: particularly in the case of *The Smart Set*. In its earlier incarnation as a risqué high society magazine, in the first decade of the century, its sales were around 140,000 (Hamilton, "The First" 94). Leick notes that *Vanity Fair* did not reach "the enormous audiences of popular magazines like *Life* or the *Saturday Evening Post*, but the many discussions and reprints of its (uncopyrighted) articles in the daily press accounted for many more readers" (130).

the American public. *The New Yorker*, which began where *The Smart Set* left off[7] and was first, edited by Harold Ross, numbered Louise Bogan, e.e. cummings, Marianne Moore and Langston Hughes among its contributors. *Vanity Fair*, edited by Frank Crowninshield, published authors including Jean Cocteau, Djuna Barnes, Gertrude Stein and D.H. Lawrence. In addition, it reproduced modernist paintings and experimental photography, and commissioned covers from artists such as Fortunato Depero and Marie Laurencin.[8]

Lawrence Rainey points out that the three periodicals Eliot considered for the publication of *The Waste Land* in America were *The Little Review*, *The Dial* and *Vanity Fair*. He argues that *Vanity Fair* belonged entirely to the market economy and that its publication of modernist texts represented a commodification of "the works of a literature whose ideological premises were bitterly inimical towards its ethos and cultural operations" (91). Edward Bishop concurs, adding that:

> publication of the poem in *The Little Review* would have been a look backwards to modernism's beginnings, where with a circulation of 400, and no news-stand sales, there was a direct relationship with the reader. *Vanity Fair*, with advertising revenue of $500,000 a year and a circulation of 92,000 represented modernism's future [… in] the market economy. (311)

Michael Murphy likewise categorizes *Vanity Fair* as "a piece of market-driven mass culture" (68), Mark Morrisson classes it with the *Ladies' Home Journal* and *Cosmopolitan* as a "mass market magazine" (176), and Michael North refers to it in connection with what he terms "offensive" public relations techniques" (211). But these judgments are all based on the traditional dualistic understanding of commercial and elite culture, a model which fails to acknowledge the middle ground: that is, the range of cultural production which lay between the experimental and the popular, and engaged with both.[9] The books and periodicals falling into this range do not relate to the literary marketplace in the same ways as either mass-market publications or high-culture texts. Morrisson's book, *The Public Face of Modernism* (2001), offers an invaluable study of little magazines and their relationship to the marketplace and to mass-circulation periodicals, but throughout he maintains the division between "little" and "mass market," allowing no category to intervene between them. Therefore, he can only characterize *Vanity Fair* as an oddity, noting: "one mass market magazine that made an exceptional effort to support modernist art and literature [was] Frank Crowninshield's *Vanity Fair*" (205).

---

[7]   *The Smart Set* ceased publication in 1924. Hamilton argues that it was not *The American Mercury* (which Mencken and Nathan went on to edit) but *The New Yorker* which was the true inheritor of *The Smart Set*'s style and ethos ("Mencken" 101).

[8]   As Murphy notes, the magazine also promoted modernist visual styles by using "futurist, vorticist, dadaist, and surrealist visual effects" (63).

[9]   For more discussion, see Hammill, *Women, Celebrity* (9–13).

Vanity Fair was never straightforwardly a product of the market economy. This conception of it may result from the fact that it was owned by Condé Nast and launched as a sister magazine to his profitable American *Vogue*, but Crowninshield's showcasing of modernism entailed distinct commercial risks: for instance, he drew criticism for reproducing paintings by Van Gogh, Matisse and Picasso which some of the magazine's advertisers termed "decadent and distorted" (Bradlee 11). The publication of the paintings directly threatened advertising revenue. Crowninshield also devoted considerable space to experimental artists and writers who were at the time unknown and whose work was often "difficult" and unlikely to appeal to mass audiences. In later years, he and his various managing and literary editors (including Robert Benchley and Edmund Wilson) could boast of having introduced numerous leading modernists to the American public. Stein's 1934 piece "And Now," for example, appeared with an introduction referring to her recent success: "*Vanity Fair* views all this with a certain smugness, for it has been publishing Miss Stein's work [...] for seventeen years" (Stein 280). *Vanity Fair*, then, was prepared to challenge current definitions of artistic good taste,[10] and Crowninshield carefully balanced aesthetic against commercial considerations rather than understanding them as mutually exclusive. Indeed, his risk-taking with unknown modernists often paid dividends, as their growing fame, the controversy generated by their work, and the cultural capital which their signatures and their faces had accumulated sold more copies of his magazine. But the same is true of little magazines, as critics such as Rainey and Morrisson have amply demonstrated. Therefore, *Vanity Fair* and similar magazines should be understood as mediating between popular magazines and small literary journals, since they shared certain editorial and marketing practices with each type of publication.

Edward Bishop suggests that: "in *Vanity Fair*, *The Waste Land* would have been next to pictures of movie stars; in *The Little Review*, in good company but isolated from the mainstream" (311). The implication, of course, is that movie stars are bad company. But considering the productive interplay between modernist and popular cultures which has recently been the subject of several important studies,[11] Bishop's judgment seems problematic. New meanings are produced by the juxtaposition of culturally disparate texts and images in *Vanity Fair*. In terms of the specific preoccupations of this essay, by bringing well-known authors and artists into relationship with the stars of the entertainment industry, the magazine became a site of encounter between popular and high-culture forms of celebrity. At the same time, it encouraged a detached attitude by frequently including cartoons, features and parodies which reflected critically on celebrity culture, or

---

[10] A comparison with *The Smart Set* is useful here—as Hamilton points out: "Part of this magazine's influence upon the development of American modernism related to its ability to push the boundaries of the permissible" ("The First" 93). It published stories by Fitzgerald, Cather, Lawrence, Joyce and Dreiser which most other periodicals, seeking to maintain a respectable image, would have rejected.

[11] See, amongst others, Ardis; Ayers; Dettmar and Watt; North.

which mocked either the excesses of experimental art or the inanities of popular culture. This is one way in which the magazine works to disrupt boundaries between high and low, commercial and artistic.

Vanity Fair and the Sophisticated Reader

Vanity Fair, then, provides a middle space, located between the author-centered production model of the avant-garde magazines and the market-driven arena of the daily papers and mass-circulation weeklies. It addresses a reader who is literate in both high and popular culture, and who possesses or aspires to wit, discriminating tastes, style and current knowledge. In the early twentieth century, the term "sophistication" functioned as shorthand for these qualities. But the etymology of "sophistication" reveals more complex resonances that are also relevant here. Its oldest meaning, dating back to the fifteenth century, is roughly equivalent to adulteration or falsification, and this could refer to fraudulently mixed commodities, or to misleading rhetoric and specious argument (sophistry).[12] The first occurrence of "sophistication" in terms of "worldly wisdom or experience; subtlety, discrimination, refinement" is dated by the *OED* to 1850, and in the interwar years, whilst "sophistication" was generally a term of praise, it still retained traces of its earlier meanings. Joseph Litvak proposes in an article on Thackeray's *Vanity Fair* that, "the distinction between snobbery and distinction [is] precarious: naturalized or not, sophistication—which means adulteration or denaturing before it means refinement—is by definition pseudo" (229). Anxieties about this "pseudo" quality surface in the magazine *Vanity Fair* in various forms, and are particularly visible in its satiric features and cartoons (such as those by Fish that are discussed below). The ambivalence of the term "sophistication" also corresponds to the magazine's ambivalent positioning in relation to the marketplace, and the idea of fraudulent mixing of commodities may seem to be (implicitly) invoked by those critics who object to the proximity of film stars and experimental poets in *Vanity Fair*'s pages.

Jessica Burstein notes: "Like the dynamic of fashion, sophistication works by relentlessly defining itself against its immediate past, or immediate context" (234); arguably, this might also serve as a preliminary definition of modernism. Burstein engages with the complex relationship between modernism and the sentimental, inserting "sophistication" as an additional term in the debate. While Suzanne Clark, in *Sentimental Modernism* (1991), urges "that we should restore the sentimental *within* modernism" (4), Burstein argues a different position: "It's less useful to think of modernism as refusing sentimentalism, or, in a revisionist account, embracing it, than to understand modernism as privileging urbanity, with

---

[12] "Sophistry" is etymologically related to "philosophy" (both stem from "sophos," meaning wisdom or the love of knowledge), but whereas "philosophers" were genuine lovers of wisdom, "Sophists"—itinerant professors in ancient Greece—came to be regarded as purveyors of fake wisdom and misleading rhetoric.

its concurrent aggrandizement of sophistication, pleasure, and boredom" (228). Burstein exposes the false logic that sets up straightforward oppositions between sentimentality and modernism or else between sentimentality and sophistication. She cites Dorothy Parker's theatre reviews for *The New Yorker* and *Vanity Fair*, in which she "distinguishes herself as *uncommon* by ironically parading her tendency to weep. This activity is distinctive precisely because of its context, the urbane and critical milieu of the Algonquin Round Table" (234).[13] Burstein describes this move, which Parker used repeatedly, as "the ne plus ultra of sophistication by virtue of disdaining it," adding: "The logic is simple: if everyone else does it, I don't" (235). This concept of sophistication as entirely relational illuminates both the editorial and the promotional practices of *Vanity Fair*.

In his editorial for the first issue of *Vanity Fair*, Crowninshield launched his search for "originality and genius" and "an inventive, forward [...] spirit" (13). He promoted the magazine on the basis of the individuality and distinction of its contributors. In contrast to more popular magazines, which tended to use a large amount of anonymous text or pieces signed with pseudonyms or initials,[14] *Vanity Fair* prominently identified the author of each contribution. This practice compares to the author-centered approach of the small literary magazines, but one key difference was that *Vanity Fair* often illustrated features with a photograph of the writer. In general, as Aaron Jaffe observes: "the matrix of associations supporting [modernist] reputations is not intrinsically image-based but predicated instead on a distinctive textual mark of authorship" (1). Yet in *Vanity Fair*, images do interact with, or partly constitute, modernist signatures. For example, a photo of T.S. Eliot appeared in 1923 on a page reprinting some of his early poems, one of Lawrence was placed above his "Polemic Against Mass Thinking" (1928), and Jean Cocteau's 1922 article "The Public and the Artist" is accompanied by a shot of him performing in his nonsensical musical play, *Les Mariés de la Tour Eiffel* (1921). These are all previously published, recognizable images, and the small-sized reproductions take on the quality of a visual signature.

Modernist artists, writers and musicians were also frequently included in the "Hall of Fame" features, or in themed photo spreads. These larger pictures were accompanied by captions indicating the subjects' newsworthiness and describing their careers over the longer term. Reasons for Hall of Fame nominations ranged from commercial, artistic or political success through aristocratic descent to wit, charm and glamour. Among the experimental artists who appeared were Rachmaninov and Yeats (1920), Proust (1923), Picasso, Mann, Diaghilev and Hemingway (1928), Woolf and Strachey (1929), Klee and Hindemith (1930), Joyce (1931), Stravinsky and Shoshtakovich (1935). Michael Murphy remarks

---

[13]   On Parker's construction of herself as celebrity through her reviews, see Hammill, *Women, Celebrity* (27–54).

[14]   In its early years, *The New Yorker* also used a lot of anonymous text, and for signed contributions the name was generally placed at the end, in small type. *Vanity Fair* was ahead of its rival in capitalizing on the value of modernist signatures.

on *Vanity Fair*'s: "especially skillful appraisal of and traffic in the celebrity values of the most important 'bohemian' figures, photographed stylishly by serious 'art' photographers" (62). The magazine laid claim to highbrow culture by assuming its readers' familiarity with the key figures of modernism and bohemia. At the same time, the Halls of Fame make meaning through diversity; Jaffe remarks that the similar spreads in British *Vogue* represent a "gallery of mixed worthies knowingly juxtaposing the elite and the popular," and point to "the kind of qualified reintegration of high and low forms first undertaken by Gilbert Seldes" (237n2). This sort of celebrity-watching was deliberately eclectic, advocating a generous understanding of culture and beauty which could at once value the elegance of Greta Garbo, the popular appeal of Pearl Buck and the stylistic innovation of James Joyce.

This eclecticism was, however, combined with an emphasis on discrimination. Whilst stars from Gertrude Lawrence to Gertrude Stein earn inclusion in the *Vanity Fair* hall of fame because they are much discussed and widely admired, nevertheless the detailed captions suggest that their true value will only be understood by sophisticated elites. Stars whose appeal has no dimension of intelligence or distinction are denigrated: the film actress Clara Bow, for example, is described in the caption to a 1928 photograph as "the little lady prancing and dancing"; her attempt to write her autobiography is ridiculed, and her representative quality is referred to contemptuously: "in one person, in one pose, we have the *genus* American girl, refined, washed, manicured, pedicured, permanent-waved and exalted herewith." In contrast to Clara Bow's reproducible, rather infantile charms, *Vanity Fair* presents the nightclub hostess Texas Guinan (also featured in 1928) as a true original, with a "genius" for words: "She sits atop the piano in a kind of savage Parcae glory, maintaining an unceasing and genuinely funny running comment, keeping everything going."[15] According to *Vanity Fair*, Guinan's combination of unpretentiousness and sophistication attracts "those who know they're wise and those who are willing to get wise," while Bow's appeal is far more general: "Ladies, and gentlemen (not to mention children): regard, observe and otherwise behold [...] the vivacious, the audacious, the orchidaceous Clara Bow! Feast your weary optics upon this super-flapper of them all—the hyper-reality and extra-ideality of a million or more film goers."[16] The inclusion of the Bow portrait brings *Vanity Fair* into momentary alignment with movie fan magazines, even as the sarcastic caption, with its parodic citation of Hollywood promotional discourses, seeks to distance the magazine from mass-market celebrity.

Whilst pandering to public interest in the famous, *Vanity Fair* nevertheless maintained a certain skepticism towards the modern celebrity system. The "Hall of Fame" was occasionally replaced by a "Hall of Oblivion," nominating people who should be quickly forgotten, and many features and stories lampooned would-be

---

15 Parcae: Roman goddesses of fate.
16 Portraits reprinted in Amory and Bradlee 153 (Bow) and 142 (Guinan).

stars or analyzed cultures of publicity.[17] Crowninshield also encouraged satire of the excesses of modernists and their imitators, and this skepticism is crucial to the pose of sophistication which *Vanity Fair* constructed for itself and its readers. Many modernists were named in its high-profile 1923 symposium on "The Ten Dullest Authors," in which widely read journalists and authors such as H.L. Mencken, Edna Ferber and George Jean Nathan challenge the dominance of modernist aesthetics by repeatedly selecting Lawrence, Stein, Whitman and Proust among their nominations for "the Most Unreadable of the World's Great Writers." In addition, *Vanity Fair* printed numerous parodies of the very modernist writers whose work it had previously published.[18] The parodies compromise modernist cultural authority, but simultaneously contribute to the fame of elite artists by citing the recognizable conventions of their work. They interpellate an audience already familiar with avant-garde texts, flattering readers by implying that they are too sophisticated to be intimidated by experimental writing, but that they can also recognize the *over*-sophistication (speciousness, obscurity) of certain highbrow postures.

The witty cartoons by "Fish" (Anne Harriet Fish), often captioned by Dorothy Parker or by Crowninshield, epitomize *Vanity Fair*'s occasional skepticism about the modernist celebrity. Fish reduces the stars of bohemia to a series of "types." One cartoon spread, "Advice to the Lovelorn: What Every Girl Should Know Before Choosing a Husband," includes a drawing of a young man declaiming dramatically to an inattentive girl, captioned:

> Beware the modernist poet. There is a time in every girl's life—usually around Spring—when she falls in love with the Professional Poet. He wears his hair in the manner made popular by Irene Castle, and he believes in free speech, and free verse, and free love, and free everything. His favorite game is reading from his own works—such selections as his "Lines to an Un-moral Tulip." (Fish 40)[19]

The girl is equally bored by "The Futurist—with a Past," who "can show her how, at a glance, to tell the difference between a Matisse painting and a Spanish omelette," and considers himself "simply ripping at designing costumes—he tells you how Lucile is battling to engage him, if he would only descend to commercialism" (Fish 41). Another Fish contribution, "The Art of Fashionable Portraiture: You Can't Quite Be 'It' Without the Aid of a Modernist Artist," suggests that the society woman might have her "portrait done by one of the cubist sculptors, who are causing such a furor—among themselves." She is advised: "Just ask the first sculptor you meet at dinner if he won't do a bust of you; he is sure to be a cubist.

---

[17]   See for example Lippmann; Ross; Wells.

[18]   On the parodies of modernist writing which appeared in *Vanity Fair*, *Life*, *The New Yorker*, the *Saturday Evening Post* and regional American newspapers, see Leick (132–3).

[19]   Fish was one of the most regular cartoonists for *Vanity Fair*, especially in the late 1910s, though she also drew for other magazines. Her work is most easily accessible via her large-format books, so I quote here from *High Society*, which reproduces features from *Vanity Fair*.

He will [...] oblige with a charming trifle, looking rather like an egg after a hard Easter" (Fish 45). The fraudulence of Fish's artist figures consists partly in their susceptibility to fashions and partly in their pretended denunciation of the commercial (in reality, they want to be given "free everything"). Their recognizability as "types" destroys their claim to the distinction and individuality which are the supposed hallmarks of fame.

Novelty and Nostalgia in *Vanity Fair*

The primary satiric target of the smart magazines was pretension. They rejected, in particular, those who seek distinction through fraudulent intellectual posturing or an adulterated "bohemianism." Yet at the same time, the whole success of magazines like *Vanity Fair* depended on the operation of pretension, in the sense defined by Pierre Bourdieu:

> Pretension, the recognition of distinction that is affirmed in the effort to possess it, albeit in the illusory form of bluff or imitation, inspires the acquisition, in itself vulgarizing, of the previously most distinctive properties; it thus helps to maintain a constant tension in the symbolic goods market, forcing the possessors of distinctive properties threatened with popularization to engage in an endless pursuit of new properties through which to assert their rarity. (251–2)

The appeal of the sophisticated magazines was founded precisely on their readers' quests for distinction, and the novelty of each new issue depended on a movement beyond—even a rejection of—what was celebrated in earlier issues.[20]

Vanity Fair—like modernism itself—continually marketed itself in terms of novelty and making new: the 1918 promotional text quoted at the start of this article appealed to "forward-minded Americans," while an advertisement dating from January 1916 ran: "We promise you, solemnly, that *Vanity Fair* is not just one more magazine; or even a new magazine of an old kind—but an altogether new kind of magazine. It is an entertaining magazine for Moderns" (11). The rhetorical modern-ness of *Vanity Fair*, *The Smart Set* and others is, though, interestingly balanced against their endemic nostalgia. As Susan Stanford Friedman explains:

> Modernity and tradition are relational concepts that modernity produces to cut itself off from the past, to distinguish the "now" from the "then." Modernity invents tradition, suppresses its own continuities with the past, and often produces

---

[20]   An interesting comparison might be made with *Cosmopolitan*, a highly successful general interest magazine established in 1886. The ethos of cosmopolitanism is related to sophistication, although there isn't space to explore the connection here. But as Berman notes, *Cosmopolitan* included many articles on new technologies, especially of transportation, and: "The implication, of course, is that what is new is cosmopolitan and that the magazine will be a harbinger of the new" (39).

nostalgia for what has been seemingly lost. Tradition forms at the moment those
who perceive it regard themselves as cut off from it. (434)

The nostalgia of the sophisticated magazines clearly inflects their construction of
celebrity images. They often harked back to an imagined era—usually identified
with the eighteenth century and Regency periods—when only genuinely original
people became famous. *Vanity Fair*, of course, shares its name with a novel set in
the eighteenth century, and was explicitly modeled on the British *Tatler*,[21] which
took its name from Richard Steele's paper, set up in 1709 to report on news and
gossip heard in the London coffeehouses. In keeping with this, Crowninshield ran
items such as a feature on dandyism and an imaginary letter from David Garrick
to John Barrymore, while many of the society features and satires are reminiscent
of eighteenth-century conduct literature (a genre which had been revived in the
popular etiquette books of the 1910s and 1920s).[22]

According to Anita Loos: "Crownie's magazine, together with *Smart Set*,
had an enormously civilizing effect on the United States; but while Mencken's
policy was to boot our native land into an awareness of culture, Crownie's was
to lead us there with a gentle, properly gloved hand" (*Girl* 145). Crowninshield's
repeated evocation of a lost age appears to contradict *Vanity Fair*'s claim to be
a harbinger of the new, yet the logic of sophistication actually depends on a
continual negotiation between an impulse towards novelty and a contrary longing
for a past era of elegance and intellectual polish. This approach is epitomized
by contributors such as Noël Coward, who combined the ultra-modern,
brittle style of the twenties with a nostalgic vision of aristocratic English life.
P.G. Wodehouse, a regular contributor, similarly offers access to a rose-tinted
country-house world, complete with witty butlers and dotty or dastardly lords.
Of course, the leisured aristocratic way of life retained a precarious existence in
England itself during the interwar years, but for American readers of *Vanity Fair*
(and, indeed, for middle-class readers everywhere) it was pure fantasy. For the New
York magazines, the feudal system apparently appealed because its elite is small
and membership cannot be achieved through the mechanisms of the marketplace.
(A comparison with the modernist ethos immediately suggests itself here.) Frank
Crowninshield repeatedly published texts which celebrated upper-class manners
and lifestyles, and with these gestures of his "properly gloved hand," he partially
concealed the economic basis of his operation and disguised the primarily middle-
class identity of his readership. This was essential because, as Litvak explains:

---

[21]   An advert stated: "In London alone there are seventeen papers like the 'Sketch'
and the 'Tatler'. In America there is not one [...] It is along the lines of these English
publications that we have planned 'Dress and Vanity Fair'." (*Vogue* 42.7 [1 Oct. 1913]: 16.)
Vanity Fair, though, rapidly became a more culturally rich magazine than its British models,
and retrospectively, it is clear that it owed much less to them than to *The Smart Set*.

[22]   See John Peale Bishop (on dandyism); Young (on Garrick). Emily Post's immensely
successful *Etiquette* (1922) represented the culmination of an extensive literature on modern
conduct and manners.

"once the ambitious, endemically imitative middle class buys into sophistication as a cultural value, as both a means and an index of social success, the arbiter of taste risks becoming [...] redundant" (229).

Vanity Fair, seeking to consolidate its authority in the sphere of taste, anxiously policed the boundaries of its supposedly select readership, occasionally publishing articles in foreign languages or difficult modernist poems. Yet in order to maintain itself financially, the magazine needed to attract an audience beyond the metropolitan elite to which it was ostensibly addressed, and its primary appeal was, of course, to those who aspired towards that elite.[23] This tension is legible in an advertisement which appeared in *Vogue* to herald the launch of *Dress and Vanity Fair*, as it was then called:

> Our ambition is not towards a popular magazine with a big subscription list. We don't expect everybody to be interested in "Dress and Vanity Fair," and, frankly, we shall not try to interest everybody. On the other hand, there are, we believe, a great number of people, who will thoroughly enjoy the cleverness, the variety, the dash and appreciate the fastidiousness and luxuriousness that shall in time make "Dress and Vanity Fair" the most distinctive among all American magazines.[24]

Despite the magazine's reiterated suggestion that these qualities of style and distinction are natural and inherent, its cross-class appeal actually depends on the assumption that such sophistication can be *learned*. Publicity material promised readers entry to a new world; for example, one promotional text, signed "D.P.," for Dorothy Parker, presents *Vanity Fair* as: "a whole course of study in the art of being a New Yorker," adding, "It's a Who's Who in New York." Parker's copy suggests that in order to operate successfully in the higher levels of New York society, it is necessary to be well informed about the current celebrities. *Vanity Fair*, she promises, will teach readers to "distinguish a musical comedy star from a débutante" and to "tell which were imagist poets, and which moving picture heroes." The modernist celebrity is here temporarily brought into alignment with the heroes of the entertainment industry, but at the same time, the text clearly suggests that regular readers of *Vanity Fair* will learn to discriminate confidently among these different—and differently valued—kinds of stars.

Frank Crowninshield positioned his journal as a tasteful arbiter of modern celebrity, and sought to accrue cultural authority by discriminating judgments between worthy and unworthy stars. *Vanity Fair*'s emphasis on originality is visible, on the one hand, in its mocking delineation of the predictable social "types" and disposable celebrities to be met with in modern society and, on

---

[23] Compare *Cosmopolitan*, with a readership encompassing the middle class and those who aspired to it: "Marketability pervaded the editorial pages as well [as the advertisements], providing voices, positions, and cultural experiences which [...] reinforce the desired social position of their audience" (Berman 43).

[24] *Vogue* 42.7 (1 October 1913): 16.

the other hand, in its celebration of individuals—often modernist artists—who are considered to have transcended these types and achieved "distinction." The magazine thus represents a site of intellectual curiosity and cultural aspiration combined with a healthy skepticism about pretension. Its repeated juxtaposition of modernist poems with full-page portraits of glamorous film stars epitomizes the complex ways in which the magazine contributed to the production of celebrity across cultural divides.

Many modernist artists and writers became famous not only through the circulation of their texts and signatures in restricted fields of literary production, but also through the exposure of their work, their names and their images, in medium-circulation periodicals. In turn, the modernists' growing cultural capital consolidated the smart magazines' reputations as taste-makers, and allowed them to participate extensively in the making of modernist reputations. Yet in their ambivalent relationships to the literary marketplace, magazines such as *The New Yorker*, *Vanity Fair* and *The Smart Set* disrupted stratified cultural organization, refusing to fit neatly into the hierarchy of populist weeklies, fashion glossies, and small literary magazines. Although "smart" and "slick" are useful ways of referring to these journals, I would argue that the best term for them is "sophisticated." This word sums up the qualities the magazines sought to embody, and gestures towards their strategy of maintaining their distinctiveness by means of continual repositionings in relation to a changing cultural context. Both the existing literary history of modernism, and the newer project of understanding modernism and celebrity, has been amplified and reevaluated through attention to these magazines.

Chapter 9
Reaching for Stars:
Jean de Tinan's "Essay on Cléo de Mérode Considered as Popular Symbol"[1]

Michael D. Garval

I have no reason not to continue philosophizing about Cléo.
—Jean de Tinan, *Think Success!* 203

Perhaps Jean de Tinan's unpublished "Essay on Cléo de Mérode considered as popular symbol" never existed; probably the manuscript has just been lost. But the idea of such an essay figures in Tinan's novel, *Think success! Or, the many and diverse loves of my friend Raoul de Vallonges* (1897), in which Vallonges, Tinan's largely autobiographical protagonist, tries but fails to write an "Essay on Cléo de Mérode considered as popular symbol," while suggesting much about what such an essay might say, if it could be written. Yet maybe it is the juxtaposition of the essay's desired success, and *mise-en-scène* of its failure, that best captures the elusive nature of celebrity, as mass cultural phenomenon, and as object of reflection for the modern intellectual.

Jean de Tinan (1874–1898) and Cléo de Mérode (1875–1966), largely forgotten today, were emblematic figures within the extraordinary cultural ferment of fin-de-siècle France. A promising young writer, Tinan frequented with such avant-garde luminaries as Henri de Toulouse-Lautrec, Claude Debussy, Colette and Willy, Pierre Louÿs, Jean Lorrain, Rachilde, Alfred Jarry, Stéphane Mallarmé and Paul Valéry.[2] He shared this creative cohort's early modernist sensibilities and strove for, but never achieved, comparable recognition: after a few years of intense literary activity, he died at 24. Mérode, a dancer, capitalized on her exceptional beauty and on the opportunities of a nascent celebrity culture, to propel herself to international renown. At the height of her career, in the decade surrounding 1900, she was the most photographed woman in the world, or at least her image was most widely and abundantly reproduced.[3] A key, transitional figure in the

---

[1]   All translations are mine.

[2]   Pseudonyms Colette, Willy and Rachilde refer to: novelist and dancer Sidonie-Gabrielle Colette; her husband, author and impresario Henri Gauthier-Villars, for whom Tinan worked as a ghostwriter; and novelist Marguerite Eymery.

[3]   Mérode's memoirs refer to her as "the most photographed woman in the world" (119). Likewise, a contemporary commentator calls her "the most photographed performer

history of celebrity and visual culture, she departed from the still-prevalent "great man" conception of fame *à la* Victor Hugo, to anticipate pop culture icons—film stars, singers, models—who would command public attention over the century ahead.[4] Eclipsed in turn by idols she heralded, Mérode lived out her long existence like a phantom from an earlier time: a more lucid, distinctly Parisian Norma Desmond. Tinan's and Mérode's divergent paths crossed however in his "Essay" project, a probing, if appropriately slippery, reflection on the emergence of mass media-driven stardom.

Amid growing tension between mainstream culture and avant-garde experimentation, there were important lines of convergence, but also critical fault lines, between the world of show business celebrities, and that of the intelligentsia. An artist like Toulouse-Lautrec built much of his reputation depicting popular entertainers; dancer Liane de Pougy indulged her literary ambitions by publishing thinly veiled *romans à clef*, encouraged in this by her partner in scandal and self-promotion, writer and journalist Jean Lorrain; conversely, aspiring author Colette achieved a certain notoriety as a stage performer, spurred on by her husband, the man of letters and impresario Willy, for whom she also worked as a ghost writer. For Tinan and Mérode, these worlds intersected most suggestively at crucial, early moments in their respective careers. Tinan aspired to the literary spotlight, first with an essay on Mérode; then, putting this manuscript aside, with a novel recounting the failed composition of such an essay. Before she was famous, Mérode apparently received a flattering, hand-written homage from a then-unknown author: Marcel Proust. Both Tinan and Mérode assigned great importance to these manuscripts that later disappeared—a coincidence perhaps, but evocative of the highly charged, troubled relationship between celebrity and modernist creative endeavors.

"Gloria, in excelsis Cléo ..."[5]

> Cléo de Mérode, probably the most beautiful woman alive. Her head, everyone knows.
>
> —Paul Klee, *Diaries* (1902) 94

Mérode entered the Paris Opera ballet at seven and as she worked up the ranks her beauty caught the public's eye. At 16 she debuted her trend-setting, hallmark

---

in France and throughout the world" (La Bicyclette, L'Opéra Cycliste: Les Danseuses [Bibliothèque Nationale, Opéra, clippings file C 657, c. 1896–1899, based on internal evidence]). Christian Corvisier notes, "While one cannot be sure that she was the most photographed woman of her day, she was the one whose image was reproduced the most, worldwide, on postcards" (53).

4   See my *A Dream of Stone* 204–6.

5   According to Mérode, the journalist and novelist Félicien Champsaur, who was obsessed with her and persecuted her with marriage proposals, coined this revealing phrase (271).

Fig. 9.1   Charles Ogereau, *Cléo de Mérode*. Postcard (c. 1895). Author's collection.

Fig. 9.2   Photo spread of Cléo de Mérode, *Metro Magazine* (August 1896).
              Anonymous. Author's collection.

hairstyle: over the ears, often in a chignon, often worn with metal bands. This already suggests Mérode's sense for cultivating her public image, maneuvering through a rapidly evolving cultural landscape, as earlier veneration of male literary idols gave way to an obsession with stage performers, especially female performers. Their enchanting effigies disseminated by ever more powerful and compelling visual media—the illustrated popular press, posters, postcards, all prefiguring cinema and television.

In 1896 Mérode became *the* hot new celebrity in Paris. Events cast her in an alluring if morally dubious role: as a hetaira, a high-class courtesan or concubine; in particular, as a modern incarnation of the ancient Greek courtesan Phryne, a favorite femme fatale figure in *fin-de-siècle* France, like her biblical counterpart Salomé. In late 1895 an alleged, probably apocryphal affair with Belgium's King Léopold II first attracted attention; the story continued into 1896, and well beyond, keeping tongues wagging and caricaturists busy for years. In spring 1896 Mérode won, overwhelmingly, a newspaper contest for the most beautiful woman on the Parisian stage. Soon thereafter, prominent sculptor Alexandre Falguière exhibited a full-length nude statue, titled *Dancer*, that depicted her face and distinctive coiffure. It was the *succès de scandale* of the 1896 *Salon*. Mérode probably did pose nude for the whole work, as Anne Pingeot has demonstrated, and Falguière was thought to have used plaster casting to render every contour of the ballerina's celebrated body. But she only admitted sitting for the bust (i.e., head and shoulders); the ensuing controversy provoked public curiosity and extensive press coverage.

Finally, that summer, Louis Ganne's ballet *Phryne* premiered in seaside resort Royan, with Mérode in the title role. It was a sensation—particularly the closing, courtroom scene. Sheathed in pink tights, Mérode simulated the nakedness that secured Phryne's acquittal. Her presence at the resort, on the beach, offered a public spectacle beyond her official nighttime performances, recalling a long, mythological, archetypal tradition of Venus Anadyomene (Venus rising from the sea) and anticipating the celebrity trope of seaside sensuality, from Mack Sennett's "Bathing Beauties," to Brigitte Bardot at Saint-Tropez, to *Baywatch*. All watched the star of the show, "the famed 'beauty queen,' 'the Phryne' applauded at the Grand Casino" (Mérode 146), her svelte silhouette concealed and revealed in the period's modest swimwear, ogled by "100 pairs of binoculars" (146)—anticipating the paparazzi's telescopic lenses, scanning for famous flesh.

For Mérode's contemporaries, the story of ancient Greek courtesan Phryne provided a key heuristic device for understanding the rise of modern stardom. Phryne's incomparable beauty drove wealthy and powerful men to ruin, yet she longed for fame, and gave herself for free to artists who would immortalize her. She is said to have posed for Praxiteles' Venus of Knidos, Western art's archetypal female nude, heralding so many Venuses to come. In the most celebrated episode of her life, Phryne was accused of profaning the Eleusinian mysteries, but acquitted when her unadorned body was revealed to the male judges. Yet perhaps their second ruling, beyond her acquittal, was of greatest interest. In Jean Richepin's 1896 version, the "stunning spectacle" of Phryne's nudity at her trial persuaded the magistrates that such beauty should be shared with the people. They ordered her to appear once a year and bathe naked in the sea, before crowds ashore, who would sing: "Blessed be divine Phryne, for she has given men's eyes and hearts the dazzling experience of Beauty itself!" (Richepin 169). Serving up famous beauty, offering the masses a dream of intimacy from afar, the scene already acts out a star-fan dynamic at the heart of celebrity culture. Phryne's official consecration, as a transcendent beauty for public consumption, also recalls Mérode's triumph, in that year's newspaper contest. While limited to Parisian performers, this prefigured the rise of competitions for national titles like Miss France or Miss America— a development Tinan anticipated, contending that Cléo de Mérode should serve as an official, "national representation" of beauty (204).

Her renown continued to blossom and in the following year, on leave from the Opera, she performed at Koster and Bial's in New York, an enterprising vaudeville theater. Amid tremendous hype, Mérode's Broadway run flopped. Her "chaste" classical dancing did not meet expectations for French naughtiness, heightened by her reputation as nude model, royal inamorata and latter-day Phryne (*Los Angeles Times* 31). But, back in Europe, the luster of a New York engagement launched her lucrative solo career. By 1899 she left the Opera for good, continued touring in France and across Europe through the eve of World War I, then occasionally until 1934.

As a performer, Cléo de Mérode was best known for her "Cambodian" dances at the 1900 Paris World's Fair, which struck a resonant chord at the height of French colonial expansion, amid fascination with exotica. Yet her greatest triumph was not on stage, but on postcards. By 1900 the postcard had come into its own as a medium, mass cultural phenomenon, and means for promoting celebrities. Still young, extraordinarily photogenic, and already famous, Mérode offered an ideal subject, in abundant guises and poses, sporting tutus, togas, tiaras, furs, feathers, gloves, hats. Such images usually originated in Parisian photographic studios, but competitors the world over made reproductions, emblazoned with greetings, captions, decorative elements. Circulating everywhere from Varna to Montevideo, these provided a new vehicle for international fame, disseminating celebrity effigies inexpensively, efficiently, with a seductive illusion of intimacy intensified by close-ups.

However good a dancer she was, Mérode's greatest gift lay in self-fashioning. Between her initial Phryne phase and emergence as international star of the not yet moving pictures, she seemed to trade her beautiful body for her lovely face, and alluring flesh for the second skin of her dazzling wardrobe, abandoning a conventional, courtesan model of female notoriety, to pioneer a new kind of stardom, at a time when film had been invented, but film stars had not. Visual evidence and contemporary accounts suggest she managed her photographic image masterfully, well before movie studio publicists or celebrity consultants and handlers, cultivating remarkable variety yet fundamental consistency, across myriad likenesses, displaying a studied awareness of herself, not as frankly sexual object, but as exquisite *objet d'art*.

Closer examination reveals a more complex picture. While reigning as the worldwide postcard queen of 1900, Mérode continued to perform courtesan-type roles that seemed a throwback, particularly the title part in a 1904 *Phryné* revival. At very least there was a gap between her postcard and stage personas. In a larger sense, Mérode may have exerted substantial control over the making of her photographic images, but far less over her broader public "image." She was "completely bewildered" by the dimensions that the "tale" of her liaison with Léopold assumed, "s[peeding] along, across France, throughout Europe, and around the world" (Mérode 155). Later in life and beyond, despite whatever she had accomplished in her career, despite subsequent decades of a quiet existence, teaching young girls to dance and working for Catholic charities, she would be remembered most—if at all—as a courtesan, notably in Simone de Beauvoir's *Second Sex*.[6] Even the part of Mérode's celebrity that seemed most within her grasp, her photographic portraits, could spin out of control, once images entered circulation:

> When I began to frequent [photographers'] studios, it was as if, like a sorcerer's apprentice, I had opened floodgates that were impossible to shut. Unscrupulous people copied the best photos, and used them to make an infinite number of postcards. These cards circulated all over the place; and, for a few pennies, anyone could buy himself a picture of "Cléo" […].

> When I would go dance in major cities abroad, what I noticed first of all were the racks, at newsstands and railway station bookshops, filled with postcards of me. If I ventured a few steps in the street, young girls would rush to buy these cards, and run after me, asking me to autograph them. This became such an obsession that often I gave up on going out, and preferred to stay shut away in my hotel room. (121–4)

This offers a virtual road map of celebrity culture in the century ahead—self-promotion gone awry, overzealous media, crazed fans, tormented stars—from Garbo's legendary reclusiveness, through Beatlemania, to "Brangelina fever."

While America spurned Mérode, it would embrace what she pioneered. In her meteoric rise to fame, her savvy (if by no means infallible) media manipulation, the dubious equation of her beauty with talent, and the international diffusion of her image—culminating in Belle Époque postcard mania—Mérode prefigured the reign of Hollywood stars, music idols, supermodels. Her elder contemporary Sarah Bernhardt, the great tragedian, claimed much the same cultural space as the great writer Victor Hugo had before, both in France and abroad, enjoying tremendous renown grounded in tremendous talent. But Mérode achieved celebrity far beyond what her distinction as a performer could justify.

This quality in particular—a fundamental emptiness, a remarkable degree of celebrity-for-celebrity's sake—makes her fame seem so modern. At worst,

---

[6]   Beauvoir referred to her as a "hetaira" in the first edition (390); Mérode won a symbolic franc in damages, and the passage was ordered cut from later editions.

Mérode rehearses the vacuous, short-lived stardom of figures like Britney Spears, or Loana Petrucciani, the go-go dancer turned television personality who won the French reality show *Loft Story* in 2001—figures who seem more mastered by their stardom than masters of it. At best, she heralds more enduring icons like Greta Garbo, Marilyn Monroe or Madonna, better able to control and successfully manipulate their public persona, despite the potential for tragic dissonance with whatever might remain of their private lives—thus Garbo's reclusiveness, or Monroe's suicide. Perhaps it's a dubious distinction, but Mérode deserves credit for recognizing new opportunities and figuring out how to exploit them, exploring the largely uncharted territory of mass celebrity, and of celebrity self-fashioning in particular.

Mérode and Tinan shared early insight into the emergence of modern stardom: she as practitioner, he as commentator. This is all the more remarkable since Tinan did not live to see Mérode's international apotheosis from 1900 onward, but rather examined what preceded and foreshadowed it: the initial French, largely Parisian, phase of her renown, as the press lavished attention, and shops hawked photographs—often those later disseminated, yet more widely, on postcards. His prescient observations anticipated much about the broader rise of celebrity as transcendent ideal, opium of the people and puzzle for the intelligentsia, obsession and mirage.

Tinan's Essay

Published in 1897, *Think success!* was written between 1894 and 1896. The title highlights the novel's overriding theme, the futile yet rewarding quest for "success" (literary, intellectual, romantic). The novel, which Mallarmé saw as an update of Flaubert's *Sentimental Education*, relates Vallonges's amorous adventures from adolescence to manhood. Blending fictional material with passages from his own journals, Tinan relates events with a disarming mix of cynicism and vulnerability, idealism and lucidity, while vacillating among narrative voices: third-person (the narrator), first-person (Vallonges), even second-person (in the "long letter" that makes up much of chapter eight, which Mallarmé considered a "marvel"). Hybrid, exploratory, experimental, perhaps but a "preface" for more mature works to come (as the epilogue claims), *Think success!* is truer in its essayistic approximations than more polished pieces would be, more 'touching' in its imperfections than whatever might follow (295–6).

Written largely in 1896—Cléo de Mérode's *annus mirabilis*—chapter six considers her sudden celebrity. Its full, mock-epic title is ORIGIN, RISE AND FALL OF AN 'ESSAY ON CLÉO DE MÉRODE CONSIDERED AS POPULAR SYMBOL.' Vallonges first lingers in bed, perusing morning papers "quite preoccupied with Mlle Cléo de Mérode" (197), indeed "haunted by her" (203), from the headlines to the classified ads ("Yng. orphn., grt. rssmblnce. to Cléo…

requests...pass[age de l']Opéra 27."[7] He is supposed to pick up his mistress Suzette for lunch, but seems in no rush. While readying himself, his thoughts on provisional immortality, prefiguring Warhol's 15-minute fame for all, drift toward the star of the day: "Everything is immortal—at least for a while; and this morning Mlle Cléo de Mérode strikes me as particularly immortal" (200).

Considering Mérode's effect on the populace, Vallonges harks backward, while reflecting upon new developments. She is preceded by other legendary beauties ("a few graceful or fierce women to concentrate the attention of overly civilized crowds"), but the public's relation to such figures has been transformed by modern media—journalistic discourse on celebrity (with its attention to "little scandals that are just ploys" or its "daily drone of innocuous prattle"), and also photography:

> Our neo-byzantinism has transformed ancient crowds' thunderous enthusiasm for prostituted empresses...but the same feeling that in past sent admiration and furor hurtling toward the palaces now makes curious or breathless passersby linger before shop windows crammed with photographs. (200–201)

Photos in shop windows, transfixing passersby, evoke modern celebrity culture's visual turn, and paradoxical mix of distance and proximity. New media allow celebrities to appear close but remain far. Fans reach futilely for stars, thus Tinan's "mix of curiosity and pity for all whom a sheet of glass separates from something useless that they watch intently" (201–2). But, above all, the public's obsession with Mérode exemplifies the paradoxes of celebrity stargazing, as admirers

> get a little pang in their chest when yet another image—and often they have never seen *Her*—makes its way into the little ideal album through which we leaf in our dreams and reveries.
>
> Ah! Imagine someone *loving* her with an impossible love, loving her from across display windows, and jealous...curious psychoses... . (202–3)

These "psychoses" are "curious," but common. Impossible love for celebrity icons becomes part of modern sentimental education, as individual experiences of love, beauty, desire get filtered through celebrity culture's mass machinery. Tinan's contemporaries internalize such pre-packaged stuff of dreams: "a little ideal album," much like the published albums of stage beauties popular at the time (e.g., *Nos jolies actrices*, including Mérode, published in 1895–1896). The modern Pygmalion—modern Everyman—no longer frames and animates his own vision of an ideal woman; the media supplies an image, brought to life through countless fans' collective gaze.

The multitude votes with its eyeballs, electing Mérode its idol. So why not make this official?

---

[7]   This Cléo look-alike's come-on calls to mind a story about prostitutes disguised as Hollywood actresses (Braudy 579).

It would be appropriate, from generation to generation, that a priestess be named, to make the people understand—they would perhaps understand, after all—that Beauty has a "national representation." Juliette Récamier was necessary, but she had a "salon"…which displeases me. I would however be pleased to see required of Mlle Cléo de Mérode, in exchange for a large state subsidy, that she be there where her presence can best move the elite or the crowd. At Gallery openings, at Dress rehearsals and Premieres, at Great Receptions of an official sort, at racetracks, adorned with all the luxury one could desire, accompanied by a special escort, poised upon the velours of her box or reclining upon the pillows of her carriage…she would convey the idea that, during the twilight of latin culture's reign, it is fitting to exaggerate as much as possible the homage we owe to exceptional beauty…[H]ow much more interesting it would be, more flattering for the posterity of our civilization, if it were legislated and official. (204)

Juliette Récamier (1777–1849) was a celebrated beauty, painted by Jacques-Louis David and Baron Gérard. Her image continued to be reproduced widely in Tinan's time, through popular prints, porcelain, advertising, making her a de facto national beauty for nearly a century. She prefigured the role Tinan envisions for Mérode,[8] that would indeed become "legislated and official" in the twentieth century, through the Miss France contest, and the patterning of Marianne, the personification of the French Republic, on female celebrities.[9] Yet, with an influential salon, Récamier was also a key intellectual player, however displeasing this might be from the later nineteenth century's generally misogynistic, anti-bluestocking perspective (articulated by figures like Guy de Maupassant and Jules Barbey d'Aurevilly). Tinan envisions a tribute to sheer pulchritude, devoid of concern for women's intellect. While such an "exaggerated homage to exceptional beauty" anticipates the rise of beauty queens, celluloid sex symbols, supermodels—the triumph of celebrity eye candy—Tinan remains preoccupied with the role of the implicitly male intellectual. Mérode should appear "where her presence can best move the elite or the crowd" (204). He notes elsewhere the "dissatisfaction of the anxious crowd, to which we too belong" (201). Such turns of phrase betray a necessary but uneasy juxtaposition: the intelligentsia and the crowd stand together and apart, in their mutual fascination with shimmering but unattainable stars.

The chapter's middle section ponders this relation at length:

The shifting, moving crowd flows along the boulevards, beneath arcades, around parks, at each point renewed and resembling itself; beyond the abstract term that designates it, the crowd's clearly defined sensibility, the latent power that

---

[8]   Mérode remembers baritone Lasalle always greeting her with, "Bonjour, Madame Récamier!"(110); in the 1920s, American-born German movie star Fern Andra played both Mérode and Récamier in respective film versions of their lives.

[9]   The Miss France contest began in the 1920s. Since 1970, a series of French actresses and models, including Brigitte Bardot, Catherine Deneuve and Laetitia Casta, have been chosen to pose for the official bust of Marianne.

its concerted action would unleash, affirms a perseity, independent, amid our reveries…[*une perséité indépendante de nos reveries…*]. (206)

"Perseity," from "per se," means the quality of being in itself, and "our reveries" refers to intellectuals' musings. But does the crowd's "perseity" somehow stand out as an "independent" *and* integral part of our reveries? Or is it rather "independent of," i.e., separate from "our reveries"? What continuity or discontinuity exists between the intelligentsia and the crowd? Is the crowd the quintessence of the intellectual's reflections, or a world apart? Tinan's ambiguous syntax captures his ambivalence.

To make sense of mass celebrity, you need to figure out what the crowd is thinking, plumb its "collective soul" (207). But intellectuals and common folk perceive "a given spectacle" (207)—a manifestation of entertainment culture, in which modern celebrity flourishes—with differing degrees of intensity and awareness. Intellectuals make "innumerable connections which they note with care…tenuous connections that amuse the cultivated mind" (207). For "vulgar" laborers, "it's like a bullet shot into a wall," spawning "general ideas…perhaps more powerful in their simplicity" however "almost never…known by those for whom they could illuminate the general meaning of life." Intellectuals' greater subtlety and self-awareness may attenuate the emotion of their brushes with celebrity, whereas common men can be plugged into something more primal, but remain barely conscious of this. The intellectual therefore interprets the crowd's reactions, piecing together fragments, to envision its mindset:

> it is rare to find gestures or sentences through which we can gather the intimate feelings of those who do not yet manage to think. An attitude, an exclamation makes us see them, in an instant, truer than if they tried to explain themselves with great difficulty; and, for this reason, these are infinitely precious things, worth noting precisely. (208)

Above all, beauty stirs the crowd: "[T]he emotion of beauty" is omnipresent, its two most common forms being "admiration of the starry sky, and admiration of women…the infinite twinkling of the stars, and the Life force, whose splendor appears in Women." Paradoxically, apprehension of beauty is also "among the most distant and inaccessible" (208) of sentiments, difficult to articulate and evaluate. However, "latent thoughts that remain hidden in confused minds sometimes can be inferred through an unconscious gesture or exclamation, signifying the entire collective soul of a race, the entire soul of the living crowd" (209). Scrutinizing how beauty affects the populace would offer particular challenges, but also particular rewards—a royal road to understanding modern society's obsessions.

If women and stars are Tinan's exemplars of beauty, wouldn't his ideal object of study be a woman who is, metaphorically, a star? He does conclude the central part of his chapter by setting sights on Mérode:

> To motivate an essay on the real, profound emotion that a brush with beauty gives life, even for hurried passersby whose humdrum existence makes one shudder,

I have chosen the delicate face framed by tresses, smiling behind all the shop windows. Sounding the depths of all these souls for the spell she has cast upon them, I aim to compose, beside Cléo de Mérode's graceful effigy, the image of Herself seen through the prism of attentive or accidental admiration—of Herself CONSIDERED AS POPULAR SYMBOL.

Vallonges stood up: "I'll make a preface out of this," he declared. (210)

Tinan teases with this apparent thesis, only a slippery statement of intention—neither a beginning nor an end, but a project for a project, further refracted through the lens of his double Vallonges. So where—if anywhere—might his essay be?

Lost Manuscripts

And I really like the little game of epigraphs.
                    —Jean de Tinan, "A Document on the inability to love"

Chapter six's remaining two sections further enhance the mystification. Encountering his friend Lionel Silvande (Pierre Louÿs's double), Vallonges vaunts his "admirable," "unique" subject, projecting

developments on the Idea of Beauty, on the Idea of Elegance, on the Idea of Dance, on Aperitifs, on the Idea of Royalty, on the Aesthetics of Photography […]; on the Aesthetics of Statuary; on the Idea of Scandal; on the Idea of Advertising; on the Ideal of Sensual Pleasure […] On the value of Smiles; on the Philosophy of Fashion; on the meaning of the Bicycle; on the Idea of hair […]; on Botticelli; on new trends in Commercial Display; on Modesty, from Antiquity to the present day […]. (211)

Silvande adds "…Ice pops, mint drops, caramels, oranges…," and Vallonges, "…Barley water, soda pop, beer,—in short, God, Man, and the World! It's a subject that really lends itself." "With little interest," retorts Silvande. Whether Mérode's celebrity is the most substantial or inconsequential of subjects, the question remains: will Vallonges write his essay? He ventures only that he "will have the intention of doing it" (212). Finally, we learn that the essay "was never completed—and it's quite a shame" (212).

Like a hall of mirrors, Tinan's chapter creates the illusion of an essay, particularly through paratextual manuevering. The chapter's ostensible heart, Vallonges's "li'l meditation" on Mérode, begins and ends with spurious epigraphs—first, a paradoxical, probably apocryphal quotation:

Really—there is a line from Leconte de Lisle (no doubt) that seems especially destined to serve as an epigraph for whatever treatise one might wish:
What matters whatever's not immortal! (200)

The second epigraph proves more slippery still. Had he written his essay, Vallonges would have borrowed from Leontios (cf. Anthology) an adequate epigraph:

> *"O Rhodocleia, the tenth Muse, the fourth Grace, you enchant mortal man and adorn the city,—you have such eyes, such winged feet, such eloquent fingers, as neither the Muses nor Graces do have."*

It would have been quite good. (212–13)

Not Leontios however but Rufinus, in the *Greek Anthology*, lauds lovely Rhodocleia—a name no doubt chosen here as a partial anagram of Cléo de Mérode. Superlative yet superfluous, Rhodocleia would be the most charming in each cohort, but cannot belong to either (nine Muses, three Graces). By this point we also know Vallonges won't write his essay, making its second would-be epigraph as illusory as Rhodocleia—and perhaps as Mérode herself, in her sudden celebrity.

These epigraphs betray a broader pattern. The chapter builds up to then retreats from its supposed subject. In a series of procrastinatory activities, rhetorical throat-clearing exercises, Vallonges dallies, lingers, luxuriates, dresses slowly, smokes cigarettes, before embarking upon his "meditation," that yields only what he says he will make into a preface. There follows his conversation with Silvande about what he hasn't written; regrets that the essay will never be completed; the second bogus epigraph; and, an ultimate, isolated, parenthetical comment: "(April 1897…'*No doubt it's quite late to still talk about it…*')." This proffers closure without saying anything, except perhaps that, with everything deferred and delayed, nothing ends up said. When Vallonges envisions publishing his essay, he imagines the trappings ("A portrait of Cléo by Léandre, pink and apple-green cover […] Prolegomena. Paralipomena. Numerous philosophical notes and methodical iconography" (211–12) without mentioning the essay itself. And, as it appears— or rather doesn't appear—in his novel, Tinan's essay is all prologue and epilogue, words before and words after, with the body missing.

Much ado about nothing? Not exactly. At very least, chapter six's elaborate mise-en-scène acts out the absence of Tinan's own essay on Cléo de Mérode— unpublished during his lifetime, likely lost afterward. By spring 1896, Tinan had published several articles and two slim volumes, *A Document on the inability to love* and *Erythrée*, in small print runs. These had attracted some attention in literary circles, but the ambitious 22-year-old yearned for more. For some time Tinan had admired Cléo de Mérode, delighting in photos of her in classmates' desks and, when they lived nearby, conspiring to run into her, prompting "delicious bouts of insomnia" (Goujon 203). When she rose to stardom in 1896, he thought to capitalize on this by writing an essay about her. In March, Tinan plugged his "forthcoming" *Essay* in *Erythrée*, and published in the journal *Le Livre d'Art* the brief "preface" that figures, unchanged, in chapter six of *Think Success!* (202). He seems to have written the rest of the essay in March and April; read it to Valéry, who offered advice; planned its release for the fall, indeed Lorrain's popular weekly column announced its imminent publication. Meanwhile Louÿs, who had urged Tinan to write and publish this, decided that his friend needed a novel to jumpstart his career. Tinan put the manuscript in a drawer—with regrets, since his essay *"was finished"* (Goujon 205; Tinan's emphasis)—and set to work on *Think Success!*

What became of the manuscript? The only trace, in a 1941 auction catalogue, provides a brief description: a dedication to a beautiful woman, followed by a *Note on epigraphs*; Tinan himself then Vallonges waking up lazily; three friends and their mistresses (Vallonges, Suzette, et al) at a restaurant lunch, trading clever banter, freewheeling opinions, quotations from leading authors, before going their separate ways (Goujon 204). It would thus have contained similar elements as chapter six, though arranged more elaborately, with similar emphasis on mise-en-scène, rather than exposition. Perhaps this somewhat fuller treatment of the same material likewise acted out Tinan's difficulties vis-à-vis his subject. He may not have managed to say much about Mérode or her fame, at least not much more than in his novel. But he felt compelled to try.

Tinan valued his essay project, intending it to establish his literary reputation in a way previous publications had not. Vestiges of this hope still inform chapter six's subtitle: "To impress upon the reader that Vallonges is a 'man of letters'" (195). Fragments of argumentation in the chapter (on crowds, the press, photography) also show that, through Mérode, he aimed at something essential about his society, about modernity—the rise of a pervasive celebrity culture. In the process, he tried to strike a deal with this new order, framing a symbiosis between himself and Mérode, the intellectual and the star. His essay would explain, elevate, exalt her stardom, ennoble her "popularity." In return, her fame would provide a springboard into his own. Like contemporary academics' MLA sessions on Madonna, it promised (though did not exactly deliver) a double illumination—the thinker shining his lofty analysis upon her celebrity, the star projecting her celebrity upon his intellectual endeavors. In the post-Hugo universe of *fin-de-siècle* France, writers could no longer aspire to their illustrious predecessor's monumental radiance. But they might bask in the reflected light of the period's new show-business idols, like moons set aglow by the sun. Perhaps, in exchange, entertainers might gain some of the respectability, legitimacy, and high cultural prestige that French writers had retained, while relinquishing transcendent fame.

Such aspirations also inform a lost manuscript anecdote in Mérode's memoirs. Since 1890 or 1891 she had befriended young composer Reynaldo Hahn. In 1894 or 1895, he introduced her to his "best friend" (and lover at the time), Marcel Proust. They would converse about music and poetry, with Mérode sharing her taste for Verdi, Wagner, Baudelaire, Verlaine, Rimbaud:

> Marcel Proust seemed surprised; no doubt he did not think a simple dancer capable of understanding great music or subtle poetry. Together we three had conversations as free and confidential as those I had with Reynaldo alone. Marcel Proust...spoke to me of my art, my face, my poses, with such infinite loveliness and delicacy. After a certain number of meetings, he gave me a manuscript entitled: *Portrait. To Cléo de Mérode.* Ten full pages, his quite curious handwriting covering the paper with its flowing lines, and letters intertwined

like vines. I should have learned this text by heart, it was admirable. His thought
shone through, like a vein of ardent gold, amid the twists and turns of a style
filled with images of stirring poetry, and events whose every word was charged
with meaning. Had I been a prophet, I should have seen the author's great literary
future in this portrait of me, sumptuous and shimmering like a Ravenna mosaic.
I preserved carefully this magnificent gift, a testimony of great value, of which
I had every right to be proud. Alas! I did not hide it well enough; during the last
war it was stolen from my home, along with several other valuable documents.
I was devastated by this loss. (98–9)

Rival dancer and courtesan Liane de Pougy prided herself on luring Hahn away
from his homosexual predilections for a memorable one-night stand; Mérode, on
conquering Hahn and his lover, the future great writer, with her intellect, her art.
Casting its golden aura, Proust's *Portrait* confirms her distinction as far more than
a "simple dancer." The lost manuscript is also a lost origin: just before Proust
published his first book, *Pleasures and Days* (1896), Mérode would already have
inspired him to realize the potential of his "great literary future."

The manuscripts for Tinan's *Essay* and Proust's *Portrait* share much, from
their common focus on Cléo de Mérode; to their genesis in Paris, during the mid
1890s, amid aspiring artists; to their disappearance during World War II. Together,
they tell a story about a key moment in modern intellectual and cultural history,
amid modernist ferment in the arts, in parallel with the rise of early mass celebrity.
What kind of story? It's a utopian reverie of mutual fascination, understanding,
and inspiration, between elite intellectuals and show business stars—but also a
cautionary tale of their failed, perhaps impossible dialogue. And these extremes
would continue to frame the difficult yet productive relationship between
modernism and celebrity.

Perhaps France's tradition of public intellectuals would give this a particular
inflection. At mid-century, Simone de Beauvoir and Jean-Paul Sartre played to the
media spotlight, styling themselves as models of literary excellence, philosophical
rigor, and intellectual *engagement* (ironically, while disparaging Mérode in her
magnum opus, Beauvoir also had an American adventure, that recalled and in
some ways outstripped the dancer's).[10] In 1964 Sartre reaped far greater publicity
from refusing the Nobel Prize for Literature than he would have by accepting it,
but two decades later, when Claude Simon was awarded the 1985 prize, few in
France or abroad had heard of this arduous, experimental writer. The year before,

---

[10]   On Beauvoir's and Sartre's celebrity, see Garval 231–5. During her visits to the U.S.
in the late 1940s, Beauvoir achieved a level of success and abandon that eluded Mérode.
The press celebrated this exemplar of French style and sophistication, who likewise sported
a severe and distinctive hairdo. She also embarked upon a torrid romance with the gritty
American writer Nelson Algren, and did not object as his friend the photographer Art Shay
captured her nude, with her back to the camera, when the bathroom door was left open
(reproduced, amid controversy, on the January 3, 2008, cover of the French magazine *Le
Nouvel observateur*).

however, Marguerite Duras's challengingly avant-gardist memoir, *The Lover*, became a best-seller, due largely to its erotic-exotic appeal, with the author's self-portrait as a "little white prostitute" in colonial Indochina like a distant echo of Mérode's courtesan pose and "Cambodian" dances—or perhaps, more recently, of the tremendously popular soft porn film series *Emmanuelle*.

More broadly speaking, despite potential for cross-fertilization between the realms of the modern creator and that of the show business star, there are dangers: self-destructiveness, superficiality and, ultimately, polarization. Ernest Hemingway, the iconic writer who frequented movie stars, and Marilyn Monroe, the iconic movie star once married to a great playwright, would both be driven to despair and suicide. Artists like Andy Warhol or Jeff Koons would toy relentlessly with the trappings of celebrity, spurring dissenters to cry charlatanism and pandering. Today there seems to be an increasing gap, with an arcane avant-garde condemned to marginality or irrelevance, while a triumphantly narcissistic celebrity culture revels in its own shimmering but hollow image. Perhaps then it is the fate of Tinan's and Mérode's lost manuscripts, rather than whatever they promised, that remains most prophetic, and most poignant.

Chapter 10
Leni's Hitler/Hitler's Leni

Annalisa Zox-Weaver

Go laughing down the way of your great calling. Here you have found your
heaven and in it you will be eternal.[1]

— Julius Streicher to Leni Riefenstahl, 1937

[S]he was not only the sole motion-picture director, she was the only woman
on the great parade field—one white linen skirt moving freely before fifty four
thousand green-woollen, mechanical men, one professional woman on her
job…among the quarter-million spectators assembled there wasn't a person who
didn't know who she was.[2]

— Janet Flanner, *The New Yorker*, 1936

In her notoriously unreliable memoir, Leni Riefenstahl provides an impressively
detailed account of a 1937 conversation with the Austrian-American auteur Josef
von Sternberg. As she recalls, Sternberg praises the director's work in *Triumph
of the Will*, draws favorable comparisons between Riefenstahl and Marlene
Dietrich, and makes a plea for insider knowledge about what Hitler is "really
like." Characteristically, Riefenstahl recounts the dialogue as an opportunity to
substantiate her desirability and to pronounce upon the misery of her obligations
as the Führer's filmmaker and the many "conspiracies" she was victimized by as
a result of the privileges such work afforded. The exchange ends with Riefenstahl
dejectedly remarking that, "Fame doesn't bring happiness" (219).[3]

While the accuracy of the Sternberg conversation is disputable, the realities it
betrays are nonetheless meaningful for what they tell us about Riefenstahl's lifelong
project to self-fashion and self-mythologize. From her early career in dance and
her daring performances in Arnold Fanck's Alpine films, to her transformation
into auteur for *The Blue Light*, unsurpassed cinematic glorification of Hitler for
Triumph of the Will, and celebration of the human bodies, Hellenistic aesthetics,
and physical exertion in *Olympia*, Riefenstahl never wavered from her pursuit of

---

[1]   Qtd in Bach, 83.

[2]   Flanner, 22.

[3]   Riefenstahl titled the English edition of her memoir *The Sieve of Time* after an Albert
Einstein quotation, which she uses as an epigraph: "So many things have been written about
me, masses of insolent lies and inventions, that I would have perished long ago, had I paid
any attention. One must take comfort in the fact that time has a sieve, through which most
trivia run off into the sea of oblivion" (219).

fame. She doggedly promoted herself and her work, casting aside all expressions of loyalty and personal obligation, revising and recrafting her personal history at will. If celebrity is indeed, as the *OED* has it, "the condition of being much talked about," such circumstances were the norm for her, beginning with the mixed acclaim she received for the dance hall performances of her teen years. Riefenstahl basked in the glories of praise and enviability for the first 15 or so years of her adult life; for the remaining 65, she parried condemnation and infamy by busily shifting blame, issuing denials and rationalization, erasing the names of Jewish collaborators, engaging in litigation, and enduring numerous denazification tribunals (Luckhurst and Moody 1). Over the course of her 90-year career, she earned the admiration of Walt Disney, Charlie Chaplin, and Jean Cocteau, and in her later years gained highly dubious cult status among feminists and film aestheticists as well as a bizarre assortment of celebrity admirers from Mick and Bianca Jagger, Siegfried and Roy, and Madonna, to George Lucas and Andy Warhol, whose cult status is a source of particular interest in her memoir. Although Riefenstahl would never escape her designation as "the Nazi Filmmaker," she was "much talked about" for her entire life and beyond, demonstrating in her own way that, as Leo Braudy has put it, "[i]n a world preoccupied with names, faces, and voices, fame promises acceptability, even if one commits the most heinous crime" (562).

Still, the peculiar, protean quality of Riefenstahl's stature makes her difficult to categorize. Admired and famous in Germany, while loathed and famous in most of the western world, Riefenstahl was, in her day, indisputably a celebrity. In a strange way, her prominence demonstrates an unlikely example of an assertion Noël Coward once made of his dual identity as famous entertainer and spy: "Celebrity was wonderful cover" (Koch 24). Though the remark's context and implications differ radically for the two, it captures the spirit of Riefenstahl's persistently irreconcilable location at the convergence of modernism, celebrity, and fascism. In her hands, cinematic avant-garde technique serves the ultimate seduction and mobilization of the masses; what results is charismatic leader as commodity, a figure of racial purity and unassailable superiority who embodies and advances the will of the dispossessed. He is, at once, icon and everyman, as much celebrity as ideological leader. To Riefenstahl, Hitler was a muse and a proxy, an investment in her own career and a direct path to her own celebritydom. And yet, very quickly that fame became its own sort of cover, a duplicity and a distraction from understanding the extent to which Riefenstahl ever believed in the Nazis she so carefully promoted. Indeed, Riefenstahl had no shortage of covers; her early love of stage and then screen readily demonstrated her craving for display and performance, disguise and impersonation, so that in her role as filmmaker of *Triumph of the Will*, Riefenstahl configures Hitler as yet another cover for herself. Her cover is not only Hitler but also the cinematic medium itself, which allowed her to expand and exploit modernist affections for transcendent value and atemporality, myth and mythification, self-transformation and stylization of the body. As the quintessential document of fascism, *Triumph of the Will* promulgates illusions of wholeness (the all-meaning Hitlerian body, at-one-ness between leader and people, total projection and identification, the will to sacrifice to the larger good), but does so with an unabashed rehearsal of the techniques of cinematic modernism—aesthetic self-consciousness, fragmentation, montage technique, abstraction, and so on. But these spectacular techniques themselves come to cover the moral reprehensibility and ideological horror of the film and transmute Hitler from brown-shirted politician to hyper-visualized celebrity.

In *History of the German Film*, cultural theorist Siegfried Kracauer added several pages of analysis on *Triumph of the Will*. Originally composed for the Museum of Modern Art, and under the auspices of museum curator Iris Barry, "Propaganda and the Nazi War Film" explicates the film's gratuitous exploitation of the triad of "commentary, visuals, and sound" (298). Strangely, Kracauer refers to the film as a "very impressive composition of mere newsreel shots," but then proceeds to devote close analysis to its "cinematic techniques…of constant panning, traveling, tilting up and down," adding extensive commentary on its "total movement," "officially fabricated mass ornament," and "*tableaux vivants*" (300, 302). Though this piece would later bear an enormous influence over "Fascinating Fascism," Susan Sontag's infamous excoriation of Riefenstahl's *oeuvre*, it in fact spends very little time discussing the authority or intentions of director, instead speaking of the film as more or less a patented rehearsal of Nazi film and totalitarian propaganda in general. That Riefenstahl indulged her own personal and professional agenda does not appear to be of critical concern to Kracauer.

Riefenstahl Rise

The Sternberg anecdote—and its facile retrospective insight—is fortuitously placed in her timeline, as 1937 was, in many ways, the final year before her fame transformed, irrevocably and with far-reaching consequences, into infamy. Traveling to America in the following year, Riefenstahl would be forced outside of the hermeticism of her brazenly ignorant fantasy of a benevolent Third Reich. But while America's radical departure from the comforts of a propagandized Nazi fatherland jarred her from the comforts of her extreme narcissism and threw her into an even more entrenched stance of personal defensiveness, it was Hollywood's mobilization of hostile forces that finally forced Riefenstahl to confront the fixed outer limits of her fame. The media frenzy that surrounded Riefenstahl in America peaked and fizzled during the course of her visit, so that by the time she departed she was, for the first time since she had gained fame, not talked about. She found that obscurity brought even less happiness than notoriety.

Beyond Hitler, beyond the world of German cinema, and beyond her unprecedented accomplishments as an auteur, Riefenstahl had always held out success in the Hollywood studio system as the ultimate form of professional validation and the certain measure of cinematic celebrity. It was her cherished ambition to join the coterie of German talent that had hastily fled the purified new Germany she vigorously promoted in her films. Instead, America would serve as the site of moral reckoning for Riefenstahl, who not only arrogantly believed that her fame held universal currency, but also grossly underestimated the public's perception of her image as interconstituent with that of Hitler. Before the scope and potential of Hitler's dark intentions had become internationally apparent, American publications rather uncritically promoted her on its covers, dubbing her "Hitler's Friend" (*Newsweek* 16) and "Hitler's Leni Riefenstahl" (*Time* 38). Riefenstahl eagerly embraced these characterizations, seeing collaboration with the Nazi leader as symbiotic and mutually beneficial. Even while the German studio system remained indifferent to her talents, the Third Reich embraced her. Propaganda minister Joseph Goebbels, identifying Riefenstahl as a vital advocate to the grand intentions of the Nazi superstructure, enthused in a diary entry from 1933: "She is the only one of all the stars who understands us" (qtd in Bach 109). Eager for recognition beyond the cultish successes of the Alpine film genre, Riefenstahl positioned herself as Hitler's cinematic maker, to this end calculatedly implicating herself in his very image, cultivating intimacy and promoting a selective (and morally careless) relationship to the power apparatus that sustained him. Controlling his public image became a direct way for her to cultivate her own.

With *Triumph of the Will* (1934) Riefenstahl eagerly and inextricably hitched her star to the rising Nazi Party, producing the cinematic apotheosis of "fascist aesthetics" and staging Hitler's visual and corporeal image as an exploration of her own projections and assumed shared affinities. Whatever fascination Hitler may have held for Riefenstahl as an ideologue was immaterial compared to what he offered as a cinematic subject: her celluloid Hitler signals her own desire for absolute authority and self-invention as an icon. Though Riefenstahl is not exceptional for producing a career through an unholy alliance with Hitler, she does present a unique case study for the professional implications of appropriating *his* iconization in order to enact her own artistic superiority. Thus her film's hypervisualized Hitler becomes symptomatic of her deep anxieties about professional achievement and ambivalent longing to have a captivating public image. If *Triumph of the Will* demonstrates Hitler's love of the stage, over-focus upon the body, parasitic reliance upon spectacles, and need for mindless adoration, it also reflects how Riefenstahl sought to represent herself just as vigilantly through these same modes of image and authority production. Making *Triumph of the Will* was pivotal in Riefenstahl's effort to proclaim her self image as filmmaker, representing at once a culmination of almost 20 years of professional ambitions and a death knell to the cinematic career and public adoration she so keenly set her sights upon.

"Germany's Garbo"[4]

Before Hitler, there was Hollywood, although such aspirations seem thoroughly quixotic as Riefenstahl never even achieved any measurable success in Weimar

---

[4]   Frank Deford, "The Ghost of Berlin," *Sports Illustrated* (4 August 1986): 50.

cinema. Her place in the film studios of Ufa, Universum-Film Aktiengesellschaft—
"the world's only meaningful rival to Hollywood"—was limited to work in her
twenties as an unbilled day player in *Ways to Strength and Beauty*, described by
her biographer, Steven Bach, as "a full-length 'culture' feature devoted to physical
fitness and exercise, mostly in the out-of-doors and mostly in the altogether" (3).
While the careers of Marlene Dietrich and Asta Nielson were gathering momentum
on the sound stages of Ufa, Riefenstahl lived out the rise and fall of a fairly
impressive dancing career (from October 1923 to May 1924 she performed in 70
engagements), took minor modeling jobs, and entered beauty contests. Along the
way, she jealously archived all reviews of her work, putting together a scrapbook of
strategically edited articles she would use as a tool of fervent self-promotion (29).
For Riefenstahl, crafting and chronicling her reputation were simultaneous and
equally imperative undertakings. Hers was, from the very beginning, a highly self-
conscious project of public packaging and mediation through which subjectivity
would be willingly conceded in a high stakes bids for increased public exposure.

As she recalls it, her transformation into an actress occurred on the platform of
a train station, where a poster for Arnold Fanck's Weimar mountain film *Bergfilm*
(*Mountain of Destiny*) propelled her to meet Luis Trenker, an Austrian-Italian
actor who earned his reputation with Fanck but would go on to become one of
Nazi propaganda's most beloved actors. "I am going to be in your next picture,"
she informed her future leading man, pronouncing her imminent successes with
characteristic assurance and determination (43). And when a knee injury ended her
dance career, the move to film acting seemed like part of the inevitable trajectory
of her calling as an illustrious performer.

The Alpine dramas of Arnold Fanck, a geological engineer turned "father of
the alpine film," soon defined and delimited Riefenstahl's place as a screen actress.
Beginning in 1926, she emerged as a star in *The Holy Mountain*, and went on to
make half a dozen or so other films with Fanck, all of which single-mindedly
promoted the virtues of vigorous physical culture and dare-devil athleticism among
the glacial elements. The romantic melodrama of the plots—Siegfried Kracauer
derided them as "a mixture of sparkling ice-axes and inflated sentiments"—were
by design secondary to the muscular display. Riefenstahl performed all of her own
stunts and—suffering behind the scenes as she always would—formidably faced
the endurance test of her will and physical prowess (111).

Though highly successful, these films quickly became rote undertakings for
Riefenstahl, who yearned to work with directors certified through success with
Ufa or, better yet, Hollywood. Because Fanck's direction of actors was notoriously
mediocre, G.W. Pabst, famous for having directed Greta Garbo in *The Joyless
Streets* (1925), was hired to film the acting scenes of *The White Hell of Piz Palü*
(1928). As Riefenstahl recalls it, the experience had a transformative effect upon
her screen performance and confirmed the direction her career should be taking.
Just as *Joyless Streets* had paved the way for Garbo's Hollywood career, perhaps
Pabst's attentions could provide just the enhancement Riefenstahl's work needed.
Along these lines, her memoir insists upon the need to pursue the more dramatically

complex and racy roles played by Pabst's former and future stars Greta Garbo and Louise Brooks:

> It was a new experience for me to be directed by G.W. Pabst. I felt for the first time that I too was an actress. I couldn't work as well under Dr. Fanck's direction because he completely misunderstood me and projected on to me his own female ideal—to which I did not correspond. His ideal girl was a naïve, gentle type, a sort of *ingénue*, very different from me. (69)

While American reviews praised Riefenstahl's work, they provided little indication of cinematic viability outside the limited frame of the mountain genre. "Riefenstahl is convincing as Maria, the brave girl of the group," wrote one *New York Times* journalist of her performance in *Piz Palü*, while another reviewing *Peaks of Destiny* credited her as "an actress with no little charm" ("Alpine Romance" ?; Hall, "A Drama of the Alps" 31). But a review of *S.O.S. Iceberg* best summarizes the hopelessness of asserting screen personality in the face of Fanck's spectacular panoramas of icebergs and glaciers: "Leni Riefenstahl is acceptable… It is, however, a picture in which nature outshines both the players and the story" (Hall, "Rod La Rocque" 18). Her athletic exertions suited Fanck's canon but could never vie with the intense eroticism or provocative vulnerability of the Weimar or Hollywood screen starlet. She was, as a 1929 issue of *Variety* explained, "a typical German sporting type but too buxom for the average American taste" (qtd in Bach 55).

   That she ever really deserved the moniker "Germany's Garbo"—or was a contender for any significant studio films—is part of the self-fashioning and retrospective biography Riefenstahl continuously engineered for herself. As the undisputed female star of the Alpine film genre, Riefenstahl was still an incalculable distance from cinematic celebrity of the studio variety. As her biographer starkly interprets it, "She was pretty and could pantomime passably on skis or while climbing cliffs, but no one thought of her for plum roles, the ones that made you a legend or took you to Hollywood" (Bach 60). In typical fashion, Riefenstahl glosses over these failures in her memoirs, supplanting rejection and indifference with tales of just-missed opportunity and grandiose desirability.

   It is perhaps her envy of and fascination with Dietrich that most clearly betray her frustrations about failing to make the honor roll of the day's cinematic talent. We have already glimpsed how her memoir's sanguine interpretation of her relationship with Josef von Sternberg elucidates the need to draw similarities between herself and the enviably accomplished German film star. But Riefenstahl also suggests that she had been, by turns, a contender for *The Blue Angel*'s legendary femme fatale role of Lola and a cherished professional consultant on the film. While daily conferences sought by Sternberg lead to Riefenstahl's conclusions, "I almost felt as if I were working with him," her appearance on the set of *Blue Angel* presents nothing less than a threat to the rehearsing Dietrich (77). Simply watching Dietrich perform "Falling in Love Again," on the sound stages of Ufa, Riefenstahl provokes severe irritation, and a "defiant pout." Marlene threw a "tantrum," she explains, "threatening to walk out for good if I ever showed up on the set again" (78). Of such creative interpretations, Riefenstahl's biographer concludes, "Leni's losing the prize role to Dietrich did not end her campaign for Sternberg's attention: Hollywood was on her mind and would remain there…Leni had made up her mind that if G.W. Pabst and Josef von Sternberg were not going to 'discover' her and cast her in a star-making film, she would do so herself" (Bach 68). And so she would not only cast herself in *The Blue Light*, but would also convert herself into an *auteur*, directing, acting, and producing, far from the prominence, glamour, or encouragement of the established film industry. Of her first feature film, Sternberg remarked, "It's a beautiful film and you are wonderful. There is no greater antithesis than that between you as Junta in *The Blue Light* and Marlene as Lola in *The Blue Angel*. I made Marlene: she is my creature. Now she's an international star. And you—when are you coming?" (Riefenstahl 131). Indeed it would not be the likes of a von Sternberg, Lubitsch, Lang, or Wilder who would "make" her, but rather the concerted phenomena of Riefenstahl's own mercenary ambition and the generous authorization of a high profile figure on the German political stage, the soon-to-be chancellor, Adolf Hitler.

Cinematic Authority

In a 2002 interview on her 100th birthday, Riefenstahl flaunted her former subject's admiration for her work: "Hitler was absolutely crazy about *The Blue Light*" (Forster, Harms, and Skupin 254). According to her version of events, the film, first released in 1932, not only gratified her aspiration to auteurship, but also converted her most consequential viewer into an enduring fan. By this account, it is Hitler's attraction to *her* aesthetic that inspires cinematic history's most controversial enterprise, *Triumph of the Will*. Where her "dance on the sea" in Fanck's 1926 film *The Holy Mountain* had stirred his admiration for her physical elegance and beauty, *The Blue Light* captivated him for her cinematic ingenuity. Taken together, her careers as a dancer, then actress, and, finally, director led to the Nazi film that conclusively determined her professional and personal life. As her memoir describes it: "[*The Blue Light*] was pivotal in my life … because Hitler was so fascinated by this film that he insisted I make a documentary about the Party Rally in Nuremburg. The result was *Triumph of the Will*" (210a).

While this anecdote leaves out Riefenstahl's own confessed admiration for Hitler and abridges the complicated sequence of events that led to the famous documentary—including her production of its less known antecedent, *Victory of Faith* (1933)—it succeeds in enlisting Hitler for her own self-exalting narrative. Ernst Jäger, Riefenstahl admirer and editor-in-chief of the trade publication *Film-Kurier* had encouraged her to attend her first Führer event, held at the Berlin Sports Palace in 1932. There, she reportedly experienced an "apocalyptic vision" and temporary paralysis. Her attraction would soon find mutual gratification with his pleasure upon viewing her arresting performances on the screen (104).

While *Triumph of the Will*'s Hitler serves as effigy and eroticized object, he more importantly functions as on-screen proxy for Riefenstahl, who saw in his image an opportunity to promote her own devotional status cinematically. For this reason alone, her lifelong effort to distance herself from the Nazi party remains impossible to reconcile with her compulsion to enfold Hitler into a personal narrative of life-as-myth.[5] Throughout *Triumph of the Will*, one senses a deep conspiracy with form: though the body at the center of the film's focus may be "Hitler," the director's authorial signature plays promiscuously across the image's surface. That Riefenstahl presents a uniquely "authorized" version of Hitler is insisted upon through image construction and a cinematic language of access; *Triumph of the Will* is a hermetic, imaginary world sealed by the imprimatur of an innovative woman artist, adulating "Hitler" and doing so to exalt the filmmaker he commissioned to "produce" himself. As we shall see, the accretion of visual meaning around Hitler's body produces the film's centripetal effect. He is seen seeing; his gaze endows meaning to the expanding tableaux. But his pleasure in surveying the crowd—his privilege as super-spectator or master of the scene— competes with the camera's persistent designation of his body as object. Spectacular gestures exist very much within the economy of Riefenstahl's embodied gaze.

The 1934 Nazi Party Rally documentary opens with an ideologically suggestive collusion among viewer, camera, and subject: seen through Hitler's eyes, this sequence taps into prevailing cultural fantasies and fetishizations of Hitler's body, at the same time obliquely commenting on issues of embodied viewing and mediated perception. Foregrounding subjective, human control over technology, the film's prologue disavows the wholly transparent viewing subject by connotatively locating the gaze in a body that flies the plane and watchfully scans the panoramic view from the cockpit. Importantly, however, we do not *see* the body, but see *from* it: Hitler's viewing power, such perspectival alignment suggests, is materially and phenomenologically grounded at the same time that it appears omniscient, all-encompassing. Such seeing is, in large measure, an exercise of his natural authority, but this opening sequence also demonstrates Riefenstahl's access inside Hitler's plane—an alignment that effectively advertises Riefenstahl's politically sanctioned camera. In undercutting Hitler's claims to point-of-view, Riefenstahl emphasizes her role as the formative agent of the unfolding images, immobilizing the Führer in a tableau of infinite self-reference. To submit to Riefenstahl's visual choreography, to display libidinal intoxication as object and image of self-reflection gratifies the illusion of a totally dispersed, totally visual Hitlerian super-subject. Riefenstahl participates in the submission dramatized by her own "overpresent" character, a self-reflexive indulgence she repeats later in saying of her documentary's Hitler: "I wanted to form *my own* image" (101).

For her part, Riefenstahl fulfills this objective, and to this end strategizes a critical reciprocity: namely, her own insinuation into the mutually empowering economy of leader-viewer-follower. Riefenstahl's lens and angle work underscore Hitler's

---

[5]   See, especially, her memoir's chapter entitled "A Fateful Meeting."

transformation into the film's visual locus while gesturing back to the physical presence of the filmmaker. The blurriness of our very first glimpse of Hitler—and numerous ones that follow—emphasizes the act of looking and signifies the ways that human skill ratifies the work of the photographic apparatus. Riefenstahl asserts the filmmaker's perceptual act through manipulated compositions and textures that abstract the visual subject. Emerging from the airplane, Hitler presents a rigid embodiment of shadow and light entering the top right corner of the frame. Five shots later, Hitler comes into focus.

In the following sequence, Hitler progresses from the airfield to his hotel. With an exterior camera shooting into a diplomatic automobile, this scene films a rigid, iconic Hitler from behind, by turns zooming in and moving out, capturing a full range of compositions from upper torso to luminous palm.

In showing us once more what Hitler *sees*, Riefenstahl quotes the opening scene's intimate perspectival alignment. However, for the duration of the film Riefenstahl makes little effort to align the camera with Hitler's point of view. Where the vantage point (just to the side of and behind Hitler) establishes Riefenstahl's authority as almost interconstituent with the leader's, the camera's mobility articulates her free circulation within that agency.

Extensive of this identification is the looming sense we get of the technological apparatus: airplane and, later, camera gesture toward the film's maker, toward the authoritative presence controlling it.[6] Twin scenes feature the shadowy presence of the airplane and camera, respectively: in which the plane's silhouette appears like a black scar against a building's starkly white exterior, anticipates the later moment when a cameraperson's inky outline sails past a sunlit monument. Not only do glimpses of the machinery speak to power's circulation *within* the film—and certainly the machinic bodies of the followers are metonyms in this sense—but they also index Riefenstahl's determined attendance at the scene.

Echoing one another, these subtle allusions to technology make reference to the constructedness of the event, while perpetuating the opening scene's pattern of identification and self-reflection. Complementing the value system of luminosity and iconolatry surrounding Hitler, such shadows suggest the imprint of a story-telling agent, of narratorial scaffolding. In this interpretation, I strongly disagree with Russell Berman's assessment that the latter scene evidences "the self-effacing signature of the director" (100). What we see, his argument goes, is a "glimpse" of the shadow of the apparatus, "not a glimpse of the apparatus itself

---

6   According to Jean-Louis Baudry, critical use and application of the term "apparatus" suffers from inconsistency. Baudry distinguishes among the "*basic cinematographic apparatus*," "*the apparatus*," and "*the apparatus of projection*." "Thus, the *basic cinematographic apparatus*," he explains, "involves the film stock, the camera, developing, montage considered in its technical aspects, etc. as well as the apparatus [*dispositif*] of projection [and] is a long way from being the camera by itself" (763). At the risk of confusing matters, my usage refers explicitly to the photographic apparatus and to the cameraperson. This operator is often but not always Riefenstahl herself, so I speak metonymically when I conflate the appearance of the camera with Riefenstahl's implied or introjected presence.

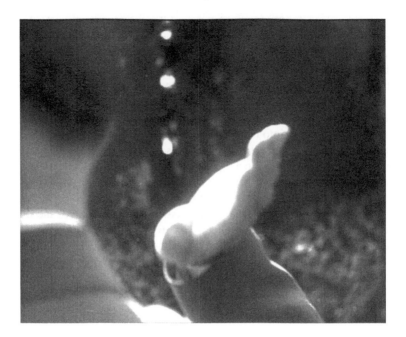

Fig. 10.1   Hitler's hand, in *Triumph of the Will*, dir. Leni Riefenstahl (1935).

(*technology is excluded*) but its shadow projected onto the wall as a metaphor of the cinematic screen" (italics added, 100). However, what serves as a "glimpse" of the apparatus's shadow in this setting, proliferates into at least 12 scenes in which Riefenstahl films her own equipment; meticulous as her editing was, these inclusions of technology can only be regarded as intentional.

In making the camera present, Riefenstahl imposes a directorial fiat (the presence of the maker) that works contrapuntally to the autotelic world of fascist power. This exposed apparatus foregrounds fascism's representational conundrum, in which aesthetics manufacture state as much as state manufactures aesthetics. The incorporated machinery insists upon the double helix of fascism and film, as Riefenstahl presents an iconographic equation between Hitler and cinema that, through the present camera, configures her as the *sine qua non* of that world. Indeed, she literalizes this interpolation in the final parade sequence, featuring a tableau of Hitler arriving by car, a cluster of equipment and cameramen, and, presiding over the scene, Riefenstahl herself.[7]

---

[7]   *The Wonderful, Horrible Life of Leni Riefenstahl*, Ray Müller's 1993 documentary, formally signifies his own camera's narrative agency by making visible the iris's darkened edges. Perhaps offering a riposte to Riefenstahl's implicative resonance throughout *Triumph of the Will*, Müller formally and conceptually reframes Riefenstahl's image, documenting the documentarian in a way that both imitates and interrogates her own cinematic strategies. Müller does not raise the issue of his subject's self-referentiality but registers his own

Fig. 10.2   Shadow of Hitler's airplane, in *Triumph of the Will*, dir. Leni
             Riefenstahl (1935).

The appearance of the apparatus throughout the course of *Triumph of the Will* purposely betrays Riefenstahl's own embeddedness in the diegetic space and interrupts the smooth assumption of spectatorial control implied during Hitler's arrival at Nuremberg. The self-abnegation of those in the crowd and the sheer interchangeability of the political legions mark the limits of Riefenstahl's directorial devotion. For even as her 32 cameramen camouflaged themselves in SA uniforms throughout the shooting, Riefenstahl's costume—as Janet Flanner recounts—consisted of visually striking all-white combinations of blouse and skirt. And, while the camera makes her metonymically legible, it can only do so while marking her as separate from the scene, "at once immanent and transcendent with respect to the masses" like some kind of double for Hitler himself.[8]

---

mediating gaze not only through his often aggressive use of the camera but also by showing his crew and including scenes in which he directs an ornery Riefenstahl on how to act when film is rolling.

[8]   In discussing crowds, Italian fascism, and mass panoramas, Jeffrey T. Schnapp reads such doubling in a rally image, writing: "Nested in the image is the dictator's double, the cameraman [... .] He does not simply reproduce tidal flows, but rather produces them just like the dictator-demiurge who is at once immanent and transcendent with respect to the masses" (257).

Fig. 10.3   Hitler arriving at Nuremberg, in *Triumph of the Will*, dir. Leni
                 Riefenstahl (1935).

With *Triumph of the Will*, Riefenstahl assured that Hitler's image would be
indelible in the minds of viewers and that her own role as producer, framer, and
editor of the spectacle would be forever inextricable from its ideological force.
The extent to which she believed she could regain control of her public image is
unclear. "I felt a sense of relief," she writes in her memoir, "and tremendously
encouraged by the thought that I would be completely free after this project and
able to do whatever I wished" (159). She would not, however, as she claims
here, be able to sustain a selective relationship to all that the Nazi propaganda
film represented. Whether she truly held such a naïve belief or only claimed to
as a retrospective cleansing of her beliefs and affiliations is almost impossible
to discern.

Leni Goes to Hollywood

It is difficult to imagine what Riefenstahl's reception in America would have been
upon her arrival had Kristallnacht not erupted in Germany three days earlier. But
the violent oppression and mass exportation of Jews to concentration camps did
occur on November 7, 1937, securing a hostile reception for "Hitler's honey," as
the American media dubbed her, much to her own amusement (Bach 170). The
aims for her American tour were multiple. As her biographer has succinctly put it,

"If *Triumph of the Will* made Hitler safe for Germany, a film of the 1936 Olympics in Berlin could make him safe for the world" (Bach 143–4). Failure was not a consideration, nor had it never had been for Riefenstahl, as she never contemplated distinguishing between critical reception in Germany and critical reception in the rest of the world. To her, the lavish openings throughout Europe confirmed her work's universal appeal. Munich, Venice, Stockholm, and Copenhagen, celebrated her accomplishments. And so Riefenstahl set off for America, prepared to market and promote *Olympia*, Hitler, and, above all, herself. *Olympia: Festival of Nations* and *Olympia: Festival of Beauty*, the two-part documentary record of the 1936 Olympics hosted by the city of Berlin, were Riefenstahl's follow-up to *Triumph of the Will*. She took with her to America three prints of the documentary: in the official version, Hitler is the superspectator, applauding the real heroes of the film—presiding while passively taking in the spectacle; the others were sanitized versions excising any and all sign of Hitler. She was characteristically politic when assessing her audience and choosing which version to screen.

Though Riefenstahl set off for America under the pseudonym "Lotte Richter," the urge to mingle and form advantageous connections with the ship's other passengers compelled her to pronounce and publicize her presence on the ship. "[S]he became," as historian Cooper C. Graham put it, a "shipboard celebrity" (212). Along with her for the tour were Werner Klingeberg, a member of the German Olympic Committee for 1940, and Ernst Jäger, now, the former editor-in-chief of *Film-Kurier* and publicity chief for both documentaries Riefenstahl produced for the Nazi party.

In the few short months Riefenstahl spent in America, she grudgingly confronted the fierce opposition to the Nazi party, Hitler, and, to her utter frustration, to herself. The initial enthusiasm that greeted her on the docks of New York, as well as the trivializing, but prevailingly favorable characterizations that filled American publications, quickly faded. Walter Winchell, creator of the celebrity gossip column had dubbed her, "Pretty as a swastika," another noted "the gal ... has charm to burn," while, as she reports it, journalists "pestered and photographed [her] on all sides." (Winchell 10; qtd in Graham 435; Riefenstahl 236). But even before Kristallnacht, the Non-Sectarian Anti-Nazi League presented formidable challenges to Riefenstahl, believing, correctly, one might say, that it was her intention to spread Nazi propaganda in America. That all opportunities and invitations quickly evaporated in the wake of Kristallnacht did not prevent Riefenstahl from pressing on to Hollywood, where, she believed, her German émigré contacts would redeem the string of rejections she had received in New York, Washington, and Chicago. So naïvely did she interpret her potential, Riefenstahl did not even consider the extent to which Jewish-born entrepreneurs—Sam Goldwyn, Carl Laemmle, Louis B. Mayer, and the Warner Brothers to name a few—were the architects of the motion picture industry.

Hollywood greeted her with everything ranging from coldness and indifference to vigorous and tactical resistance. Far from the throng of press members in New York, Los Angeles had four people awaiting her arrival on the *Super Chief* from

Chicago on November 24, 1938. One particularly pitiless first-hand account
described Riefenstahl's appearance in the following way:

> Slowly a compartment door opened. Leni Riefenstahl appeared, long-stemmed
> roses effectively arranged in the crook of her arm. Dreamily she stepped
> down the short stairs to a little clearing...She assumed a photo pose, ready for
> Hollywood's adulation...With closed eyes she awaited the explosion of flash
> bulbs, the chatter of reporters as they pressed in on her...It would be like all the
> movies about Hollywood she had seen, Josef von Sternberg would be there—
> once he had begged her to sign a movie contract. (*Hollywood Reporter* 13)

Dramatic interpretations aside, the reality was a politically organized lockout. Five
days after she arrived, the Hollywood Anti-Nazi League ran an advertisement in
the *Hollywood Reporter* damning "emissaries of Fascism," announcing that "Leni
Riefenstahl, Head of the Nazi Film Industry, has arrived in Hollywood," and
making a plea for all readers to "SIGN THE PETITION FOR AN ECONOMIC
EMBARGO AGAINST GERMANY!" (*Hollywood Reporter* 5). Connections
at Paramount Pictures and MGM failed to manifest, while promised invitations
from the likes of Gary Cooper and Greta Garbo never came through and "Josef
von Sternberg remained silent" (Bach 176). Even inspired praise for *Olympia* in
the *Hollywood Citizen-News* and the *Los Angeles Times* could not compensate
for her toxic affiliation with the Third Reich. Traveling companion—and
former Hitler promoter—Ernst Jäger would later vengefully relay his first-hand
experiences with Riefenstahl in a series of sensational articles published in the
Hollywood Tribune. Titled "How Leni Riefenstahl Became Hitler's Girlfriend,"
the extensive chronicle depicts its already unsympathetic subject as venal, petty,
and narcissistic to distraction. According to Jäger, Riefenstahl consoled herself
through recourse to the Nazi line: "If only this damned Jewish question would
get out of the headlines. The American public would quickly forget about the
whole business if they had a new sensation to talk about" (Jäger 13). Doubtless,
Riefenstahl felt that she embodied the very "sensation" America needed in order to
recover from all that nasty business in Germany; instead, she simply served as an
odious reminder of Nazi hatred. In the end, the only Hollywood celebrity she met
was Walt Disney, whose *Snow White* had lost out to *Olympia* for the Golden Lion,
the Venice Biennale's prestigious film award. And even he would not screen her
film for fear that his union projectionists would leak the news to Hollywood.

In a report filed sent to Hitler shortly before she left America, Riefenstahl
composed a careful narrative of excuses and accusations. The trip had been an
utter failure because of the "character of the American people." "Jews" were
emboldening the "negro," while Bolshevism and a "low level of culture" made
revolution imminent. "There was nothing left for her," reported Jäger, "but to
return to Germany a martyr" (14). Not one newspaper reported her departure from
Hollywood on January 13, 1938. The press neither celebrated nor maligned her;
for the first time in her 15-year career, she was neither "much talked about" nor
mentioned by the media at all.

Final Frontier

By way of conclusion, consider a photograph of Riefenstahl taken in Santa Barbara during her disastrous promotional visit to America. The director sits poised on the railing of a horse stable against the backdrop of a barn, hands folded between her knees, a resigned slump to her shoulders, toes turned inward, a diffident smile on her face. Set against the reticence in her presentation is the incommensurate, even absurd, costume she wears: a cowboy hat and boots, dark stiff-looking blue jeans with a generous cuff, a plaid western-style top, and bolero tie. Her self-fashionings and self-proclamations as the triumphant and adored are undercut by the posture and uncharacteristic gaze away from the camera's eye. And still the effort to adapt her own image to that of the iconic American cowboy betrays her deep affection for and identification with the masculine hero image. As much as the authentic attire sets off her failure to gain approval or even acceptance from the American film industry (and the American public), it also brings to the fore some of the thematic correlations between the iconic American image of the cowboy and the career of the German director. Indeed the Alpine film genre that established her cinematic celebrity was, in many ways, the Weimar equivalent of the Western. Unspoiled nature, human survival in and spiritual communion with the rough elements, the spectacle of man's endurance, minimal dialogue, and arousing panoramas: the genres share many visual motifs and thematic similarities. In her role as undisputed star of the Alpine genre and as much so in her professional and personal life, Riefenstahl was nothing if not pioneering, an intrepid explorer of new frontiers. And yet the poorly calculated appropriation of the iconic cowboy image speaks equally of Riefenstahl's lifelong belief that self-creation was only as limited as her imagination, that self-promoting was as simple as aligning with the right icon at the right time. But her professional and cinematic alignments with Hitler's image had taken her very far, so far in fact that claims to any other identity could never, ever be possible.

Chapter 11
Four Elvises

Edward P. Comentale

A point which I want very much to establish is that the choice of these "Readymades" was never dictated by esthetic delectation. This choice was based on a reaction of visual indifference with at the same time a total absence of good or bad taste…in fact a complete anesthesia.

—Marcel Duchamp, "Apropos of 'Readymades,'" 1961[1]

Readymade Elvis

Of course, there are all kinds of Elvis to love—Southern Elvis, Tender Elvis, Trucker Elvis, Cadillac Elvis, Black Elvis, Queer Elvis, Vegas Elvis, Zoroastrian Elvis, Army Elvis, Karate Elvis, Bloated Elvis, Dead Elvis, Saint Elvis. At the risk of crowding the stage, my essay adds four more to the mix: Ready-made Elvis, Machine Elvis, Mother Elvis, and the Third Elvis. By presenting these undeniably willful constructions of "The King"—I hope to conjoin my interests as a fan and a scholar and thus expose the primarily affective dimensions of the entire Elvis phenomenon. More than anything else, I believe, Elvis's fame rests upon an affective openness that became available with both the new recording technology and expanding consumer culture that redefined the public sphere during the modern era. His aesthetic, if one may apply that term to such an incoherent and undeniably spontaneous process, begins with an anxious dissociation of sensibility, a radical decontextualization of experience, voice, and language that nonetheless entails the release of otherwise illicit affects and emotional states. In this, Elvis's modernism—his avant-gardism, say—proves decisively popular and non-literate; on records, at concerts, and in photographs, it works at the level of the sensual body and serves to reconfigure its habitual relations with an increasingly mechanical world. Here, then, with Elvis and his fame, we may trace the outlines of a popular or vernacular modernism, of the kind first defined by Miriam Hansen, one that exhibits its own structures of feeling, its own relations to the pains and promises of modernity, and its own modes of address and reparation.

Approaching the 1950s, though, I must contend with a moment of popular culture that is often reviled as a moment of betrayal. Here, specifically, the production of popular music becomes enmeshed with the practices of big business and seems to lose much of its transgressive power in its growing connection to alien media such

---

[1] Duchamp 141.

as photography, television, and film. The sad arc of Elvis's career represents the stale packaging of an otherwise defiant folk culture, and, if anything, remains a cautionary tale of the ways in which the culture industry manages the unruly desires of modern life. At the same time, I must address academic work on Presleyana and the Culture Industry at large, one that enforces a similarly static view of the phenomenon, locking both Elvis and his music into an ideological grid of rigid cultural significations. From today's scholarly perspective, Elvis figures largely as a pulsating semiotic star; at once black and white, male and female, poor and rich, he shimmers with the ideological tensions that define Cold War America at large.[2]

Alternately, I propose to explore Elvis and early rock-n-roll as a down and dirty transmission of affect. I'd like to confront the Elvis phenomenon in terms of experience rather than meaning, and approach his stylized performances not as "texts" to be "read," but events that gripped the body of the fan in a number of ecstatic ways. If anything, this is the terrain of Melanie Klein, not Freud or even Marx, where a pre-Oedipal play of dirty drives precludes coherent selfhood and stable subjective relations. The Elvis phenomenon harks back to an infantile, prediscursive terrain, generating new affective states that elude the structures of what we may come to understand as personal or cultural maturity. My analysis finds support in Lawrence Grossberg's claim that the allure of rock music depends on the play of bodily affects and the alliances thus created. As Grossberg explains, rock does not produce narratives or even representations. Rather, it generates affects and moods that are at once physical and significant—more immediately significant because they are physical (Grossberg 152–3, 154, 156). This chapter, similarly, abandons *meaning* for *mattering*. Fans seek objects that matter, impressively, in their lives, in relation to their experiences, needs, and desires. Behind such mattering lies a theory of affect as a kind of embodied judgment, at once corporeal and evaluative, sensory as well as sensible, capable of generating and sustaining significant differences. Affect, working at the fringes of desire, seems to complicate the differential logic of the sign and the related desires of a castrated subject. To me, it implies a kind of valencing, a turning, as opposed to a structured relation of desire; it is a pervasive and open-ended mode of engagement rather than a readymade system of presence and absence, frustration and satisfaction.

Thus, chance, indifference, tastelessness—Duchamp's blueprint for readymade art—implies not only a cunning dissolution of aesthetic pretension but also the clumsy production of a very modern kind of fame and its attendant pleasures. Before all else, Duchamp's project serves as an attempt to turn the ordinary into the extraordinary and thus exposes the production of public aura as an arbitrary designation of the generic as the unique. The random selection and indifferent regard of otherwise common, tasteless, and even slightly raunchy things underlies both the success of the culture industry at large and the terms of fanaticism in twentieth-century America, the very first country to recognize the cheap genius of

---

[2]   See, for example, Barbara Ehrenreich, Elizabeth Hess, and Gloria Jacobs; David R. Shumway; and Erika Doss.

both Duchamp and his perversely displayed objects.[3] In this regard, we'd be wise to trace the homologies not between Elvis and Duchamp, or even between Elvis and Duchamp's shimmying *Nude Descending a Staircase*, but between Elvis and the no less sensual *Fountain*. If the alignment of famous human and famous thing seems forced, we should only recall the shrieks of indignation that accompanied the unveiling of both. More significantly, though, we will find that an economy that produces both urinals and superstars consistently blurs this boundary in order to sell its wares. Indeed, the very technologies of mass production and mass marketing consistently deny the expressive humanism of its objects in order to generate sensual currents that far exceed the demands of any individual ego. Simply put, these objects are at once common and sensual, open and charged, thus capable of sustaining attention on a mass scale. On the one hand, then, a blank industrial object is carefully chosen by an idiosyncratic artist for its supple physical form, its suggestive curves and orifices, and thus appears endowed with an uniqueness akin to personal character. On the other, a decisively grubby and eccentric teen wanders into a shoddy Memphis studio, and, quickly, before the blank machinery of musical production and the amoral regard of his manager, becomes the kinky object of an entire culture's arrested gaze. The critical challenge, though, lies not merely in locating the origins of said gaze, but in defining its attendant pleasures, and more specifically, the ways in which these pleasures inform a specifically popular modernism.

As Duchamp famously explained, his experiments with found objects were designed to move art beyond the ego and the bourgeois cult of expressivism. Random selection, mechanical drawing, academic jargon, punning—these strategies have been often seen as signs of Duchamp's increasingly cerebral approach to aesthetic categories, but they also served to free the work of art from its expressivist coordinates and thus restore its affective potential within a wider cultural context.[4] Hence, the shovel, the bottle rack, the urinal—despite the heady ironies that the casual repositioning of such objects might imply, they are solidly objects in the world, and their unnatural selection draws attention to the sensual currents they typically generate and sustain. By removing objects from their everyday contexts and associations, from their every day "uses," Duchamp asserted the primacy of their aesthetic qualities and invited a new attentiveness to the pleasurable sensations of just looking. Hence, Duchamp's famous declaration of the "beauty of indifference" (30). If this indifference lies somewhere between Pyrrho's great apathy and Kant's aesthetic purposelessness, its practitioner is a lazy sensualist carelessly enjoying a decisively artificial world.[5] Thus, despite the

---

[3]   Calvin Tompkins 117 and Dawn Ades, Neil Cox, and David Hopkins, *Marcel Duchamp* (London: Thames and Hudson 1999), 166.

[4]   See Duchamp's comments in "The Great Trouble with Art in this Country," in Duchamp 125; Katherine Kuh 89; and commentary in Arturo Schwarz 19–20, 26.

[5]   For Pyrrho's indifference, see Jean-Michel Rabaté 223. For Kantian purposelessness, see Margaret Iverson 46.

artist's oft-declared revolt against bourgeois canons of taste, he himself frequently suggested that the readymade serves a wider commitment towards nothing less than a restoration of everyday wonder:

> For me, this is an infinite field of joy—and it's always right at hand. Sometimes four or five different levels of meaning come through. If you introduce a familiar word into an alien atmosphere, you have something comparable to distortion in painting, something surprising and new. (Qtd in Kuh 89)

The radical populism of the readymades, though, exists in their ability to effect transformations in a common human body and its habitual relations with the world. Duchamp typically began with a useful object, one that implies a consistent set of corporeal expectations and investments. The shovel, the urinal, the coat hanger— each suggests a blindly productive mode of relation to an increasingly mechanical, or "readymade" world, but each, by its casual and often ironic reframing, confounds that relation and its agent. Thus, Jean-François Lyotard describes the readymade as the culminating moment of an industrial revolution in which continuous innovations and applications of machinery effected radical recoordinations of the human body. The readymade, as a surreal product of a modern art-factory, demands a complex shift in the shape and capacity of the human form, revealing "The old European peasant-aristocrat body cracking and falling to pieces, according to the demands of a different mentality and a different sensorium." By working through the body and its mechanical relations, Duchamp—as we'll find with Elvis—is less an artist, than a transformer, whose work entails a channeling or redistributing of human energy: "The *performer*," Lyotard writes, "is a complex *transformer*, a battery of metamorphosis machines. There is no art, because there are no objects. There are only transformations, redistributions of energy. The world is a multiplicity of apparatuses that transforms units of energy into one another" (15, 36).

Ultimately, if Duchamp's own emphasis on "things" trips us up, we should recall that the artist endowed each readymade with suggestively human qualities, and, conversely, modern spectators respond to their idols as always somewhat less than human. In fact, less a theory of the object than a theory of a specifically modern kind of vision, the readymade calls attention to a gaze at once ecstatic and indifferent, both charged and blank, by which art, commodities, and human bodies are momentarily raised above their generic horizons and just as quickly abandoned. If anything, the readymade implies a pleasurable swerving across the glossy surfaces of the everyday world; freed from the demands of the ego, the eye careens across the rim of the urinal, slides down the wooden shaft of the shovel, and tumbles into and out of the marble cubes in the bird cage, never piercing through, never claiming ownership, only always slipping away. One can read desire and signification in these passive, receptive images, but their pleasure is specific to the fluid currents of an affection. As Margaret Iverson explains, the readymade seeks to circumvent the "whole complex of relations that normally governs our lives," specifically the anxious logic of castration and fetish, and proposes instead "an aesthetic practice that tries to circumvent selfish desire, power, possessiveness." For Iverson, the readymade and the *objet trouvé* are two sides of the same aesthetic experience, both of which displace the coordinates of the subject, but whereas the former occasions a free-floating experience of aesthetic judgment, the latter is the traumatic focus of structured fantasy and desire. Equating Lacan's formulation of *objet petit a* with the Surrealist notion of *trouvaille*, she explains, "The contrast between the Duchampian rendezvous and the Bretonian encounter should now be clear. While the readymade is essentially indifferent, multiple, and mass-produced, the found object is essentially singular or irreplaceable, and both lost and found" (46, 50).

At this point, history—and Elvis—enters our analysis. Duchamp's project responds to world of photographic reproduction and wall-to-wall advertising, corporate branding, auratic commodities and plate-glass window-shopping, the mass production of difference and the very public eroticism of the consumer. While the initial gesture of the *Fountain* shifts attention from the artist to the factory worker (R. Mutt), the exhibition of the work declares a shift from aesthetic connoisseur to contemporary consumer (Rrose Sélavy). In this regard, the Duchampian gaze—at once public and passionate, indifferent and erotic—entails not necessarily the death of art, but its desublimation into the heart of the modern public sphere. With the readymade, as with any object commercial brand, a single chancy gesture constitutes both the thing to be seen and a specific way of looking. Random selection of the generic implies a phenomenal doubleness of both subject and object. Every item on the shelf is just an ordinary thing that submits to a common, careless response, but each is also an extraordinary object that commands an ecstatic gaze. With this, the most basic drives are put in the service of a fleeting surface pleasure, given free reign across the wondrous surfaces of an artificially constructed world. According to Dawn Ades, Neil Cox, and David Hopkins, the readymade would not be possible without the "ironic recognition of the industrial object as the perfect union of natural and artificial aspects so long desired by artists." More positively, we might contend that the readymade reveals the very real pleasures that lie everywhere on the fringes of commodity fetishism and its presumed passivity; its spectator "remains outside the all-powerful system, by converting the ordinary commodity into this own pleasure-machine, by using it privately and even inappropriately, not according to the manufacturer's instructions" (Ades, Cox, and Hopkins 155, 162).

However, in the marketplace of the readymade, which mimics the market of the mass-produced commodity, commonness also implies a certain tastelessness. The object's extraordinary ordinariness sanctions an indulgent pleasure: the very real pleasure of misusing or misperceiving the object or one of its many alluring hooks and holes. In this, Duchamp and his readymade signal not just a gripping anesthesia, but a certain cheapness, a trashiness, with which the terms of fame and fanaticism have been overturned in twentieth-century America. In America, specifically, Duchamp's objects have been both mocked and adored in the spirit of carnival, and in this they point toward the incredible tumult that lies just at the fringes of the culture industry and its cheap gimmickry.[6] Thus, we might recall, in a rather unexpected way, Guillaume Apollinaire's early claim regarding the implicit populism of Duchamp's work: "Perhaps it will be the task of an artist as detached from esthetic preoccupations, and as intent on the energetic as Marcel Duchamp, to reconcile art and the people" (qtd in Tompkins 121).

Ultimately, it is the cheapness of the readymade and its fame that links Duchamp's high-concept experiments in art with Elvis's low-concept popularity. Elvis too was a random creation, an accidental star; his presence was received by the ecstatic gaze of a decisively tasteless public. His atomic pelvis is perhaps the quintessential readymade—at once ordinary and extraordinary, tacky and sublime; divorced form context and the static structures of signification, it points all the more forcefully towards a common body and its affective modes. In other words, with Elvis, Duchamp's great indifference becomes a more common form of cool, a rock and roll shrug, an everyday kiss-off—one that frees and commits the public body to a more radical way of mattering. As we'll find, it takes a radical lack of command to swagger with such grace; Elvis taps the readymade immediacy of the hopeless, the unprotected, and betrayed. His largely poor, largely rural Southern fans found something of the century's promise and wonder in his derelict thrust—not just sex, and certainly not reason, but a vital affective responsiveness, a more supple emotional range, and thus a more supple body politic.

Machine Elvis

"I've never made a record with an established star yet," Sam Phillips proudly told a reporter at the *Memphis Press-Scimitar* in 1955. This article—one of the first to describe the Elvis phenomenon—recounts Phillips's early days as an engineer for WREC and his early aspiration to build a studio that would record "anyone who wanted to play." Phillips's Sun Studio, the article explains, provides an open space for untutored (and often unwashed) musicians, its machinery tuned to rough American sound and rough American feeling:

> As word got around, Sam's studio became host to strange visitors. Negroes, with field mud on their boots and patches in their overalls, came shuffling in with battered instruments and unfettered techniques. Most tried to impress him with white man's music. Sam outwaited them, listened for a wisp of original melody, a happy sound, or an unconventional riff. (Qtd in Rjiff 34)

Phillips wasn't the first record producer hoping to mine the South for sonic gold, but he was perhaps one of the most idealistic. As a whiz-bang technician with a dream of democratic expressivity, he sought to draw deep, untainted feeling out of the recesses of the country. His Sun logo, emblazoned in rustic yellow on

---

[6]   See commentary in Tompkins 117ff. and also the extended history of the *Fountain*'s American reception and manipulation in Camfield 62–142.

each single, suggested a new dawn for American culture. Its motto—"We record anything, anywhere, anytime"—was both an economic and a social proposition for a disenfranchised community.

Phillips, though, was neither musician nor businessman; rather, his genius resided in matching technology to feeling, opening the former to all of the subtleties and intensities of the latter. As a studio engineer, he did all he could to inspire intimacy. He worked only with amateurs untainted by the business. He sat eye level with his artists and coached them to sing and play freely, according to their most immediate needs and drives. Most importantly, though, Phillips allowed the tapes to roll freely, immune to the passage of time so they could pick up anything of interest as it occurred. The console was ready to catch the slightest gesture, the spontaneous cry, the most fleeting emotion, and its otherwise indifferent master was willing to sustain and amplify those moments until they became objects of interest in their own right. "I saw myself as being the facilitator," Phillips explained, "the man who listened to an artist for his native abilities than tried to encourage and channel the artist into what would be a proper outlet for his abilities" (qtd in Escott 156). In this, Sun resembled a number of new recording outlets, such as Chess Records in Chicago or Norm Petty's Studio in Clovis, where independent spirit and advanced technology (specifically newly cheap magnetic tape) were allowed to coalesce freely. As these studios briefly flourished in the South and Midwest during the fifties, their working methods tended to replace artistry with accident; in an instant, mistakes became hits and nervy amateurs turned overnight stars. You didn't need to be good all the time, just once; each take could as easily lead to greatness as to the waste bin; each tossoff could become the stuff of history.

Most importantly, these self-enclosed spaces freed sound from the demands of human expression and the expected relations of any material context. Whereas blues inevitably recalled the life of the jukes and cabaret, and country music echoed the space of the honkytonk or barn dance, the rock recordings of the fifties resounded in the utopian realm of the self-contained studio. Early rock sounds—with their decisively clean tones and eerie echoes—were decisively extrinsic to any cultural space, drawing attention to themselves and their inherent aesthetic values over against any lived or shared musical experience. Phillips deployed a range of techniques to exploit this non-space and generate previously unheard sounds. Stuffing a speaker cone, adding an echo, a slight change of tape speed—with each gesture, the engineer widened the gap between sound and the activity of its making. The slapback echo was the most famous intervention; by bouncing the signal between two recorders, and thus adding a slight delay, the human voice attained a mysterious depth and its own self-syncopated rhythm. Similarly, on the bass, by placing a mike below the bridge to amplify the percussive slap of hand on neck, the activity of sound-making emerged at the center of the recording, becoming at once more primitive and more abstract. In these ways, Sun recordings were never simply expressive, but neither were they merely inhuman. With each abstracted noise, the human always became a bit more of itself—its very estrangement became something like its realization. At once freeing and estranging the activity of human sound-making, each recording seemed to hit upon the dialectical urgency of mediation itself. In this, one is recalled to Duchamp's only sonic readymade: "With Hidden Noise." Duchamp instructed a friend to insert a small object into a ball of twine sealed on both ends by metal plates. The "accidental noise," one created beyond the artist's back, so to speak, refers to no space or any human motive beyond the experience of work itself, throwing the activity of listening—and all its sensual pleasures—back onto the listener. Similarly, the music recorded at Sun was defined by its own uneasy disarticulation, the way in which each extreme noise, each barbed riff or shout or drum kick, threatened to derail the entire song; sounds flew out of the groove, kicked against the song itself, carrying the listener, errantly, away from any obvious relation of space or address. Yet these uncanny sounds became a source of interest in their own right, and, in their very freakishness, called forth a more direct, a more committed response from otherwise distracted fans.

"Rocket 88," recorded by Jackie Brenston and Ike Turner at Sun Studio in 1951, has been called the first rock-and-roll record, but it owes its (perhaps dubious) distinction—like Duchamp's *Three Stoppages* or the cracks in his *Large Glass*—to the engineer's Duchampian respect for chance. As the story goes, the band's main amp, having fallen off the top of the Turner's car on the way to the studio, had been hastily repaired by stuffing paper into the speaker cone. According to Sam Phillips, "We had no way of getting it fixed, so we started to play around with the damn thing, stuffed a little paper in there and it sounded good" (qtd in Escott 24). As with many technological innovations in music, the amp, a practical device for producing loudness, becomes—in the hands of a few bored teens—a significant object of novel aesthetic pleasure. In the same way, the song's lyrics divest the titular car of any convenient uses, presenting it instead as an object of sheer aesthetic contemplation and pleasure, capable of blasting all riders far beyond the confines of the everyday world:

> You women have heard of jalopies,
> You heard the noise they make,
> Let me introduce you to my new Rocket '88.
> Yes it's great, just won't wait,
> Everybody likes my Rocket '88.
> Baby, we'll ride in style,
> Movin' all along.
> V-8 motor and this modern design,
> Black convertible top and the gals don't mind
> Sportin' with me,
> Ridin' all around town for joy.
> Blow your horn, Raymond, blow.

Conceived in excess, consumed as mere frivolity, the "Rocket '88" races past all vulgar need and habitual contexts. In fact, with joyriding, the readymade is set in motion, along the highways and airwaves of the region. Movement trumps direction, and the listener is carried along for a pleasurable swerving that is at once physical and aesthetic. Ultimately, with the horn solo, the sound of the song merges with the sound of the car (a connection perhaps backed by the use of a car radio). This final abstraction carries the listener by the ear into a space that is neither real nor habitual, a movement that defies the placement of the body itself.

All of these forces were at work during the recording session which produced Elvis's first accidental hit—Sun #209 "That's All Right"/"Blue Moon of Kentucky." Elvis had been playing with Scotty Moore and Bill Black for several weeks, searching for a new sound to cut through the airwaves. Urged by Phillips, they wanted to make a record greater than the sum of their very talented parts, but the feeling was inchoate and the goal vague, and only by stumbling freely in the studio did they have any chance of hitting on something interesting. Elvis tried each song on their list from a number of angles, moaning and warbling and sometimes whistling his way along, trying to find a mood, a groove vibe that felt right. Finally, late that evening, they realized they needed a break and, as the boys in the band sipped Cokes, Elvis started goofing off, hamming up a version of Arthur Crudup's "That's All Right (Mama)." As Scotty explained, "Sam, I think, had the door to the control booth open…and he stuck his head out and said, 'What are you doing?' And we said, 'We don't know,' 'Well, back up,' he said, 'try to find a place to start, and do it again'" (Marcus 147, 132).

The very title of the song, "That's Alright" is matched by the accidental, take-it-or-leave-it performance. The phrase can be taken in any number of ways, and Elvis plays with all of them. In turn, it becomes an aggressive howl, a hurt moan, a mocking sneer, a drunken murmur. By the end of the song, though, the lyrics fall away altogether, and Elvis, hooked by the antsy groove, shouts out a string of scat syllables that signify little more than their own gleeful sounding. Ultimately, the vocal performance gives us sound without referent, as nothing more than its own affective experience, asserting everything and nothing. The melodic structure of each verse, in fact, models a kind of divestment of authority. Elvis starts out tentatively and rises in confidence with both the melody and the more aggressive strumming of Scotty's guitar, only to shrug off all desire and turn to the pleasure of singing itself by the fourth line. At the same time, a number of spontaneous tics in the sound tear attention away from the expressive performance itself. Not just Elvis's mannered burps and slurs, or Scotty's spindly licks, but more accidentally, a shaky stammer, the sound of Scotty's plectrum hitting the neck, and, most incredibly, the loss of the lead guitar track at the end of the first solo, these tics or thrusts—Deleuze might call them "zips" or "lines of flight"—carry the ear elsewhere, break up the already roiling surface of the song, and demand a reconfiguration of the listener's investment.

Here, at his best, then, Elvis is not so much creating new meanings, but reeling off new modes of feeling, exploring sound as such, as a medium of great affective suppleness. Specifically, though, most of Elvis's performances draw their force from a central tension between humility and conceit; his voice soars and cracks by turns, at once hurt and then cocky, hesitant and then haughty. In fact, vocal triumph is born—again and again—of complete dereliction; it is the cheap freedom to withdraw and assert the self at will, to create and recreate life at its most affective before an indifferent world, represented perhaps by the studio machinery that records and redeems him. As Greil Marcus explains, "It's the blues, but free of all worry, all sin; a simple joy with no price to pay"; Elvis's best performances reveal a "will to throw yourself all the way after something better with no real worry about how you are going to make it home. And it was this spirit, full-blown and bragging, that was to find its voice in Elvis's new blues and the rockabilly fever he kicked off all over the young white South" (147, 132). Within months of his first successes, of course, Elvis had realized the nature of his genius and milked it dry. Songs such as "Baby, Let's Play House" and "Good Rockin' Tonight" reveal an ever more radical vocal suppleness, one in which the slightest inflection of tone or timbre send off affective sparks too quick to even register. In the first song, going, coming, love, and betrayal—all options are sustained by a spirit of reckless fun; they matter precisely because they don't really matter at all, because they couldn't matter less, and in this they allow his voice to run through all manner of affective stances. Yes, we can hear regret, anger, the kiss-off, and we can imagine all sorts of typical scenarios regarding duck-tailed greasers and their bobby-soxing squeezes. But then we also hear a needlessly strained grunt, a purposelessly cracked cry, a hiccupped leap, and then the voice lures us elsewhere, into its own raucous vocal space. As we can hear in his sly reference to the Cadillac, Elvis signals the markers of conventional joy and success only to shrug them off. It is not just his own growing wealth, though, but his liberated voice that allows him to play all sides of the great class divide. "Good Rockin' Tonight" begins with a wild burst and never lets up. Elvis rides the affective current like a rodeo pro, shaping the vibe with each line. "We're gonna rock" is sung in an entirely new way each time— as dare, as command, as come-on, with triumph, with urgency, as simple statement of fact. By the fourth or fifth repetition, though, it doesn't matter how he's singing it, because we're already rockin.' In fact, at the end of the song, Elvis is merely shouting the word "rock" over and over, whipping the affective vibe into a tight circle, pushing, driving it into a greater frenzy. Future tense becomes present tense, living gerund—rockin' in space.

Here's a voice subject to accident, humility, and confounding alienation, and yet free to sing of something new, daring, exhilarating. It transmutes the most damning terms of poor white modernity into something akin to tasteless fun—fate becomes carelessness, poverty becomes risk, and alienation becomes a truly affective joy. As Lawrence Grossberg writes, "Rock and roll transforms the despair of its context into an embracing of its possibilities as pleasure. But it cannot dismiss the despair…it must always place these back into the context of a world that undermines all meaning and value…Rock and roll celebrates play— even despairing play—as the only possibility for survival" (*Dancing* 40). Again, though, this humility and this play are linked through the very machinery that generates and records both. When asked about how he found his groove, Elvis replied, "Well, sir, to be honest, we just stumbled upon it." In fact, whenever Sam asked him to repeat his performance for the tapes, "Elvis would say 'What did I do? What did I do?' Because it was all so instinctive that he simply didn't know" (qtd in Guralnick 133). This inarticulacy, which will become important when I turn to the issue of music and the drives, was matched by that of band, producer, and then DJ and the dozens of callers who tried to contact the station after the single's first spin. If anything, Elvis's music was uncategorizable—almost unhearable— as it referenced nothing but its own release. In fact, as a phenomenon, it shrugged off the very need for categorization; as Sam Phillips laid it down, "they didn't give a fuck about classifying him in Memphis, Tennessee, *they liked what they heard*."[7] Importantly, this strange success, this accidental success, derived precisely from the most rigid forms of mediation. Elvis dilates and contracts first and foremost as a media star, as a technological mediation that releases as it restrains the affective needs of a manic culture. However, with SUN #209, as with a host of other sides, the manipulation of popular form did not necessarily dampen its potential liberations. Rather technology—reproductive and redistributive—allowed accidental pleasures and surreptitious moods to enter the public sphere on a scale hitherto unimagined.

Mother Elvis

Elvis stumbles onto a stage in the summer of '56—some dusty, overheated club or assembly hall in the South, perhaps Shreveport, perhaps Jacksonville, or the Kessler Air Force base in Biloxi, Mississippi. He has three different kinds of grease in his hair. The seam on his left pant leg is split and his cuffs are worn thin. His face scans the crowd, eyes popping with a wild fear, a certain devilment. Then, he shrugs his shoulders, wipes his nose on his upper sleeve, and starts frailing on his guitar. After the first verse, he spits a wad of pink gum into the crowd and burps into the mike. At the end of the song, he mutters, "Fuck you very much" and smiles back at the boys. As he loosens up, his hair breaks its oily mold and flops over the front of his brow. Each limb seems to wander off on a rhythm all its own—shoulders lurch, thighs pump and crisscross, his head flops to his shoulder and dangles. Then, after a series of quick hip jerks across the stage, he thrusts crotch into guitar for a few mindless pumps. Unsatisfied, he tosses the guitar around his back and falls to the floor. He slithers over to Nipper, the RCA company dog and sneering madly, humps the plastic canine icon, whose typically bemused expression seems to shift slightly towards gruff annoyance.[8]

On the other side of the stage, the girls scream and shriek. They pull out their hair, tear at their breasts, fall to the ground. Some seem to be in a fugal trance, swaying in place, tears poring out of blackened eyes. Others have passed out in the heat, face down in the dust. This is not fanaticism, but apocalypse. On the fringes

---

[7]   Details in Escott 70 and Guralnick 101.

[8]   These details are repeated in many first-person accounts and historical overviews. A wealth of details about Elvis's performances and stage antics can be found in Guralnick and Pierce.

of the arena, fans toss themselves onto the guards. Some bang their heads against the doors, trying to escape. Some stand up defiantly and carve Elvis's initials into their arms with broken shards of glass. In New Orleans, six girls bound and gagged an elevator operator. At a theatre in New York, the manager had to replace a quarter of the seats because they were soaked with urine. When Elvis announces that he'll meet the girls backstage, they surge forward. They rampage through the hotel, looking for totems of their hero—they will steal dirt, grass, blood, and spit, and lick the dust from what they believe is his car fender.[9]

Elvis's revolt takes the body itself as its object, and works quickly, thrillingly, to destabilize the nodes and vectors of an otherwise obsessively conditioned corpus. All is tension and release, dilation and contraction—a series of tics and spasms, which became monstrous, outrageous on the auratic space of the stage. As he once tried to explain, "It's like your body gets goose bumps, but it's not goose bumps. It's not a chill either. It's like a surge of electricity going through you" (qtd in Guralnick 319). Unlike Valentino, the cool sheik, who toyed with the erotics of the look and thus the recently emancipated female consumer, or Sinatra, the crooning existentialist, who brought stylish disaffection to the suburban middle classes, Elvis addressed his audience at the level of the drives in all their raunchy sloppiness. His revolt was decisively subterranean, appealing to the lower regions of both the body and the body politic. Whether listening to Elvis, watching Elvis, dancing with Elvis—we find pleasures of abjection, a public celebration of life beneath the law. As Gael Sweeney explains, Elvis offers trash as the "denigrated aesthetic of a people marginalized socially, racially, and culturally … an aesthetic of bricolage, of random experimentation … gorging, license, and excess" conducted in a state of absolute "powerlessness" (Sweeney 250, 263).

This was a decisively public revolt and a spectacular excess, and Elvis's fans detail ever stranger bodily states occasioned by the concert experience—moments of ecstasy, gestural compulsion, doubled consciousness, unbearable pain, exhaustion. According to one, "I was so completely entranced by him that he was all that filled my mind and my consciousness" (qtd in Olmetti 58). "On a deep level," another describes, "I was totally 'there,' but on a conscious level, I was not there. It is a rare occurrence" (qtd in Olmetti 144). In the lingo of the time, this initial surge was called "flipping," what one fan described as a simultaneous experience of "love, hate, anger, hero worship, anxiety and a few other [extreme emotions]." The confusion is telling here. The stage show brought about a convulsion of the body, an affective overload at once pleasurable and painful, welcomed and feared. Many fans, unsurprisingly, responded with confused violence—striking themselves, tearing out their hair, begging "More, Elvis!" and then "Please stop, Elvis!" In photos, their gestures suggest less desire than a wild mix of affections.

---

[9]   Several dozen books and articles offer comprehensive accounts of the experiences and shenanigans of the Elvis crowd. The most outrageous details can be found in Jane and Michael Stern; Bob Olmetti and Sue McCasland; and Anne Mandlsohn.

Fig. 11.1   Elvis fans, *St. Louis Post-Dispatch* (March 30, 1957).

They hold out their arms, they hug themselves, they grip their heads as if they might explode.[10]

Ultimately, though, after the initial surge died down, fans found themselves caught in an affective vice, uncontrollably mimicking the gestures of the figure on stage and, ultimately, each other. In many accounts, the exchange seemed to be immediate and inescapable. A report from Spokane described, "White-sweatered arms swept in imitative circles and once, when he gave his famous thumb-twirling gesture, the stadium was a waving field of twirling thumbs" (reported in DeNight 97). Another press report, from Tacoma, more sinisterly describes Elvis as a gestural magnet, one whose struts and gyrations allowed him to "blend his personality into theirs" (qtd in Rjiff 170).

With these accounts, the fanatic body seems lit up, set aflame, not so much by desire, but limitless, free-floating states of shame, anger, hatred, and love. In any case, the extremity of the situation reveals much of what we now take for granted regarding the relationship between image and affect. While the psychology of identification and projection provides a certain abstract stability to the dynamics of fandom, it accounts for very little when it comes to the physical intensity and

---

[10]   See related commentary in "Elvis Sings Here, but Squeals of 11,000 Often Drown Him Out," *St. Louis Post-Dispatch* (March 30, 1957); and John Fislayson, "Elvis Wiggles and Wails as 24,000 Scream and Sob," *Detroit Free Press* (April 1, 1957); both reprinted in Rjiff 124–5 and 130–34, respectively.

Fig. 11.2   Elvis fans, *Detroit Free Press* (April 1, 1957).

affectionate currents that play across a crowd. In the same way, some clarity can be found if we turn away from strictly Freudian models of object relations and explore Klein's work on the infant's earliest interactions at the mother's breast. Klein draws attention to the drives that inform the infant's pre-oedipal play of mouths, fingers, and breasts and give rise to affective experiences of pleasures and displeasure. "The earliest feelings," she writes, "are experienced in connection with external and internal stimuli" and "leave their imprints on the mind which do not fade away but get stored up, remain active, and exert a continuous and powerful influence on the emotional and intellectual life of the individual." For Klein, though, the infant's affective relations to the world are untame, extreme, and confused; the same object, such as the mother's breast or hand or voice, may inspire feelings of intense love as well as anger. Equally important, the objects that inhabit this child's world are unformed, unrelated, disassociated from any particular body. Most famously, Klein argues that these "partial objects" occasion fantasies of introjection and projection, experiences that refuse any boundary between self and world. For Klein, "the breast of the mother is the object of [the infant's] constant desire, and therefore this is the first thing to be introjected. In phantasy the child sucks the breast into himself, chews it up and swallows it; thus he feels that he has actually got it there, that he possesses the mother's breast within himself, in both its good and in its bad aspects" (Klein 290–91).

As Klein suggests, the affective body operates according to an informed physiology, one that is both more supple and more acutely judgmental than anything structured by desire. It does not so much "read," let alone "desire," the objects of its environment; rather, a complete lack of oedipal structuration informs a more radical openness to the world and free-floating experiences of affect, a kind of extrinsic swerving through and around the charged masses on the horizon. Arguably, the Elvis experience recreates a similar affective experience and reconceives sociality in its terms. Desire gives way to affect in a field of dissolving bodies and free-floating partial objects—not least of which is sound— that wreck havoc on the body and its habitual relations with the world. Drawing upon Klein, Teresa Brennan stresses the notion that all affect is social in origin and physical in effect. Affect, she argues, emerges in an open encounter between two bodies and felt in the nerves and muscles of the soma. This means that "we are not self-contained in our energies. There is no secure distinction between the 'individual' and the 'environment'" and thus "between the biological and the social." For Brennan, social identity is sustained and often superceded by somatic transmission or contagion, a rhythmic linkage across bodies affected through chemical and nervous entrainment. The social group reignites and, at best, redesigns the affective experiences of the infant. It taps—particularly in a concert experience—something of the extremity and the content of the infantile affects, and thus works through "valences" rather than significations to establish more intensive communal bonds (Brennan 6–7, 65–6).

Not surprisingly, Elvis's oft-proclaimed innocence often took form as sheer infantilism, and his fans were accused of engaging in a perverse regression. Elvis's obsessive orality, his love of teddy bears and dodgem cars, his romantic relationship with his mother, his privately weak sex drive—again and again, the biography points towards an arrested development, a perverse, yet singularly compelling performance of infantile pleasure. Indeed, one might reasonably claim that Elvis basically transferred his intense bond with his mother to the stage. With his pet names, his scarves, and his chaste kisses—his performance was built upon an intimacy that was by turns sweet and tough, intimate and intense, surely Kleinian in its intense ambiguities. As he sang "Baby, Let's Play House" and "(I Wanna Be Your) Teddy Bear," he addressed the listener as cooing other and sadistic cribmate, and his voice exhibited all the narcissistic joy of baby babble, replete with hiccups, burps, coos, shrieks, and whispers.

For fans, of course, Elvis seemed to alternate between reckless child and tender lovin' caregiver. Detailing various Elvis encounters, they recall not only the dramatic and often conflicted affections of childhood, but also the intense focus and myopic perspective of the infant. One stage-side fan reported, "The closer I'm getting, [Elvis's face is] coming to life, getting bigger and bigger as you get closer and closer … and [he] just looks like he's going to crash into your face, coming down so fast [and lovingly], and he gave me a blue scarf" (qtd in Olmetti 62). Another fan directly links this infantile perspective with a sense of illicit drive:

> But I couldn't sit through this show like a good little girl…When I got to the second row I didn't think I would make it any closer…Right after that somebody in front of me raised their arms and I ducked under. There I was, I had made it!

I was actually standing right at Elvis's feet. The stage was about 6 ft. high and looked like a mountain. (Qtd in Olmetti 2)

Again and again, these accounts also reveal a Kleinian dynamic of pain and pleasure, hostility and adoration, marked especially by a gift-giving economy that Klein sees as the hallmark of infant/parent negotiation:

I was in the front row and Elvis was singing many songs and giving me more kisses and scarves than I had ever received. I said to my girlfriend that I wasn't feeling well and just after I said that, Elvis came over to my table again and gave me another kiss and scarf. (Qtd in Olmetti 6)

To be true to our sources, we should remember that these exchanges involved a whole range of bodily functions—crying, shrieking, pissing, spitting, and shredding. In the midst of any encounter with Mother Elvis, the body becomes infantile once more and the boundaries between inside and outside become fluid, supple, capable of transmutations otherwise impossible in the world outside the auditorium.

Importantly, Elvis and his handlers typically countered threats of deviant sexuality with a sense of childlike directness and emotional honesty. "I can't help it, Mama," the star once explained, "I just have to jump around when I sing. But it ain't vulgar. It's just the way I feel. I don't feel sexy when I'm singin'. If that was true, I'd be in some kinda institution as some kinda sex maniac" (qtd in Booth 165). These claims recall early defenses of Duchamp's *Fountain*, which similarly sought to counter charges of indecency by celebrating the object's sensual innocence.[11] As innocent, Elvis's body is nothing less than the potential out of which a whole range of new social feelings and experiences developed; the restoration of the body politic and a redrafting of laws inscribed upon it. In fact, watching Elvis's spastic body, we might recall Giorgio Agamben's claim that "By the end of the nineteenth century, the Western bourgeoisie had definitely lost its gestures." For Agamben, early twentieth-century art, particularly the obscene histrionics of stage and screen, reveal a cultural obsession with the failure of public communication. The distorted, flailing bodies of modern art and cinema exemplify the death-throes of a middle-class public culture, a last-ditch effort of the bourgeois world to record, scientifically, the expressive language of gesture as it slipped through their fingers. Gesture, in this regard, exists outside the orbit of either mundane communication or aesthetic wholeness; instead, it offers the exhibition of mediality, it is the process of making the body visible as a means. As Agamben explains, "If dance is gesture, it is so, rather, because it is nothing more than the endurance and the exhibition of the media character of corporal movements. *The gesture is the exhibition of mediality: it is the process of making a means visible as such*" (Agamben 49, 58). Perhaps modern dances—the twist, the lindy, the hop, Elvis's entire repertoire—function as a jumbled collection of more or less reified gestures calling for their liberation. These dances—isolated, frantic, mute—arise out of communicative

---

[11] Both texts quoted in Camfield, 38 and 40.

failure, but they also, following Agamben, expose communicability in its purist form. Elvis's song, with its seemingly disconnected and anti-expressive strings of burps, hiccups, and coos, may be nothing more than a compendium of vocal gestures. On stage, Elvis's body offers a more immediate, more directly public version of this mode, his flailing limbs revealing the medial character of public being as such. In both cases, though, a significant loss of coherence proves a great affective gain, charging the perceiver with a renewed sense of engagement.

The Third Elvis

In 1957 Evelyn Fraser, age 14, from Long Beach, California, sent *Movie Teen* a 19-point list of reasons of why she is "so ape" over Elvis. Amidst the usual adoration of the King's manliness and "yum-yum electricity," she offers extended descriptions of her idol's voice, face, expressions, gestures. Writing from the comfort of her four-postered, pillow-stuffed bed, Evelyn details the ways in which her idol's movements play upon her adolescent sensibilities. Interestingly, her account continually slips away from her professed desire; rather, her keen pleasure seems to exist in her visual detachment and the affective responses it allows:

> Elvis is so handsome the sight of his picture gives me goose bumps. No one has those blue eyes with the merry-lovin' twinkle behind them. And I wish I had a slow-moving film of that smile. I'd like to watch the crinkles start at the corners of his mouth, the way his full, lower lip opens downward and spreads, showing his wonderful even, sparkling white teeth. I could spend the rest of my days just watching this slow-motion picture of his smile...

While her specifically visual attention wanders across the surfaces of her image collection, Evelyn is responsive to the subtle feelings that arise within her body. Each photo is matched by a nearly nameless affection that manifests itself in chills, goosebumps, and other resonant states. Throughout, the fan—who claims to "sleep under an acre of Elvis pictures"—conflates Elvis's various moods with her own changing state. By the end, the boundary between gaze and object seems to dissolve entirely, description becomes creation and the fan's affective potential matches that of her adored object: "I've never met Elvis, it is true, but you can't say I don't know him...Elvis is IT with me." But she doesn't stop there, because Evelyn's great big teenage heart extends beyond Elvis to include a whole legion of fans, all bound by an affective tie that she can certainly feel, but never describe: "I'm sure I speak the sentiments of the thousands—hundreds of thousands—of girls who feel the same way."[12]

As an Americanist, I'm here inclined to borrow from Whitman: Evelyn Fraser—*you are large! you contain multitudes!* As a modernist, though, I'm drawn to Flaubert's more elusive pronouncement: *Evelyn Silber—c'est moi!* I must confess,

---

[12] "An Elvis Fan Tells All," 23.

when it comes to images of Elvis, my responses are less than scholarly. I can flip through Elvis scrapbooks for hours, ogling at each still. Every image inspires the same response, which is really no response at all, just a nearly empty amazement that seems to emerge from neither photo nor brain, but the very act of looking itself. My critical purchase (if you can call it such) takes shape as a simple, awestruck urgency: *Hey, you gotta see this. Do you see it? Look again—do you see it?!* Surely, here, with the image, when all of the immediacy of the music or the stage show becomes static, stagnant, contained by technology and commerce, affect should be checked by the most rigid structures of meaning. Here, though, even in this glossy glamorized form, Elvis seems to elude inscription to attain something like an apotheosis of affective being. Looking at these images, then, I hope to expose the continued importance of affect in a culture that otherwise seems to have been given over to mimetic reproduction and mass disenchantment.

Given any photograph of Elvis, we can easily locate its origins. We can name where and when it was taken, and we can reestablish a set of material forces— region, industry, and technology—that came together for such an image to exist. At the same time, we can read its symbolic coordinates; we can translate hair, skin, suit, and shoes, not to mention posture and other forms of body language into legible cultural meanings, a syntax of class, gender, and race. And yet, as in the famous 1956 photo used to promote Elvis (see Fig. 11.3), the eye is drawn to a number of seemingly irrelevant and perhaps irreverent details—the peculiar position of the feet, the odd twist of the hip, the dissymmetry of arms and uneven dynamism in the hands.

It is not so much that these features suggest awkwardness, but they elude any kind of posturing we might encounter in our everyday lives, and reveal a confluence of force that nearly collapses the body in upon itself. Simply put, this image convulses, and thus pushes us both towards and away from a certain corporeality, captures as it dissolves an experience of the body as such. This double movement—towards presence and absence, immediacy and mediation—seems to be augmented by the medium itself, which here serves to annul as it exposes the body's dynamism. It is not enough to say that the photographic image allows us to see what would otherwise go unnoticed in the rush of real time. Rather, the photograph amplifies the convulsion of the body, gives us a gestural body in action, at once surging and fading, obvious and elusive.

At times, Elvis's body takes a more directly abstract turn. In Fig. 11.4, Elvis reaches out, limply, lightly, with his right arm, while his left hangs bent, rigid, charged with a different quantum of energy and breaking the symmetry. His head hangs to his side, offsetting the straight line of his padded shoulders, but extending the line of his opposite arm. His face—as we see in the relations of mouth, nose, brow— is a marvel of Euclidean geometry, Cubist portraiture, and Beale Street flash.

The tracking the curves of this form occasions a disjointed, but undeniably compelling play of feelings. However, our responses to these photos depend precisely on the fact that these images are at once posed and corporeal, empty and full. Our judgment, if one may refer to this dumb experience as such, becomes

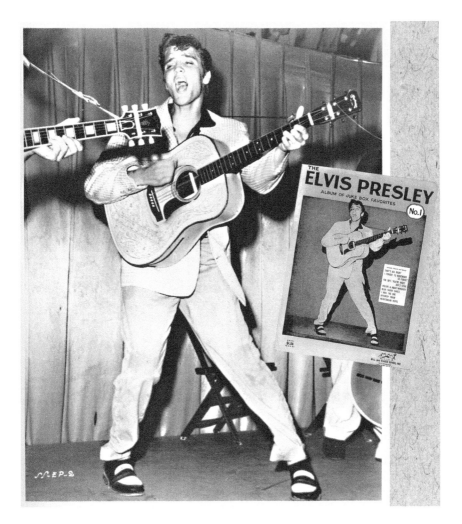

Fig. 11.3   Elvis publicity photograph (1956).

possible precisely in the double play of detachment and drive. Take, for example, the famous photo of Elvis stretched out against his bed (Fig. 11.5). Here, too, we find a conflation of otherwise opposed affects and gestures—fists raised over the head in a gesture at once defiant and weary, eyes turned upward in a mixture of love, curiosity, and resignation. The key feature, though, remains Elvis's chest, which spreads openly across the frame, available for a range of meanings and investments. It is at once exposed and weak; present, hunky, available, and yet silent, empty, blank; we can, and might, find everything and nothing written on this chest.

Fig. 11.4   Elvis performing.

Helpfully, the confluence of historical forces that pushed Elvis to mimetic fame also inspired, across the Atlantic, French semiotician Roland Barthes to develop a startling theory of the image and its increasing social significance. Here, I am most interested in an essay titled "The Third Meaning," in which Barthes explores the affective voluptuousness of the image as such. Barthes begins with the idea of the photographic image as a "message without a code." A photograph, as a form of signification, "reduces," but by no means "transforms" its referent, and thus maintains a direct connection with the fleshy world. In this, the photograph is always situated at the limit of meaning; neither simply denotative or connotative, natural or discursive, it is—like Elvis's chest—at once too full and too slight, at once bloated and meager as a form of signification (Barthes 32, 54). For Barthes, though, as perhaps for Evelyn Fraser and a host of other teenage gawkers, this slippery dimension of the image is precisely what holds attention. The image is open at both ends, meaty and measly, present and detached, but never quite either, and thus both alluring and free. Once denotative and connotative readings are exhausted, Barthes writes, "I am still held by the image. I read, I receive… a third meaning—evident, erratic, obstinate. I do not know what its signified is, at

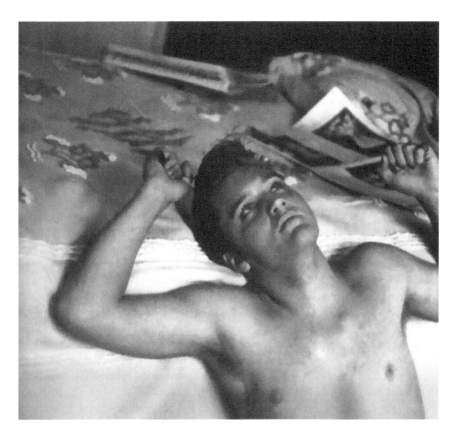

Fig. 11.5   Elvis at rest.

least I am unable to give it a name, but I can see clearly the traits, the signifying accidents of which this—consequently incomplete—sign is composed" (53). As opposed to denotation and connotation, the third meaning is an "obtuse" meaning. At once provocative and plastic, engaging and ethereal, it inspires a slippery sort of attentiveness, a pleasurable careening of the sensibilities. It communicates by valences and vectors, shifts and swerves of attention, leading the reader, affectively, but not necessarily cogently, across the surface of the text.

For me, this analysis works as a theory of popular reading, describing how fans find themselves moved in relation to often cheap objects of affection. Barthes reads just like 14-year-old Evelyn Fraser—their common responses are linked by the common, expansive, ridiculously inarticulate logic of the drive. Indeed, their method reveals that the difference between drive and desire is the difference between mattering and meaning, between a pleasurably swerving aim, open to all sorts of cheap diversions, and a significant goal, hammered out by rigid discourse. As Mladen Dolar explains, describing the voice as an object cause of the drive, "there is the dimension of the drive which does not follow the signifying logic, but, rather, turns around the object…as something evasive and not conducive to signification" (Dolar 72). Importantly, though, while the drive may be common, sluttish, game, it still feels its way with precision and it judges without hesitation. At once dumb and distinct, incredibly vague and yet acutely felt, the drive informs not only our most eager, but also our most earnest, most sincere responses to popular culture. In fact, Barthes never truly shies away from the language of value and judgment, for it is precisely at his most deconstructive that he turns to something like an evaluation: "I believe," he writes, "that the obtuse meaning carries a certain *emotion*…it is an emotion which simply *designates* what one loves, what one wants to defend: an emotion-value, an evaluation" (59). Thus, the third meaning moves silently, without friction, across the face of an otherwise rigid, mediated world, casually dislodging its stubborn values and judgments.

As I've been arguing, Elvis's fame and significance resides in his affective, rather than his symbolic body. His revolt is cultivated through spontaneous gestures and their affective resonances; at once primitive and posed, engaged and detached, his body discloses itself as a socially mediated body and thus becomes something like a compelling ethical proposition, a public proposition. Perhaps the most telling moment of Elvis's career occurred during his junior year of high school, when he showed up to shop class wearing a scarf (Guralnick 50). Just like that—no explanations, no excuses, no precedent even—just a shy boy in a scarf working the drill press. No biographer has been able to track the cause of this impulsive and seemingly empty declaration. No psychologist has unearthed the original trauma that may have tied up this flimsy, casual knot. No cultural theorist has been able to link the hard chains of historical causality to this insubstantial charm. Perhaps, though, the significance of this scarf—as with any readymade—resides precisely in its unaccountability, its flamboyant uselessness. Elvis's scarf is like his song: an emphatic gesture, a forced expression of self-mediation. In this, it does not cancel or even challenge history as such; rather, it operates within its own gambit, its own circuit of affective intensity, in ways that only indirectly impact the chronicle of events and their assumed meanings. Like a dark star or hidden magnet, Elvis polarized everything he touched, reeling out all manner of subatomic moods, feelings, and tones. His was an accidental, indifferent fame, at once oblivious and obtuse, powerful in its very shallowness. Elvis's pompadour, drenched with Rose Oil tonic and Vaseline. Elvis's shirts, bought by the dozen from Lansky's on Beale. Elvis's pink and white Cadillac. Elvis's columned mansion. Elvis's kung fu fighting. Elvis's peanut butter and banana sandwich. Elvis's monkey. With every useless stylish thrust, he recreated both his body and the body politic. And through records, radio, television, and film, this revolt has been extended across time and space, sanctioning legions of unruly kids to try out anything on their own gangly, outcast frames.

PART 3
Stellar Afterimages

Chapter 12
Modernism Is the Age of Chaplin[1]

Jonathan Goldman

In 1918 Charlie Chaplin released *Shoulder Arms*, a short film that makes a large claim. *Shoulder Arms* suggests that its writer/director/producer/superstar deserves to reside in the stratospheric heights where his literary contemporaries were locating themselves through linguistic and narratorial experiment. Though the film comprises a comedic look at life in the World War I trenches, it is neither the imperative of its title, nor the underlying high seriousness of its subject matter, nor the fact that at its New York premier at the Broadway Theater it was paired with a Verdi aria that claims to elevate Chaplin to the authorial ferment. Rather, it is the film's announcement of a new kind of filmmaker—an idealized figure of the author as both source and endpoint of all meaning—which makes *Shoulder Arms* a text that formally echoes the machinations of literary modernism. Chaplin invents himself as a figure who might match not only Foucault's description of the author who appears "so transcendent…that, as soon as he speaks, meaning begins to proliferate, to proliferate indefinitely" (221) but also those modernists—Joyce, Stein, and company—whose idiosyncratic representational techniques imagine a similar, irreproducible, godlike creator.

The film's opening constitutes what at a glance seems an unremarkable title card, displaying the words "Shoulder Arms written and produced by"—above a blank space. Alongside these words is an image of the Tramp, already by 1918 Chaplin's universally recognized screen persona. This particular iteration of the Tramp wears doughboy garb, but remains identifiable by his hallmark mustache and splayed feet. The convention of the static title card is immediately disrupted by motion, as a real (celluloid) human hand, monstrously huge next to the Tramp, moves in front of the camera from off-screen. Its index finger first mimes underlining the printed words, then points at the illustration. The hand produces a piece of chalk (it seems) then elaborately signs "Charles Chaplin," filling the blank slate that has been reserved for the author's signature. In this way the opening announces the film as a product of one single author, represented by a giant, godlike hand.

---

[1]   Some of the material and language in this essay appears in a previous version of the piece, which can be found in the online journal *M/C* under the title "Double Exposure: Charlie Chaplin as Author and Celebrity" (http://journal.media-culture.org.au/0411/05-goldman.php).

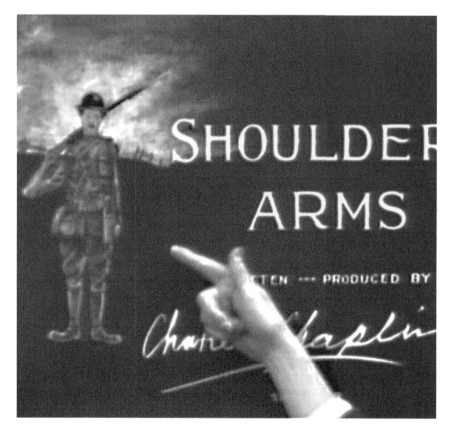

Fig. 12.1   The godlike hand of the author, in *Shoulder Arms*, dir. by Charles
              Chaplin (1918).

But there is another Chaplin here, embodied in the immediately identifiable image: that the Tramp is disfigured by the uniform but remains "the Tramp" underscores the image's universal recognizability. So, if the hand of Chaplin provides an inimitable signature of the author, a literalizing of what Jaffe calls the authorial imprimatur, then the Tramp, the trademark image of Chaplin, provides an inimitable signature of the celebrity. But wait; there's more. For its final gesture the superhuman hand pantomimes shooting a gun at the movie star Tramp. The same index finger that had pointed at the Tramp as if to remind the audience, that image there refers to me, now becomes the barrel of a gun, trained on the image. The relationship between the celebrity icon and the film's "writer" is co-dependent but antagonistic. The hand that signs the author's name (in the less familiar, non-diminutive form) wishes violence on the body.

Thus at the opening of *Shoulder Arms* Chaplin combines the creation of himself as author with ambivalence if not antipathy toward his cinematic image. To compound matters, we might take into account the historical events surrounding

Chaplin's relationship to WWI; criticized for not fighting the war, he used his celebrity stature to sell war bonds and fund the allies' efforts. The split between author and image therefore also works in contextual material, as Chaplin plants the seeds of division between himself and the doughboy who only dreams of fighting the Kaiser. (Indeed, the Tramp's wartime heroics in the film are revealed as a dream.)[2] This reading reinforces the sense that Chaplin is using his image on screen as a way of asserting that he himself is elsewhere. The body of the Tramp emerges as what Slavoj Žižek, in a reading of Chaplin's *City Lights* (1931), calls "the remainder" of the text—that which is "left over" from the narrative (7). Žižek notes that the Tramp's body is always in the way of things; he becomes "a disturbing stain one tries to get rid of as quickly as possible" (4). The disturbance, I will argue here, stems from the fact that Chaplin, unlike his modernist writer counterparts, creates his immaterial authorial persona while keeping his body on display, and therefore must find something to do with the image. The gesture seems paradoxical for a filmmaker, perhaps, but not for a modernist. *Shoulder Arms* creates a distinction between the body that appears on camera and the authorial consciousness that resides beyond the confines of the text, a stratagem that would resonate throughout the rest of Chaplin's career, and, I will suggest, throughout twentieth-century culture.

In the context of this volume my treatment of Chaplin will serve several purposes: it constitutes both a case study of perhaps the greatest celebrity during the modernist moment, and an argument that Chaplin uniquely reveals the commonalities between celebrity and modernist authorship. By de-authorizing the image of his body—shoulder, arms, and all—as a representation of the author, Chaplin further aligns himself with, and suggests that his works be considered alongside, those writers who were simultaneously forging distinct literary mannerisms which point to the idea of the unique author. Chaplin thus shows us that the kind of imprimatur we associate with modernism extends its influence into the realm of popular celebrity. I conclude the essay by arguing that Chaplin, while establishing his authorial consciousness as separate and above his image, recuperates the celebrity icon. Particularly in *Modern Times*, as I will show, Chaplin treats the Tramp as an indexical marker, a representation of his historical moment (the Age of Chaplin), and an image through which the multitudes achieve self-realization. Through his treatment of the Tramp, Chaplin suggests that his own universal familiarity authorizes the image to represent history itself, and that celebrity has become a way of narrating collective experience. This version on celebrity persists to this day. In other words, via Chaplin we learn to see the celebrity ferment as the guiding lights to understand our own culture.

---

[2]   I am indebted to Pearl James for drawing my attention to how the author/image split invokes the WWI contexts specifically.

Birth of the Author

As my discussion of the *Shoulder Arms* title card suggests, Chaplin's works are marked by a particular division between author and image, of body and subject. That bifurcation is rooted in Chaplin's improbable early fame, improbable because of the genre in which it developed.[3] Chaplin broke into moving pictures in 1914 as an ensemble performer in Mack Sennett's Keystone productions, an arena supposedly resistant to the star system that was taking over much of the film industry. Sennett's studio "promote[d] its stock company and studio formula over individual stars" (Riblet 168–9). Indeed, the slapstick genre, which Sennett helped codify, leaves little room for performers' individualization. These films put both people and things interchangeably at the mercy of unpredictable physical laws. Within this genre Chaplin's characters are often barely able to control the body's movements. A scene from Sennett's only feature-length work, *Tillie's Punctured Romance* (1914), also the first feature-length slapstick production, offers an example. Chaplin, fleeing the jilted Tillie (Marie Dressler), almost runs full-tilt into a police officer, braking just in time with a hopping stutter-step of the sort familiar to anyone who ever has watched classic slapstick such as the Keystone Kops, or MGM's Tom and Jerry cartoons. He repeats this motion three times, using it to counter his momentum, as he careens into the street, trips and falls over the curb, finds another police officer looming above him, rushes in the direction of the camera, reverses direction and rushes back. Susan McCabe describes Chaplin in such moments as having an "elastic body [that] is never rendered entirely volitional" (433). The film grants Chaplin only a limited degree of agency, imperfect authority over the body's movements. It reinforces this lack of control by bouncing Chaplin's image between more powerful bodies, those either larger (Tillie) or bearing insignias of the state (the policemen). We might say that, within Sennett's films, Chaplin's image makes him more object than subject.[4]

With the image of his body stripped of agency and subjectivity, Chaplin's rise to stardom belies most accounts of early cinema celebrity. The Hollywood stars of Chaplin's day were thought to "reveal purified feelings within [the body]" and provide "models of the well-integrated self" (Fowles 27). Richard Dyer has written influential analyses of this logic, arguing that stars "articulate what it is to be a human being in contemporary society; that is, they express the particular notion we hold of the 'individual.'" This star-function relies on "the idea of the separable, coherent quality, located 'inside' the body and variously termed 'the self,' 'the soul,' 'the subject' and so on" (15). Early film stardom, in these critical

---

[3]   Charles Maland's *Chaplin and American Culture* is one of the best and most recent of the many accounts of Chaplin's rise to fame. See 3–55 in particular.

[4]   Fernand Léger picks up on this construction of Chaplin's image, depicting the Tramp as a marionette for the opening sequence of his *Ballet Mécanique* (1924), alongside the words, "Charlot présente le ballet mécanique." Similarly, in "A Look at Chaplin," Walter Benjamin writes that Chaplin's "mask of indifference turns him into a sideshow marionette" (310).

accounts, proposes that the celebrity images articulate, in fact incorporate, a coherent interiority, a fully realized subject; celebrities offered both a reaffirmation and an embodiment of the subject to a culture beset by these anxieties concerning justification of the self. While these scholars establish a basis for understanding the rise of mass-mediated celebrity, they do not entirely explain the particularities of a figure like Chaplin, as I will show.

The Chaplin story further contradicts the standard accounts of cinema celebrity insofar as his early persona is not created in close-ups. The cinematic device of the close-up was conceived as a way to make the interior life legible; D.W. Griffiths, credited with popularizing the technique in the nineteen-teens, claimed that the close-up was his way of "photographing thought" (Schickel 47). That close-ups were nearly a ubiquitous component of the production of stars during the silent era is noted by Mary Ann Doane, who writes: "with the formation of a star system heavily dependent upon the maintenance of the aura, the close-up became an important means of establishing the recognizability of each star" (46). Such remarks underscore a critical consensus that early film stardom relies on a notion that images somehow reveal the subject residing within the body, proposing an interrelation of surface and depth that is at least correlative, if not actually indexical. In other words, the image is proposed as a sign by which the subject, housed within, can be read and understood.

Chaplin's initial screen appearances diverge from accounts of celebrity-production, in part by eschewing the close-up.[5] *Tillie's Punctured Romance*, for example, unfolds almost entirely in medium-range shots, with an absence of close-ups even at moments when the narrative seems to call for one. In one scene, Chaplin and his partner in crime (Mabel Normand) escape to a movie house screening a film about a con artist. Watching this film-within-a-film, the two characters fidget and exchange glances. At this moment of self-reflection, however, the film never isolates one image, severely restricting the sense that these images can be considered as representing subjects. This is the style of film in which Chaplin's star is born; it foreshadows that Chaplin's treatment of his image will complicate the version of celebrity attributed to his contemporaries in the film industry.

Rather than imbuing the Tramp with an interior, Chaplin, as he began writing and directing films himself,[6] transformed his image into an emblem of authorial control, one that, in fact, matches his involvement with practically every aspect of film production. In this way he dramatizes his production of an author who generates and governs meaning. Chaplin takes the very conventions of slapstick and manipulates them to establish the Tramp as less prone to the chaos of physical objects—a stark contrast with the limited agency granted to characters in

---

[5]   The only actual close-up I have found in Chaplin's early films occurs in *A Woman* (1915), which features Chaplin in drag. It depicts Chaplin's face minus the mustache, as if to use a close-up to defamiliarize him.

[6]   This move itself was not unusual, as many of the performers at Keystone took turns at directing.

Sennett's films. So Chaplin's characterization of the Tramp in *The Vagabond* (1916), for instance, associates his image with control. Here, the Tramp, embroiled in a barroom brawl, runs toward the saloon's swinging doors and neatly sidesteps before reaching them; he has learned to overcome cartoonish stutter-step by now. The Tramp's pursuer, however, has not. His momentum carries him through the doorway and out of the frame. This moment, like the scene in *The Rink* (1916), in which the Tramp literally skates circles around the other characters who slip and fall all over the ice, grants the Tramp a degree of volition that marks him as different from the other images. Other characters are holdovers from the slapstick genre, but the Tramp seems to exist in a less chaotic genre of film. These treatments of the celebrity image announce that the films are controlled by one unified subjectivity.[7] In a 1924 article Gilbert Seldes comments on this change in Chaplin's films: "It was foreordained that the improvised kind of comedy should give way to something more calculated" (36). Seldes observes the more disciplined universe of Chaplin's films. The Tramp, acting as a fulcrum of control, obliquely but unmistakably refers to the author who has created the text.

This treatment of the image is instrumental in generating the idea of the author. It makes visible the machinations of authorship of the sort considered by Foucault, who writes, "[w]e are used to thinking that the author is so different from all other men, and so transcendent...that, as soon as he speaks, meaning begins to proliferate, to proliferate indefinitely. The truth is quite the contrary: the author does not precede the works" (221). Instead, the author is defined by "a series of specific and complex operations" (216). In this formulation, authors do not create meaning; rather, formal attributes of the text create the idea of the author. The intertwining formal and narrative shift in Chaplin's work, marked by films such as *The Rink*, create the idea of Chaplin, beyond the film, beyond his celebrity image, as author. As Chaplin's career flourished throughout the decade of high modernism, his films continued to enact this author-production. In Chaplin, however, the text that creates the author also relies on the author's celebrity, assumes audiences' familiarity with the Chaplin of the industrial apparatus. As Richard deCordova has written, "discursive practices produce the star's identity, an identity that does not exist within the individual star...but rather in the connections between and among a wide variety of texts—films, interviews, publicity photos, etc." (120). Chaplin's films, increasing in length and complexity, increasingly gesture beyond their diegesis—beyond that representation of a bounded fictional world—and toward the figure of Chaplin as author of the film, known from previous films and intertextual discourses.

---

[7]   By announcing himself as, literally, an "author," Chaplin participates in a critical discussion concerning whether film should be seen as a product of one mind or many—"the controversy," as Rudolph Arnheim puts it, "between the individuals and the collectivists" (67). In "Who is the Author of a Film?" Arnheim writes of "a recent conception [which] implies an exaltation of the director...He alone was said to be the author of a film" (63).

In *Modern Times* (1936), for example, synchronized sound repeatedly invokes the extra-diegetic Chaplin. The use of sound incorporates into the film Chaplin's famous reluctance to film dialogue, making Chaplin's well-known choice of production methods part of the film's meaning. Although the talkies started to appear in the late 1920s, Chaplin had held out against dialogue throughout the 1930s. *Modern Times* continues to eschew dialogue except for the two moments when a voice emanates from the radio or from the factory boss' giant two-way screen—two moments, that is, when voices are mediated through technology (within the diegesis, as well as without). These instances bear crucial implications in light of *Modern Times'* obvious distaste for the increased mechanization of society.[8] Of greater import here, however, is that both the plot of the film and Chaplin's author-production reach a catharsis, through the issue of sound, when the moment comes for the Tramp to perform the singing half of his job as a singing waiter—when the Tramp is supposed to use his voice.

The film has provided an intense buildup to this moment. The Tramp needs work to survive, and needs to sing in order to keep his job. Chaplin's voice, of course, had never been heard in his movies. When the manager asks "Can you sing?" the Tramp touches his neck as if wondering whether there is a voice in there at all, a motion clearly invoking the extradiegetic figure of Chaplin and his resistance to sound. At this point the film clearly becomes about Chaplin the author, as much or more than it is about the plot surrounding the Tramp. As the crucial moment approaches, Chaplin draws out the suspense; the Tramp loses his lyric sheet, causing him to look about in a panic over what words to sing. He finally sings nonsense syllables. His gesticulations convey the song's meaning (though his intonation participates). It is a polemic, readable in context of the fame of Chaplin's strident resistance to dialogue in film. The significance of this entire sequence, of sound in *Modern Times*, lies in its insistent creation of the author.

While Chaplin situates his author-production around the Tramp, he maintains a separation between his cinematic persona and the extradiegetic Chaplin. As if suspicious that the image can adequately represent the subject, he uses the image but only to suggest the author who is located elsewhere. For instance, Chaplin usually places the Tramp in the role of the protagonist, in fact the hero, of his narratives, a stratagem that elevates the image in relation to the other characters. He does so, however, without endowing the Tramp with the particular physical abilities that distinguish the hero of other genres of film. The Tramp, that is, rarely performs deeds with guns, swords or fists. The Tramp's brand of heroism corresponds to Siegfried Kracauer's argument that slapstick makes the hero a figure of luck. Kracauer writes that slapstick does not "highlight the performer's proficiency in braving death and surmounting impossible difficulties; rather, it minimize[s] his accomplishments in a constant effort to present rescues as the

---

[8]   Barnard writes that the film is "clearly intended to strip the phrase 'modern times' of its associations with technological boosterism" (22).

outcome of sheer chance."[9] In other words, while Douglas Fairbanks dons the mask of Zorro and swashbuckles around with swords and guns, denoting a hero with superior physical attributes, the slapstick hero achieves success without his abilities having had much to do with it. In Chaplin's films, however, the Tramp's "luck" invokes the superior physical attributes of the extradiegetic Chaplin. For example, in *The Circus* (1928), the Tramp finds himself performing a high wire act without the hidden rope he had meant to attach. The Tramp, in Žižek's description of this scene, "starts to gesticulate wildly, trying to keep his balance, while the [diegetic] audience laughs and applauds, mistaking this desperate struggle for survival for a comedian's virtuosity" (4).

The irony is that this performance does, of course, represent a comedian's virtuosity: Chaplin's. The circus audience is so wrong that it is right; though the crowd erroneously identifies the Tramp's actions as a demonstration of his abilities, their response invokes the Chaplin situated outside of the narrative. This scene withholds physical prowess from the character, displacing it, extradiegetically, on to the celebrity.[10] To be sure, the virtuosity of Fairbanks similarly gestures toward the celebrity's real body. Fairbanks's physical skill, however, plays a diegetic function that suggests no separation between celebrity and image; Zorro's abilities have an indexical relationship to Fairbanks's abilities, matching them exactly. Chaplin's ironic play with the Tramp's clumsiness while the circus audience cheers for a virtuosic performance invokes the historical Chaplin, beyond the diegesis, delimiting the character's capacity to represent him.

Chaplin, indeed, enforces the separation of image and subject inherited from Sennett's films, continually demonstrating that the Tramp is not to be equated with Chaplin. As Devin Anthony Orgeron and Martha Gabrielle Orgeron argue, "Chaplin produces a double discourse: as the Tramp he is the unknowing, perhaps ambiguous sign, but as Chaplin the director he is creating a critical and specific reading of that sign." In other words, the Tramp figure serves as an object which points to an author outside of the text. For instance, *The Idle Class* (1921) casts Chaplin in two roles in order to signal the inadequacy of either as a location of the subject. Chaplin plays, and the title refers to, both the penurious Tramp and a wealthy, tuxedoed alcoholic

---

[9]   For Kracauer, slapstick's emphasis on chance at the expense of physical abilities registers "the emergence of a public sphere that is unpredictable and volatile." See *Theory of Film* 26. He therefore claims it as a pluralist, in fact anarchic, move. Clearly, Chaplin's treatment of his cinematic image revises these pluralistic possibilities. Kracauer's comment underlines how Chaplin's treatment of the celebrity image imposes order rather than anarchy. The tightrope scene points toward the particular abilities of the celebrity, rather than the public sphere–hardly an invitation to anarchy.

[10]   Michael North recently noted something similar: "the more helpless the comedian is in the role of dramatic hero, the more skillful he has had to be in handling the technical demands of filmmaking" (*Machine-Age Comedy* 11). North uses the observation to compare filmmaking styles of Chaplin, who "mute[s] this fact," and Buster Keaton, who uses Rube Goldberg-style machines to draw humorous attention to technology. Chaplin, I am arguing, uses the same dynamic to create a separation between the image and the author.

named Charles. Although Maland contends that these dual personas allegorize Chaplin's biographical contradictions as a rich celebrity born into the working class (60), the film does not merely provide two separate images of Chaplin; it complicates the notion that images have a direct correlation to a subject located inside the body. The plot of *The Idle Class* stems from a case of mistaken identity, as the revelers at a masquerade ball assume the Tramp is really Charles in costume. It thematizes the question of which image contains which identity. The film only shows both on screen simultaneously when Charles dons a suit of armor whose helmet visor is jammed shut, masking his face. Trying to prove his identity as the real millionaire, Charles enlists the Tramp to help remove the helmet, resulting in the evocative sight of two supposed images of Chaplin trying to wrestle the disguise off of one of them, struggling to remove the exterior in order to verify the interior. Once the visor is lifted, with the Tramp still visible, the film provides a brief glimpse of Charles's face—but only from medium-range, as a close-up of Chaplin at this moment would literally reaffirm the correspondence of the image to the subject in a way that the film is resisting.

The Idle Class makes use of the celebrity image to stage a separation between the image and the extradiegetic Chaplin, registering suspicion that a single image can adequately represent a single subjectivity. Although Michael North considers *The Idle Class* one of Chaplin's "allegories of unwilling reproduction, Chance dropping the tramp into situations in which he must face and in some cases fight his mirror image," he misses the way the film is always sure to reject any assertion that the images on screen contain the subject (*Reading 1922* 168). In this way Chaplin devises a metonymic relationship between author and image; the Tramp cannot encompass the author, only refer to him. Chaplin's films exhibit a distrust, if not actual rejection, of the idea that an image can embody the author.

This suspicion toward the image reverberates in critical receptions of Chaplin's work, transforming the films by establishing, in some perspectives, their credentials as art rather than mere entertainment. For instance, Walter Benjamin's take on Chaplin simultaneously lauds Chaplin's elite qualities and re-enacts the division between author and image. Benjamin compares Chaplin with Shakespeare, arguing that, as Shakespeare's stage acting is the least important aspect of his work, so the image of Chaplin on screen is less noteworthy than his writing and directing. He writes, "Chaplin's relationship to film is fundamentally not that of the actor-protagonist at all, let alone that of a star…one can almost say that Chaplin, seen in his totality, is as little a performer as the actor William Shakespeare was… he is the poet of his films, that is, as director" ("A Look at Chaplin" 309). Benjamin opposes the "star" that performs to the "poet" who composes. The comparison to Shakespeare specifically, and poets generally, proposes that true artists work off-stage or off-camera, not as figures of display. (There is no audience for watching someone write.) The image of Chaplin's body disturbs Benjamin to the extent that he tries to wish it away altogether. Referring to Philippe Soupault's treatment of Chaplin, he writes, "Soupault, unlike virtually all previous commentators, sees the peak of Chaplin's work in *L'Opinion Publique* [*A Woman of Paris* (1923)], a film in which, as is well known, Chaplin himself did not appear at all" (310). Benjamin emphasizes the irreconcilability of author and image implied by Chaplin's works. His approach suggests that in order for a work to achieve elite status its author must remain invisible.

The Body is History

As the opening of *Shoulder Arms* reminds us, despite Chaplin's conception of himself as an author whose subjectivity transcends the image, the Tramp remains present, if not quite accounted for. Here, Foucault's theory of the author finds its limitations, unable to completely explain the operations of author-production that relies on the image even as it situates the author outside the narrative. The Tramp, which Benjamin and Chaplin's godlike hand both want so badly to get rid of, seems to get in the way of the idealized model of the author. But it remains an image that is recognizable even when reduced to its simplest components of mustache, bowler, baggy pants, splayfeet, and some combination of cane, tails, and plaid waistcoat. For example, the plot of *The Kid* (1921), hinges on the need of the Mother (Edna Purviance) to track down the Tramp. To this end, she places a personal ad in the newspaper (depicted in a close-up) that announces her search for a "little man with large flat feet and a small mustache." The narrative depends upon whether characters will identify the Tramp using these indexical clues and therefore invokes the image's recognizability, its ubiquity within Chaplin's films and intertextual discourses. *Sunny Side* (1919) unfolds similarly, opening with the Tramp in bed, encased in a nightgown that it turns out he wears over the baggy pants and waistcoat. Gradually removing the outer garment to reveal his outfit, Chaplin creates the joke that he sleeps dressed this way, and thus reinforces this image's trademark quality. By enlisting his image's familiarity, Chaplin insists on it, making the image recognizable by assuming its recognizability.

Chaplin thus makes his image into an icon, a "universal symbol" as Seldes calls it (35). "The iconic quality of any celebrity is also the zenith of a career" writes P. David Marshall, adding, "what the icon represents is the possibility that the celebrity has actually entered the language of the culture and can exist whether the celebrity continues to 'perform' or dies" (17). Chaplin's films promote his Tramp as an image that represents more than himself. Rather, it becomes an emblem of the collective experience provided by his films, proposing that his work unifies everyone in his audience, possibly the largest audience in the world during his career's apex. He casts the Tramp as the insignia of the masses who consume his movies.[11] In other words, while granting the image only a metonymic relation to

---

[11]   Marshall offers a detailed analysis of how celebrities articulate a particular audience in terms of consumption practices throughout his *Celebrity and Power*, particularly 56–76. Whereas he focuses on the particular audience identity, the "audience-subjectivity" generated by each audience, my concern is with the way Chaplin enlists the sheer size of his audience, characterizing his appeal as universal.

the author and leaving it over as Žižek's "remainder," Chaplin also asserts that the celebrity image makes legible his mass audience.

As an emblem of the masses, the icon becomes, in *Modern Times*, a close-up of history. Unusual within the Chaplin canon, *Modern Times* takes pains to announce that it is set in a specific period, the early 1930s, a moment indicated first by the title and second the film's striking scenes of social unrest. The narrative unfolds against a backdrop of historical change, onto which Chaplin superimposes the Tramp, who exists, as usual, somewhat apart from the urban sets and Hollywood extras. Chaplin withholds the icon during the first section of the film, putting the character in factory clothes. When the Tramp emerges in his trademark regalia after a stay in the "hospital," his appearance has the effect of those moments in *The Kid* and *Sunny Side*, invoking the familiarity of the icon. Moreover, the arrival of the icon coincides with the arrival of a new historical stage. Chaplin indicates the temporal transition through a montage of filmmaking techniques: abrupt cross-cutting between shots at tilted angles, superimpositions, and crowds of people and cars moving rapidly through the city, all set to jarring, brass-wind music. The film then situates the Tramp contiguously with signs of social upheaval, first placing him against a backdrop of a closed factory and, then putting him at the vanguard of a socialist demonstration (to which he remains oblivious). This sequence unites signs of social upheaval, technological advancement and Chaplin's own cinematic skills to indicate that the film has entered "modern times"—all spurred by the appearance of the celebrity image. In fact, some of the most vivid and famous scenes of the film, such as when Chaplin is subjected to the feeding device or takes a trip through the giant gears of the factory, are established as the film's past, a moment prior to the modern times and social unrest that ensue.[12] *Modern Times* thus uses the icon as a marker of historical change. The celebrity image becomes at once a universally identifiable emblem of Chaplin's mass audience and a sign of this moment in history. Modern times, Chaplin suggests, are Chaplin's times, the age of Chaplin and his audience.

In such scenes Chaplin authorizes his icon to function as a sign of history, a figure that connotes the celebrity, his mass audience, and their specific moment in time. The logic behind this production of the icon is clarified by Benjamin's concept of the dialectical image that furnishes a culture with a method of identifying itself:

> What distinguishes images from the "essences" of phenomenology is their historical index...For the historical index of the images not only says that they belong to a particular time; it says, above all, that they attain a legibility only at a particular time...Every present day is determined by the images that are synchronic with it: each "now" is of a particular recognizability...[I]mage is that wherein what has been comes together in a flash with the now to form a

---

[12]   The factory sequence mimics such iconic 1920s films as *Ballet Mécanique* and Fritz Lang's *Metropolis*. The influence further suggests that these scenes represent a prior historical moment within the narrative.

constellation. In other words: image is dialectics at a standstill. For while the relation of the present to the past is purely temporal, the relation of what-has-been to the now is dialectical: not temporal in nature but figural.

Benjamin argues that although images and time are in a sense opposed—as images are static but time moves from "what has been" to "now"—images can provide a static figure of temporality. In this system images achieve "a particular recognizability" at a specific historical moment and define that moment by crystallizing the dialectical relationship between past and present. That is to say, graspable images put temporality in stasis. Clearly, Benjamin and Chaplin are pursuing similar lines of thought in different forms of production. In Benjamin's terms, *Modern Times* elevates Chaplin's Tramp icon to the status of historical emblem by suggesting that its familiarity makes it a static figure of his moment, defined against and incorporating the "what-has-been" of the past. Justus Nieland, in his assessment of Chaplin as modernist, sees Chaplin in a productively similar way. He writes that Chaplin constitutes "a story of the modern person's relationship to temporality and historicity…that is everywhere synonymous with the potential— and threat—of Chaplin's eccentric personality" (252). Though Nieland's focus is on the affect of the eccentric, he points out that Chaplin's identification with his moment is exactly what constitutes his modernism.

My thinking springboards from Benjamin and Nieland in that I see Chaplin's work demonstrating that the celebrity image, specifically, acts as historical marker—that the mass audience, specifically, legitimates his Tramp as the sign of its times. Chaplin thus assigns celebrity the social function of signifying history. Richard Schickel, for one, has retrospectively identified Chaplin's time with the inception of this model of celebrity. Schickel calls the celebrity image "a walking context [that] we apprehend instantly" (*Intimate Strangers* 70). He claims that these images contain their own historical backdrop and become figures for their eras, and that this cultural function for celebrity images as tokens of their historical moments all starts in the 1920s: "[F]or no previous era is it possible to make a history out of images…for no subsequent era is it possible to avoid doing so. For most of us, now, this *is* history" (70–71). Schickel proposes modernism as a moment that provides the techniques and the logic to treat the celebrity image as history. Considered alongside this argument, Chaplin appears to be participating in a broader cultural imperative of distilling the passage of time into an image that, by virtue of being ubiquitous during a particular era, now embodies that era.

By gesturing beyond the supposed boundary of the text, toward Chaplin's audience, the Tramp image makes legible that significant portion of the population unified in recognition of Chaplin's celebrity, affirming that the celebrity sign depends on its wide circulation to attain significance. As Marshall writes, "The celebrity's power is derived from the collective configuration of its meaning" (65). The image's connotative function requires collaboration with the audience, the Tramp's recognizability to that audience, as it moves through scenes of historical change, whatever other discourses may attach to it. North writes that to critical admirers, "Chaplin appealed as the symbol of a symbol, one so purified of the abstract and arbitrary that it could be read and understood universally" (166). That is, Chaplin's universality was understood as encoded within the Tramp image, turning the icon into a figure around which a culture organizes itself.

The attempt to separate author and image that permeates Chaplin's work thus enables this principal role of the celebrity. Despite working in film, or perhaps because of it, Chaplin evinces a deep distrust of the image as a suitable location for the subject. Instead, wedding the devices of literary modernism with the popular medium of film, he generates an idealized figure of the author, which leaves behind the image. Denuded of the authorial subjectivity, yet an icon of the celebrity's mass popularity, the image becomes an embodiment of Chaplin's audience—the millions around the world who can apprehend his image at a glance. In other words, Chaplin's echoes of literary modernism, his preference for articulating the author through the narratives and formal devices of his work rather than through his Tramp icon, are what allow us to understand the way celebrity images have become our close-ups of historical moments, though which we see, not the subject within, but the mass movements of culture.

Chapter 13
On Retrofitting:
Samuel Beckett, Tourist Attraction

Stephen Watt

> Do we give up fighting so the tourists come
> Or fight the harder so they stay at home?
> —Derek Mahon, "An Bonnán Bol," *The Yellow Book*, 1998

In a recent essay in *The London Review of Books*, Colm Tóibín walked the streets of city centre Dublin: recalling a coffee shop he once frequented, his days reading at the National Library on Kildare Street, and one frightening explosion in 1974 when the Troubles in the North migrated south for the summer in the form of a car bomb on South Leinster Street. For Tóibín, these memories and the press of daily responsibilities—paying bills, traipsing along O'Connell Street to the General Post Office (GPO) to mail letters, finding a quiet place to enjoy lunch—usually trump more literary and cultural ruminations. Moreover, he observes, some Dublin streets possess such a "peculiar intensity," a quality that has grown ever "more gnarled and layered" over the years, that the past and the books that record it "hardly matter" any more and seem almost a "strange irrelevance" (10). He thus admits to seldom thinking of Leopold Bloom's trek along these streets, and yet on this day he does, which through a chain of other associations leads him to the sign "Finn's Hotel" where James Joyce famously met Nora Barnacle. Other flotsam from *Ulysses* drift into his consciousness, lemon soap and the racehorse Throwaway, for instance, as does one bit of arcana concerning Beckett's novel *Murphy* and the exact distance between the floor of the GPO and the posterior of Cuchulain's statue prominently displayed there. In actuality, Tóibín's essay has nothing to do with Joyce, *Murphy* or Cuchulain's arse; rather, it is a brief biography of Jack MacGowran and Patrick Magee, two actors who rose to prominence in the 1950s impersonating Clov and Krapp, respectively, in *Endgame* and *Krapp's Last Tape*. MacGowran in particular, who occupies the limelight of Tóibín's thoughts, was long associated with Beckett, in large measure because of his celebrated one-man show comprised of scenes from Beckett's work and his role as the Fool in Peter Brook's famously Beckettian 1971 film production of *King Lear* in which Magee played Cornwall. (Here, the term "Beckettian" resonates in a totally untheorized, almost banal way: lines from Beckett are transposed into Shakespeare's play, Lear's throne room resembles Hamm's shelter, and of course the presence of MacGowran in the cast all support the use of this adjective.)

An essay on Beckett's actors that starts with Joyce is perhaps surprising, and it may seem almost eccentric to pause at the statue of Cuchulain or to recall Joyce and Nora's first date, which began with their rendezvous outside the office of Sir William Wilde's surgery. More intriguing for my purposes are Toíbín's playful allusions to Ireland's largest industry—tourism—and its relation to the nation's literary history and culture. "Tourists must love" the sign at Finn's Hotel, he reflects, just as they flock to see the "funny colourful statue" of Oscar Wilde in Merrion Square opposite the office in which his father practiced, the same statue unveiled in 1997, as Paula Murphy reminds us, that irreverent Dubliners refer to as the "quare on the square" (127).[1] Such thoughts then give way in this network of associations to the attic in which Beckett temporarily resided over his father's quantity-surveying business on nearby Clare Street, which in turn inspires Toíbín's notion of having a plaque inscribed and positioned conspicuously on the building: "This is where Beckett got away from his God-forsaken mother." And then he adds: "Must tell tourist board." In a city littered, if this is not too flippant a term, with statues of well-known figures from Irish mythology, of acclaimed writers and influential politicians, even of fictional characters—the most infamous being the often vandalized Anna Livia monument, known more familiarly as the "floozy in the Jacuzzi"—Toíbín's epiphany seems oddly appropriate, yet prompts an obvious question: Why would tourists, especially those Americans of Irish heritage who pour into Ireland every summer, be interested in Beckett in the first place? True enough, *Waiting for Godot* was once heralded by *Variety* as the "laugh sensation of two continents," but Americans have scarcely crowded into theatres to see Beckett's plays, save perhaps for the 1988 Lincoln Center production of *Godot* starring Steve Martin and Robin Williams. And even this much-anticipated revival was far from an unqualified success, as reviews were sufficiently negative to motivate Martin to swear he would never act on stage again.[2]

Toíbín's musings, however, reflect an even more striking phenomenon, one that has transformed the very streets he walks: namely, the robust "Celtic Tiger" economy of Ireland in which multinational corporations have made enormous investments both in the North and in the Republic. One of the engines driving this economy as, among others, that Andrew Kincaid has examined, is cultural tourism and the reimagining of history as "heritage." More particularly, a globalized economy, of which the Celtic Tiger serves as a conspicuously successful example, "appropriates the past to anchor itself more thoroughly and to present itself as the logical outcome of history." In Ireland, the results of this appropriation have contributed to a sharp increase in the number of visitors to the country—during the decade of the 1990s alone, the number soared from 2.2 million per year to some 5.5 million by the decade's end—which in turn has sparked a rise in hotel

---

[1]   As Murphy points out, the statue is in fact polychromatic, so Toíbín's use of the term "colourful" should be taken literally.

[2]   While early audiences seemed entertained by this production, many reviewers were not, blasting in particular Robin Williams' numerous improvisations.

constructions. In Dublin, the number of hotels rose from 80 to 115 between 1998 and 2000 with some 20 more in the planning stages. (Kincaid 177).[3] (Those tourists who love garish statues and old signs have to sleep somewhere.) But, again, such projects prompt a number of more serious questions, ones that like Dublin streets are more layered and mottled than the one raised earlier about why tourists would want to bother with Beckett in the first place (a conundrum Toíbín clearly has considered and through which he can spoof the entire enterprise). Paramount among these is perhaps too obvious a query: What damage is done both to Irish culture and history—and to the land itself—in the names of progress and prosperity? More specifically, what sort operations—or distortions—could turn Beckett into a tourist attraction?

As my epigraph implies, writers like Derek Mahon have expressed palpable unease over such issues; others, like Brian Friel in his early and controversial play *The Mundy Scheme* (1969), have lampooned the idiocy of Irish politicians as they pursue the almighty dollar and the tourists who might dispense them. The "scheme" of Friel's high-flying politicians in *The Mundy Scheme* involves the development of several western counties into lavish cemeteries for foreigners, particularly Americans. After all, as the Minister of External Affairs explains to the Taoiseach in Act One, when cities like New York and London grow, "ground becomes more scarce and therefore more expensive…and as these cities expand, more and more cemeteries are required" (Friel 203, 202). The solution? Look to the future and author a "new trend": identify tracts of land unsuitable for farming, preserve their "natural state" except in those locales where "landscaping would be desirable, and the building of all roads, airstrips, and communication links," and create graveyards for wealthy foreigners. The "suitable climate" and "religious atmosphere" of Ireland that already obtain would enhance the attractiveness of the country for this purpose. In addition, the plan's champions argue, the Mundy scheme would bolster, perhaps even treble, the tourist industry in the West, as families and friends of the deceased will almost certainly want to make pilgrimages to the gravesites; as a result, the demand for "hotels, souvenir shops, wreaths, headstones," and so on should increase sharply. In short, just as Switzerland is the acknowledged center of world banking, Ireland could become known as the world's "eternal resting place," or so the Mundy scheme's proponents argue to those colleagues wary of its possible consequences (Friel 204).

America, as Friel has revealed in interviews, rested heavily on his mind while writing this play. He feared for the futures both of Irish writers, who seemed to him doomed to failure unless they could cultivate an American audience, and of a country that was devolving into a "shabby imitation of a third-rate American state." No longer describable as "West Britons," Molly Ivors' deprecation of Gabriel Conroy in Joyce's "The Dead," Irish men and women were slowly becoming "East Americans" (Friel 49). The speakers of several poems in Mahon's volume *The Yellow Book* are equally direct. While recalling his strolls down the sidewalks

---

[3]   Kincaid reports the data on hotel construction, 182.

of New York in "American Deserta," Mahon laments the "post-Cold War, global-warming age/of corporate rule, McPeace and Mickey Mao" (46). In this age, the ascent to discursive power of "glib promotional blather" is corroborated daily by the busloads of tourists who descend upon Ireland. For this reason, in "Night Thoughts" Mahon extols the virtues of the early morning hours before the first buses arrive loaded with "aliens, space invaders clicking at the front door/goofy in baseball caps and nylon leisurewear" eager to be thrilled by a "Georgian theme-park" (12–13). In "shiver your tenement," he remembers with affection a different sort of visitor in the "demure" 1960s before the country "discovered sex." Then, young would-be writers traveled to Dublin by the busload to crawl down Dawson and Grafton Streets, pursuing at times a night of "roguery," but just as often searching for the rich assembly of writers and intellectuals who frequented pubs there. These neophytes found hospitable gathering places, where they sipped "watery Jameson" and enjoyed a "life of the mind" among established literati and other artists, who preferred the "unforced pace" of Dublin to the thoughtless speed of London and elsewhere. This was a time, Mahon recalls, before celebrated writers were reduced to familiar icons—or promotional hucksters:

> Those were the days before tourism and economic growth,
> before deconstruction and the death of the author,
> when pubs had as yet no pictures of Yeats and Joyce
> since people could still recall their faces, their voices. (18)

By sorry contrast, living in the "pastiche paradise of the postmodern" and its myriad simulations, people today feel more at home with the "ersatz, the pop, the phony." This hyperreal Eden, of course, has been underwritten by tourist dollars, francs, pounds, and now euros; and it has necessitated both the leveling of certain neighborhoods—especially low-income districts located in city centres to make room for the headquarters of multinational corporations—and the metamorphosis of others into faux-historical "theme-parks."

If city space can be so transformed, what might happen to a figure like Beckett if *Bord Fáilte*, the Irish tourist board, were to act upon Tóibín's puckish suggestion? In what specific ways might Beckett be turned into the "ersatz, the pop, the phony"? In another essay in which Kincaid assesses ways in which the Celtic Tiger induces the Irish diaspora to return home for a visit, a partial answer to these questions emerges, in this instance in the design of landscapes:

> Contemporary artists, architects and landscapers have incorporated the history of emigration into their work, re-writing emigration *on the landscape*...Cultural geography is a form of history-writing. Contemporary shapers of space profit from the ordeal of emigration. In order to do so, they do not whitewash its trauma, but they engage in a more subtle glossing-over...[4]

---

[4]   Andrew Kincaid, "What They Left Behind: The Irish Landscape After Emigration," an unpublished manuscript, 6. My thanks to Andrew Kincaid for permission to quote from this essay.

One *not*-so-subtle instance of this process, as Kincaid explains, is Ireland's emergence as a destination for golfers, a project envisioned by Bernard Shaw's Tom Broadbent in *John Bull's Other Island* over a century ago. Shortly after World War II, Irish political leaders were advised that, for the tourism industry to flourish, the country would need not only to expand and improve its hotel accommodations, roads, and airports, but also develop venues for entertainment (golf courses, spas, even casinos were specifically recommended) and a coherent cultural program of attractions, one of which was the checkered *Tóstal* festival.[5] Responding to this call, some 110 new golf courses have been built during the 1990s alone, often—as Kincaid wryly observes—"out of the remains of former Anglo-Irish landlords' houses and the remnants of the garden estates that once surrounded them" (9). Even a cursory inspection of the advertising campaigns of some of Ireland's most celebrated newer courses confirms this point. The hotel of the K Club Golf and Spa Resort near Dublin, for example, which opened in 1991 and hosted the prestigious Ryder Cup matches in 2006, was built around the 1832 Hugh Barton House. The K Club's promotional literature sketches the history of the house and foregrounds its "idyllic rural setting," as it also highlights the challenge of the Club's 36 holes designed by golfing legend Arnold Palmer. The Big House, as Kincaid archly notes in reference to this widespread revision of cultural geography, has now been restored as "the clubhouse" (10).

A lot has happened, in other words, to reverse the admission Seán Lemass made in 1960, the same year in which he assumed the office of Taoiseach, that Ireland was "new to, and somewhat inexperienced in, the organized international tourism business." In the early 1950s, when tourism ranked as Ireland's second-leading industry behind agricultural exports, some politicians viewed the nascent project as a kind of anathema.[6] It is no longer. Yet in the past half-century or so since Lemass made this confession to the Congress of International Hotel Associations, the country has scarcely slowed down to draw a deep conceptual breath and consider the entire range of effects of this investment. I intend to speculate about one such case—or, rather, possible effect—of this investment, taking seriously the suggestion of placing a plaque on William Beckett's surveying office on Clare Street and turning his son Samuel into a tourist attraction. What sorts of refashioning or the cultural equivalent of plastic surgery would this project require? How could Beckett attract tourists to Clare Street after lazy mornings kissing the Blarney stone, playing a round of golf at Lahinch or Ballybunion, or fishing for salmon in the Shannon River?

Acting upon Tóibín's brainstorm would require Ireland's tourist board to engage in a concerted *retrofitting* of Beckett, a process that, as we shall see, is already underway. I employ the term "retrofitting" purposefully, appropriating it

---

[5]   For a discussion of these mid-century plans, see Irene Furlong.

[6]   Furlong notes that in 1950 tourism trailed agricultural exports by some 12 million pounds (173); in the early 1950s, Lemass spearheaded several legislative initiatives to install a tourist board and gradually altered political opinion of this topic.

from the architectural jargon in which it initially gained currency. The process connotes the remodeling of an older architectural structure to accommodate a present-day purpose; or, through the installation of more technologically advanced equipment or the redesign of space, retrofitting allows an older structure to comply with safety or other codes enacted since its original construction. One of the more spectacular—and tragic—examples of architectural retrofitting came as the result of the 1980 fire at the "old" MGM Grand Hotel in Las Vegas in which 84 residents were killed and nearly 700 were injured. After spending between $110 and an estimated $223 million settling claims brought against the Grand after this almost unparalleled disaster, billionaire owner Kirk Kerkorian—and every other hotel-casino operator in the city—spent millions more installing automatic sprinklers in ceilings, redesigning stairwells, emergency doors, and other parts of emergency exits systems, and considering a unique array of precautions so that the tragedy would never be repeated.[7] If nineteenth-century Big Houses and all they connote about the Famine, absentee landlordism, and the class system of nineteenth-century Ireland can be remodeled into clubhouses with all the amenities American and other golfers demand, surely a writer, even one as aloof as Beckett was, can be refurbished to satisfy the tastes and pique the curiosities of wealthy visitors. But how?

At least three possibilities present themselves: one adapted from the long-established marketing strategy that induces consumers to visit a place and purchase goods they might find there; another derived from recent staging practices and the repertories of contemporary Irish theatres; and yet a third that finds its provenience in a chameleon-like *presentism* that some commentators believe has already affected our understanding of Beckett for the worse. The first strategy for retrofitting Beckett, as I have mentioned, has already begun; its goal, or one of its goals, is to make him a more Irish, even more romantic, figure than he might have been. It works, in short, to position Beckett in a tradition within which he is ill described; and, in so doing, inaugurates what can only be regarded as a series of telling, in some cases unfortunate, ironies. One such irony, in many ways the sharpest, concerns an analogous "move" in the broader discipline of Irish Studies, one James Chandler describes as produced by the "Irishing" of writers. The critical exfoliation of a writer's "Irishable" qualities—Chandler develops the examples of Edmund Burke and Maria Edgeworth—makes possible an "elevated perspective" that has heretofore been occluded. In a crucial metaphor, Chandler argues that yet another model of Irish Studies resembles a photographic negative or, more cinematically, a reverse shot of the typical view afforded by literary history or history told from a predominantly British point of view. It, too, depends upon making Irish writers more legibly Irish:

---

[7]   As recently as 2005, national safety organizations were issuing reports and analyses of this fire. Some insist that as many as 85, or even 87, deaths are attributable to this accident, and several identify the hotel's "systems of egress" as the largest cause of death and injury.

In many of these examples, and Burke's is an especially good case in point, the question of an author's being "Irishable" is intensified by the sense that, internal to his or her *ouevre*, we can find not only another side to the story but beyond this, an anticipation of what it means to be able to see or not to see the story from the other side. (Chandler 27)

Chandler goes on to ask what the "Irishing" of an author might mean and what effect such a process might exert on our ability to locate this author on a larger "cultural map" (31). That Beckett can very easily be seen as Irishable is beyond question; this has been one of the informing premises of this chapter. That Beckett might be understood from an "elevated" or other perspective instantiated by Irish Studies is equally certain; but that he can be located on the precise cultural map created by Irish tourism is another matter altogether.

To date, the most prominent means of drawing this map are posters seen throughout Ireland of the country's four Nobel Prize winners in literature: William Butler Yeats, Bernard Shaw, Beckett, and Seamus Heaney. (I first saw the poster in 2006 at the Dublin International Airport, where it was widely displayed.) One effect of the poster, based on a stamp collection of Nobel laureates printed by Sweden Post Stamps in 2004, is to repatriate both Shaw and Beckett, two writers who left Ireland at relatively young ages and, in Beckett's case, did not often look back. To be sure, Shaw took an active interest in all things Irish and from afar commented on them, from Home Rule to the Stage Irishman, from Irish melodrama to—of all things—Irish tourism. (In fact, he wrote an article in 1916 praising the quality of Irish hotels, of fishing in the Shannon River, and of Irish golf courses, among other things.)[8] Beckett, conversely, can hardly be accused of a similar engagement with tourism or Ireland. (Though, ironically enough, he maintained a life-long interest in golf.)[9] John Banville observes that both Joyce and Beckett, "who took so much from this impoverished little bit of rock on the edge of Europe, had shaken the dust of Ireland from their heels and never looked back" (29).[10] Banville, like Beckett's biographers Deirdre Bair, Anthony Cronin, and James Knowlson, emphasizes that Beckett's short stint teaching at Trinity College in 1930–1931 only exacerbated his disdain of Ireland in general and Dublin in particular. "He was not happy in Ireland," Banville notes, and he found "Dublin life suffocating" (26).[11] By December, 1931, Beckett could no longer tolerate Trinity or Dublin and escaped to Germany and then Paris, only to "crawl home" again in August of 1932.

---

[8]   See "Touring in Ireland."

[9]   In their commentary in *Images of Beckett*, John Haynes and James Knowlson emphasize Beckett's long-time interest in sports. He read a French paper dedicated to sports, was an avid viewer of cricket and rugby on television and followed it on the radio, and discussed golf with a small circle of enthusiasts (12–13).

[10]   John Banville, "Memory and Forgetting: The Ireland of de Valera and Ó Faoláin," in *The Lost Decade: Ireland in the 1950s*, 29.

[11]   In *Damned to Fame*, Knowlson quotes from one of Beckett's letters written at this time: "This life is terrible and I don't understand how it can be endured" (123).

He remained in Ireland for a little over a year, but again he was unhappy. (His father's death in May, 1933 complicated his life even further.) Bair puts the matter about as strongly as it can be put: "Beckett had no pride in his Irishness; national identity meant nothing to him" (Bair 120). Consequently, "being Irish" was something he "avoided at all costs," or so some critics have alleged.[12]

But national identity means everything to tourism; thus, sentiments like these, much like the historical traumas that have riven the land itself, need to be "glossed over." The iconic gesture of putting these four Irish writers in a single design attempts such a concealment; and the positioning of the resulting image in venues like the Dublin International Airport must be regarded as a mechanism to accomplish this revision in the cultural imaginary, even if such an intention may not fairly be attributed to the Swedish postal service that conceived of the stamp series. That is to say, the message conveyed by the juxtapositioning of this quartet of Nobel laureates seems equally clear: these are *all* Irish writers, connected irrevocably to the wild coastline in the background of the stamp celebrating Heaney and, more indirectly, to the Abbey Theatre building in the background of the stamp for Yeats.

Such a thesis is *least* applicable to Beckett, perhaps one reason that the background of the stamp features a duo in bowler hats from *Waiting for Godot* and not a natural vista or other visual cliché associated with the Irish landscape. Nonetheless, the poster posits a national unity that does or did not exist.

But there are other glossings over as well. Yeats, as is well known, disliked Beckett's early prose, though Bair characterizes his disapproval as circumspect, in large part because his brother Jack was a close friend of Beckett's. Yeats regarded Beckett's work as "amoral," and "neither approved of the direction in which Beckett's writing took him, nor did he enjoy reading it" (qtd in Bair 122). In his "Preface for Politicians" that preceded the 1906 first edition of *John Bull's Other Island*, Shaw recounts Yeats's request of a play to add to the repertory of the nascent Irish Literary Theatre and remarks that in *John Bull*, "Mr Yeats got rather more than he bargained for." This was so, in part, because from Shaw's perspective the play is "uncongenial to the whole spirit of the neo-Gaelic movement, which is bent on creating a new Ireland after its own ideal," while he insists instead upon an "uncompromising presentment of the real old Ireland" (Shaw 443). So, *John Bull's Other Island* opened at the Court Theatre in London to enthusiastic audiences, in part because Shaw's and Yeats's Ireland were very different places (and, more prosaically, because the play's staging demands exceeded the capacity of a young theatre to realize them). Nationalism, as Terry Eagleton observes, "speaks of the entry into full self-realization of a unitary subject known as the people." So, to a great extent, does cultural tourism (28).

Just as Shaw's "real old Ireland" is not Yeats's Ireland, *these* Irish writers are not Beckett's Irish writers. In addition to his well-documented admiration of Joyce, Beckett enjoyed J.M. Synge's comedies, particularly *The Well of the Saints*,

---

[12]   See Fintan O'Toole 17.

Sweden Post Stamps

Fig. 13.1   Irish Nobel Laureate plate block of commemorative stamps
(Sweden, 2004).

which he had seen at the Abbey Theatre, and the "knockabout comedy" of Sean
O'Casey's *Juno and the Paycock* and his one-act "curtain raisers" *Nannie's Night
Out, Cathleen Listens In,* and *The End of the Beginning.* Indeed, Joyce, O'Casey,
and Beckett are permanently linked in Irish cultural history—and, in yet another
irony inherent to this topic, in the history of Irish tourism—in a fashion far more
substantial than any perception of aesthetic or national unity implied by the stamp
series. For in 1958, in connection with *Tóstal, Bord Fáilte* announced that the
Dublin Theatre Festival, inaugurated a year earlier, would feature O'Casey's
new play *The Drums of Father Ned,* a theatrical adaptation of *Ulysses* called
Bloomsday, and several works of Beckett's because, in the Board's own words,
"the *Bloomsday* and O'Casey productions would be likely to have the greatest
effect toward inducing people to visit Ireland for the festival" (qtd in Whelan and
Swift 114). What happened then, as Carolyn Swift, cofounder of Dublin's Pike
Theatre where *Waiting for Godot* received its first Irish production, describes, was
"a hugely complicated comedy of errors typical of the times, with double and triple
dealing," the upshot of which was the cancellation of the festival and Beckett's
subsequent imposition of a "blanket ban of any of his plays being performed in the
Irish Republic" (Whelan and Swift 114–15).[13]

Christopher Murray underscores the absurdity of the festival's cancellation by
recalling that when *Tóstal* was conceived in the early 1950s, its *raison d'être* was
not only to attract tourists to the country, but also to "showcase Ireland in forms

---

[13]   Beckett's decision damaged the future of the Pike Theatre, spearheaded by Alan
Simpson, Swift's husband, who bravely produced such controversial plays as Brendan
Behan's *The Quare Fellow* and Tennessee Williams' *The Rose Tattoo,* the latter of which
led to his trial for obscenity.

which would revive cultural nationalism." Murray quotes Lemass's endorsement of the program as "designed to express the Irish way of life and to revive the spirit which animated the traditional Gaelic festivals for which Ireland was famous when Europe was young" (qtd in Murray 124). We will never really know how Beckett's plays might have contributed to an expression of the "Irish way of life," because after Archbishop John Charles McQuaid refused, in protest over the inclusion of Joyce and O'Casey, to preside over a special mass, the festival was quickly scuttled. McQuaid felt little need to explain his refusal; according to Murray, he "merely had to sit back" and "let the *Tóstal* committee work itself into a lather over the bad publicity that [his] disapproval would bring" (125). For her part, Carolyn Swift indicted the "utter spinelessness" of a committee that capitulated to the "public and private pressure" exerted upon it by McQuaid's "lay allies, particularly his close associates in the Knights of Saint Columbanus" (Whelan and Swift 114). Beckett was livid at this turn of events.

As the ill-fated 1958 Dublin Theatre festival suggests, the history of cultural tourism in Ireland has not always been one of unprecedented success, as ideological battles—and real ones in the North—have risen at times to undermine its ambitions. More important for my purposes here, Sean Lemass's understanding of the cultural work such festivals achieve also indicates the extent to which they are calibrated to invoke a nostalgia analogous to that inherent in the practices employed in the marketing of other commodities. In her formulation of the "commodified authentic" cultivated to market consumer goods at such London department stores as Selfridge's earlier in the century, for example, Elizabeth Outka describes how skillfully designed advertising campaigns combined with the *mis-en-scène* of the store itself (transforming into an "urban village") to produce a "nostalgic version of the authentic" for its shoppers (314). The result was the invocation of an "originary and unified past before mechanical reproduction and fragmentation," a simulation that cast a "misty glow over the production process" of the various commodities available for purchase (316). A similar process obtains in an advertising campaign that attempts to repatriate Beckett in the way the Nobel Prize poster does, foregrounding the faces of the laureates against an iconically Irish background and thereby connecting all four to the national landscape. Needless to say, the poster remains silent about Beckett's disillusionment with Ireland in the early 1930s, his support of Alan Simpson during his trial for obscenity in producing Tennessee Williams' *The Rose Tattoo*, and his outrage over the power of the Church so strikingly in evidence during the 1958 Irish Theatre Festival fiasco. "Beckett was Beckett," Irish journalist Brian Fallon once quipped, an "odd individualist" who, to become a tourist attraction, has to be made both familiar and "Irishable" (14).

At this point, one might reasonably object that historical distortion is inherent to tourism, especially where celebrities are concerned, and there is doubtless some truth to such a rejoinder. Indeed, that is one of the points I'm laboring to make. But I want to conclude this part of the discussion with one further amplification of Toíbín's fanciful plaque on the Clare Street office—"This is where Beckett got away from his God-forsaken mother"—which provides yet another register within which to market and (mis)read Beckett. For aren't many Irish and Irish-American writers, at some point, forced to negotiate an impossible relationship with their mothers? Think here of May Joyce's fatal illness and its effect on her son (and on *Ulysses*); or Ella O'Neill's drug addiction and its centrality to Eugene O'Neill's *Long Day's Journey into Night*; or, to take a more recent example, Brigid Regan's battle with cancer and Paul Muldoon's elegy "Yarrow." Toíbín's imaginary engraving traffics in such romanticized and clichéd portrayals of the pained son-author. Thus, while the engraving possesses the merit of a partial truth, Beckett in the early 1930s *did* seek refuge above his father's office, it remains silent about his several reasons for doing so: initially, to flee his mother's intense anger over both his writing and his apparent disinterest in finding gainful employment; and, more important, after his father's fatal heart attack on June 26, 1933, to escape a home that his mother had turned into a "mausoleum" that lasted for "weeks on end." He fled, in his own words, not just his mother but all the "vile worms of melancholy observance" (Knowlson 167). No plaque intended for the perusal of tourists can record all of this.

Were *Bord Fáilte* to act upon Toíbín's suggestion, then, it could rely on the Nobel poster to help refashion Beckett as a "commodified authentic" Irish writer. To assist in this kind of marketing strategy, to help conceal the fact that Beckett wrote most of his major works in French, for example, the Board might also consider a second kind of retrofitting: namely, the redaction of earlier writers' work by way of more contemporary conventions. Such a revisionary process is not entirely new and may prove almost unavoidable, as Jack MacGowran once intimated when describing his impersonation of Fluther Good in O'Casey's *The Plough and the Stars* after playing in *Waiting for Godot*: "I began to notice Vladimir creeping in. This jovial old Fluther from O'Casey suddenly turned into Vladimir" (qtd in Toíbín 20). A similar, but much more concerted revision of Synge's plays on the twenty-first century stage might help illuminate this point. As Adrian Frazier identified in the Druid Theatre's 2003 production of *The Playboy of the Western World*, director Garry Hynes introduced a kind of "postmodern paddywhackery" into Synge's text by transporting such a sensibility from the plays of Martin McDonagh. Frazier describes the curious result:

> Now in 2004, through a sort of feedback loop in the Syngean tradition of Irish drama, *The Playboy* manifests the traits of these more recent playwrights and productions. Their radical and postmodern aestheticizations of Irish rural life inspire a non-naturalist and almost 19th-century melodramatic extravaganza. (124)

Nicholas Grene responded similarly, connecting *The Playboy* to Druid's earlier productions not only of McDonagh's plays, but also of John B. Keane's *Sharon's Grave* (2003) (126). Grene employs the term "redesigning" to characterize this redaction of earlier works by way of later ones, but in my view this term is too tame. That is to say, if "Irishing" a writer defines one kind of potential retrofitting of Beckett, this recasting of Synge might better be termed, after Beckett, one of Proustian or "reverse" influence. Recall that in *Proust*, Beckett insists that there is "no escape from yesterday because yesterday has deformed us, or been deformed by us" (2). For much of the previous century, the discipline of *literary* criticism was obsessed with the former process—the effect of past writers and texts on later ones—and post-graduate students just a generation or two ago were trained in the protocols of tracing influence and literary reputation.[14] A revised *cultural* criticism needs to privilege the opposite process, defining the ways present aesthetic conventions and thematic preoccupations modify, even deform, the past. Reverse influence, then, may not make Synge—or Beckett—more "Irishable," but it may make them more like McDonagh or another figure from the contemporary scene, as it may also impact their status as commodities.

Adaptation is perhaps the most familiar form of reverse influence, and here again Synge's plays have proven fertile material for contemporary playwrights: Vincent Woods' *A Cry from Heaven* (2005) adapts *Deirdre of the Sorrows*, and Bisi Adigun and Roddy Doyle have collaborated on a new version of *The Playboy of the Western World* (2007). Among the numerous and significant modernizations of these texts, Woods' play foregrounds both violence and sexual desire in the Deirdre legend, including Conor's rape of Deirdre, that was notably muted in or absent from Synge's unfinished original. Indeed, the play's concluding tableau combines a disturbing reprise of the symbolic oppositions between day and night, sexuality and violence, that underlie the legend and play. And the Adijun/Doyle *Playboy* shifts the scene of the action from Mayo to a Dublin suburb, recasting the play's protagonist as a Nigerian immigrant to Ireland. In addition to both adaptations' repositioning of the canon of Irish drama more centrally in Dublin's postmodern and multinational present, both invariably reread and retrofit the Syngean originals into this cultural moment. Without deprecating either of these more recent plays, this kind of reverse influence suggests the potentially "poisonous ingenuity" of Time that Beckett describes in *Proust*; in so doing, it also reveals another model of retrofitting Beckett in the twenty-first century.

The processes of "Irishing" and reverse influence might be subsumed under a third, larger kind of retrofitting: *presentism*, the warping of a text or cultural form from the past into a comment on the present moment. One might hope that the mere assertion of Shakespeare or Beckett's contemporaneity does not signal a presentist bias, and certainly the history of Shakespearean adaptations can not be read as constituting such a chronicle. Nahum Tate, to cite perhaps the most egregious example in a long chronicle of theatrical and filmic adaptations, actually argued that his *King Lear* rectified an aesthetic error in Shakespeare's play by revising Cordelia's unwarranted fate. While Tate's doing so might have made the play more appealing or legible to a Restoration audience—rather like casting the witches in *Macbeth* as punk rock druggies in an early 1980s Royal Shakespeare

---

[14]   See, for example, Richard D. Altick, *The Art of Literary Scholarship*, especially the chapter "Some Scholarly Occupations."

Company production I shall always remember—such an adaptive revision nods to the present, but does not necessarily apprehend the play to comment on contemporary realities or dilemmas. Presentism works differently. In her recent book *Hamlet's Heirs: Shakespeare and the New Millennium* (2006), for example, Linda Charnes offers no Tate-like "improvements" of Shakespeare, but does find highly persuasive ways of reading George W. Bush's presidency into them: or, rather, of finding ways in which Shakespeare can illuminate this deeply flawed administration.

Is such a presentist reading also an example of retrofitting? A better question would ask if such a reading necessitates the addition to the original of the textual or interpretive equivalent of sprinkler systems or more effectively illuminated emergency stairwells. Stated somewhat differently, the question urges a defetishizing critique to probe the extent to which at any historical moment the term "Beckett" or "Beckettian" is socially, hence contingently, constituted.[15] This question encourages a meditation of how precisely our—or any—historical moment revises the past to suit its own purposes, and as this brief note is intended to suggest, how late capitalism can "glocalize" a figure like Beckett: that is, make him more local to appeal to a potentially global clientele.

This, I take it, is the tenor of Lydia Davis's short story "Southward Bound, Reads *Worstward Ho*" (2007), in which a woman prepares for a long bus ride by taking two books to read: Beckett's *Worstward Ho* and *West with the Night*. She specifically chooses to read Beckett during the first half of the trip "when she is fresh," and Davis's narrator describes her several struggles with the text, particularly with one passage:

> Soon after, with confusion she reads: 'Said is missaid. Whenever said said said missaid.' She misunderstands and reads again: 'Whenever said said said missaid.' Then a third time, and when she imagines a pause in the middle of it, she understands better. (70)

The myriad ways in which Beckett will remain our contemporary will require such readerly vigilance. We will of necessity be required to assess the operations of such retrofittings as reverse influence and presentist distortion. And to do so we shall need to "remain fresh" in contending with the successive Becketts with whom we will most surely be confronted. On.

---

[15] I am borrowing this language from Seyla Benhabib, 70.

Chapter 14
Defiling Celebrity[1]

Steven Connor

This Is Me, With Rolf

I saw Rolf Harris[2] in our street the other day. I was just parking the car and there he was, walking along the road. He came right by me, and then turned into the little park opposite our house. I didn't say anything and, funnily enough, he didn't say anything to me either, though I sensed he was on the point of it. This is not an entirely unprecedented experience in our street. The lead singer of Jamiroquai lived for a while a few doors down, and I gather he sold his house on to the lead singer of Travis, who then caused flutters in the parish by persuading his band to do unscheduled performances at the infant school where his son went. Still, this is a pretty ordinary Victorian terrace in Crouch End, not Highgate (where I once saw Ruby Wax having breakfast), Hampstead or even Hackney, and this kind of encounter is not at all the sort of thing you have to learn to be blasé about. In truth, I don't really know what the lead singer of Travis looks like, even though, thinking back, there is a good chance that it was him I lent my hedge-trimmer to over the summer. Whereas you could not possibly make a mistake about seeing Rolf Harris. This was a definitive event, a conjunction of worlds.

Richard Schickel points out two interlocking fantasies of the life of the celebrity. The first is the "dream of autonomy": the celebrity lives a life unrestricted by necessity. The second is "a dream of intimate, almost familiar connection," or what we might call the Valhalla fantasy: that to be a celebrity is to sport and feast in continuous fellowship with other, equally celestial entities (Schickel 255). Whereas Rolf Harris was alone. He was just walking along the road, on his own. I found this fact perplexing and unnerving. Surely somebody like Rolf Harris must always be accompanied by some kind of retinue—minders, makeup artists, agents? My first thought was to take a panicky look round: seeing Rolf Harris, whom I have never seen except when he was being watched, by me, made me certain that he must be being filmed, which meant that I too might be in shot. This was altogether an ointment to which I was unwilling to supply the fly. I sat in my car and fiddled with my keys until he had gone by, but could see no camera crew

---

[1]   Based on a paper originally given in the Cultural History of Celebrity seminar at the Humanities Research Centre of the University of Warwick, 24 October 2005.

[2]   Born in 1930, Harris is a celebrity Australian television painter and singer, best known in the UK.

Fig. 14.1   Rolf Harris publicity photograph (2009).

anywhere. Then I watched him for a bit from behind, just carrying on walking. My seeing him from the back made me feel obscurely guilty; it seemed a kind of liberty or violation. The backs of celebrities are not generally available for scrutiny and thus rather vulnerable. Vulnerable to whom, or what? (To me?)

So put out was I at this astonishing behavior of the part of Rolf Harris, walking along the road, my road, on his own, that I now realize I assumed he must be having some kind of breakdown. This impression was firmed up when he turned off the road and into the little park just across from my house. Evidently, he was going for one of the many unoccupied benches, which are often favored by crooning derelicts or the sort of characters evoked in Philip Larkin's "Toads Revisited"— "the men/You meet of an afternoon:/Palsied old step-takers,/Hare-eyed clerks with the jitters,/Waxed-fleshed out-patients/Still vague from accidents" (Larkin 18). I could easily imagine him a bit later on, being tenderly led away by the loyal P.A. who had been searching for him all day, sobbing a little, trousers soaked in wee, still clutching his noggin of rum in a paper bag.

Part of my astonishment came from the fact that something in me had imagined that Rolf Harris was dead, like Margaret Thatcher or Jimmy Saville. He certainly looked impossibly old, as celebrities seen in the waning flesh always, always are. Why did this upset me? I remembered the story that Melanie Klein tells of a young child who is being held up to the window by his grandmother, when, suddenly looking round to see the face of an elderly stranger who has entered the room, he is plunged into anxiety—because, says Klein, his "bad (grand)mother" has suddenly appeared in the place of the "good (grand)mother" (Klein 103). Bad Rolf (vengeful, vulpine, his very name a hoarse, convulsive bark) had somehow insinuated himself in the place of avuncular, animal-loving Rolf, and what big eyes he had. What was Bad Rolf doing here? (*On his own?*) Did I know where my children were? (Did he?)

Now, Freud suggests that there is a straightforward reason for our fear of the revenant, reverend dead. It is because we think they will have found out posthumously about our homicidal intentions towards them in life. That we wanted them dead. We may even ourselves feel that their conveniently dropping dead like that, just when we had wanted them to, was no coincidence. We may suspect we seen them off through our secret ill-will, and that they have returned to get their own back (Freud 116–17). The menace of the bad mother comes from a similar fear of the recoil upon the child of the murderous fantasies she has entertained towards the figure she has violently segregated from that of the good mother.

Freud and Klein doubtless hope to reassure us that these are fantasies, which, once confronted and armed against, will seem as unreasonable as they are. But the thing is, it would not be at all unreasonable for the undead Rolf Harris to be out to get me, dead or alive. For the dossier of my dealings with Rolf Harris does not make edifying reading. While never having had anything against him personally, I can't remember ever having thought about or referred to Rolf as anything else but an idiot, loser, or affable kind of goon. Like all the schoolboys of my generation (you see how old he must actually be?), I could always summon a passable Rolf Harris accent when I needed a character to guy. I was an energetic purveyor of all the many Rolf Harris jokes in circulation, and in search of cheap laughs there was a Rolf Harris character in a revue we put on at university (oddly enough, in my overheated reminiscence, the character was played by the young Tony Blair, no doubt material for rich and extended analysis, for which I have neither time nor stomach here). Seeing Rolf Harris walking along our road like that made me realize that I was afraid he must know about all the casual derision and lampooning to which I, like everybody else, had subjected him all my life, and most of his. But why should he pick on me? Everybody did it. That was what Rolf Harris meant, what he was. He encouraged it, he went along with the joke, like all good victims of bullying, he was able to laugh at himself, good old Rolf, turning up every year to wobble out "Tie Me Kangaroo Down Sport" to the mock-affectionate roars of the Glastonbury crowd.

But he certainly didn't seem to be in a laughing mood as he walked along our street. On inspection, he seemed to have a rather dragging gait, which increased his air of unstable menace. While I am spilling the beans about my career of casual thought-crime, I may as well tell you of the most humiliating episode of Rolf-baiting of all. I once actually wrote a fan letter to Kate Bush about her superlative album *The Dreaming*, in which I swottily lectured her on my appreciation of the playing off of different musical styles and registers in the album. I congratulated her in particular for the way she had sent up Rolf Harris in the title track, which, as you will perhaps recall, features Rolf playing the didgeridoo, with Kate manufacturing a just-passable Harrisian Strine in the vocals, which are all about kangaroos and aboriginals being run over. Shortly afterwards, I read an interview in which she spoke of what a privilege it had been to work with someone who understood the nature and possibilities of indigenous music so well, and how underestimated his musicianship was. I felt it as a direct reproof. Oh my god: I had put my address in the letter! Clearly I had something to expiate.

Celebrity Power

After these revelations of my complex psychological entanglement with the figure of Rolf Harris, it will be no surprise that I will be speaking about the ambivalence of our relations to celebrity. I'm going to be saying that the contemporary culture of celebrity is intricately and intrinsically threaded through with envy, hostility, fear, and rage. Writers about celebrity regularly affect surprise and mystification when confronting the evidence of this kind of negative feeling. How can adoration, admiration and adulation coexist with the desire to do such dirt on their subjects? Graeme Turner notes that "the pleasures of certain kinds of celebrity material are derived from their capacity to be invasive, exploitative and vengeful" (Turner 122), but he finds such practices anomalous and "difficult to interpret from the outside." Indeed, he clearly regards them as a kind of perverse modification of mainstream celebrity 'consumption': 'the practices I examine here take us beyond the specific contents of production within which I have situated celebrity in this book, emphasizing the mobility of celebrity and its availability for appropriation into other domains of commodification and consumption' (Turner 122).

P. David Marshall also notes in passing the fact that celebrities, unlike the famous, are subject to negative responses: "The sign of the celebrity is ridiculed and derided because it represents the center of false value…The celebrity sign effectively contains this tension between authenticity and false cultural value"

(Marshall xi). And yet, in the analysis of the power invested in the figure of the celebrity that follows this comment, this possibility of ridicule and derision dwindles to invisibility. Marshall even has a section on Freud's theory of the primal horde which institutes law in its murder of the first father, but he ignores the ideas of murder and guilt in Freud's quaintly fantastic myth, drawing from it instead only an achingly obvious point about "the process of identification and idealization that the celebrity embodies for the population" (Marshall 25). Though Marshall recognizes the process whereby celebrities are constructed and disseminated, he also insists on the power—principally the power to focus affect (Marshall 199)—possessed by the celebrity. Since the celebrity is the very opposite of the self-made man, one is surely entitled to wonder where this power might come from. Well, it's from the "system of celebrity" itself,

> that is positioned as a means of comprehending and congealing the mass into recognizable and generally nonthreatening forms. Simultaneous to the emergence of the popular will and democratic constructions in government was the building of means and methods of understanding and controlling the expression of the popular will. The system of celebrity is one of the ways in which the crowd/mass is housed/categorized and understood. (Marshall 203–4)

So, for Marshall, power is always exercised upon the mass. He acknowledges the possibility of "the threat… in the play with affect" (Marshall 207), the fact that undesired responses to a public figure can bubble up and quickly propagate, but only in order to emphasize how carefully responses are engineered in order to contain this threat (Marshall 207). The point is always to show how the unruly stew of public feelings is channeled, ordered, and domesticated into what he calls "public subjectivity" (Marshall 241–7). So nowhere in the chapter that is promisingly entitled "The Embodiment of Affect in Political Culture" is there any reference to any other affects than those held to be thus "positioned," "constructed," or otherwise constituted from above. The book concludes sonorously, but somehow also serenely, with the judgment that

> Celebrities, as the affective economy's construction of public individuals, are sites for the dispersal of power and meaning into the personal and therefore universal. They represent the reorganization of collective identities into the affective economy of the contemporary capitalist democracy. (Marshall 247)

This is odd, given where the book begins, which is in pointing out how flawed or dubious the meaning of celebrity is: "The air of inauthenticity that rings through these last examples describes the current meaning of celebrity. It has become a term that announces a vulgar sense of notoriety" (Marshall 5). So how, one wonders, given this ambivalence, does the "system of celebrity" come to exercise its power to render populations so docilely excitable?

Somewhat more positively, others emphasize the ways in which the celebrity acts as a vehicle or channel for feelings and beliefs displaced in commodity capitalism. Celebrities like Princess Diana are often said to generate, in the words of Graeme Turner, "para-social interactions that operate as a means of compensating for changes in the social construction of the communities within which many of us live" (Turner 23). In such accounts, celebrity constitutes a sad, but not entirely contemptible compensation for the alleged alienations and destructions of "community" effected by modernity.

In all of this, one finds a systematic inattention to the systematically negative feelings and actions to which celebrities and the category of the celebrity are subject, which seems all the more systematic in that so many writers on the subject of celebrity first acknowledge and then ignore this dimension. I want to show in the remainder of this essay that celebrities and celebrity are not accidentally at risk from shaming, debasement, defilement, and ritual humiliation. I'd like it if we stopped not noticing how inseparable celebrity is from such feelings, and from the forms of violence from which they arise or which they can provoke.

The Dream Scheme of Celebrity

It is not hard to see that the culture of celebrity involves profound and complex states of subjective feeling and fantasy. To understand the workings of celebrity it is necessary to grasp what Schickel calls "the larger dream scheme that has evolved out of this century's countless billions of fantastical encounters between the celebrity elite and the anonymous mass" (Schickel 2000, 255). The encounters are not always comfortable or straightforward. Let us first of all consider some of the work done by the word *celebrity* itself. Celebrity is different from both fame and renown. Both of these latter categories suggest a kind of achieved or objective position. Celebrity, by contrast involves prestige or charisma, both of which depend upon a participation or circulation of affects. It doesn't matter whether or not I think Charles Dickens or Che Guevara or Saddam Hussein are famous, they just are and that is that. If I have never heard of them, so much the worse for me. But for me to acknowledge a public figure as a celebrity is to assent to the fact that they are the object of celebration. The celebrity is not just well-known; they are in-celebration, to-be-celebrated. To have fame means to be famous, the noun and the adjective closing together like the pages of a book. Fame is fate: celebrity is being fêted. To be a celebrity is to stand in present need of celebration.

Because the celebrity is in need of celebration, the celebrity makes an implicit claim upon us. One is thereby doubly subjected. On the one hand, celebrities have power over us, in all the obvious ways; they are rich, privileged, admired, desired, made much of, free. But they also have the power that comes from the solicitation of our admiration of these qualities, the call they make to us to assent to their celebrity. Hence one aspect of the ambivalence of celebrities, namely our resentment of their presumption in soliciting acknowledgement of their celebrity. Fame makes no such demands on us: but we may well resent the expense of spirit that is entailed by this work of active assenting to celebrity. This is one of the reasons that insecurity and transience are built into the notion of celebrity. It may also help account for the scornfulness that attaches to the lower ranks of celebrity's angelic throng—the Z-list or scum-of-the-earth celebrities who populate the reality shows. You cannot be slightly famous in this way. But because the condition of celebrity always involves presumption or demand, we feel entitled to deride those who claim to be celebrities without our ever having heard of them, even though the oxymoronic category of Unknown Celebrity is swelling all the time.

Celebrity culture mediates the mass and the individual, embodying one of many solutions to the distinctly modern problem of how to bring together the distant and the intimate. Celebrity culture is among the most striking forms of the condition of extimacy, or the intense exteriorization of intimacy, which media society effects. Is there violence in the vicinity of this intimacy? There certainly seems to be violation, the possibility that the closeness and familiarity of celebrities might become frightening and oppressive. Starstruck fans often feel that the celebrity is wholly theirs, their voice, their gaze fixed uniquely on them. But this narcissism can tip over into the sense of invasion. The stalkers and persecutors of celebrities often report their conviction that their targets are persecuting or even stalking them, looking out of the screen into their souls, embedding secret messages in their lyrics, walking around on their own outside their houses, and so on.

The celebrity is the also bearer of the power that, since the late nineteenth century, has been generated in abundance by the apparatus of mass communication, namely the power of fascination. This is not simply the power to mesmerise, captivate, or enchant. This is to say that the power does not simply flow (as in popular fantasies of "influence") unidirectionally from the fascinator to his or her subjects. In fact, the dream scheme of celebrity involves complicated circulations of powers, in which agency and passivity undergo strange reversals and convolutions. The fascinator's power is the power to awaken in the subject of enchantment the desire to be subjected to power. Where, though, does this power come from? It is not itself self-sufficient or self-originating, but comes from an acquiescence on the part of the celebrity—actor, sportsman, singer, politician—to the demands of the celebrity condition: an acquiescence, that is, to the demand that the celebrity assume the power to induce the powerful, insatiable, infinitely demanding surrender of conscious will characteristic of the fan or the celebrity watcher. Hence all the strange paradoxes of the celebrity dream scheme: the impassioned, intractable, domineering passivity of the celebrant, the helpless, involuntary imperium of the celebrity; the determination of the star not to surrender their ordinariness, and the audience's refusal to permit the celebrity to give away their precious privilege, of being uniquely, passively exposed to ordeal, extremity and ruin.

Some of these affective knots do occasionally appear in writing about celebrity. Graeme Turner points to the occasional flarings among fans of the desire for revenge, arising from "a class-based sense of exclusion, a response to privilege" (Turner 125). Virginia L. Blum's book *Flesh Wounds* focuses in rather more detail on the dynamics of envy, disappointment, and rage that are enacted through the very public open secret of cosmetic surgery. She describes a number of websites which offer visitors the chance to inflict digital damage on the faces or persons of celebrities. Often, as in the case of the *Smack Pamela Anderson* site, the target is a celebrity who has already obligingly subjected herself to improving self-harm via the surgeon's scalpel. (Blum 224–6). As Blum shows, cosmetic surgery seems to represent a particular provocation to viewers to magnify and intensify the celebrity's self-injury. The obvious example here is Michael Jackson, who is held to be subject to a mysterious inner compulsion to deface his own visage and person and is also subject to caricaturing excoriation of his foolishness and self-destructive narcissism in doing so. If he had not himself so obligingly and ruinously rearranged his physiognomy, it seems there would have been plenty who would have done it for him. Blum analyses these phenomena as the expression of an unresolved relation of identification with the celebrity, which alternates violently between rapturous merger with what is taken to be an image of self-sufficient completeness, and angry, disappointed envy at the realization that full identification with such a condition is impossible. The result is "a narcissistic hell of unresolved rivalry with ideal counterparts" (Blum 221).

Of course there are bound to be actual bearers of these feelings for whom this analysis may or may not be plausible. But I do not think that one can simply read the operations of what is a dynamic interpersonal system in terms of a matching intrapersonal dynamic. What is being described here does not belong to the realm of psychology, because nobody feels any of these things. These are not conditions of mind, but mobile dispositions of affective actions. Like the quasi-objects spoken of by Michel Serres in *The Parasite* (Serres 225), they are quasi-affects, which jump from person to person like a hot potato or an epidemic. The point at which it is possible to find these feelings captured or personified in a particular individual is the point at which the circulations and substitutions are temporarily arrested: the moment when the music stops and somebody gets to open the parcel, or is left without a chair. As soon as somebody securely knows what they or somebody else is feeling, the game is derailed or denatured.

In discussing the downfall, or "status-stripping ceremonies" (Rojek 82) of stars and celebrities, Chris Rojek distinguishes between *auto-degradation* "in which the primary exponent of status-stripping is the celebrity" and *exo-degradation*, in which "external parties, usually situated in the mass media, are the architects of the status-stripping process" (Rojek 80). His descriptions of the collapses into anorexia, drug addiction, and alcoholism of celebrities like George Best, Alex "Hurricane" Higgins, Paula Yates, and others give little indication as to how this discriminator is to be applied to the narratives in question. Perhaps the most obvious example of the indissoluble ambivalence of this process is the trope of the projective first-person, in the form of phrases like "My Cocaine Hell," "My Rape Ordeal," "My Night of Shame." Nobody has ever used these phrases *in propria persona*, just as nobody outside the world of newspapers ever nowadays utters a "vow" or commits an act of "slaying." Here, where the *auto-* is so obviously the artifact of the *exo-* (though perhaps never completely or definitively so), is the prototype of a more general displacement or, as we might call it, *dispropriation* of feeling.

Comic Strip

Celebrities exist to be exposed. This is true literally as well as metaphorically. It used to be the case that important persons and persons of renown were insulated by layers of outward show and ceremony which were unavailable to ordinary people. The story of "The Emperor's New Clothes" makes it clear how little it matters whether one is actually clothed or not. The well-known distinction between the nude and the naked rests on the same distribution of privilege. The nude is cloaked in his or her display. The naked is abjectly deprived of this protection. Interestingly, there is no word to correspond to "the nude," which names a certain kind of subject. "The naked" simply means someone with no clothes on, while the nude means someone who is, if only for the time being, not only an unclothed being, but also a *being unclothed.* "The nude is a form of dress," as John Berger puts it. When the stripper in a skuzzy pub with no stage or curtains finishes her act and has to stoop to pick up her discarded fishnets and garter belt, she moves from the condition of the nude to the naked.

It is said that one can always defeat feelings of social intimidation by imagining the judge, teacher, policeman, prime minister, etc., naked. But celebrities are of course skilled exponents of the art of bodily self-exposure. With the pansexualization, the pornalization even, of visual culture, celebrity and sexual display have come closer and closer together, to the point where it sometimes seems as though the nude photographic session has become a rite of passage for the celebrity, an examination which one must pass in order to get on to the fabled A-list. Celebrities thereby render themselves immune from the humiliation of being imagined in the nude. Unless, that is, their willed nudity, their fully self-possessed exposure, can be degraded in some way, thus restoring the celebrity to the condition of nakedness: hence the rise of the celebrity nude. Ruth Barcan finds in the appetite for unauthorized naked images of stars—telephoto-lens sunbathing snaps, stolen sex videos, footage from injudicious early appearances in porn movies ("I was young and needed the money")—a mixture between "the endless and impossible quest for authenticity" and a rather more dubious voyeurism, delivering "the thrill of the forbidden and the stolen" (Barcan 245). Barcan is unusual in the seriousness with which she takes the question of celebrity nudity, perhaps because her real focus is on the contemporary meanings of nudity rather than celebrity. Writers on celebrity itself tend to be less attentive. Graeme Turner follows the links from celebrity sites to celebrity porn sites, noting how close they are, but still unaccountably holds to on a fundamental distinction between the realms of glamour and sleaze: "the distance between regarding celebrities with wonder to regarding them as whores is surprisingly short, but the kinds of images available in the latter context are significantly different," he unconvincingly reassures us (Turner 124).

In fact, the institution of the celebrity porn site is the most telling example of the inseparability of admiration and degradation. The ambivalent reaction of celebrities themselves to such material is telling. Celebrities may attempt to deny that images in circulation are really them, may acknowledge their veracity, but attempt to restrict their circulation, on the grounds that they have been obtained illegally or represent an infringement of privacy, or may attempt to appropriate the profit from images, claiming violation of copyright. As Barcan observes, a celebrity will often launch a lawsuit with one logic, and then lurch across to another. (Barcan 246–7). The growing ease with which images can be digitally modified and manufactured makes for a whole new cycle of offence without harm. Of course there is an appetite, indulged by magazines like *Now!*, for warts-and-all pictures of celebrities who have dieted themselves to cadavers, gone gratifyingly to fat, or just dared to go out for a pint of milk without makeup. But celebrity porn pictures defile celebrities by displaying them in their essential condition of not really having their own body. It is a kind of enforced digital surgery, which no doubt encourages the more corporeal bodily kind. Where defilement and degradation has traditionally stripped objects of their dignity by reducing them to their bodies, these images deny the celebrity a body in which to be naked; this is defilement through idealization.

The Machine of Disgrace

It is often suggested that celebrity has moved into the place occupied by religious values—that the celebrity is the last embodiment of the *mana* or *charisma* that in pre-modern societies was invested in powerful leaders or religious figures (Rojek 57–8). Once again, this tends to be taken as an indication of the positive power of the celebrity or the idea of the celebrity. But the fact that the celebrity seems to be a kind of democratic demigod, the inheritor in a secular age of religious powers and functions, may offer a clue to some of the ambivalence attaching to the celebrity. For, as has often been noted, the sacred figure is often set apart not only in order to be adored or revered, but also to be the target of purgative or propitiatory violence. René Girard observes that the scapegoat is nearly always one who does not properly belong to a society, because of religious, ethnic, or physical difference. We may nowadays be slow to recognize that this can be as true of a king or an aristocrat as it is of a beggar or leper. "A mere glance at world history," writes Girard, "will show that the odds of a violent death at the hands of a frenzied crowd are statistically greater for the privileged than for any other category…Crowds commonly turn on those who originally held exceptional power over them" (Girard 1986, 19). Girard coins the term "marginal insider" to designate such vulnerable embodiments of privilege or power (Girard 1986, 18).

Girard was surely right to point out, in a much-reproduced interview for *Le Monde* on November 5, 2001, that what we call the clash of civilizations embodied in the war on terror is in reality an example of "mimetic rivalry on a planetary scale" (Girard 2001), in which violence both produces and is itself produced by profound identifications. Not the least of these identifications is the coalition of religion and celebrity. The 9/11 attacks made Osama Bin Laden a celebrity, which is to say, allowed him to take the place of the negative, becoming a conduit for energies of disidentification and defilement that had previously been diffuse and unbound. Postcards and caricatures multiplied after 2001, showing Bin Laden raped by goats, gay Bin Laden, and so forth.

Because the Royal Family themselves embody the movement from religious or charismatic culture to secular culture, it is natural that its members should be made to suffer disproportionately from the demands of celebrity. Once the entry of Princess Diana into the Royal Family had introduced the virus of premier-league, no-holds-barred celebrity into the Palace, the role of its members was to be fattened up for various sacrificial acts of public roasting. Perhaps the present monarch's determination to outlive even Rolf Harris comes from her understandable abhorrence at the prospect of the role of Defender of the Faith passing to a man who sent telephone calls to his lover saying how much he would like to be reborn as her tampon. In reality, the declaration of a republic would throw the affective economy of the nation and the world into crisis, and would certainly require the completion of the process of celebritizing the political head of state.

In his *Violence and the Sacred* (1977), Girard articulated the theory of violence that he has been elaborating in his work ever since. Girard's claim is that violence is related to the sacred, because the sacred means that which is most apt to be sacrificed. Sacrifice arises as an effort to contain what would otherwise be the endless cycle of violence which any violent act or rivalry can propagate. This is said to be a particular risk in premodern societies, which tend to have close-knit kinship structures, which in their turn mean that inaugurating acts of violence can easily prompt the desire for vengeance or reprisal. The very bonds of society become the engine for destroying it, in an unstoppable sequence of substitutions:

> Vengeance…is an interminable, infinitely repetitive process. Every time it turns up in some part of the community, it threatens to involve the whole social body. There is the risk that the act of vengeance will initiate a chain reaction whose consequences will quickly prove fatal to any society of modest size. (Girard 1977, 14–15)

The reason that the victim of sacrifice tends to be socially marginal is to ensure that there will be no reprisals as a result of his or her death. Only in this way, according to Girard, can a violence to end violence be effected. The function of sacrificial ritual is therefore "to "purify" violence; that is, to "trick" violence into spending itself on victims whose death will provoke no reprisals" (Girard 1977, 36). Girard sees all religion as based upon the distinction between these different kinds of violence—profane, or contagious violence, and holy, once-and-for-all, unanswerable violence. Indeed, he suggests that it is the principal role of religion both to institute and obfuscate this distinction. Religion is therefore only

> another term for that obscurity that surrounds man's efforts to defend himself by curative or preventative means against his own violence. It is that enigmatic quality that pervades the judicial system when that system replaces sacrifice.

> This obscurity coincides with the transcendental effectiveness of a violence that
> is holy, legal, and legitimate successfully opposed to a violence that is unjust,
> illegal, and illegitimate. (Girard 1977, 23)

Since the beginnings of celebrity culture, perhaps in the eighteenth century, there
have been those who have sought celebrity through murder or violence. Schickel
says of this growing group that they "require no metaphors whatever to apprehend
the meaning of celebrity in today's world, who understand the demands of that
role and, more important, the demands of winning it in open audition, with deadly
directness" (Schickel 2000, 276). He goes on to characterize the view that "murder
is a hop, and a skip, a hoot and a holler, from 'certification' by the media" as a
kind of "perverse celebrity" (Schickel 276), but points nevertheless to the close
association between crime, especially crimes of violence, and celebrity. To be
sure, these attempts to use violence to break through from obscurity to celebrity
sometimes have celebrities as their objects: notable victims include John Lennon;
Monica Seles, who was stabbed by an obsessed fan; George Harrison, also stabbed,
by a fan who thought he was a witch; and the newscaster Jill Dando. The imagery
of sacrifice surrounded the death of Princess Diana, and, indeed, tends to break out
whenever a celebrity dies suddenly or violently.

Nevertheless, actual violence against celebrities is rarer than the presence of
electric fences, security cameras, and bodyguards might suggest, though celebrities
are absolutely right to sense that they need protection from us. Much more routine
and significant is the symbolic violence of defilement, defacement, and desecration.
These all have one conspicuous advantage over homicide, namely that they leave
the celebrity available for further symbolic assault. It is important that celebrities
not only be disgraced and derided but also that they continue to exist visibly in
their humiliated condition: like a hanged man, the celebrity must be brought low
on high. It is for this reason that celebrities do not cease to be celebrities after they
have been defiled: indeed, one might say that they only really become celebrities
once they have reached this point, and not just because they have been inoculated
or hardened to their condition. It is the destiny and function of the celebrity to
be exposed to scandal and absurdity and to bear its mark forever. Celebrities are
there not to be murdered, but rather to be *mortified*, indefinitely preserved in a
condition of fate-worse-than-death. Hugh Grant's arrest for receiving oral sex
from the prostitute Divine Brown, which cost him $1,225, of which only $45 went
in payment to Ms Brown for her services, meant that Grant had to act out for real
his screen persona of the slightly dizzy, but fundamentally decent and ultimately
self-deriding Englishman. As he publicly confessed on the Larry King show
"I could accept some of the things that people have explained, 'stress,' 'pressure,'
'loneliness'—that that was the reason. But that would be false. In the end you have
to come clean and say 'I did something dishonorable, shabby and goatish'" (CNN
Showbiz News 1995).

"There is good and bad in everyone," tootle Paul McCartney and Steve Wonder
in their why-can't-we-just-get-along song "Ebony and Ivory." Melanie Klein

also regards the toleration of ambivalence as the mark of psychological maturity, after the violent, pathological splittings of good from bad which characterize the "paranoid-schizoid" phase of development. But not all ambivalence is desirable, nor is tolerance always a virtue. The defilement of celebrities, or, as I have been arguing here, the production of celebrity for the purpose of defilement, is an example, not of paranoid "othering," but of an ambivalence that allows defilement to continue indefinitely. Even if their hurt is gratifyingly larger than life, celebrities, like toys or cartoon characters, cannot be hurt because it is well known that they don't exist. Besides which, they always deserve the ridicule they attract, because of the power we think that they think they have over us. Just occasionally, they may mistake the nature of the game and harm themselves; but what we really want is for them always to be there, at once adored and detested, our adoration the alibi for the vileness we require them to carry, and the defilement they must suffer the brake on our excessive adoration. "Celebrity, in its modern form, exists as part of a long established pattern that attempts to position (and in so doing curtail) excess within the social order," warn Patrick and Kelli Fuery (Fuery and Fuery 37). But this kind of ambivalence is designed to incite and ensure excess, an infinite reproducibility of hostility, suffering and shame.

How does Girard's model fare in accounting for these actions and reactions? One of the obvious drawbacks in his model is its requirement of a separation between sacrificial and profane violence. Sacrificial violence is supposed to bring violence to an end, like the explosions that are the only way to put out a fire on an oil rig. But the defining feature of the symbolic sacrifice of celebrities is that there is never anything once-and-for-all about it. Instead, the purpose of this violence, or its symbolic form, defilement, is not to bring to an end but rather to *bring about* an infinite propagation of repetitions, reprisals, and repercussions. Of course, the shame and suffering of particular celebrities will always be exhausted—in fact it is exhausted almost straightaway—but another will always be found to take their place. Hence perhaps the huge multiplication in the number of alleged celebrities: to feed the disgrace machine.

Psychoanalytic readings assume a subject that is attempting to maximize pleasure, satisfaction, well being, or success, seeing violence as a by-product of those drives. For such readings, violence is an anomaly to be explained. My suggestion is that we view violence as primary, not as an instinct, but as a structural effect. What matters is that opportunities for violence be maximized, and the forms of violence be maximally diversified. From this perspective, there is nothing mysterious about why celebrities should attract such venomous mockery and opprobrium, and be subjected to such systematic humiliation and disgrace. The category of the celebrity exists in order to allow the exercise of symbolic violence; it is an epiphenomenon of the game of violence. It is an impulse that is exactly the opposite of the sacred violence spoken of by Girard. Here, the purpose is not to stop the cycle of substitutive violence, but to secure it. The way to maximize possibilities of violence is to ensure that its object never dies, because they are never really there. The mysterious condition of the celebrity, which is to be both there and not there, the ideal of authentic being (which is always put to the test through suffering, above all else) and the proof that one's identity can be entirely manufactured, is explicable as affording opportunities for the infinite continuation of violence. Girard thought that the problem with real violence was that it was unstoppable. But, in our situation, the problem with real violence is that sooner or later, it must meet with impediments. The dream scheme of celebrity is produced in order to enable violence never to run out of reasons or opportunities. The best violence is the kind where you cannot be sure who has done it, whether it has happened, or who it has happened to.

Perhaps, however, what is really at work here is something more or other than violence: namely, an assault on the positivity of value itself. The celebrity is simultaneously highly prized and utterly disposable, godly and profane, regal and beggarly. I have been saying that defilement allows violence to continue, but perhaps there is also a sense in which violence is just an inferior form of defilement. There must be not only a category, but also a practice of defilement, the capacity to withdraw value or see it diminish to nothing. The celebrity is not the shaman, the bearer of *mana*, or *charisma*, not, in other words, a figure in which real value is instinct or instilled. It is not absolute values that we lose when we dispense with the barbarities and infantilities of religion. It is *the necessity of the negative*. There are no negatives in nature or, as Freud astonishingly observed, in what he called the unconscious. Nature means the absence of negativity. Human values and the value of the human do not depend upon difference, as is commonly assumed. For nature is nothing but difference, as far as the eye can see. The human depends upon the specific difference of the negative, of the minus sign, the category of the barred, the unclean or the defiled. Most religious cosmogonies recognize this fact about themselves, for they date the beginning of things from the arising of a principle of division, in which negativity (evil, death, suffering, whatever ever it is that breaks into the realm of Edenic bliss or completeness of being) comes about. They thus recognize that without the specific difference exemplified by the category of the evil or the unclean, or the damned, or whatever name is assumed by this "*not-*" or minus function, nothing intelligible, or at least intelligible to humans, can happen.

The so-called problem of evil is not a theological, but a logical problem: if there is evil, how can there be an omnipotent God?; if there is an omnipotent God, what is evil doing in the world? It is solved, not theoretically but practically, by inversion. How can there be omnipotence—God, goodness, truth, life, freedom—without the negative? The problem begins with monotheism, of which global capitalism is in this sense an intensification. The more integrated and interdependent a society becomes—economically, culturally—and the more it therefore capitalizes on its differences and surpluses, the less it can afford categories of the dispensable, and the less the luxury of sacrifice is available to it. Thus, the negative needs to become the unclean, which is to say the ambivalently evil. The Church Fathers developed the doctrine of permitted evil, according to which Satan had no real power, but acts only by permission of God. Similarly, a system that aims to be more inclusive than ever needs a mechanism for producing from within itself the negativity that previously could be thought to arise from or simply was an inherent state of nature. This negativity must now be produced by defilement, which in the process changes its grammatical function. Defilement was previously a danger, the danger of what might happen to us if we did not take measures to prevent it. Now, defilement is a positive action, the transitive action of defiling, that we give ourselves leave increasingly to perform. Defilement—disgracing, defacement, desecration—is something we do to things rather than an effect produced upon us by the things that will defile us unless kept at a distance. There should be no surprise in the fact that celebrity culture has grown in proportion to the extension of protections to many of the other traditional scapegoat groups. Celebrity culture is a way of farming defilement, and conserving the possibility of destitution, undoing, and all the necessary realm of the not, under conditions of generalized positivity which otherwise threaten it with extinction.

Afterword

Nancy Armstrong

Reading this collection of essays certainly put the challenge to my longstanding assumption that thematic readings necessarily reproduce master narratives. In telling and retelling the story of celebrity, the essays in this volume suggest that, quite the contrary, the rise of celebrity culture revised the master narrative of development in a way that sheds new light on the formal innovations of modernism. Reading Wilde's *The Picture of Dorian Gray* as a disfiguration of the *Bildungsroman* form, the first essay in this collection by Lois Cucullu serves as a tip-off, just as Steven Connor clinches the deal in the last essay by calling our attention to the negative side of celebrity, the susceptibility of its superhumanity to degradation beneath the level of ordinary humanity. The persuasive power of this remarkably coherent and powerful argument to the effect that celebrity derails the story of the growth and development of an exemplary individual rests on nearly a dozen case histories of actual and fictional celebrities whose stories invariably unfold in a biographical pattern that breaks with that narrative. Prompted by decades of critical maneuvering that failed to get us over "the great divide" between high modernism and mass culture, we might expect the modernist author's celebrity to differ in this respect from that of pop icons.

How intriguing, then, to encounter essays about F. Scott Fitzgerald, Virginia Woolf, Charlie Chaplin, and Leni Riefenstahl, all of which demonstrate that celebrity conflates high and low in a performance of individuality which is really neither. Aaron Jaffe's essay initiates our encounter with a new and powerful variant of narrative by arguing "for a mutant genome that the pulp elitism of Virginia Woolf's *Orlando* (1928) shares with the elitist pulp of Baroness Orczy's *Scarlet Pimpernel* (1905)." While the high modernist tries but invariably fails to control the reception of his or her public identity, the pop icon is never simply at the mercy of popular reaction to the tawdriness of personal life. By interweaving biographical material with public performance, the essays in this collection demonstrate that individuals who become celebrities turn their private fears and longings inside-out and manage somehow to transform the materials of inner life into features of a public personality. In the face of a tenacious critical tendency to insist on our separating fictional characters from actual people, celebrity culture invites us to consider whether they are so different after all.

At least to begin with, the production of celebrity is animated by the same fantasy of self-production realized in the *Kunstlerroman*, where the artist-protagonist strives to turn him/herself into a work of art. This narrative pattern is openly thematized within works of this period so disparate as *Mrs. Dalloway* and

Modern Times, and it informs the career of Elvis Presley as surely as it does Leni Riefenstahl's. Without exception, the case studies in this collection demonstrate how twentieth-century celebrities incorporated and acted out a modification of the narrative of development, a modification specific to their moment. Through highly choreographed public performances of behaviors that ordinary individuals fervently seek to keep private, some people developed personal identities capable of attracting a mass audience. More often than not, developing such an identity did not conclude on the same happy note as the *Bildungsroman*. In the traditional narrative of growth and development, protagonists prove their worth as they assume an enviably respectable place within society as the head of a household. In this form, the narrative of growth and development not only affirmed the desirability of having such a position but also implied that happiness could not be achieved outside the limits of the modern household or beyond a society composed of such households. By contrast, celebrity identity seems to arise from the performer's self and promise certain individuals a position above and beyond the constraints of household and society. To the degree that this achievement seems to come from the beauty, brilliance, talent, or novelty of the celebrity, his or her story is not essentially at odds with the ideology of individualism. Indeed, we might be tempted to compare the development of such a public personality to the extra-social pattern of the *Kunstlerroman*. But to the degree that a celebrity depends on a popular audience, reader, or movie-goer, the story of the celebrity's development turns away from that of an artist. This principle holds true, as I will explain, even in the case of celebrated modernists who declare themselves unavailable for mass consumption.

In retelling much the same story of the celebrity's ascendance to a public personality commanding popular acclaim followed by his or her decline into death, scandal, embarrassment, or obscurity prompted by some decisive shift in public reception, the accounts of celebrity in this collection imply that the modern mass-mediated world that gave rise to modernism couldn't, in fact, tolerate an individual who was truly unique—a type unto itself. Common sense declares it impossible for an individual to be at once unique and ubiquitous, self-generated and yet available for cultural reproduction, independent of the marketplace and captive to its demands. Yet public personalities embodying this contradiction nevertheless proliferated in unprecedented numbers during the early decades of the twentieth century alongside great works of modernism (see Garval, Goldman). The ubiquity of the celebrities' uniqueness does call to mind those figures Roland Barthes describes as mythologies. I agree with the editors of this volume, however, who find the differences between Barthes's mythologies and the form and function of celebrity more instructive than their correspondences.

Like a mythology, celebrity brings together and naturalizes cultural codes in a single one-of-a-kind figure that lends itself to reproductions, each repetition of which unleashes all the expectations of previous performances. But celebrity obviously proves far less stable than "the face of Garbo" or "the brain of Einstein," as celebrity does not detach itself from the individual body but depends on repeat performances, which inevitably fail to sustain those expectations. So it is that we find accounts of celebrity starting off on much the same track of development that shapes the *Bildungsroman*, only to depart from the narrative of individual development, leaving it to the rest of us to live out that narrative. By way of contrast, the story of celebrity shifts the source of the power of fascination from the celebrity-protagonist to the mass consumer. This change inevitably transforms the celebrity into something as negative as it was initially positive, from an extraordinary individual into one that invites ridicule. As the arbiter of taste, Faye Hammill points out, *Vanity Fair* helped to produce this arc by exploiting the double capability of pretension both to elevate intellectuals to the status of celebrities and to identify them as objects of derision. Similarly, Judith Brown shows that the inertia of Garbo's characteristic pose and the double opacity of her face and sunglasses announced the very aging process she was so effective in warding off. The popularity of such an object is what makes it available to criticism.

Although the commodities associated with a public personality are very much part of celebrity production (see Mix, Watt), we won't get very far toward an explanation of the double potential responsible for the parabolic narrative of celebrity if we assume that an individual becomes a celebrity in much the same way that Marx saw objects becoming commodities. In serving as the medium of exchange between producer and consumer, Marx forecast that commodities would redefine both parties to the exchange, draining the one of his earlier purpose in making such an object and the other of her earlier sense of need in consuming it. Unlike the commodity, celebrity transforms people rather than objects by turning some people into public personalities over whom consumers exercise a curious form of power. Marx was not alone in neglecting the active role played by the consumer in the exchange of commodities; the mid-nineteenth-century intellectual—Dickens comes first to mind—was every bit as critical as Marx of people surrounding themselves with, expressing themselves through, and carrying on relationships with objects. They shared a belief that this relation to objects eroded the human qualities of spirit and will that were distinguished from objects and defined in opposition to them. To account for celebrity, I believe, we have to swim against this tide of disapproval of commodities that began with Victorian authors and intellectuals. We must not only question the claim that commodities render us passive by telling us what we need in order to be respectable, admired, happy, and so forth. We must also question the basic distinction between individuals and the objects they consume, which amounts to questioning Enlightenment individualism itself.

In their introduction, Jonathan Goldman and Aaron Jaffe explain that one motive for assembling this collection was to isolate the change between the bewildering new universe of objects that was emerging in nineteenth-century England and the full-blown culture of celebrity that marks the early twentieth century (also see Garval). I would like to pause and consider briefly one of the implications of this change. The evidence suggests that Victorian consumers equated self-fulfillment with a well-appointed home and an attractive and devoted family. To achieve public admiration, a man so often in the public eye as Dickens struggled mightily to observe the codes of middle-class gentility, as did Queen Victoria herself, when she surrounded herself with children and expensive objects. If they set the standard, as I believe they did, then England clearly entered a new cultural moment when the individuals who commanded greatest public admiration were no longer necessarily those who took up positions traditionally commanding respect. The advent of movie stardom is but one instance of a much wider transformation of "character" that encouraged and was encouraged by new modes of self-publicity, into a form susceptible to transformation into "something better, light-infused, and enduring" (Brown).

Why did the public begin to take so much interest in individual lives that for lack of such interest would fade into the obscurity of ordinariness along with Virginia Woolf's Mrs. Brown? Another way of asking the same question is to consider how celebrity culture transforms consumers into producers. To make progress toward an answer, we must concede Jennifer Wicke's point that consumption is hardly a natural activity that women in particular were born to perform.[1] Consumption does not rob the individual of subjectivity, Wicke argues, so much as create new possibilities for manifesting selfhood. Against a critical tradition that persists in regarding consumption as anything but self-enhancing, in other words, she insists on its creative potential. Guided by her counter-argument, we can entertain the possibility that consumers are called into being and empowered by the pleasure of viewing an individual clearly beyond their reach—one they cannot have, much less be. It stands to reason that such consumers would take as much pleasure in reclaiming their productive power as fans by discovering the celebrity's feet of clay and participating in his or her degradation. In shifting attention from the now tired discourse of the celebrity as "object of the gaze" to the celebrity as a subject undergoing transformation, the essays in this collection turn celebrity into a model of subject formation that revises the cultural procedures Foucault calls discipline.

Foucault's subject becomes a modern individual as it assumes the position of a mock celebrity, that is to say, as that individual is made visible and found to be lacking in certain signature respects that can be coded in terms of race, class, and gender. As it is rendered visible by the supervised spaces of family, school, and workplace, the subject internalizes the role of supervisor and takes on that function of self-monitoring. Housed within a body that routinely falls short of norms designed to be unreachable, the subject is supposed to achieve a perpetually uncomfortable state of self-government: a body always in need of government, because capable of acting on its own, and an invigilated subject ever alert to this possibility. Is it any wonder that the cultural milieu that had spawned so many "normal" individuals should give rise to such blatant failures of self-government as addiction, hysteria, and kleptomania? Nor, by the same token, should we be surprised to find one after another of the essays in this collection narrating the achievement by certain individuals of a lustrous if temporary state of plenitude that violates the norms of race, class, and gender. Of course the individuals who achieve celebrity seem to

---

[1]   This point may be found throughout much of Wicke's work. See, for example, "*Mrs. Dalloway* and the Marketplace."

have magically evaded the disciplinary mechanisms of a culture designed to turn out individuals bent on straddling a few essential but conflicting cultural codes.

The celebrity emerges as the exception to virtually any social position, as it thrusts into the public eye an individual that has eluded interpellation in some key respect. Such an individual appears to be a type unto him or herself, at once hyper-individual and the exception to the principle of self-government. Zox-Weaver's account of Leni Riefenstahl's career reveals how she and Hitler entered into a mutually mirroring relationship wherein each testified to the exceptional status of the other. To the degree that they succeed in placing themselves outside and above normative society, celebrities serve a purpose analogous to what Giorgio Agamben calls the "sovereign exception." As he describes it, the exception embodies neither the state of things as they were before the establishment of laws, nor the conditions that result from overthrowing those laws. The exception both forms and is formed by the law as a state of being outside the law. From this, we might expect the exception to draw a line between what is acceptable and can be included in society as opposed to that which must be excluded in order for society to exist. To this, Agamben adds another qualification that will further clarify the cultural dynamic of celebrity. To be exceptional, in his sense, the celebrity opens up what he calls a "zone of indistinction"—that is to say, a position within culture that is neither inside nor outside of society. I would like to play a bit with the idea of the celebrity as "the exception," or "inclusive exclusion," as distinct from the "ordinary" or "normal" individual who serves as "the example," which Agamben characterizes as an "exclusive inclusion." The chiastic symmetry of this terminology invites us to see the exemplary individual and the exceptional individual as interdependent constructs.

Their relationship sheds new light on Foucault's model of subject formation, allowing us to differentiate the culture of modernism from the nineteenth-century culture of discipline preceding it. Agamben describes the relationship of "the exception" (which alone demonstrates the power to suspend the law) to "the example" (which alone demonstrates the power of complete subjection to the law) as one that applies to all polities from antiquity to Nazi Germany. The essays in this collection suggest that, quite the contrary, the forms exceptionalism took and the work that it did varies with social-historical conditions. These essays convince me that exceptionalism could assume the form of celebrity only in a milieu thoroughly saturated by discipline, where the narrative of exemplary self formation—namely, the *Bildungsroman*—had nothing new to offer to the mass consumer. By becoming virtually a law, norm, or type unto itself, celebrity erodes the appeal of "the example," or normative individuality by exposing its limitations. (The notorious heroines of late-Victorian sensation novels made this point well before it became a fact of life by abandoning their husbands for wealthy or attractive men.) Celebrities make a spectacle of the very excesses that discipline prompts us to conceal within the self as personal deficiencies. In doing so, they transform these excesses into a public personality that attracts adulation. But this, we know, is only half the story.

In turning out modern individuals, the disciplinary institutions of modern culture arguably produce the very excesses that make the celebrity exceptional and so worthy of our attention. This human supplement not only signals the celebrity's transcendence of normative individuality, as did Elvis's signature means of making trashiness irresistibly glamorous. The supplement also signals abandonment, as it distinguishes a living body that seems no longer to belong to the world of the living. Some celebrities made the most of this fact: Garbo by personally withdrawing from public scrutiny behind her airbrushed image and sunglasses, as well as Elvis, by addressing "his audience at the level of the drives in all their raunchy sloppiness" and so "appealing to the lower regions of both the body and the body politic" (Comentale). Again, Agamben helps us understand this aspect of celebrity—how that which seems to be transcendent, because it has something that ordinary humanity lacks, can also become a major deficiency and reduce its bearer to something less than fully human in normative terms, or as Comentale says of Elvis, to a performance offering "a public celebration of life beneath the law." Rather than purging modern culture of those aspects of body, mind, and polity that discipline induces modern individuals to contain and privatize, celebrity turns the paradox of individuality—its internal singularity and external multiplicity—into a public spectacle for the pleasure of the mass consumer.

On the one hand, celebrities seem to fulfill the narrative of individual growth and development, earning public recognition for their unique characteristics. The performance of hyper-individuality exposes the upper limits of individualism, the cap that disciplinary cultures place on individual development. But this, as I have suggested, is not the only way in which the celebrity's exceptionalism exposes the limits of normative society. The desire and adulation that calls the mass consumer into being are crosshatched with fear and apprehension. In positioning themselves outside and above normative culture, celebrities also challenge the fantasy of disciplinary cultures, namely, that society is indeed an aggregate of individuals each potentially capable of governing the body through the mind. By putting on public display the human excesses that discipline induces us to conceal, celebrity culture effectively severs the "natural" connection between the modern subject and the individual body, relegating its biological component to a mass body legible in statistical terms denoting addiction, criminality, perversion, the infirmities of age, and disease. Garbo consequently withdrew her aging body from the sphere of celebrity, allowing her cinematic image to float free. In this respect, celebrity defines what might be called the lower limit of individualism, where human beings become virtually indistinguishable parts of a population. Elvis made his descent into the mass body well before drugs and bad health made it a fact of life and the cause of his early death. By concealing himself behind the figure of the little Tramp, as Goldman explains, Chaplin not only elevated himself as godlike director to a position outside the film but also established his intimacy with the very excess that disciplined individuals habitually disavow. To this point, my analysis has rested chiefly on essays concerned with popular celebrities. The real test is whether and how the logic of celebrity plays out in high modernism.

In discussing celebrity, I have been using the literary form of the *Bildungsroman* to identify what the story of celebrity does to the liberal model of individual growth and development. Let me now try to reverse the process and ask what celebrity can tell us about the novel's form. If the relatively few novels defining literary modernism abandon the traditional pattern of growth and development in order to reveal its limitations, if, further, these novels have outgrown the fantasy that becoming an artist would allow their protagonist or putative author to achieve a position outside the disciplinary mechanisms of mass-mediated culture, then what narrative does shape them? And how does that narrative transform both literary realism and sentimental fiction into the kind of reading (difficult, opaque, self-referential, or stylistically distinct) that disallows our vicariously growing up with the protagonist? I want to consider, first, what failed celebrities can tell us about the pattern they strive but ultimately stop short of realizing fully.

Allan Hepburn's analysis of the relationship between Scott Fitzgerald's yearning to command the same kind of attention as the Hollywood star and the protagonist of *The Great Gatsby* shows both author and his most memorable character falling short of becoming the kind of public personalities they perform. Are we to conclude that Gatsby, like his creator, is a celebrity *manqué* or does this disappointment imply that celebrity *is* a failed performance in that it locks the individual into a sustained performance of a cultural phantasm situated beyond the limits of social possibility? As Nick Carraway says of Gatsby, "he invented just the sort of Jay Gatsby that a seventeen-year-old body would be likely to invent, and to this conception he was faithful to the end" (Hepburn). Such imposture in earnest detaches the performing self from the physical realities being a self at the cost of the body-mind relationship on which depends our individuality. Especially revealing are the parallels between Fitzgerald's difficulty living within his own fairly anonymous skin, his self-frustrated wish to be like Douglas Fairbanks, and the abbreviated rise of the West Indian author, Eric Walrond. Having persisted and triumphed in the face of critical indifference, Walrond was about to make his crossover move into white publication, as James Davis tells the story, when "he effectively sabotaged his career at its apex." The machinery was certainly in place to make Walrond a celebrity, but the position that his publishers, friends, and contacts had created for him was one that, coming from another culture, he was apparently unable to embrace as his own invention. The case of Erskine Caldwell suggests why Fitzgerald nevertheless became a literary celebrity, precisely because he couldn't assume the position of a Hollywood star. In his chapter on Caldwell, Loren Glass argues that Caldwell's problem was his popularity. The sensational content of *God's Little Acre* did provoke an obscenity trial against Viking Press that put Caldwell in the company of James Joyce as a "highbrow champion of literary freedom." But where Joyce was celebrated for writing novels about people who would never read him, Caldwell embraced the paperback revolution and wrote for a popular audience. That he failed to sustain the tension between two systems of value personified by "genius" and "celebrity" as well as Gertrude Stein did (see Mix) explains why his relative obscurity today is something more than a class issue.

In the context of the case histories of celebrity assembled in this collection, we can single out Walrond and Caldwell as authors who refused to occupy the "zone of indistinction" enabling and created by exceptionalism. Whether they could not or would not undergo the kind of self-estrangement it would have taken to abandon the individual formed within home, schoolroom, and professional life in order to perform as a public personality is not at issue. The modernist's celebrity rested on an aesthetic performance. It is in writing that he or she must transcend the limits of the narrative of individual growth and development or sink back into relative ordinariness. Indeed, it seems clear that discomfort is also the operative descriptor for authors who achieved such celebrity, including Fitzgerald, Hemingway, Stein, Woolf, Joyce, Beckett, and others. What matters is what they wrote; their literary performance suspended the norms of their culture and marked these authors as exceptional—in this respect, outside and above the social categories that ordinary people negotiate in becoming who they are.

Whether or not the modernist led the life of a celebrity should not be our first concern. Were we to begin instead with the novels that come first to mind as examples of modernism, we find them rendering the narrative of individual growth and development spectacularly obsolete. Forster uses a bookcase weighted with the materials of a traditional education to crush Leonard Bass who seeks to develop himself by reading them. Joyce ghoulishly resurrects Stephen Dedalus' mother, exposing the futility of the artist's attempt to detach himself from her rotting flesh. Into a narrative devoted to the preparations for a party that promises to reunite all the important players in Clarissa Dalloway's emotional life, Woolf inserts the hallucinations of World War I veteran Septimus Smith that sustain his attachment to the members of his company slaughtered on the battlefield. I could go on at length suggesting that rather than insisting on the self-enclosure of consciousness, the integrity of the individual, and the capacity of any personal history to provide "the example" of a self-governing individual, modernist novels imagine life within the categories of liberal society as claustrophobic and life outside those categories as terrifying. These novels are expressions of a culture that cannot seem to tolerate unique human beings, maybe even a culture that has lost faith in the principle of individuality *tout court.*

At least this strikes me as what one must conclude when fiction abandons its stock and trade—the narrative of growth and development—for one that uses hyper-individualism to expose the viscous tissue of flesh and language connecting all human life. Finding it impossible to rescue the individual, the modernist unleashes the elements of style associated with modernism—free indirect discourse, a style that consistently announces itself as purely language, metonymic progression that makes a hash of temporalities, a literary landscape made of pornographic and commercial material, and yes, half-made traditional characters like Woolf's Mrs. Brown—to establish aesthetic continuity where the unity promised by the narrative of development has broken down. That these elements achieve coherence only as an exceptional one-of-a-kind literary performance marks the end of one phase of individualism and the beginning of another.

Works Cited

Ades, Dawn, Neil Cox, and David Hopkins, *Marcel Duchamp*. London: Thames and Hudson, 1999.

Advertisement for *Vanity Fair* magazine. *Vanity Fair* 5.5 (January 1916): 11.

Advertisement for *Vanity Fair* magazine. *Vanity Fair* 10.7 (September 1918): 9.

Affron, Charles. *Star–Acting: Gish, Garbo, Davis*. New York: Dutton, 1977.

Agamben, Georgio. *Homo Sacer*. Stanford: Stanford UP, 1998.

Agamben, Giorgio. *Means Without Ends: Notes on Politics*. Trans. Vincenzo Binetti and Cesare Casarino. Minneapolis: U of Minnesota P, 2000.

Allen, Grant. "The New Hedonism." *Fortnightly Review* 61 (Mar 1894): 377–92.

"An Alpine Romance," *New York Times* (27 September 1930): p. 24.

Altick, Richard D. *The Art of Literary Scholarship*. New York: W.W. Norton, 1975.

Amory, Cleveland and Frederic Bradlee, eds. *Vanity Fair: A Cavalcade of the 1920s and 1930s*. New York: Viking, 1960.

Anderson, B.M. *Social Value: A Study in Economic Theory, Critical and Constructive*. Boston: Houghton Mifflin, 1911.

Ardis, Ann L. *Modernism and Cultural Conflict 1880–1922*. Cambridge: Cambridge UP, 2002.

Armstrong, Nancy. *Fiction in the Age of Photography: The Legacy of British Realism*. Cambridge: Harvard UP, 1999.

Arnheim, Rudolph. "Who is the Author of a Film?" 1934. *Film Essays and Criticism*. Trans. Brenda Benthien. Madison: U of Wisconsin P, 1997, 62–9.

Arnold, Matthew. *Culture and Anarchy. The Complete Prose Works of Matthew Arnold*. Ed. R.H. Super. Vol. 5. Ann Arbor: U of Michigan P, 1965.

Austen, Jane. *Persuasion*. Oxford: Oxford UP, 2004.

Ayers, David. *English Literature of the 1920s*. Edinburgh: Edinburgh UP, 1999.

Bach, Stephen. *Leni: The Life and Work of Leni Riefenstahl*. New York: Knopf, 2007.

Bair, Deirdre. *Samuel Beckett: A Biography*. London: Jonathan Cape, 1978.

Banville, John. "Memory and Forgetting: The Ireland of de Valera and Ó Faoláin." Keogh, O'Shea, and Quinlan, 21–30.

———, "The Painful Comedy of Samuel Beckett," *The New York Review of Books* 43 (14 November 1996): 26.

Barcan, Ruth. *Nudity: A Cultural Anatomy*. Oxford and New York: Berg, 2004.

Barnard, Rita. *The Great Depression and the Culture of Abundance*. Cambridge: Cambridge UP, 1995.

Baroness Orczy. *Scarlet Pimpernel*. New York: Barnes and Noble Classics, 2005.

Barthes, Roland. "The Face of Garbo." *Mythologies*. New York: Hill and Wang, 1972.

———, *Mythologies*. Trans. John Cape. New York: Hill and Wange, 1972.

————, *Image Music Text*. Trans. Stephen Heath. New York: Hill and Wang, 1977.

Baty, S. Paige. *American Monroe: The Making of a Body Politic*. Berkeley: U of California P, 1995.

Baudelaire, Charles. *The Painter of Modern Life. Art in Theory, 1815–1900: An Anthology of Changing Ideas*. Eds. Charles Harrison, Paul Wood, and Jason Gaiger. Oxford: Blackwell, 1998, 493–506.

Baudrillard, Jean. *Simulations*. Trans. Paul Patton, Paul Foss, Philip Beitchman. New York: Semiotext(e), 1983.

————, *Fatal Strategies*. Ed. Jim Fleming. Tr. Philip Beitchman and W.G.J. Niesluchowski. New York: Semiotext(e), 1990.

Baudry, Jean-Louis. "The Apparatus: Metapsychological Approaches to the Impression of Reality in Cinema." *Film Theory and Criticism: An Introduction*. Eds. Leo Braudy and Marshall Cohen. Oxford: Oxford UP, 1999.

Bauman, Zygmunt. *Liquid Life*. London: Polity, 2005.

Beckett, Samuel. *Proust*. New York: Grove Press, 1957.

Belasco, David. *The Theatre Through its Stage Door*. Ed. Louis B. Defoe. New York and London: Harper, 1919.

Benhabib, Seyla. "The Critique of Instrumental Reason." *Mapping Ideology*. Ed Slavoj Žižek. London: Verso, 1994, 66–92.

Benjamin, Walter. "Paris: Capital of the Nineteenth Century." *Perspecta* 12 (1969): 165–72.

————, "The Work of Art in the Age of Mechanical Reproduction." *Illuminations: Essays and Reflections*. Ed. Hannah Arendt, trans. Harry Zohn. New York: Schocken, 1969.

————, "Goethe's Elective Affinities." 1922. *Selected Writings*, vol. 1. Eds. Marcus Bullock and Michael W. Jennings. Cambridge: Harvard UP, 1996, 297–360.

————, "A Look at Chaplin." 1929. Trans. John MacKay. *The Yale Journal of Criticism* 9 (1996): 309–14.

————, *The Arcades Project*. Trans. Howard Eiland and Kevin McLaughlin. Cambridge: The Belknap Press of Harvard UP, 1999.

————, "Central Park." *Selected Writings*. Vol. 4. Trans. Edmund Jephcott and Howard Eiland. Cambridge: Harvard UP, 2003.

————, "On Some Motifs in Baudelaire." *The Writer of Modern Life*. Ed. Michael W. Jennings. Cambridge: Harvard UP, 2006, 170–210.

Bennett, Andrew, and Nicholas Royle. *An Introduction to Literature, Criticism and Theory*, 3rd ed. London: Prentice Hall Europe, 1999.

Benstock, Shari. *Women of the Left Bank*. Austin: U of Texas P, 1986.

Berman, Jessica. *Modernist Fiction, Cosmopolitanism and the Politics of Community*. Cambridge: Cambridge UP, 2001.

Berman, Russell A. "'Written Right Across Their Faces': Leni Riefenstahl, Ernst Jünger, and Fascist Modernism." *Modern Culture and Critical Theory*. Madison: The U of Wisconsin P, 1989, 99–117.

Bishop, Edward. "Re:Covering Modernism: Format and Function in the Little Magazines." *Modernist Writers and the Marketplace*. Ed. Ian Willison, Warwick Gould, and Warren Chernaik. Basingstoke: Macmillan, 1996, 287–319.

Bishop, John Peale. "The Golden Age of the Dandy," Vanity Fair (1920). Rpt. in Amory and Bradlee, 46–7.

Blum, Virginia L. *Flesh Wounds: The Culture of Cosmetic Surgery*. Berkeley, Los Angeles and London: U of California P, 2003.

"Bogus Princeton Student Held in New Crime." *New York Times* (16 May 1993): Sec. A, 25.

Boorstin, Daniel J. *The Image: A Guide to Pseudo-Events in America*. New York: Harper & Row, 1961.

———, *The Image: A Guide to Pseudo-Events in America*. New York: Atheneum, 1982.

Booth, Stanley. "A Hound Dog, to the Manor Born," *The Elvis Reader: Texts and Sources on the King of Rock 'n' Roll*. Ed. Kevin Quain. New York: St. Martin's Press, 1992, 159–71.

Boscagli, Maurizia, and Enda Duffy. "Joyce's Face." Dettmar and Watt, 133–59.

Bourdieu, Pierre. *Distinction: A Social Critique of the Judgement of Taste*. Trans. Richard Nice. Cambridge: Harvard UP, 1984.

———, *The Field of Cultural Production: Essays on Art and Literature*. Ed. Randal Johnson. New York: Columbia UP, 1992.

———, *The Rules of Art: Genesis and Structure of the Literary Field*. Trans. Susan Emanuel. Stanford: Stanford UP, 1996.

Boym, Nina. *The Future of Nostalgia*. New York: Basic Books, 2001.

Bradlee, Frederic. "Frank Crowninshield: Editor, Man, and Uncle." Amory and Bradlee, 11–12.

Braudy, Leo. *The Frenzy of Renown: Fame and its History*. Oxford: Oxford UP, 1986.

Brawley, Benjamin. *The Negro Genius*. New York: Dodd, Mead, and Co., 1937.

Brennan, Teresa. *The Transmission of Affect*. Ithaca: Cornell UP, 2004.

Bristow, Joseph, ed. "Introduction." *Wilde Writings: Contextual Conditions*. Toronto: U of Toronto P, 2003, 3–38.

Brown, Bill. "Thing Theory." *Critical Inquiry* 28:1 (Autumn 2001): 1–22.

Bruccoli, Matthew J. *Some Sort of Epic Grandeur: The Life of F. Scott Fitzgerald*. Rev. ed. Columbia: U of South Carolina P, 2002.

Bryer, Jackson R., Ruth Prigozy, and Milton R. Stern, eds. *F. Scott Fitzgerald in the Twenty-First Century*. Tuscaloosa: U of Alabama P, 2003.

Burke, Kenneth. "Caldwell: Maker of Grotesques." *New Republic* 82 (April 10, 1935). Rpt. in Scott MacDonald, *Critical Essays on Erskine Caldwell*. Boston: G.K. Hall, 1981, 167–73.

Burstein, Jessica. "A Few Words About Dubuque: Modernism, Sentimentalism, and the Blasé." *American Literary History* 14.2 (2002): 227–54.

Byron, George Gordon. *The Poetical Works of Lord Byron*. London: John Murray, 1859.

Caldwell, Erskine. *Tobacco Road*. Athens: U of Georgia P, 1932.

———, *God's Little Acre*. Athens: U of Georgia P, 1933.

———, *Call It Experience*. New York: Signet, 1951.

———, "Introduction" to *God's Little Acre*. Scott MacDonald, *Critical Essays on Erskine Caldwell*. Boston: G.K. Hall and Co., 1981, 225–6.

———, "Introduction" to *Tobacco Road*. Scott MacDonald, *Critical Essays on Erskine Caldwell*. Boston: G.K. Hall and Co., 1981, 223–4.

———, *Writing in America*. New York: Phaedra Publishers, 1967.

———, *With All My Might*. Atlanta: Peachtree Publishers, 1987.

Camfield, William A. *Marcel Duchamp: Fountain*. Houston: Menil, 1989.

Carlisle, E. Fred. "The Triple Vision of Nick Carraway." Claridge, 307–15.

Carlyle, Thomas. *On Heroes, Hero-Worship and the Heroic in History. The Works of Thomas Carlyle*. Ed. H.D. Traill. Vol. V. London: Chapman and Hall, 1897.

Cashmore, Ellis. *Beckham*. London: Polity, 2004.

———, *Celebrity Culture*. London: Routledge, 2006.

Cerf, Bennett. "God's Little Acre." *Contempo* III: 7 (March 15, 1933): 1, 4.

Chandler, James. "A Discipline in Shifting Perspective: Why We Need Irish Studies," *Field Day Review* 2 (2006): 19–40.

Chaplin, Charles, dir. *The Rink*. Mutual, 1916.

———, dir. *The Vagabond*. Mutual, 1916.

———, dir. *Shoulder Arms*. First National, 1918.

———, dir. *Sunny Side*. First National, 1919.

———, dir. *City Lights*. RBC Films, 1931.

———, dir. *Modern Times*. Perf. Chaplin and Paulette Goddard, United Artists, 1936.

———, dir. *The Great Dictator*. United Artists, 1940.

Chaplin, Charles, perf. *Tillie's Punctured Romance*. Keystone, 1914.

Charles, Anne. "A Broader View of Modernism," *NWSA Journal* 15.3 (2003): 179–88.

Churchill, Suzanne W. *The Little Magazine Others and the Renovation of Modern American Poetry*. Aldershot: Ashgate, 2006.

Claridge, Henry, ed. *F. Scott Fitzgerald: Critical Assessments*. Vol. 2. Mountfield, England: Helm, 1991.

Clark, Suzanne. *Sentimental Modernism: Women Writers and the Revolution of the Word*. Bloomington: Indiana UP, 1991.

"Cléo a Flat Failure: The Beauty of the Bandeaux proves too tame for New York." *Los Angeles Times* (October 10, 1897): 31.

"CNN Showbiz News: Hugh Grant Scandal" (1995). <http://www.cnn.com/SHOWBIZ/HughGrant/>. Accessed 24 October 2005.

Collier, Patrick. *Modernism on Fleet Street*. London: Ashgate, 2006.

Conrad, Bryce. "Gertrude Stein in the American Marketplace." *Journal of Modern Literature* 19.2 (1995): 215–33.

Cook, Matt. *London and the Culture of Homosexuality, 1885–1914*. Cambridge: Cambridge UP, 2003.

Cook, Sylvia Jenkins. *Erskine Caldwell and the Fiction of Poverty: The Flesh and the Spirit*. Baton Rouge: Louisiana State UP, 1991.

Corvisie, Christian. *Cléo de Mérode et la photographie: la première icône moderne*. Paris: Éditions du Patrimoine, 2007.

Cowley, Malcolm. "The Two Erskine Caldwells." *New Republic* 111 (Nov. 6, 1944). Rpt. in McDonald, 198–200.

Crowninshield, Frank. Editorial. *Vanity Fair* 1 (March 1914): 13.

Cucullu, Lois. *Expert Modernists, Matricide, and Modern Culture: Woolf, Forster, Joyce*. Houndsmills, Hampshire and New York: Palgrave Macmillan, 2004.

Curnutt, Kirk. "Inside and Outside: Gertrude Stein on Identity, Celebrity, and Authenticity." *Journal of Modern Literature* 23 (1999–2000): 291–308.

———, "F. Scott Fitzgerald, Age Consciousness, and the Rise of American Youth Culture," *The Cambridge Companion to F. Scott Fitzgerald*, ed. Ruth Prigozy, Cambridge: CUP, 2001, 28–47.

Dance, Robert, and Bruce Roberson. *Ruth Harriet Louise and Hollywood Glamour Photography*. Berkeley: U of California P, 2002.

Davis, Lydia "Southward Bound, Reads Worstward Ho." *Varieties of Disturbance: Stories*. New York: Farrar, Straus and Giroux, 2007, 70.

"Days with Celebrities: Mr. Oscar Wilde." *Moonshine: Suitable for All and Read by Everybody. A Journal of Wit, Humor, and Satire*. 28 January 1882, 37.

de Beauvoir, Simone. *Le Deuxième sexe*. Paris: Gallimard, 1949.

de Mérode, Cléo. *Le Ballet de ma vie*. Paris: Pierre Horay, 1955.

de Tinan, Jean. *Oeuvres completes*. Paris: Union Générale d'Éditions, 1980.

deCordova, Richard. *Picture Personalities*. Urbana: U of Illinois P, 1990.

Deford, Frank. "The Ghost of Berlin." *Sports Illustrated* (4 August 1986): 50.

DeNight, Bill, Sharon Fox, and Ger Rjiff, eds. *Elvis Album*. Lincolnwood: Publications International, Ltd., 2001.

Dettmar, Kevin J.H. and Steven Watt, eds. *Marketing Modernisms: Self–Promotion, Canonization, Rereading*. Ann Arbor: U of Michigan P, 1996.

Dickstein, Morris. "Fitzgerald: The Authority of Failure." *F. Scott Fitzgerald in the Twenty-first Century*. Ed. Jackson R. Bryer, Ruth Prigozy, and Milton R. Stern. Tuscaloosa: U of Alabama Press, 2003, 301–16.

Doane, Mary Ann. *Femmes Fatales*. New York: Routledge, 1991.

Dolar, Mladen. *A Voice and Nothing More*. Cambridge: MIT Press, 2006.

Doss, Erika. *Elvis Culture: Fans, Faith, and Image*. Lawrence: UP of Kansas, 1999.

Douglas, George H. *The Smart Magazines: Fifty Years of Literary Revelry and High Jinks at Vanity Fair, The New Yorker, Life, Esquire, and The Smart Set*. North Haven: Archon, 1991.

Dowling, Linda. *Hellenism and Homosexuality in Victorian Oxford*. Ithaca: Cornell UP, 1994.

D.P. [Dorothy Parker]. "So This Is New York!: The Story of a Warrior's Return." *Vanity Fair* 12.3 (May 1919): 21.

Du Bois, W.E.B. "Five Books." *The Crisis* 33 (Jan. 1927): 152.

Duchamp, Marcel. *The Writings of Marcel Duchamp*. Eds. Michael Sanouillet and Elmer Peterson. New York: Da Capo Press, 1973.

Dyer, Richard. *Stars*. London: British Film Institute, 1979.

———, *Heavenly Bodies*. London: Macmillan, 1986.

Eagleton, Terry. "Nationalism: Irony and Commitment." *Nationalism, Colonialism and Literature*. Minneapolis: U of Minnesota P, 1990, 23–39.

Ehrenreich, Barbara, Elizabeth Hess, and Gloria Jacobs. "Beatlemania: Girls Just Want to Have Fun." *The Adoring Audience: Fan Culture and Popular Media*. Ed. Lisa A. Lewis. New York: Routledge, 1992, 84–106.

"An Elvis Fan Tells All." *Movie Teen Illustrated: Special Elvis Issue* (August 1961): 36–7. Rpt. in Stern, 23.

Emde, Robert. "From Adolescence to Midlife: Remodeling the Structure of Adult Development." *Journal of the American Psychoanalytic Association* 33S (1985): 59–112.

Epstein, Jean. "Magnification and Other Writings." Trans. Stuart Liebman. *October* 3 (1977): 9–25.

"Eric Walrond, Back in City, Feels No Homecoming Thrill." *New York Amsterdam News* (9 Sept. 1931): np.

Erkilla, Betsy. "Greta Garbo: Sailing Beyond the Frame." *Critical Inquiry* 11.4 (1985): 595–619.

Escott, Colin, and Martin Hawkins. *Good Rockin' Tonight: Sun Records and the Birth of Rock 'n' Roll*. New York: St. Martin's Press, 1991.

Ewen, Stuart. *All Consuming Images: The Politics of Style in Contemporary Culture*. New York: Basic Books, 1988.

Eysteinsson, Ástráður. *The Concept of Modernism*. Ithaca: Cornell UP, 1990.

Fahey, David, and Linda Rich. *Masters of Starlight: Photographers in Hollywood*. Los Angeles: Los Angeles County Museum of Art, 1987.

Fallon, Brian. *An Age of Innocence: Irish Culture 1930–1960*. Dublin: Gill and Macmillan, 1999.

Farmer, Philip José. *Doc Savage: His Apocalyptic Life*. New York: Playboy Paperbacks, 1981.

———, *Tarzan Alive: His Outrageous and Magnificent Life*. New York: Berkley Pub. Group, 1981.

Fernand, dir. *Ballet Mécanique*. 1924. Video. Video Yesteryear, 1992.

Fiedler, Leslie. "Cross the Border–Close the Gap." *Collected Essays*. New York: Stein and Day, 1972, 61–85.

Fish, [Anne Harriet]. *High Society: The Drawings by Fish. The Prose Precepts by Dorothy Parker, George S Chappell, and Frank Crowninshield*. New York and London: G.P. Putnam, 1920

Fitzgerald, F. Scott. *The Crack-Up*. Ed. Edmund Wilson. New York: New Directions, 1945.

———, *This Side of Paradise*. 1920. New York: Scribner, 1970.

———, *Correspondence*. Ed. Matthew J. Bruccoli and Margaret M. Duggan. New York: Random House, 1980.

————, *The Vegetable, or From President to Postman.* Intro. Charles Scribner III. 1923. New York: Collier Macmillan, 1987.

————, *The Love of the Last Tycoon: A Western.* Ed. Matthew J. Bruccoli. 1941. New York: Scribner, 1993.

————, *The Great Gatsby.* Ed. Matthew J. Bruccoli. 1925. New York: Scribner, 1995.

————, *Tender is the Night.* 1934. New York: Scribner, 1995.

————, *The Beautiful and Damned.* 1922. New York: Pocket, 2002.

————, *My Lost City: Personal Essays, 1920–1940.* Ed. James J.L. West. Cambridge: Cambridge UP, 2005.

Flanner, Janet. "Führer-I" *The New Yorker* (29 February 1936): 22.

Fontenot, Andrea. "Dandy Divas: Queer Modernism and the Performance of Celebrity." Seminar Paper. "Modernism and Celebrity." MSA 8: Conference of the Modernist Studies Association, U of Tulsa, October 19–22, 2006.

Forster, Mathias, Ingeborg Harms, and Bernd Skupin. "Der Wille Zur Schönheit." *Deutsch Vogue* (August 2002): 254.

Foucault, Michel. *The History of Sexuality. Volume I: An Introduction.* Trans. Robert Hurley. New York: Vintage, 1990.

————, "What is An Author?" *Aesthetics, Method, and Epistemology.* Ed. James D. Faubion. New York: The New Press, 1998. 205–22.

Fowles, Jib. *Starstruck.* Washington: Smithsonian Institution P, 1992.

Frank, Waldo. "In Our American Language." Rev. of *Tropic Death*, by Eric Walrond. *Opportunity* (Nov. 1926): 352.

Frazier, Adrian. "Postmodern Paddywhackery." *Playboys of the Western World: Production Histories.* Ed. Frazier. Dublin: Carysfort Press, 2004, 115–24.

Freud, Sigmund. *The Interpretation of Dreams.* 1900. London: Tavistock, 1977.

————, *Totem and Taboo: Some Points of Agreement Between the Mental Lives of Savages and Neurotics. The Penguin Freud Library.* Vol. 13. London: Penguin. 1990.

————, 1905. *Three Essays on the Theory of Sexuality.* 4th ed. Intro. Steven Marcus. Ed. and trans. James Strachey. New York: Basic Books, 2000.

Friedman, Susan Stanford. "Periodizing Modernism: Postcolonial Modernities and the Space/Time Borders of Modernist Studies." *Modernism/Modernity* 13.3 (September 2006), 425–43.

Friel, Brian. *The Mundy Scheme in Crystal and Fox and the Mundy Scheme.* New York: Farrar, Straus, and Giroux, 1970.

————, *Essays, Diaries, Interviews: 1964–1999.* Ed. Christopher Murray. London: Faber and Faber, 1999.

Frow, John, and James F. English. "Literary Authorship and Celebrity Culture." *A Concise Companion to Contemporary British Fiction.* Ed. John Frow. London: Blackwell, 2005.

Fuery, Patrick and Kelli Fuery. *Visual Cultures and Critical Theory.* London: Edward Arnold, 2003.

Furlong, Irene. "Tourism and the Irish State in the 1950s." Keogh, O'Shea, and Quinlan, 164–86.

Gagnier, Regenia. *The Insatiability of Human Wants: Economics and Aesthetics in Market Society*. Chicago: U of Chicago P, 2000.

Garrity, Jane. "Selling Culture to the 'Civilized': Bloomsbury, British Vogue, and the Marketing of National Identity." *Modernism/Modernity* 6.2 (1999): 29–58.

Garval, Michael. *'A Dream of Stone': Fame, Vision, and Monumentality in Nineteenth–Century French Literary Culture*. Newark: U of Delaware P, 2004.

Gendron, Bernard. *Between Montmartre and the Mudd Club: Popular Music and the Avant-Garde*. Chicago: U of Chicago P, 2002.

Gillis, John. *Youth and History: Tradition and Change in European Age Relations, 1770–Present*. New York: Academic Press, 1974.

Girard, René. *Violence and the Sacred*. Trans. Patrick Gregory. Baltimore and London: Johns Hopkins UP, 1977.

———, *The Scapegoat*. Trans. Yvonne Freccero. Baltimore and London: Johns Hopkins UP, 1986.

———,"What Is Occurring Today Is a Mimetic Rivalry on a Planetary Scale." Interview with Henri Tincq, originally published, *Le Monde*, November 5, 2001. Trans. Jim Williams. <http://theol.uibk.ac.at/cover/girard_le_monde_interview.html>. Accessed October 24, 2005.

Glass, Loren. *Author Inc.: Literary Celebrity in the Modern United States, 1880–1980*. New York: New York UP, 2004.

Goldman, Jonathan. "Joyce: The Propheteer." *Novel* (Fall 2004): 84–102.

———, *Modernism Is the Literature of Celebrity*. Unpublished manuscript, 4.

Graham, Cooper C. "'Olympia' in America, 1938: Leni Riefenstahl, Hollywood, and the Kristallnacht." *Historical Journal of Film, Radio and Television* 13. 4 (1993): 433–450.

Greene, David H. and Dan H. Laurence, eds. *The Matter with Ireland*. London: Rupert Hart-Davis, 1962.

Grene, Nicholas. "Redesigning The Playboy." *Playboys of the Western World*. Ed. Adrian Frazier. Dublin: Carysfort Press, 2004, 126.

Grossberg, Lawrence. *We Gotta Get Out of This Place: Popular Conservatism and Postmodern Culture*. New York: Routledge, 1992.

Guralnick, Peter. *Last Train to Memphis: The Rise of Elvis Presley*. Boston: Little Brown, 1994.

Haas, Robert Bartlett, ed. *How Writing Is Written: Volume II of the Previously Uncollected Writings of Gertrude Stein*. Los Angeles: Black Sparrow P, 1974.

Hall, G(ranville) Stanley. *Adolescence, Its Psychology and Its Relations to Physiology, Anthropology, Sociology, Sex, Crime, Religion and Education*. 2 vols. New York: D. Appleton and Company, 1904.

Hall, Mordaunt. "A Drama of the Alps." *New York Times* (29 November 1927): 31.

———, "Rod La Rocque, Gibson Gowland and Others in a Pictorial Melodrama of the Frozen North." *New York Times* (25 September 1933): 18.

Halttunen, Karen. *Confidence Men and Painted Women: A Study of Middle-class Culture in America, 1830–1870*. New Haven and London: Yale UP, 1982.

Hamilton, Sharon. "The First New Yorker? The Smart Set Magazine, 1900–1924." *The Serials Librarian* 37.2 (1999): 89–104.

———, "Mencken and Nathan's Smart Set and the Story behind Fitzgerald's Early Success," *The F. Scott Fitzgerald Review* 4 (2005): 20–48.

Hammill, Faye. *Women, Celebrity, and Literary Culture between the Wars*. Austin: U of Texas P, 2007.

Hansen, Miriam. "The Mass Production of the Senses: Classical Cinema as Vernacular Modernism." *Modernism/modernity* 6:2 (April 1999): 59–78

Hayles, N. Katherine. *How We Became Posthuman*. Chicago: U Chicago P, 1999.

Haynes, John, and James Knowlson. *Images of Beckett*. Cambridge: Cambridge UP, 2003.

Herrick, Robert. Rev. of *Tropic Death*, by Eric Walrond. *The New Republic* (10 Nov. 1926): np.

Hobhouse, Janet. *Everybody Who Was Anybody: A Biography of Gertrude Stein*. New York: G.P. Putnam's Sons, 1975.

Holland, Merlin. *The Real Trial of Oscar Wilde*. New York: Harper Collins, 2003.

Hollywood Reporter (29 Nov. 1938): 5.

Hollywood Reporter (29 Nov. 1938): 13.

Home, Gerald Joseph. *The History of Meteoritics and Key Meteorite Collections*. Bath: Geological Society, 2006.

Horkheimer, Max, and Theodor W. Adorno. *Dialectic of Enlightenment*. Trans. John Cumming. New York: Continuum, 1993.

Hovey, Jaime. *A Thousand Words: Portraiture, Style, and Queer Modernism*. Columbus: Ohio State UP, 2006.

Hughes, Langston. "Marl-Dust and Indian Sun." Rev. of *Tropic Death*, by Eric Walrond, *New York Herald Tribune* (5 Dec. 1926): np.

Huyssen, Andreas. *After the Great Divide: Modernism, Mass Culture, Postmodernism*. Bloomington: Indiana UP, 1986.

Iverson, Margaret. "Readymade, Found Object, Photograph." *Art Journal* 63:2 (Summer 2004): 45–57.

Jaffe, Aaron. *Modernism and the Culture of Celebrity*. Cambridge: Cambridge UP, 2005.

Jäger, Ernst. "How Leni Riefenstahl Became Hitler's Girlfriend." *Hollywood Tribune* (2 June 1939): 13.

Jason. *The Left Bank Gang*. Seattle: Fantagraphics, 2006.

Jevons, W. Stanley. 1871. *The Theory of Political Economy*. 5th ed. rpt. New York: Augustus Kelley, 1965.

Jones, John, ed., *Light and Illusion: The Hollywood Portraits of Ray Jones*. Glendale: Balcony Press, 1998.

Karnick, Kristine Brunovska, and Henry Jenkins, ed. *Classical Hollywood Comedy*. New York: Routledge, 1995.

Keogh, Dermot, Finbarr O'Shea, and Carmel Quinlan, eds. *The Lost Decade: Ireland in the 1950s*. Cork: Mercier Press, 2004.

Keynes, John Maynard. "An Open Letter from John Maynard Keynes to President Roosevelt."16December1933.<http://se2.isn.ch/serviceengine/FileContent?serviceID=23&fileid=229108EE-0F4F-09AB-EDE5-B88CBD3529B6&lng=en>.

Kincaid, Andrew. *Postcolonial Dublin: Imperial Legacies and the Built Environment*. Minneapolis: U of Minnesota P, 2006.

———, "What They Left Behind: The Irish Landscape After Emigration," an unpublished manuscript, 6.

Klein, Melanie. *Love, Guilt and Reparation and Other Works, 1921–1945*. New York: The Free Press, 1975.

———, "On Observing the Behaviour of Young Infants." *Envy and Gratitude and Other Works, 1946–1963*. London: Hogarth Press, 1997, 94–121.

Knowlson, James. *Damned to Fame*. 1997. New York: Grove Press, 2004.

Kobal, John. *The Art of the Great Hollywood Portrait Photographers 1925–1940*. New York: Knopf, 1980.

Koch, Stephen. "The Playboy Was a Spy." *New York Times* (14 April 2008), 24.

Kracauer, Siegfried. *From Caligari to Hitler: A Psychological History of the German Film*. Princeton: Princeton UP, 1947.

———, *Theory of Film*. 1960. Princeton: Princeton UP, 1997.

Kubie, Lawrence S., M.D. "'God's Little Acre': an Analysis." *Saturday Review of Literature* 11 (Nov. 24, 1934). Rpt. in McDonald, 159–66.

Kuh, Katherine. *The Artist's Voice: Talks with Seventeen Artists*. New York: Harper and Row, 1962.

Kyrk, Hazel. *A Theory of Consumption*. Boston: Houghton Mifflin Co., 1923.

Lacan, Jacques. "Courtly Love as Anamorphosis." *The Ethics of Psychoanalysis*. New York: Routledge, 1992, 139–54.

Larkin, Philip. *The Whitsun Weddings*. London: Faber and Faber, 1971.

Latham, Sean. *Am I a Snob?* Ithaca: Cornell UP, 2003.

Latour, Bruno. *We Have Never Been Modern*. Tr. Catherine Porter. Cambridge: Harvard UP, 1993.

Leff, Leonard J. *Hemingway and His Conspirators: Hollywood, Scribners, and the Making of American Celebrity Culture*. Lanham: Rowman & Littlefield, 1997.

Leick, Karen. "Popular Modernism: Little Magazines and the American Daily Press." *PMLA* 123.1 (January 2008), 125–39.

Lewin, Tamar. "Dean of Admissions at M.I.T. Resigns." *New York Times* (22 April 2007). <http://www.nytimes.com/2007/04/26/education>. Accessed 23 July 2007.

Lewis, David Levering. *When Harlem Was in Vogue*. New York: Penguin, 1997.

Lippmann, Walter. "Blazing Publicity: Why We Know So Much about 'Peaches' Browning, Valentino, Lindbergh and Queen Marie." *Vanity Fair* (1927). Rpt in Amory and Bradlee, 121–2.

Litvak, Joseph. "Kiss Me, Stupid: Sophistication, Sexuality, and Vanity Fair." *Novel* 29.2 (Winter 1996), 223–42.

Loos, Anita. *A Girl Like I*. 1966. London: Hamish Hamilton, 1967.

Löwenthal, Leo. *Literature, Popular Culture and Society*. Englewood Cliffs: Prentice-Hall, 1961.

———, 1944. "The Triumph of Mass Idols." *Literature, Popular Culture, and Society*. Englewood Cliffs: Prentice-Hall, 1961, 109–40.

Luckhurst, Mary, and Jane Moody, eds. *Theatre and Celebrity in Britain 1660–2000*. New York: Palgrave, 2005.

Lyotard, Jean-François. *Duchamp's TRANS/formers: A Book*. Trans. Ian McLeod. Venice: Lapis Press, 1990.

McCabe, Susan. "'Delight in Dislocation': The Cinematic Modernism of Stein, Chaplin and Man Ray." *Modernism/Modernity* 8 (2001), 429–52.

McGurl, Mark. *The Novel Art: Elevations of American Fiction after Henry James*. Princeton: Princeton UP, 2001.

Madson, Joan. "Hey Folks—Elvis is Coming to Orlando," in *Elvis Now*, 58.

Mahon, Derek. *The Yellow Book*. Winston-Salem: Wake Forest UP, 1995.

Maland, Charles. *Chaplin and American Culture*. Princeton: Princeton UP, 1989.

Mandlsohn, Anne. "The Church of Risen Elvis: Female Initiation through Sacred Souvenirs," in *Canadian Woman Studies: An Introductory Reader*. Eds Nuzhat Amin et. al. Toronto: Inanna Publication, 1999, 450–59.

Marcus, Greil. *Mystery Train: Images of America in Rock 'n' Roll Music*. 4th ed. New York: Plume, 1997.

Margolies, Alan. "The Dramatic Novel, *The Great Gatsby*, and *The Last Tycoon*." *Fitzgerald/Hemingway Annual 1971*. Ed. Matthew J. Bruccoli and C.E. Frazer Clark. Washington: NCR, 1971.

The Mark Twain Company. Dir. Adam Goldman. 1998.

Marker, Lise-Lone. *David Belasco: Naturalism in the American Theatre*. Princeton: Princeton UP, 1975.

Marshall, P. David. *Celebrity and Power: Fame in Contemporary Culture*. Minneapolis: U of Minnesota P, 1997.

Marx, Groucho, perf. *Duck Soup*. Paramount. 1933.

Mast, Gerald. *A Short History of the Movies*. Indianapolis: Bobbs-Merrill Educational Publishing, 1976.

Mata Hari. Dir. George Fitzmaurice. Perf. Greta Garbo. *MGM*. 1931.

Materer, Timothy. "Make it Sell: Ezra Pound Advertises Modernism." Dettmar and Watt, 17–36.

Matthews, John T. "Trashing Modernism: Erskine Caldwell on the Southern Poor," in Richard Godden and Martin Crawford, eds., *Reading Southern Poverty Between the Wars: 1918–1939*. Athens: U of Georgia P, 2006, 206–22.

Mellow, James. *Charmed Circle: Gertrude Stein and Company*. New York: Avon, 1974.

Miller, Dan. *Erskine Caldwell: The Journey from Tobacco Road. A Biography.* New York: Knopf, 1995.

Mixon, Wayne. *The People's Writer: Erskine Caldwell and the South*. Charlottesville: UP of Virginia, 1995.

Mole, Tom. "Lord Byron and the End of Fame." *International Journal of Cultural Studies* 11.3 (2008): 343–61.

Moore, Alan, and Kevin O'Neill. *The League of Extraordinary Gentleman*. Vol. 1. New York: Wildstorm, 1999.

———, *The League of Extraordinary Gentleman*. Vol. 2. New York: Wildstorm, 2003.

———, *The League of Extraordinary Gentleman: Black Dossier*. Vol. 3. New York: Wildstorm, 2007.

Moran, Joe. *Star Authors: Literary Celebrity in America*. London: Pluto Press, 2000.

Morris, William. "Pygmalion and the Image." *The Earthly Paradise*. Vol. 4. Hammersmith: Kelmscott Press, 1896–1897.

Morrisson, Mark S. *The Public Face of Modernism: Little Magazines, Audiences and Reception, 1905–1920*. Madison: U of Wisconsin P, 2001.

Murphy, Michael. "One Hundred Per Cent Bohemia: Pop Decadence and the Aestheticization of the Commodity in the Rise of the Slicks." Dettmar and Watt, 61–89.

Murphy, Paula. "The Quare on the Square: A Statue of Oscar Wilde for Dublin." *Wilde the Irishman*. Ed. Jerusha McCormack. New Haven: Yale UP, 1998.

Murray, Christopher. "O'Casey's The Drums of Father Ned in Context." *A Century of Irish Drama*. Eds Stephen Watt, Eileen Morgan, and Shakir Mustafa. Bloomington: Indiana UP, 2000, 124.

Nance, Ethel Ray. Interviewed by Ann Allen Shockley (1970). Charles S. Johnson Collection, Fisk University Library.

Nelson, Cary. *Repression and Recovery: Modern American Poetry and the Politics of Cultural Memory, 1910–1945*. Madison: U of Wisconsin P, 1989.

Nevins, Jess. *Heroes and Monsters: The Unofficial Companion to The League of Extraordinary Gentlemen*. Austin: Monkeybrain, 2003.

"The New Generation," *Opportunity*. March 1924, 68.

Nieland, Justus. *Feeling Modern*. Urbana: U of Illinois P, 2008.

North, Michael. *Reading 1922: A Return to the Scene of the Modern*. New York: Oxford UP, 1999.

Novak, Daniel. "Sexuality in the Age of Technological Reproducibility: Oscar Wilde, Photography, and Identity." *Oscar Wilde and Modern Culture: The Making of a Legend*. Ed. Joseph Bristow. Columbus: Ohio UP, 2008.

Nunokawa, Jeff. *Tame Passions of Wilde: The Styles of Manageable Desire*. Princeton: Princeton UP, 2003.

O'Toole, Fintan. "Shadow over Ireland." *American Theatre* (July/August 1998): 16–19.

Olmetti, Bob, and Sue McCasland, eds. *Elvis Now—Ours Forever*. San Jose: s.p., 1984.

Orgeron, Devin Anthony, and Marsha Gabrielle Orgeron. "Eating Their Words: Consuming Class a la Chaplin and Keaton." *College Literature* 28 (2001): 84–105.

Outka, Elizabeth. "Crossing the Great Divides: Selfridges, Modernity and the Commodified Authentic." *Modernism/Modernity* 12.2 (2005): pp. 245–7.

Parascandola, Louis. *"Winds Can Wake Up the Dead": an Eric Walrond Reader*. Detroit: Wayne State UP, 1998.

Pater, Walter. *The Renaissance: Studies in Art and Poetry*. London: Macmillan, 1877.

Peck, Dale. *Hatchet Jobs*. New York: New Press, 2004.

People v. Viking Press, Inc., et al. Rpt. in McDonald, 27–31.

Perelman, Bob. *The Trouble with Genius: Pound, Joyce, Stein, and Zukofsky*. Berkeley: U of California P, 1994.

Peterson, Theodore. *Magazines in the Twentieth Century*. Urbana: U of Illinois P, 1964.

Pierce, Patricia Jobe. *The Ultimate Elvis: Elvis Presley Day By Day*. New York: Simon & Schuster, 1994.

Pingeot, Anne. "Le fonds Falguière au Musée du Louvre." *Bulletin de la Société de l'histoire de l'art français"* (1978): 263–90.

Poe, Edgar Allan. "Diddling Considered as One of the Exact Sciences." *The Works of Edgar Allan Poe*. Vol. 4. New York and Pittsburgh: Colonial, 1903, 234–48.

Powdermaker, Hortense. *Hollywood the Dream Factory*. New York: Little, Brown and Company, 1950.

Prigozy, Ruth, ed. *The Cambridge Companion to F. Scott Fitzgerald*. Cambridge: Cambridge UP, 2002.

———, "Introduction: Scott, Zelda, and the Culture of Celebrity." *The Cambridge Companion to F. Scott Fitzgerald*. Ed. Ruth Prigozy. Cambridge: CUP, 2002, 1–27.

Prince, Gerald. *A Dictionary of Narratology*. Lincoln: U of Nebraska P, 1987.

Quain, Kevin, ed. *The Elvis Reader: Texts and Sources on the King of Rock 'n' Roll*. New York: St. Martin's Press, 1992.

Queen Christina. Dir. Rouben Mamoulian. Perf. Greta Garbo. *MGM*. 1933.

Rabaté, Jean-Michel. "Duchamp's Ego." *Textual Practice* 18:2 (2004): 223.

Rabinowitz, Paula. "Modernisms's Phantoms: Vernacular, Popular and Female." *Networking Women: Subjects, Places, Links Europe-America: Towards a Re-Writing of Cultural History, 1890–1939*. Ed. Marina Camboni. Rome: Edizioni Di Storia E Letteratura, 2004, 473–86.

Rainey, Lawrence. *Institutions of Modernism: Literary Elites and Public Culture*. New Haven: Yale UP, 1999.

Ramchand, Kenneth. "The Writer Who Ran Away: Eric Walrond and Tropic Death," *Savacou* 2 (1970): 67–75.

Rhodes, Gary Don. *Lugosi: His Life in Films, on Stage, and in the Hearts of Horror Lovers*. New York: McFarland, 1997.

Riblet, Douglas. "The Keystone Film Company and the Historiography of Early Slapstick." Rpt. in Karnick, 168–89.

Richepin, Jean. "Phryné" *Grandes Amoureuses*. Paris: Bibliothèque-Charpentier, 1896, 145–69.

Riefenstahl, Leni, dir. *The Blue Light*. Studio-Film GmbH, 1932.

————, *Triumph of the Will*. Reichsparteitag-Film, 1935.

————, *Olympia*. Olympia-Film GmbH, 1938.

————, *Leni Riefenstahl: A Memoir*. New York: Picador USA, 1987.

Rjiff, Ger, ed. *Long Lonely Highway: A 1950's Elvis Scrapbook*. Ann Arbor: The Pierian Press, 1987.

Rogers, J.A. Rev. of *Tropic Death*, by Eric Walrond. *Pittsburgh Courier* (5 Mar. 1927): n.p.

Rojek, Chris. *Celebrity*. London: Reaktion, 2001.

Rose, Mark. *Authors and Owners: The Invention of Copyright*. Cambridge: Harvard UP, 1993.

Ross, Claire J. "Putting Over a Prima Donna: Some Reflections on the Gentle Art of Press Agenting." *Vanity Fair* 12.1 (Mar. 1919): 100, 102.

Rowell, Charles. "'Let Me Be With Ole Jazzbo': an Interview with Sterling A. Brown," *Callaloo* 14:4 (1991): 795–815.

Rowley, Hazel. *Tête-à-Tête: The Lives and Loves of Simone de Beauvoir and Jean-Paul Sartre*. New York: Harper Collins, 2005.

Royle, Nicholas. *The Uncanny: An Introduction*. New York: Routledge, 2003.

Schickel, Richard. *His Picture in the Papers: A Speculation on Celebrity in America Based on the Life of Douglas Fairbanks, Sr.* New York: Charterhouse, 1974, 121–7.

————, *Intimate Strangers: The Culture of Celebrity*. New York: Doubleday, 1985.

————, Afterword. *Garbo*. By Antoni Gronowicz. New York: Simon and Schuster, 1990, pp. 513–18.

Schnapp, Jeffrey T. "The Mass Panorama," *Modernism/Modernity* 9.2 (April 2002): 1–39.

Schwarz, Arturo. *The Complete Works of Marcel Duchamp*. Vols. 1 & 2, 3rd ed. New York: Delano Greenidge, 1997.

Seldes, Gilbert. *The Movies Come from America*. New York: Scribner's, 1937.

————, *The Seven Lively Arts*. 1924. New York: A.S. Barnes and Company, Inc., 1957.

Serres, Michel. *The Parasite*. Trans. Lawrence R. Schehr. Baltimore and London: Johns Hopkins UP, 1982.

Shaw, George Bernard. "Preface for Politicians." *Complete Plays with Their Prefaces*. Vol. 2. New York: Dodd Mead and Company, 1963, 443.

————, *George Bernard Shaw's Pygmalion*. 1913. Ed. and intro. Harold Bloom. New York: Chelsea House Publishers, 1988.

Shumway, David R. "Watching Elvis: The Male Rock Star as Object of the Gaze," in *The Other Fifties: Interrogating Midcentury American Icons*. Ed. Joel Foreman. Urbana: U of Illinois P, 1997, 124–43.

Simmel, Georg. "The Metropolis and Mental Life." *On Individuality and Social Forms*. Ed. Donald Levine. Chicago: Chicago UP, 1971, pp. 324–39.

Smith, Christopher John. *The Roman Clan*. Cambridge: Cambridge UP, 2006.

"Some Notable Fall Books." *The Nation* 125: 3249 (12 Oct. 1928): 374.

"Some Notable Spring Books." *The Nation* 126: 3276 (18 Apr. 1929): 471.

Souhami, Diana. *Gertrude and Alice*. New York: Pandora, 1991.

Stanley, Liz. "From 'Self-Made Women' to 'Women's Made-Selves'? Audit Selves, Simulation and Surveillance in the Rise of Public Woman." *Feminism and Autobiography*. Ed. Tess Cosslett, Celia Lury, and Penny Summerfield. London: Routledge, 2000, 40–60.

Steele, Philip. *Down Pans Lane: a History of Roundway Hospital, Devizes*. Philip Steele, 2000.

Stein, Gertrude. "And Now." 1934. In Haas 36–66.

———, "And Now." Vanity Fair (1934). Rpt in Amory and Bradlee, 280–81.

———, "The Capital and the Capitals of the United States of America." 1935. In Haas 73–6.

———, *Everybody's Autobiography*. 1936. Cambridge: Exact Change, 1993.

———, *The Geographical History of America or the Relation of Human Nature to the Human Mind*. New York: Random House, 1936.

———, "Money." 1936. In Haas 106–7.

———, "My Last About Money." 1936. In Haas 111–12.

———, "Still More About Money." 1936. In Haas 109.

———, *The Autobiography of Alice B. Toklas*. 1933. New York: Vintage, 1990.

———, "What Are Master–pieces and Why Are There So Few of Them?" 1936. *Gertrude Stein: Writings, 1932–1946*. Ed. Catherine Stimpson and Harriett Scott Chessman. New York: Library of America, 1998, 353–63.

Stein, Herbert. "The Cubist Republican." *Slate* 7 Feb. 1997: 17 pars. 30 January 2009. <http://www.slate.com/id/2557/>.

Stern, Jane, and Michael Stern. *Elvis World*. New York: Alfred A. Knopf, 1987.

Stern, Milton R. "*The Last Tycoon* and Fitzgerald's Last Style." *F. Scott Fitzgerald in the Twenty-First Century*. Eds Jackson R. Bryer, Ruth Prigozy, and Milton R. Stern. Tuscaloosa: U of Alabama P, 2003, 317–32.

Stevens, C.J. *Storyteller: A Life of Erskine Caldwell*. Phillips: John Wade, 2000.

Stimpson, Catherine R. "Gertrice/Altrude: Stein, Toklas, and the Paradox of the Happy Marriage. *Mothering the Mind: Twelve Studies of Writers and Their Silent Partners*. Ed. Ruth Perry and Martine Watson Brownley. New York: Holmes and Meier, 1984, 122–39.

Strachey, Lytton. 1918. *Eminent Victorians*. Intro. Michael Holroyd. New York: Penguin Books, 1986.

Sullivan, Tom, and Erica Youngstrom. "Student Impostor Dupes Harvard, then Yale." *Yale Daily News* (13 February 2003). <http://www.yaledailynew.com/articles/printarticle/6864>. Accessed 23 July 2007.

Susman, Warren I. *Culture as History*. New York: Pantheon Books, 1973.

———, *Culture as History: The Transformation of American Society in the Twentieth Century*. New York: Pantheon Books, 1984.

Sweeney, Gael. "The King of White Trash Culture: Elvis Presley and the Aesthetics of Excess." *White Trash: Race and Class in America*. Eds Matt Wray and Annalee Newitz. New York: Routledge, 1997.

Szalay, Michael. *New Deal Modernism: American Literature and the Invention of the Welfare State*. Durham: Duke UP, 2000.

Tischler, Alyson. "A Rose Is a Pose: Steinian Modernism and Mass Culture." *Journal of Modern Literature* 26.3–4 (2003): 12–27.

Toíbín, Colm. "My Darlings." *London Review of Books* 29 (5 April 2007): 10.

Tompkins, Calvin. *Duchamp: A Biography*. New York: Henry Holt and Company, 1996.

Tully, Jim. "Greta Garbo: An Estimate of the Swedish Film Actress Who Achieved Her Greatest Success in America." *Vanity Fair* 30.4 (June 1928): 67.

Turner, Graeme. *Understanding Celebrity*. London: Sage Publications, 2004.

Twain, Mark. *Adventures of Huckleberry Finn*. Eds Sculley Bradley, Richmond Croom Beatty, E. Hudson Long, and Thomas Cooley. 1885. New York: Norton, 1977.

Underwood, Edna Worthley. "West Indian Literature: Some Negro Poets of Panama." *The Jamaica Gleaner* (March 1936): 35–7.

Valade, Roger M., ed. *The Essential Black Literature Guide*. Canton: Visible Ink Press, 1996.

Veblen, Thorstein. 1899. *The Theory of the Leisure Class*. Intro. John Kenneth Galbraith. Boston: Houghton Mifflin, 1973.

Vieira, Mark A. *Greta Garbo: A Cinematic Legacy*. New York: Harry N. Abrams, 2005.

Wade, Carl A. Rev. of *Winds Can Wake Up the Dead: an Eric Walrond Reader*, by Louis Parascandola. *Wasifiri* 30 (Autumn 1999): 69–70.

Walrond, Eric. *Tropic Death*. New York: Boni & Liveright, 1926.

Watson, Steven. *Prepare for Saints: Gertrude Stein, Virgil Thomson, and the Mainstreaming of American Modernism*. Berkeley: U of California P, 2000.

Weber, Samuel. *Mass Mediauras: Form, Technics, Media*. Stanford: Stanford UP, 1996

Weinstein, Arnold. "Fiction as Greatness: The Case of Gatsby." Claridge, 369–86.

Weiskel, Thomas. *The Romantic Sublime: Studies in the Structure and Psychology of Transcendence*. Baltimore: The Johns Hopkins UP, 1976.

Wells, Helen [Dorothy Parker]. "The Autobiography of Any Movie Actress, Set Down in the Regulation Manner." *Vanity Fair* 13.6 (Sept. 1919): 33, 110.

West, James J.L., ed. "Introduction." *My Lost City: Personal Essays, 1920–1940*. F. Scott Fitzgerald. Cambridge: Cambridge UP, 2005.

Whelan, Gerald with Carolyn Swift. *Spiked: The Church-State Intrigue and The Rose Tattoo*. Dublin: New Island, 2002.

Whipple, T.K., and Malcolm Cowley. "Two Judgments of *American Earth*." *New Republic* 67 (June 17, 1931). Rpt. in McDonald, 3–6.

Wicke, Jennifer. "Mrs. Dalloway Goes to Market: Woolf, Keynes, and Modern Markets." *Novel: A Forum on Fiction* 28 (1994): 5–23.

Wilde, Oscar. "The Decay of Lying." *Complete Works of Oscar Wilde*. Ed. Merlin Holland. 3rd Printing. Glasgow: Harper Collins, 1994. 1071–1092.

————, *The Picture of Dorian Gray. The Complete Works of Oscar Wilde.* 1890, 1891. Ed. Joseph Bristow. Vol. 3. Oxford: Oxford UP, 2005.

————, *The Picture of Dorian Gray.* New York: Norton, 2006.

Williams, Rosalind H. *Dreams Worlds: Mass Consumption in Late Nineteenth-Century France.* Berkeley: U of California P, 1982.

Winchell, Walter. "Walter Winchell on Broadway." *Daily Mirror* (9 November 1938): 10.

The Wonderful Horrible Life of Leni Riefenstahl. Dir. Ray Müller. Kino Video, 1993.

Woolf, Virginia. *A Room of One's Own.* New York: Harcourt Brace, 1929.

————, "Character in Fiction." *The Essays of Virginia Woolf.* Ed. Andrew McNeillie. Vol. 3. San Diego: Harcourt Brace Jovanovich, 1988, 420–38.

————, *Orlando: A Biography.* 1928. New York: Harcourt, 2006.

Young, Stark. "David Garrick to John Barrymore." *Vanity Fair* (1923). Amory and Bradlee, 72–3.

Žižek, Slavoj. *Enjoy Your Symptom! Jacques Lacan in Hollywood and Out.* New York: Routledge, 1992.

Index

Fiedler, Leslie, 51–2
Fish (Anne Harriet Fish), 131–2
Fitzgerald, F. Scott, 55–70, 125, 127,
    243–4
Flanner, Janet, 153, 163
Flaubert, Gustave, 91, 144, 185
Foucault, Michel, 8, 21, 193, 198, 202,
    240–41
Fowles, Jib, 6, 196
Freud, Sigmund, 32, 34, 45–6, 170, 182,
    223–5, 234
Friedman, Susan Stanford, 132
Friel, Brian, 209

Gagnier, Regina, 27–8
Garbo, Greta, 21, 107–21, 130, 143, 144,
    156–8, 166, 238–9, 242
Garrity, Jane, 124
Garval, Michael D., 7, 8, 14, 16, 238, 239
Garvey, Marcus
Gilbert, Adrian, see Adrian
Gilbert, John, 117, 118
Girard, René, 230–34
Glass, Loren, 7–9, 96–9, 243
Goebbels, Joseph, 156
Goldman, Adam, 9
Goldman, Jonathan, 7, 22, 43, 52, 88, 124,
    239, 242
Grant, Hugh, 232
Greenberg, Adrian Adolph, see Adrian
Griffiths, D.W., 197
Grossberg, Lawrence, 170, 178
Guinan, Texas, 130

Hall, G. Stanley, 24–8, 32, 35
Hammill, Faye, 7, 8, 9, 14, 239
Hansen, Miriam, 169
Harcourt, Alfred, 95
Harris, Rolf, 221–4, 231
Heaney, Seamus, 213–14
Hemingway, Ernest, 13, 53–4, 81–3, 86–8,
    91, 129, 152, 244
Hepburn, Allan, 7, 243
Herbert, A.P., 1–3
Hitler, Adolf, 14, 15, 103, 153–67, 241
Hovey, Jaime, 13
Hughes, Langston, 72–3, 75, 126
Hugo, Victor, 138, 143
Huyssen, Andreas, 5, 22, 51–2, 82

Iverson, Margaret, 172

Jackson, Michael, 31, 228
Jäger, Ernst, 159, 165–6
Jaffe, Aaron, 7, 8, 9, 14, 88, 97, 110, 124,
    129–30, 194, 237
Jason, 44, 53–4
Joyce, James, 3, 13, 22, 36, 53, 82, 91, 124,
    125, 130, 193, 207–10, 213–15,
    243, 244

Kincaid, Andrew, 208–11
Klee, Paul, 138
Klein, Melanie, 170, 182–4, 223, 232
Koons, Jeff, 152
Kracauer, Sigfried, 155–7, 199–200
Kubie, Lawrence S., 88, 92
Kyrk, Hazel, 27

Lacan, Jacques, 114, 173
Larkin, Phillip, 223
Larsen, Nella, 13, 75
Latham, Sean, 45
Lawrence, D.H., 36, 88, 126–7, 129
Léger, Fernand, 196
Leick, 98, 124–5, 131
Lieber, Maxim, 84
Litvak, Joseph, 128, 133
Loos, Anita, 14, 133
Löwenthal, Leo, 6, 27
Lyotard, Jean-François, 172

Madonna (performer), 144, 150, 154
Mahon, Derek, 207, 209–10
Maland, Charles, 196, 201
Mallarmé, Stéphane, 137, 144
Mamoulian, Rouben, 113
Marcus, Greil, 177–8
Margolies, Alan, 56
Marshall, P. David, 6, 8, 12, 23, 36, 96,
    110, 202, 204, 224–5
Marx, Karl, 170, 239
McCabe, Susan, 196
Mellow, James, 93–6
Mencken, H.L., 85, 123, 125, 131, 133
Monroe, Marilyn, 120–21, 144, 152
Moore, Alan, 52–3
Morrisson, Mark, 124, 126–7
Müller, Ray, 162